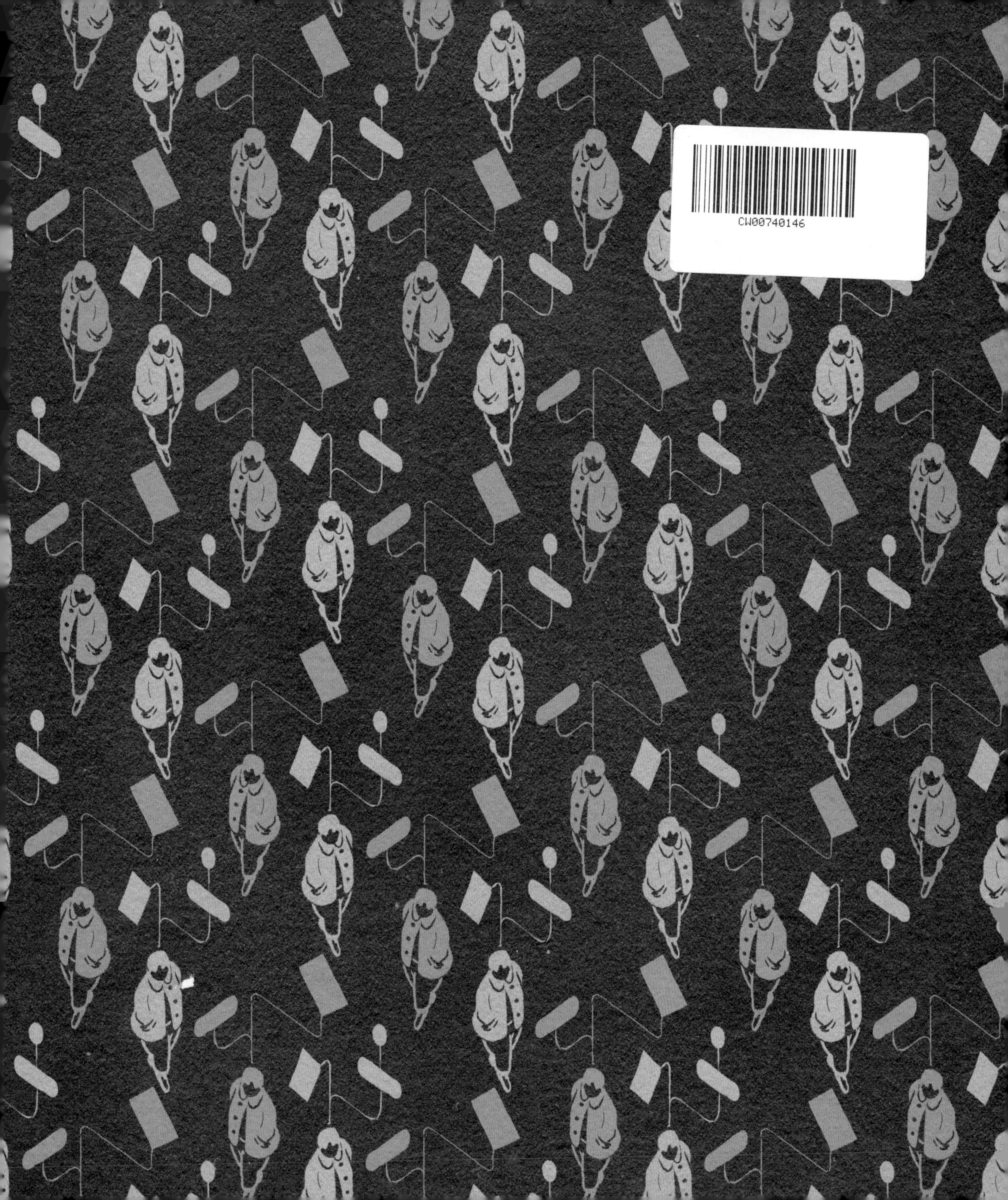

SQUARE EYES

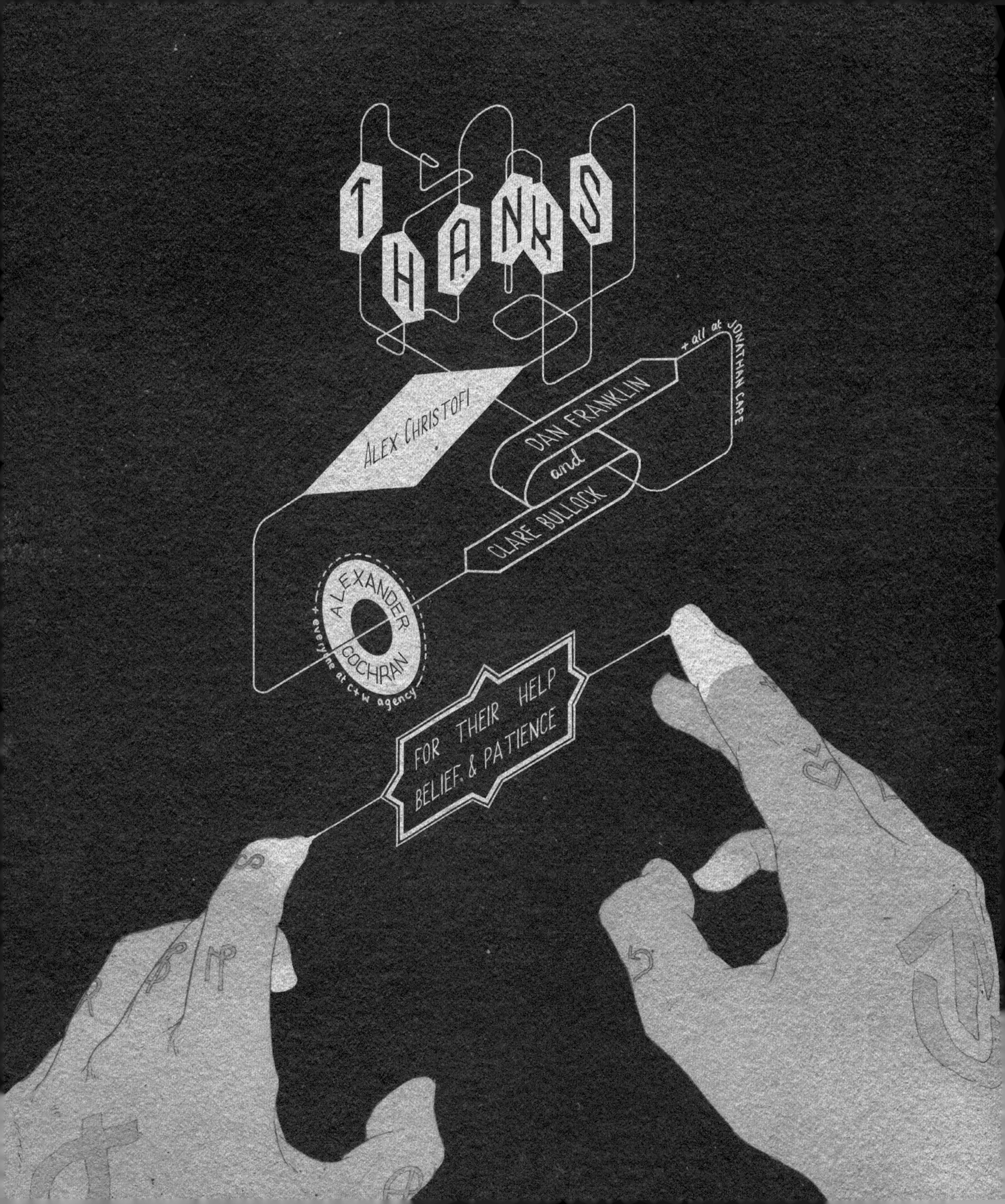
THANKS
ALEX CHRISTOFI
DAN FRANKLIN
and
CLARE BULLOCK
+ all at JONATHAN CAPE
ALEXANDER COCHRAN
+ everyone at C+W agency
FOR THEIR HELP
BELIEF, & PATIENCE

SQUARE EYES

ANNA MILL & LUKE JONES

BASED ON AN ORIGINAL PROPOSAL BY ANNA MILL, CHRIS DAY, LUKE JONES

written by LUKE JONES, ANNA MILL

ART by ANNA MILL

art + story advisor: CHRIS DAY

colouring assisted by: LEON ROZELAAR, HARRY TENNANT

5 7 9 10 8 6

JONATHAN CAPE

Penguin Random House UK

20 VAUXHALL BRIDGE RD. LONDON SW1V 2SA

an imprint of Vintage

JONATHAN CAPE IS PART OF THE PENGUIN RANDOM HOUSE GROUP OF COMPANIES WHOSE ADDRESSES CAN BE FOUND AT: GLOBAL.PENGUINRANDOMHOUSE.COM

PENGUIN.CO.UK/VINTAGE

FIRST PUBLISHED IN THE U.K. by JONATHAN CAPE 2018

A CIP CATALOGUE RECORD FOR THIS BOOK IS AVAILABLE FROM THE BRITISH LIBRARY

COLOUR REPRODUCTION BY ALTAIMAGE LTD, LONDON

PRINTED AND BOUND IN CHINA BY C&C OFFSET PRINTING CO., LTD

ISBN 9780224097222

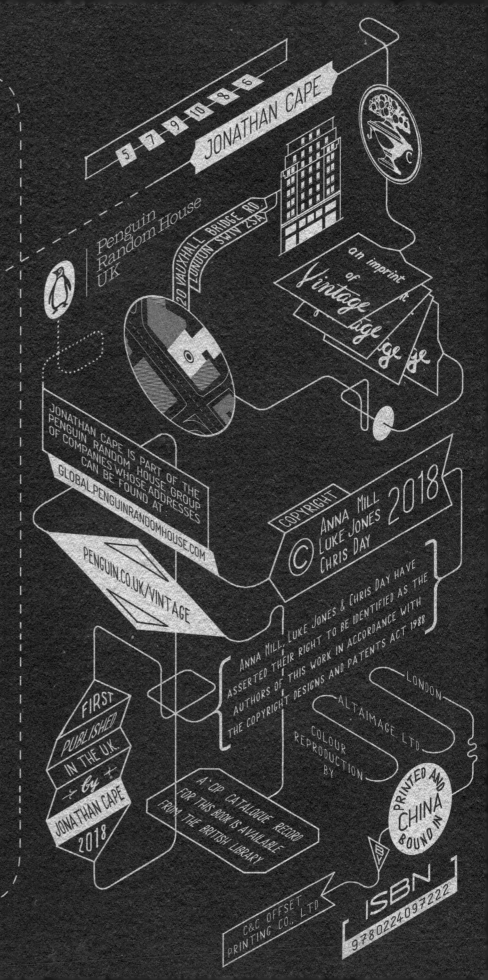

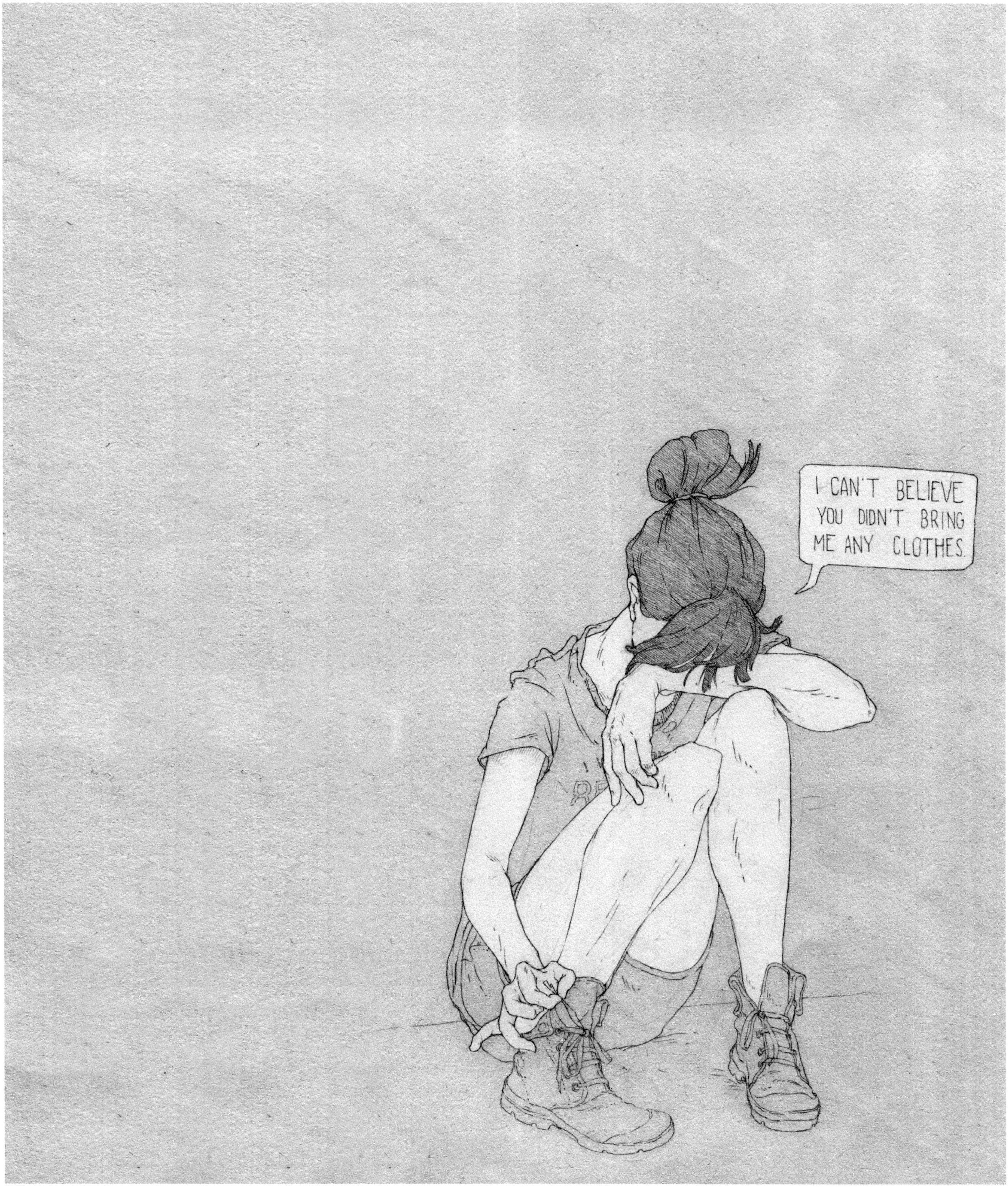
I CAN'T BELIEVE YOU DIDN'T BRING ME ANY CLOTHES.

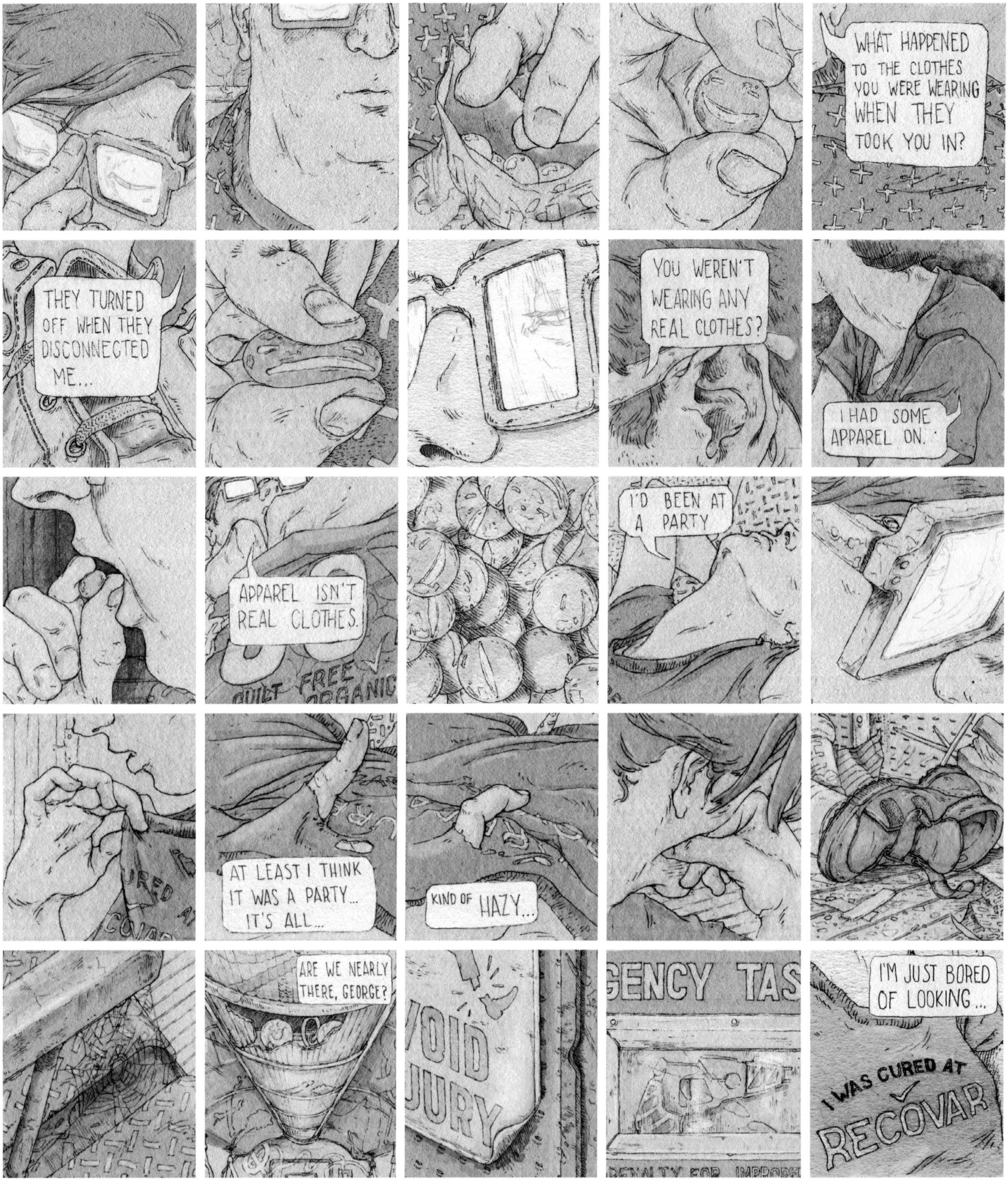
WHAT HAPPENED TO THE CLOTHES YOU WERE WEARING WHEN THEY TOOK YOU IN?
THEY TURNED OFF WHEN THEY DISCONNECTED ME...
YOU WEREN'T WEARING ANY REAL CLOTHES?
I HAD SOME APPAREL ON.
APPAREL ISN'T REAL CLOTHES.
GUILT FREE ORGANIC
I'D BEEN AT A PARTY
AT LEAST I THINK IT WAS A PARTY... IT'S ALL...
KIND OF HAZY...
ARE WE NEARLY THERE, GEORGE?
GENCY TAS
I'M JUST BORED OF LOOKING...
I WAS CURED AT RECOVAR

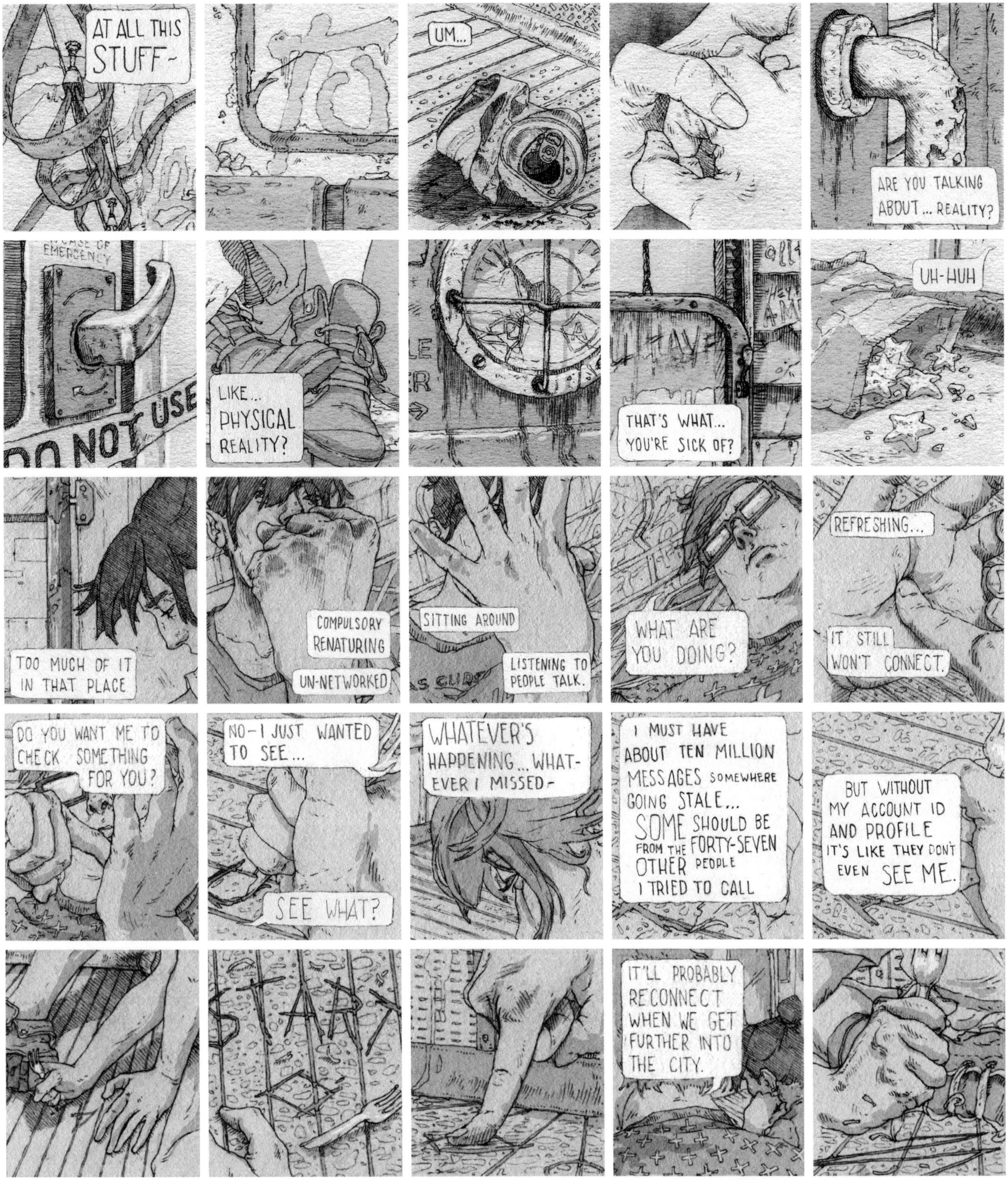
AT ALL THIS STUFF-
UM...
ARE YOU TALKING ABOUT... REALITY?
IN CASE OF EMERGENCY
DO NOT USE
LIKE... PHYSICAL REALITY?
THAT'S WHAT... YOU'RE SICK OF?
UH-HUH
TOO MUCH OF IT IN THAT PLACE
COMPULSORY RENATURING
UN-NETWORKED
SITTING AROUND
LISTENING TO PEOPLE TALK.
WHAT ARE YOU DOING?
REFRESHING...
IT STILL WON'T CONNECT.
DO YOU WANT ME TO CHECK SOMETHING FOR YOU?
NO-I JUST WANTED TO SEE...
SEE WHAT?
WHATEVER'S HAPPENING... WHATEVER I MISSED-
I MUST HAVE ABOUT TEN MILLION MESSAGES SOMEWHERE GOING STALE... SOME SHOULD BE FROM THE FORTY-SEVEN OTHER PEOPLE I TRIED TO CALL
BUT WITHOUT MY ACCOUNT ID AND PROFILE IT'S LIKE THEY DON'T EVEN SEE ME.
IT'LL PROBABLY RECONNECT WHEN WE GET FURTHER INTO THE CITY.

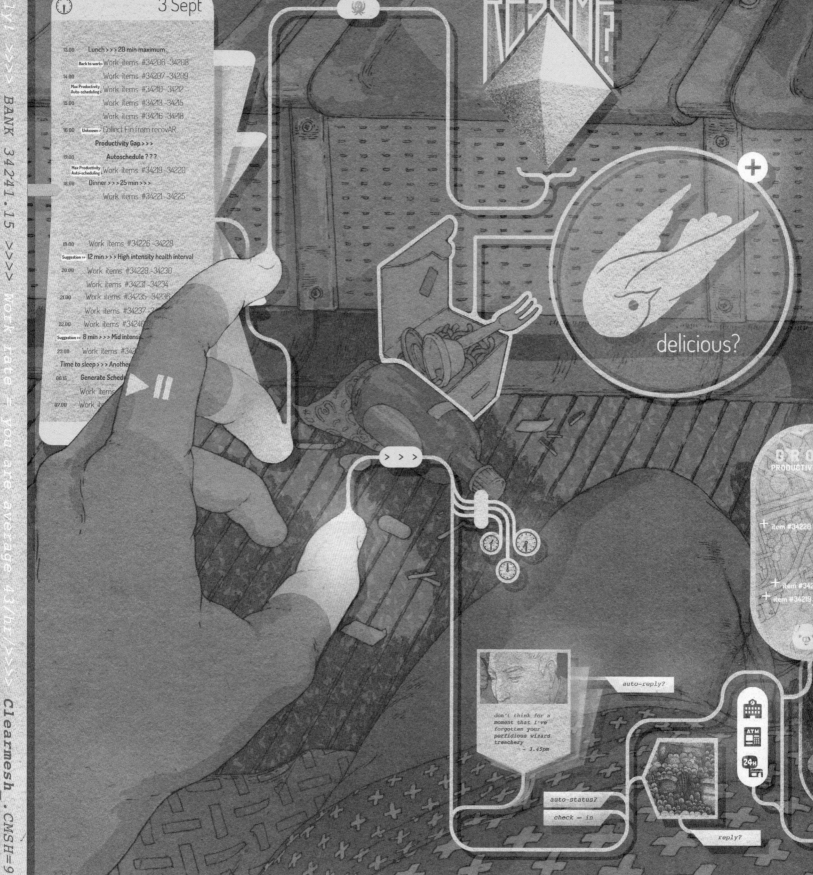

BANK 34241.15 >>>> Work late = you are average 43/hr/>>> Clearmesh.CMSH=94

3 Sept

13.00	Lunch > > > 20 min maximum	
Back to work>	Work items #34206 -34208	
14.00	Work items #34207 -34209	
Max Productivity Auto-scheduling	Work items #34210 -34212	
15.00	Work items #34213 -34215	
	Work items #34216 -34218	
16.00	Unknown > Collect Fin from recovAR	
	Productivity Gap > > >	
17.00	Autoschedule ? ? ?	
Max Productivity Auto-scheduling	Work items #34219 -34220	
18.00	Dinner > > > 25 min > > >	
	Work items #34221 -34225	
19.00	Work items #34226 -34228	
Suggestion >>	12 min > > > High intensity health interval	
20.00	Work items #34229 -34230	
	Work items #34231 -34234	
21.00	Work items #34235 -34236	
	Work items #34237 -	
22.00	Work items #34240	
Suggestion >>	8 min > > > Mid intensi	
23.00	Work items #342	
	Time to sleep > > > Another	
06.15	Generate Schedu	
	Work items	
07.00	Work it	

RESUME?

delicious?

GRO PRODUCTIVI

+ item #34228

+ item #342
+ item #34219

auto-reply?

don't think for a moment that I've forgotten your perfidious wizard treachery
— 3.45pm

auto-status?

check — in

reply?

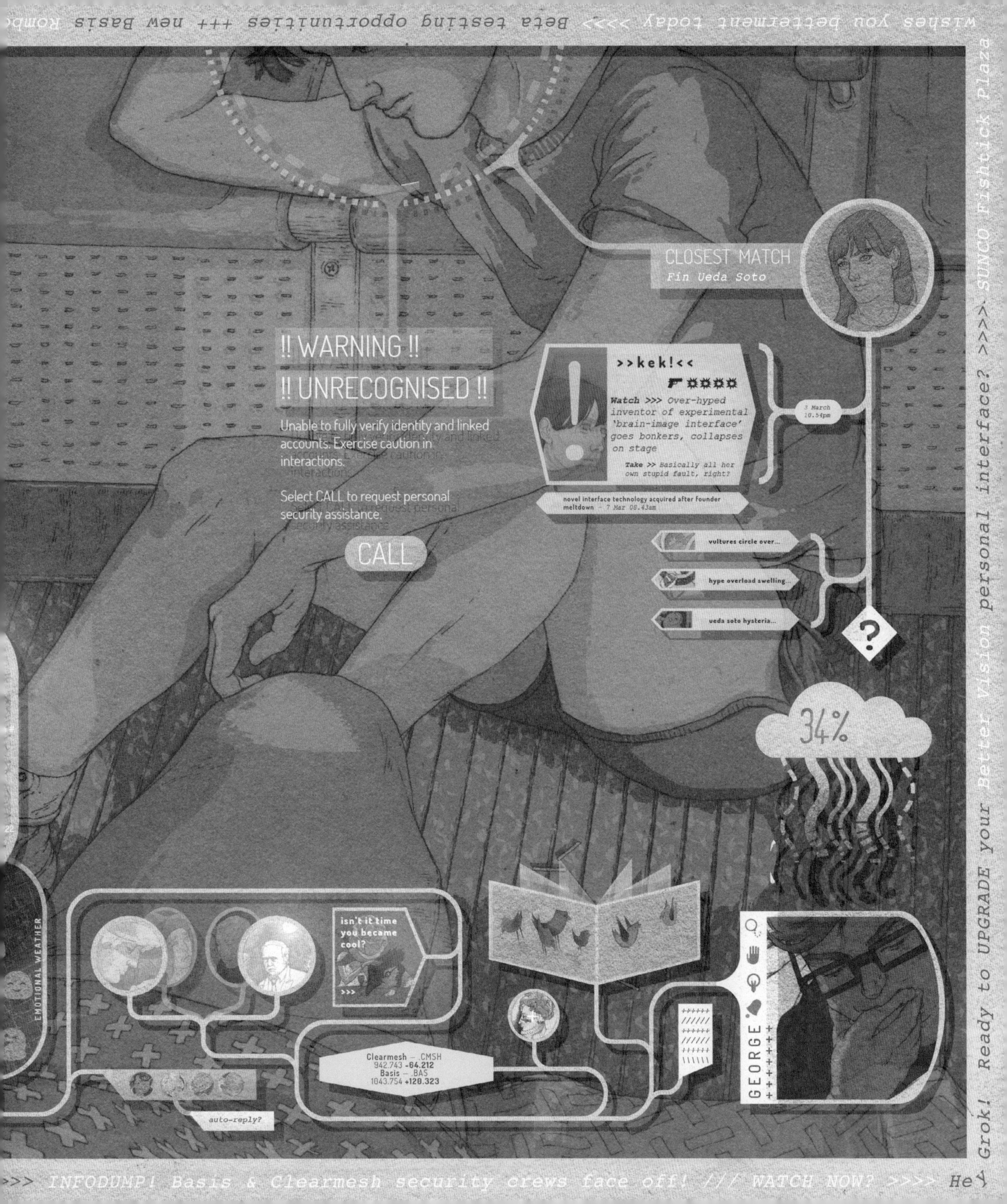

>>> INFODUMP! Basis & Clearmesh security crews face off! /// WATCH NOW? >>>> Hey
Grok! Ready to UPGRADE your Better Vision personal interface? >>>> SUNCO Fishtick Plaza
wishes you betterment today >>>> Beta testing opportunities +++ new Basis Romb
!! WARNING !!
!! UNRECOGNISED !!
Unable to fully verify identity and linked accounts. Exercise caution in interactions.
Select CALL to request personal security assistance.
CALL
CLOSEST MATCH
Fin Ueda Soto
>>kek!<<
Watch >>> Over-hyped inventor of experimental 'brain-image interface' goes bonkers, collapses on stage
Take >> Basically all her own stupid fault, right?
3 March 10.54pm
novel interface technology acquired after founder meltdown - 7 Mar 08.43am
vultures circle over...
hype overload swelling...
ueda soto hysteria...
?
34%
EMOTIONAL WEATHER
isn't it time you became cool?
>>>
Clearmesh – .CMSH
942.743 -64.212
Basis – .BAS
1043.754 +120.323
auto-reply?
GEORGE

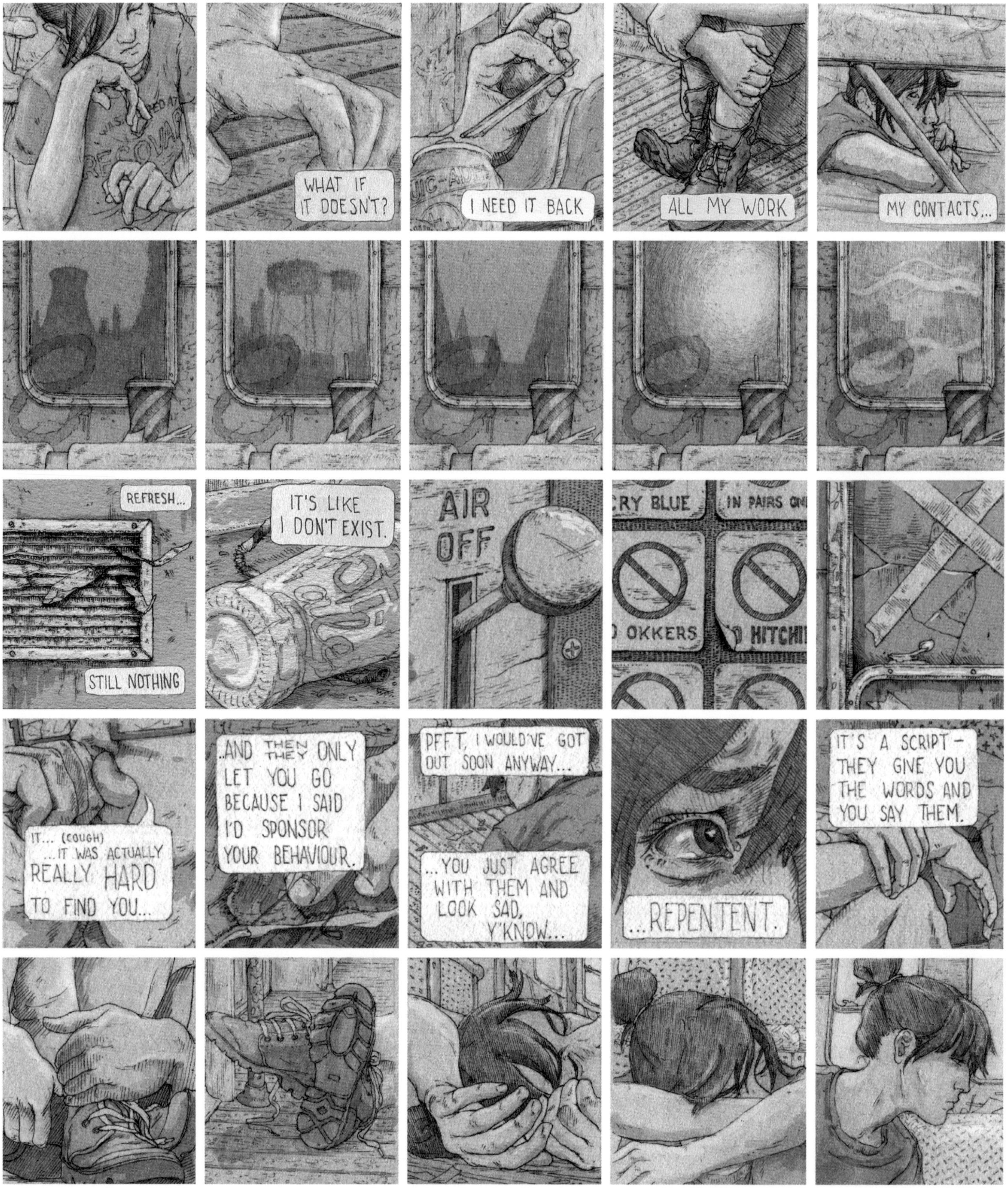
WHAT IF IT DOESN'T?
I NEED IT BACK
ALL MY WORK
MY CONTACTS...
REFRESH...
STILL NOTHING
IT'S LIKE I DON'T EXIST.
AIR OFF
RY BLUE
IN PAIRS ON
OKKERS
HITCHI
IT... (COUGH) ...IT WAS ACTUALLY REALLY HARD TO FIND YOU...
..AND THEN THEY ONLY LET YOU GO BECAUSE I SAID I'D SPONSOR YOUR BEHAVIOUR.
PFFT, I WOULD'VE GOT OUT SOON ANYWAY...
...YOU JUST AGREE WITH THEM AND LOOK SAD, Y'KNOW...
...REPENTENT.
IT'S A SCRIPT - THEY GIVE YOU THE WORDS AND YOU SAY THEM.

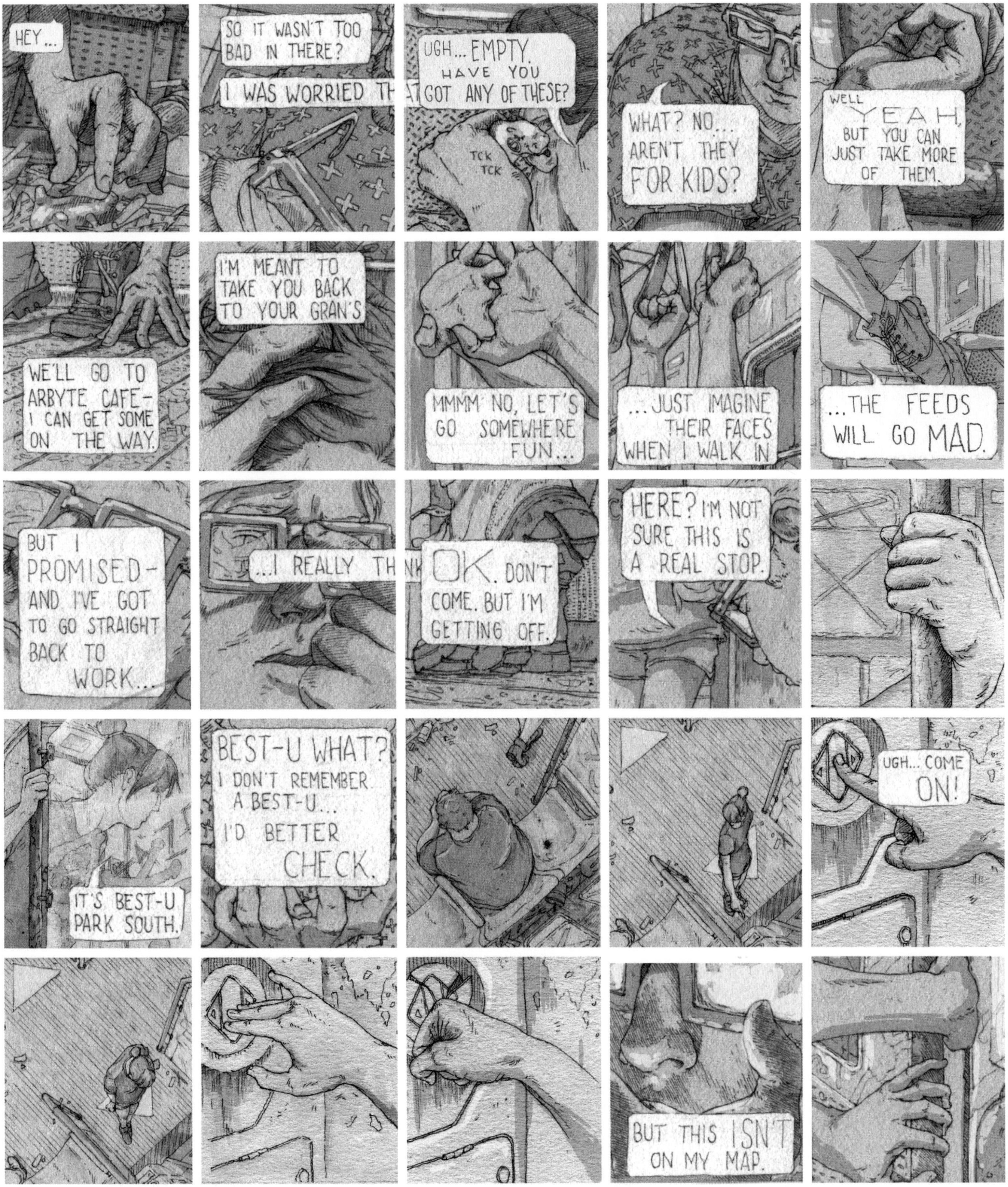
HEY...
SO IT WASN'T TOO BAD IN THERE?
I WAS WORRIED TH
AT
UGH... EMPTY. HAVE YOU GOT ANY OF THESE?
TCK TCK
WHAT? NO... AREN'T THEY FOR KIDS?
WELL YEAH, BUT YOU CAN JUST TAKE MORE OF THEM.
WE'LL GO TO ARBYTE CAFE- I CAN GET SOME ON THE WAY.
I'M MEANT TO TAKE YOU BACK TO YOUR GRAN'S
MMMM NO, LET'S GO SOMEWHERE FUN...
...JUST IMAGINE THEIR FACES WHEN I WALK IN
...THE FEEDS WILL GO MAD.
BUT I PROMISED- AND I'VE GOT TO GO STRAIGHT BACK TO WORK...
...I REALLY TH
NK
OK. DON'T COME. BUT I'M GETTING OFF.
HERE? I'M NOT SURE THIS IS A REAL STOP.
IT'S BEST-U PARK SOUTH.
BEST-U WHAT? I DON'T REMEMBER A BEST-U... I'D BETTER CHECK.
UGH... COME ON!
BUT THIS ISN'T ON MY MAP.

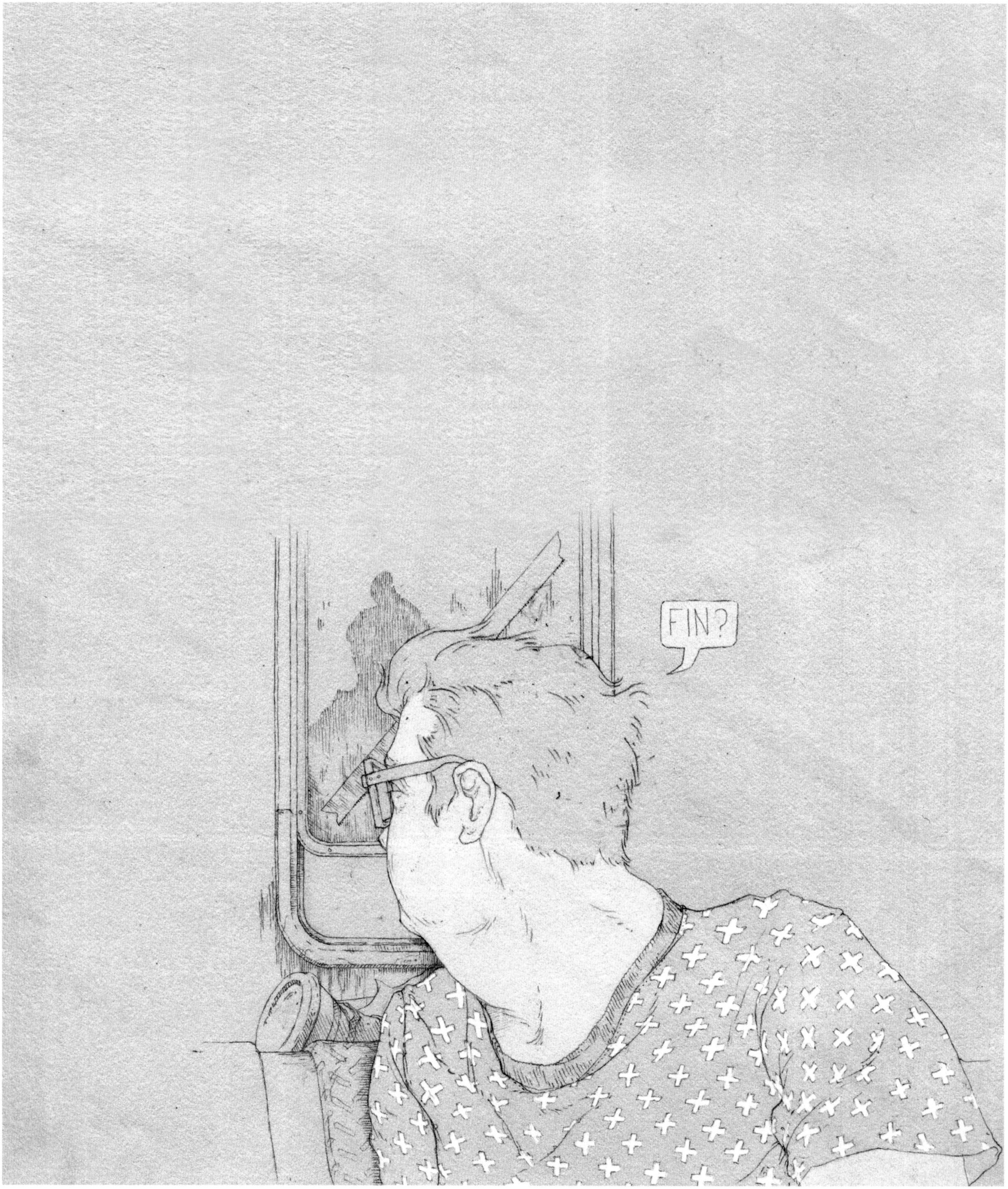
FIN?

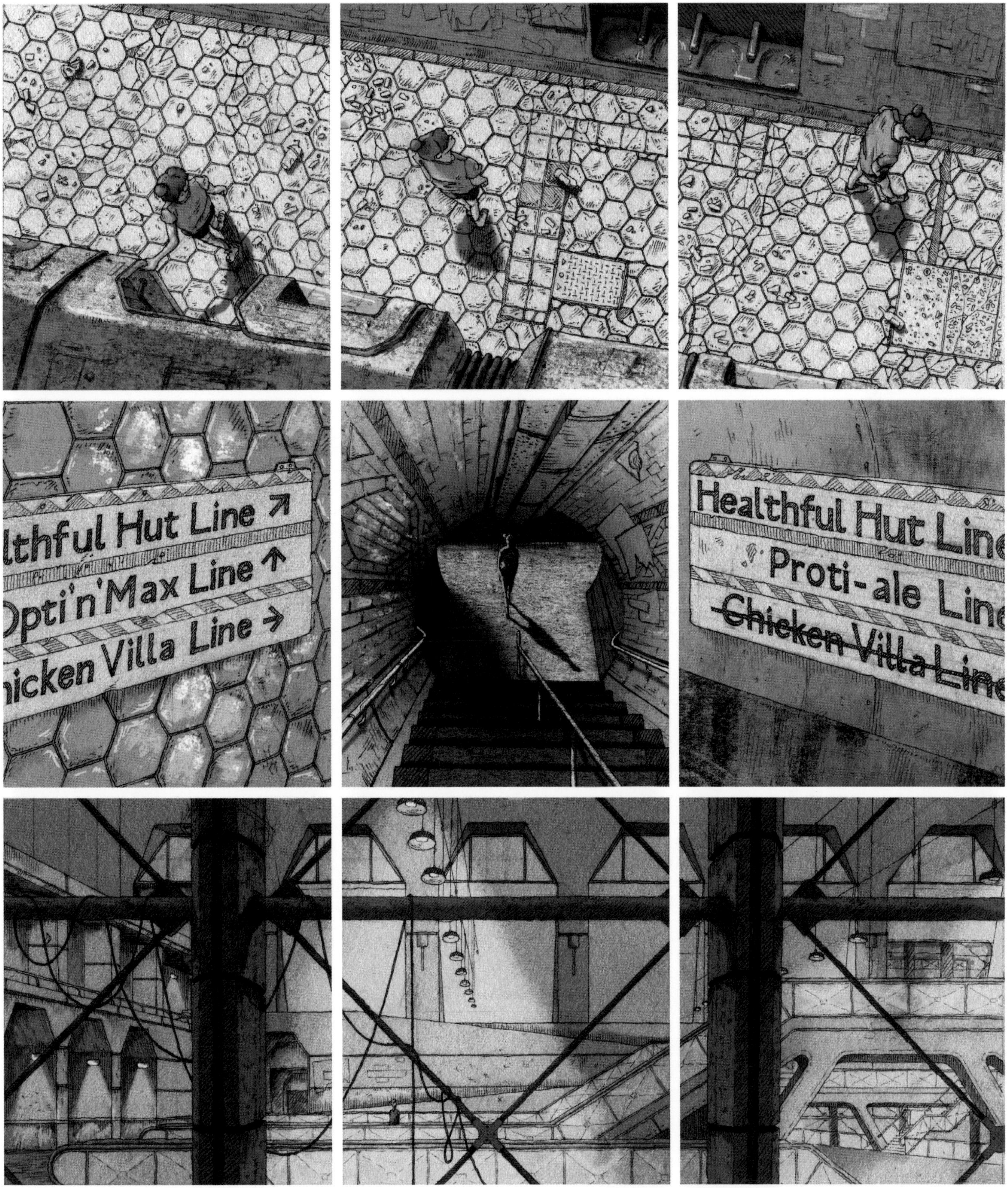
lthful Hut Line ↗
Opti'n'Max Line ↑
hicken Villa Line →
Healthful Hut Line
Proti-ale Line
Chicken Villa Line

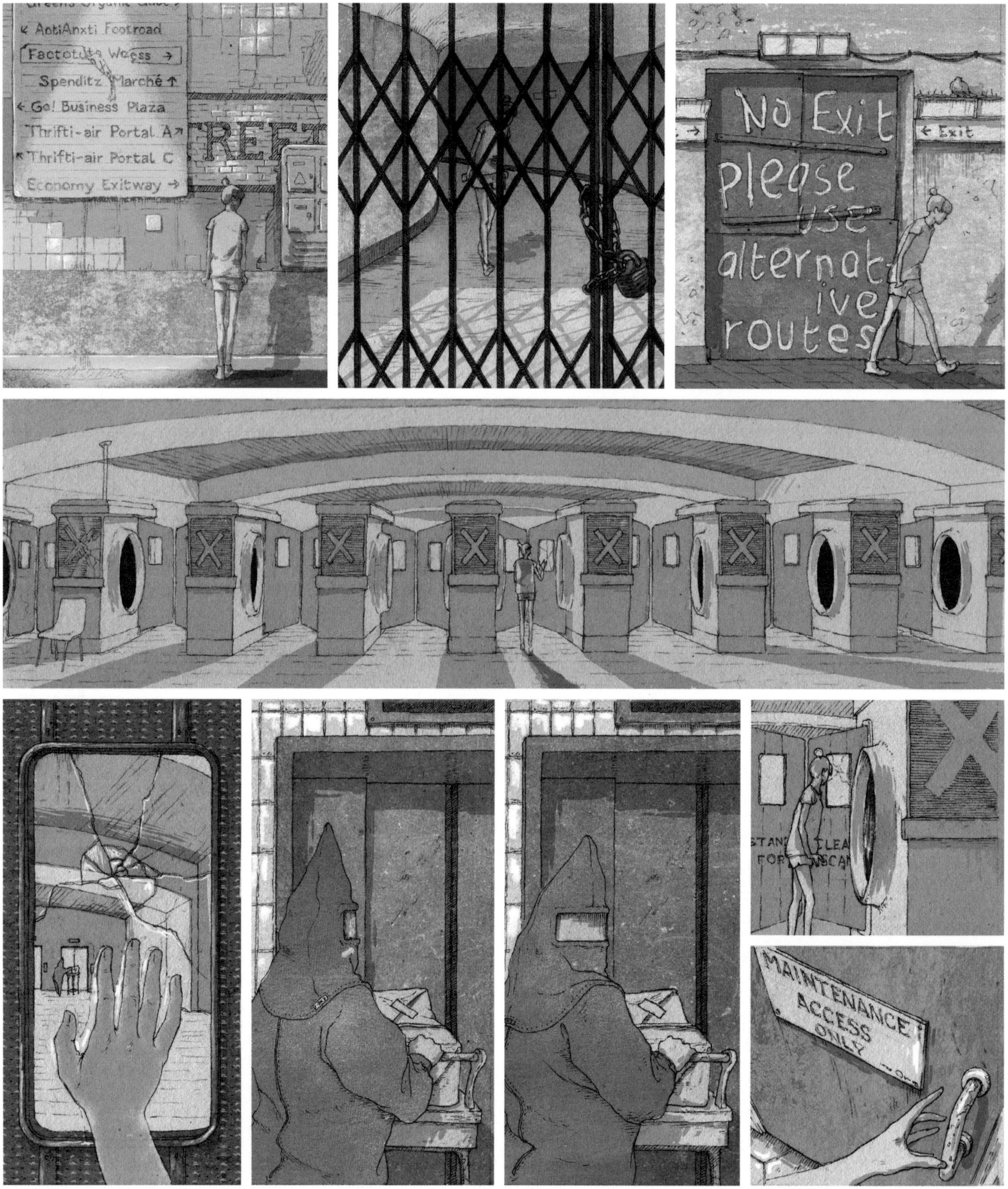
AntiAnxti Footroad
Spenditz Marché
Go! Business Plaza
Thrifti-air Portal A
Thrifti-air Portal C
Economy Exitway
No Exit
please use alternative routes
Exit
MAINTENANCE ACCESS ONLY

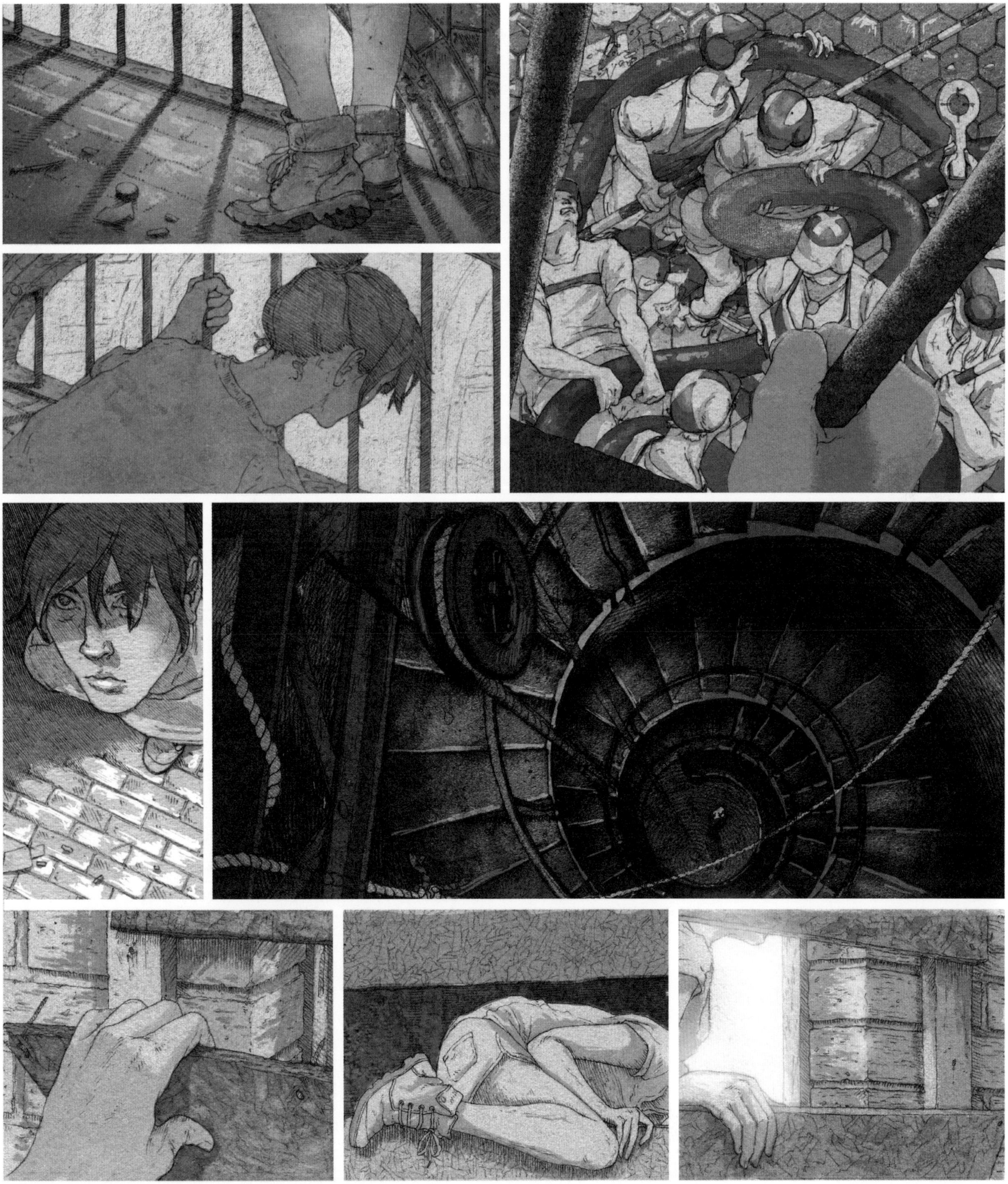

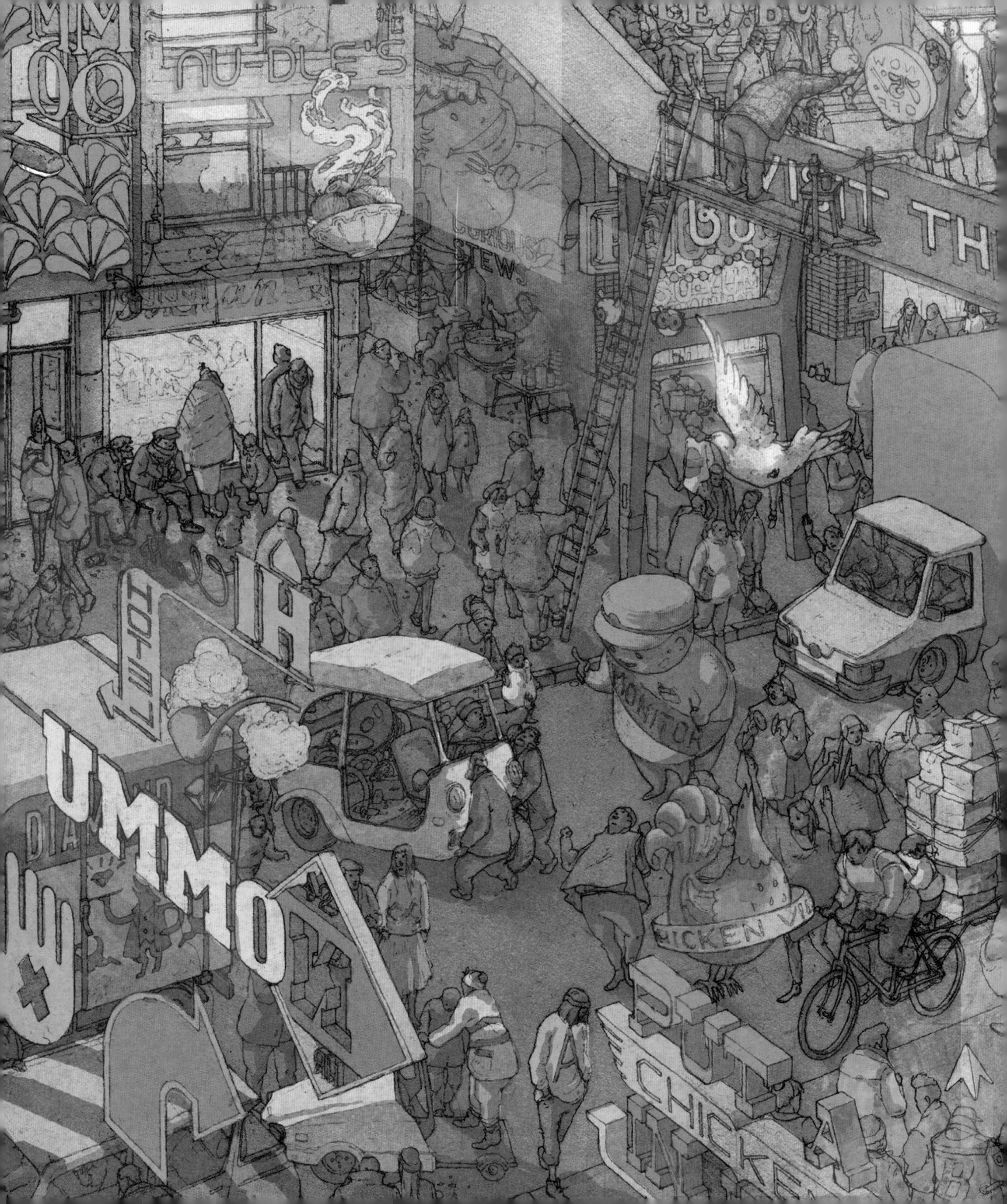
NU-DLE'S
CURIOUS STEWS
VISIT
MONITOR
UMMO
CHICKEN

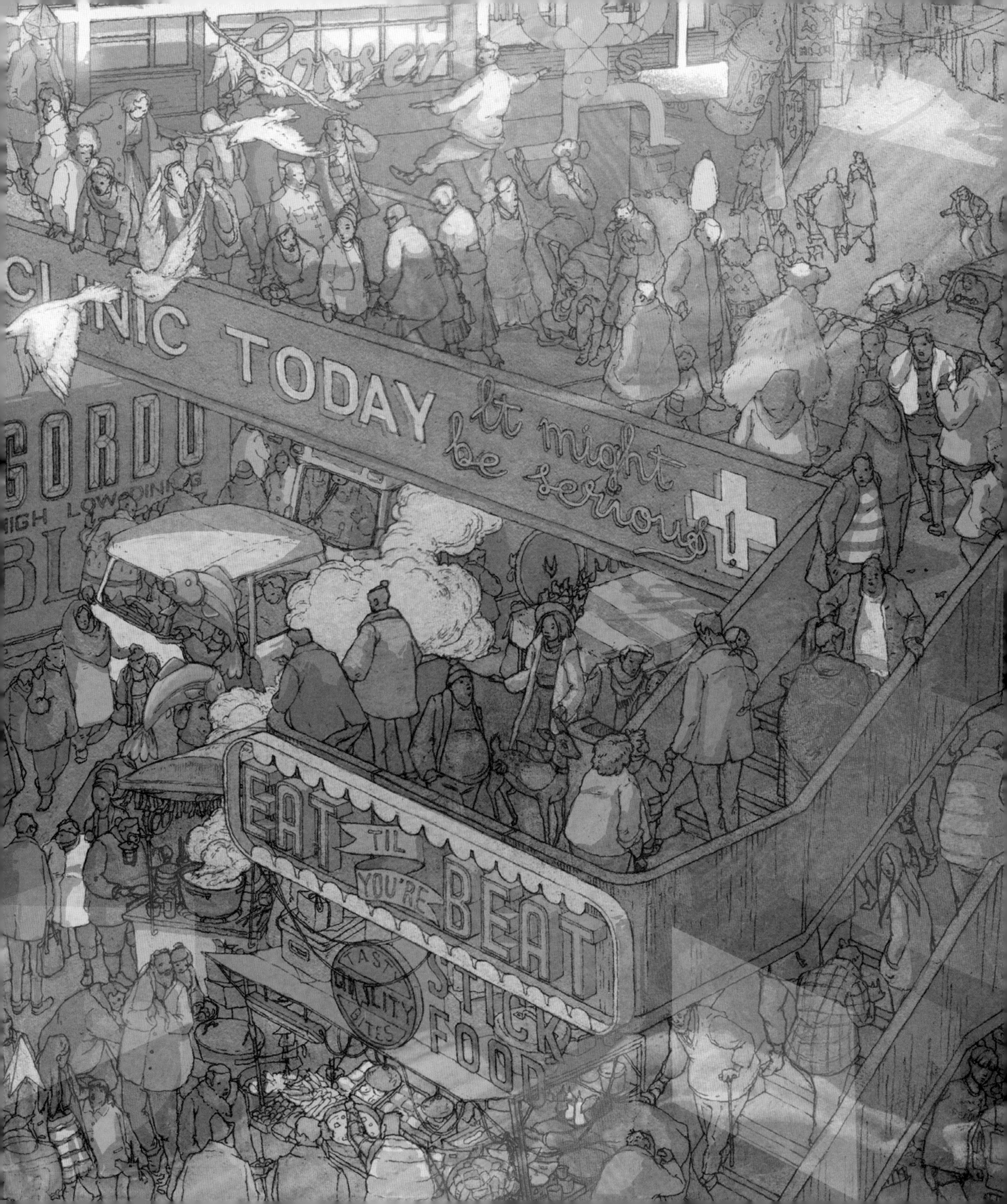
CLINIC TODAY
It might be serious!
EAT TIL YOU'RE BEAT
STICK FOOD

SQUARE

EYES

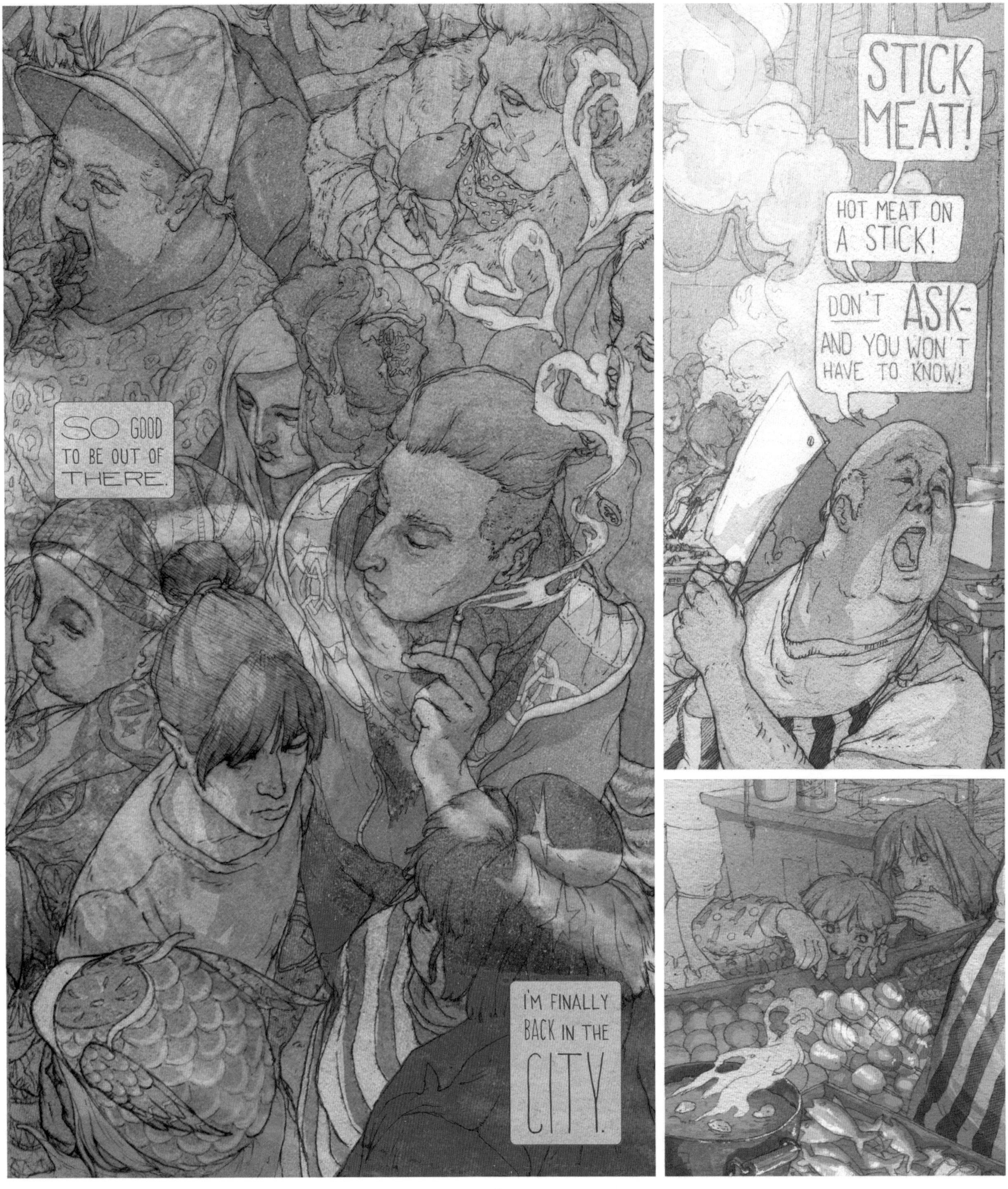
SO GOOD TO BE OUT OF THERE.
I'M FINALLY BACK IN THE CITY.
STICK MEAT!
HOT MEAT ON A STICK!
DON'T ASK- AND YOU WON'T HAVE TO KNOW!

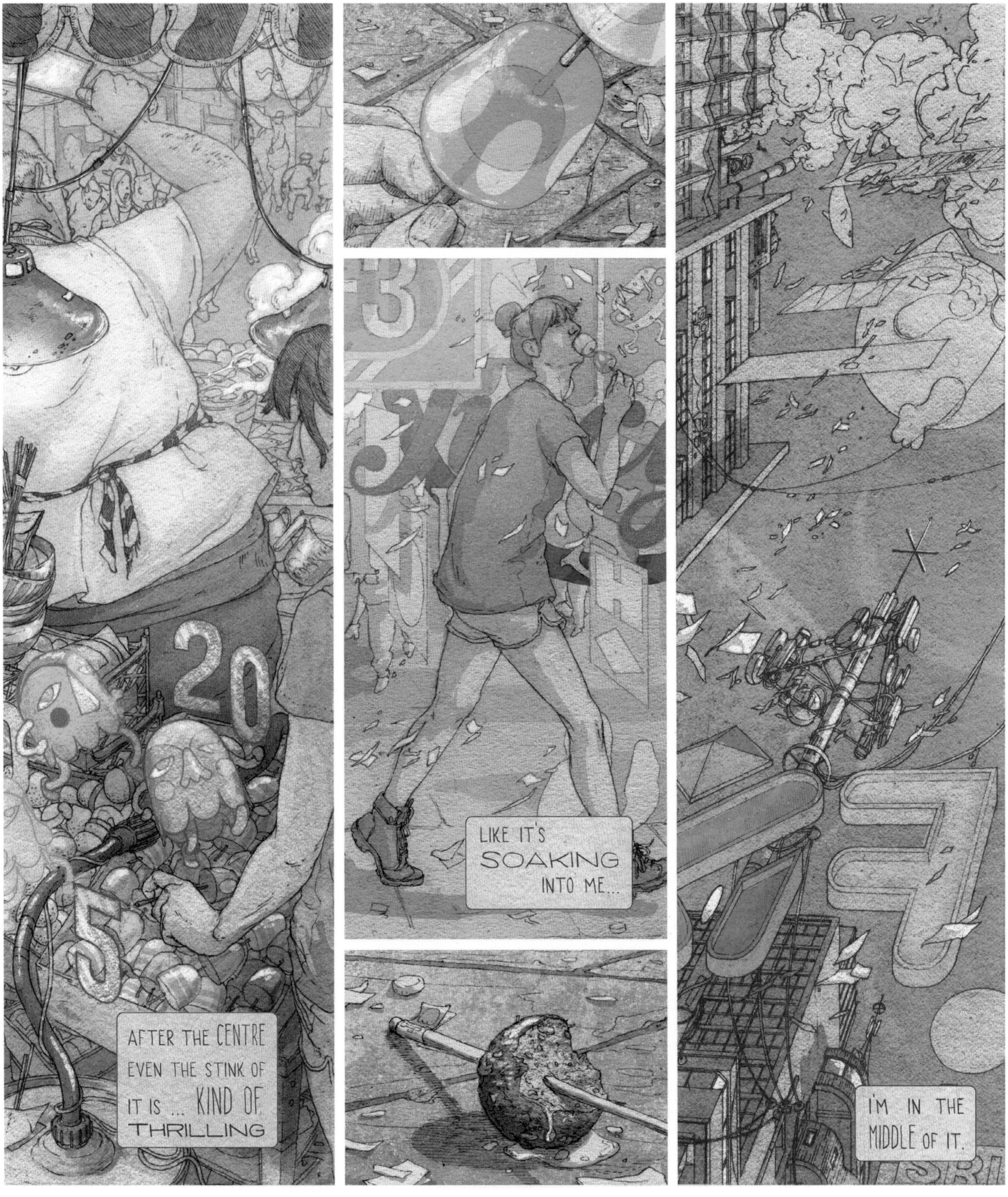
AFTER THE CENTRE
EVEN THE STINK OF
IT IS ... KIND OF
THRILLING
LIKE IT'S
SOAKING
INTO ME...
I'M IN THE
MIDDLE OF IT.

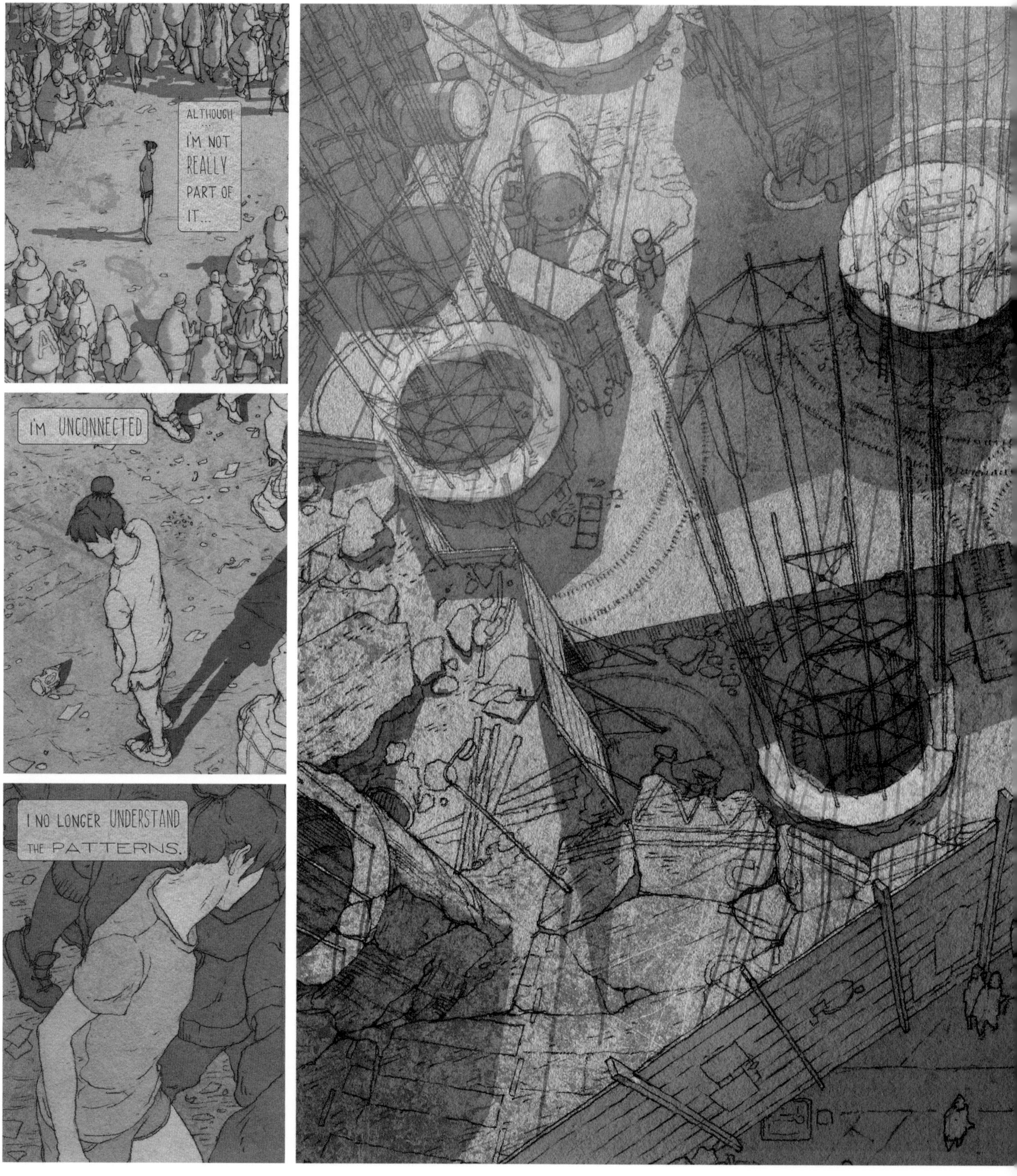
ALTHOUGH ...
I'M NOT REALLY PART OF IT...
I'M UNCONNECTED
I NO LONGER UNDERSTAND THE PATTERNS.

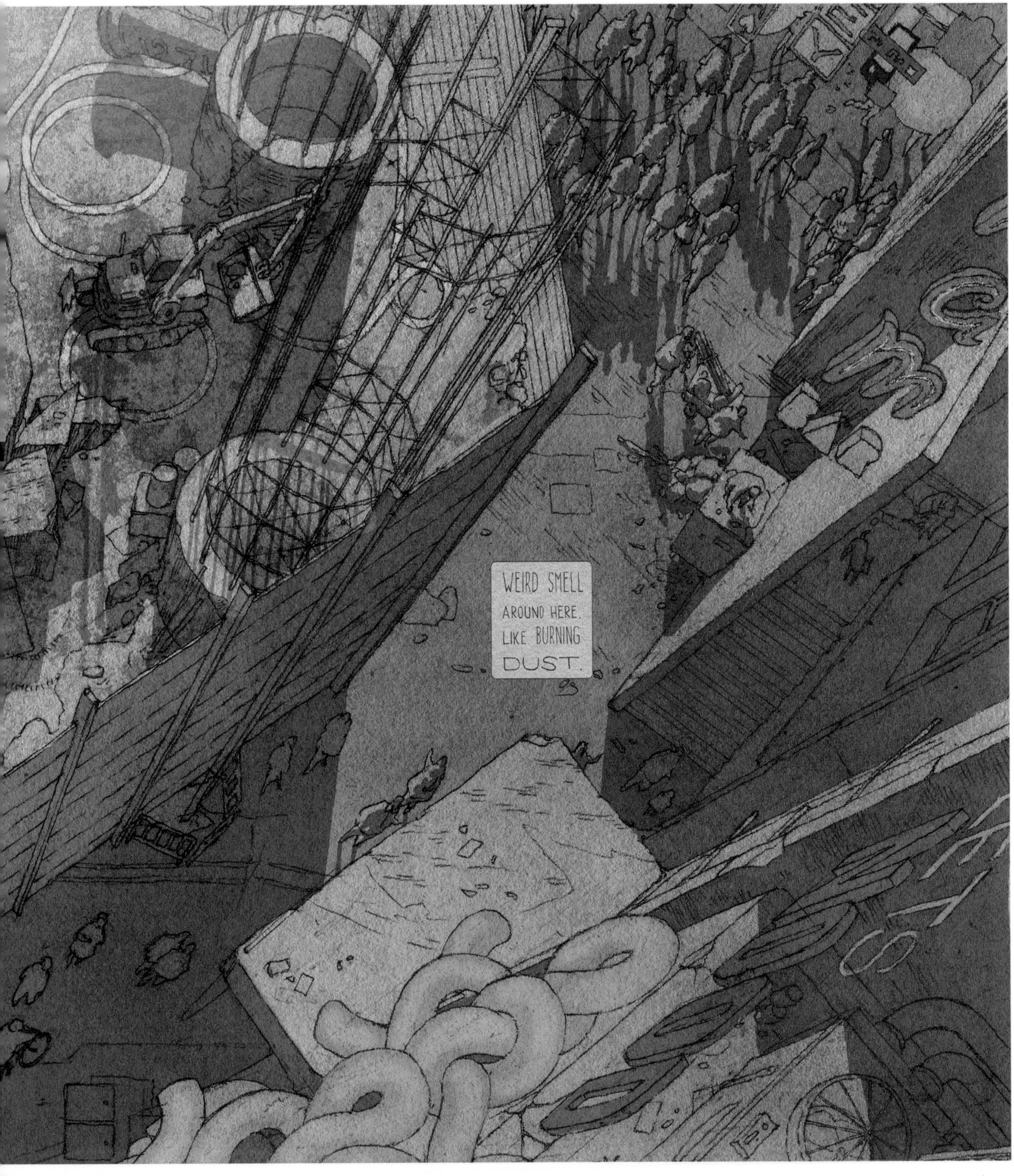
WEIRD SMELL AROUND HERE. LIKE BURNING DUST.

NOVARCADIA
Digitally integrated living
Optimal spatial efficiency
Quality milieu
Improve—just move!
HMM...
AH! IS THAT ARBYTE CAFE?
HUH.
THE CITY VANISHES

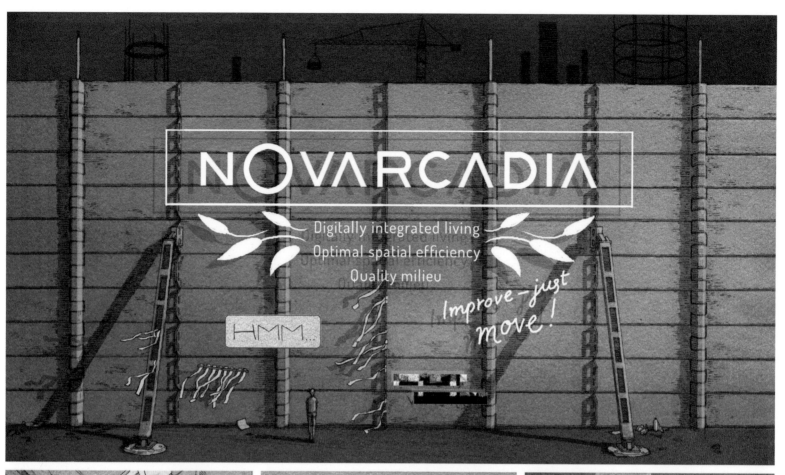

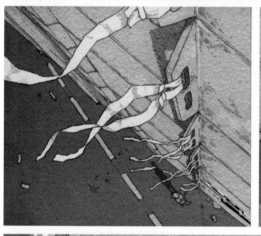

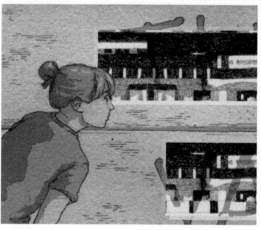

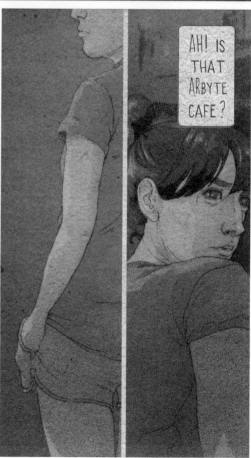

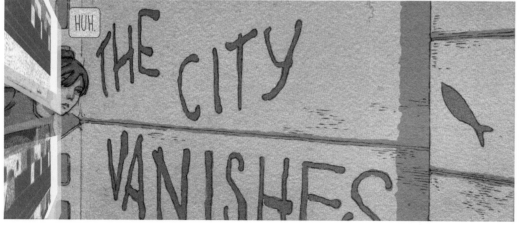

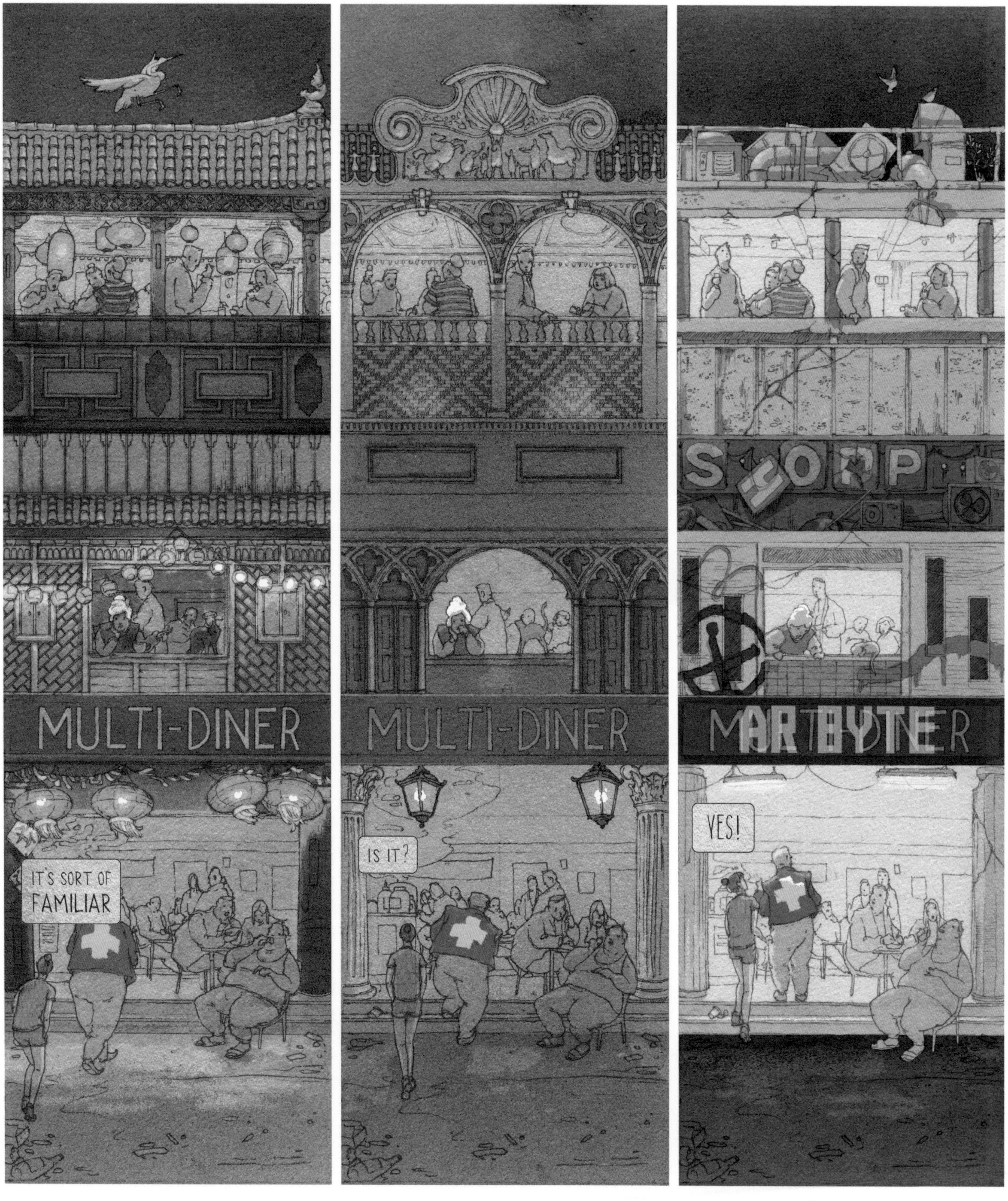
MULTI-DINER
IT'S SORT OF FAMILIAR
MULTI-DINER
IS IT?
SHOP
AR BYTE
YES!

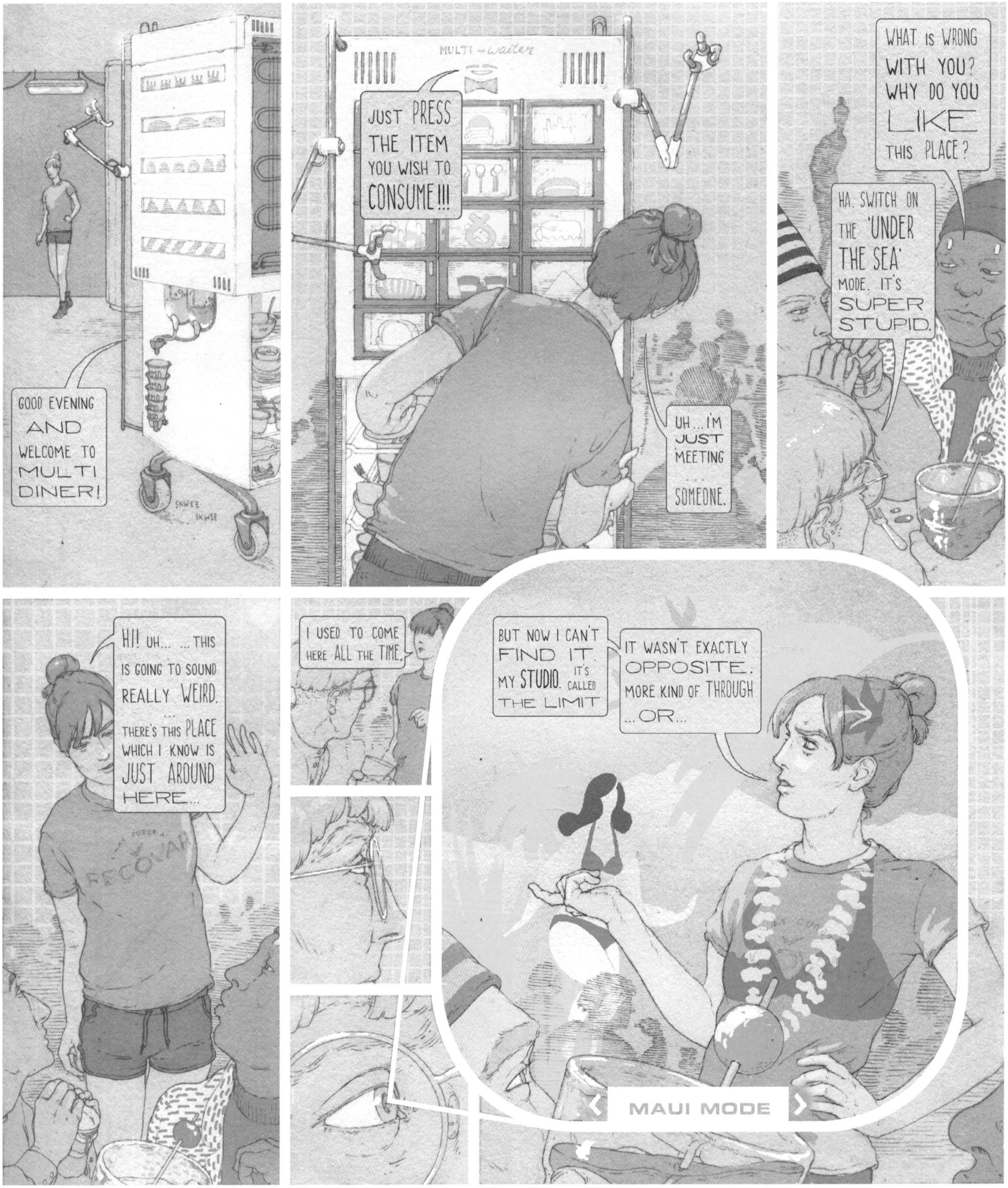
GOOD EVENING AND WELCOME TO MULTI DINER!
SKWEE SKWEE
MULTI-waiter
JUST PRESS THE ITEM YOU WISH TO CONSUME!!!
UH... I'M JUST MEETING ... SOMEONE.
WHAT IS WRONG WITH YOU? WHY DO YOU LIKE THIS PLACE?
HA. SWITCH ON THE 'UNDER THE SEA' MODE. IT'S SUPER STUPID.
HI! UH... ...THIS IS GOING TO SOUND REALLY WEIRD. ... THERE'S THIS PLACE WHICH I KNOW IS JUST AROUND HERE...
I USED TO COME HERE ALL THE TIME.
BUT NOW I CAN'T FIND IT. MY STUDIO. IT'S CALLED THE LIMIT
IT WASN'T EXACTLY OPPOSITE. MORE KIND OF THROUGH ...OR...
MAUI MODE

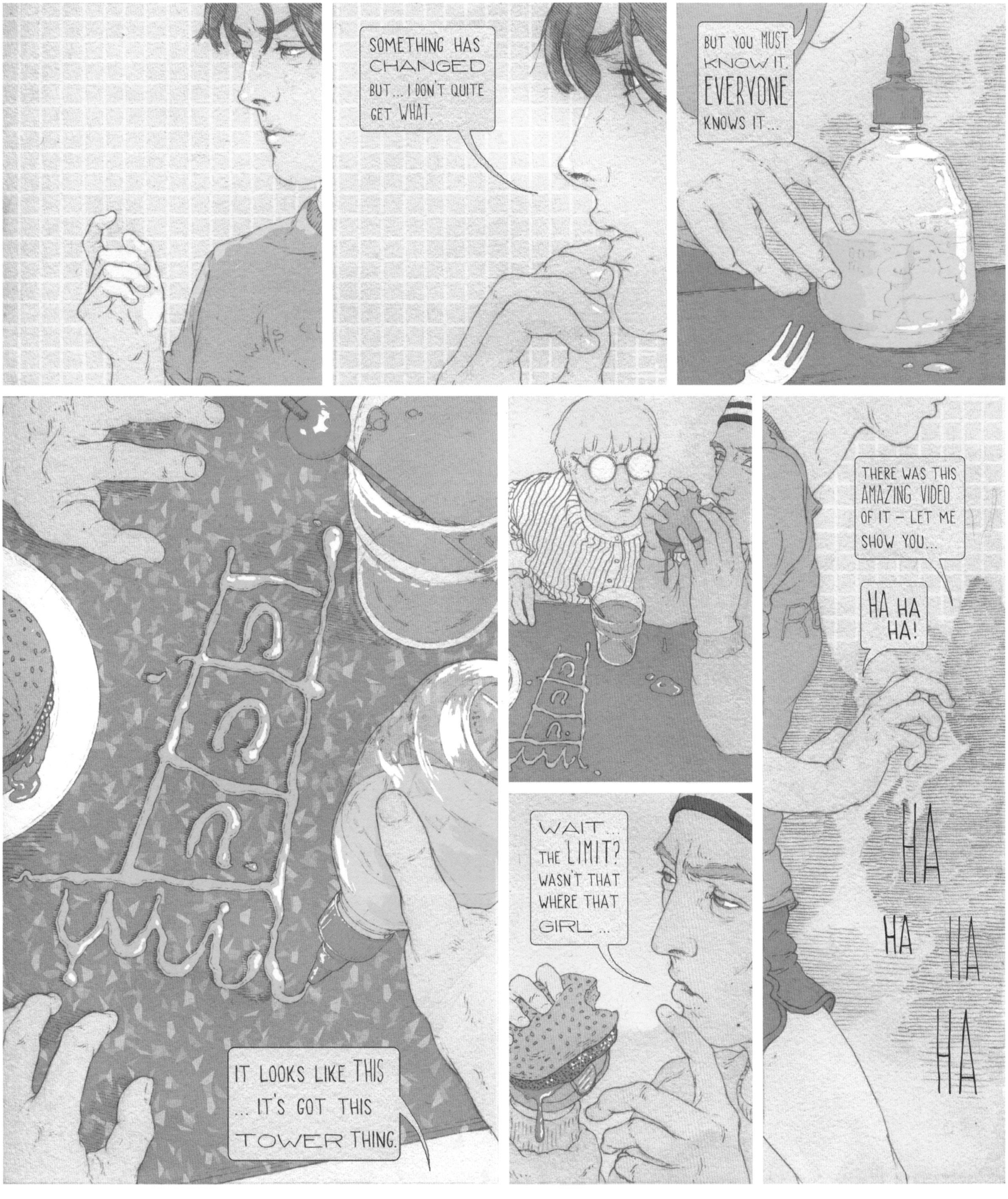
SOMETHING HAS CHANGED BUT... I DON'T QUITE GET WHAT.
BUT YOU MUST KNOW IT. EVERYONE KNOWS IT...
IT LOOKS LIKE THIS ... IT'S GOT THIS TOWER THING.
WAIT... THE LIMIT? WASN'T THAT WHERE THAT GIRL ...
THERE WAS THIS AMAZING VIDEO OF IT – LET ME SHOW YOU...
HA HA HA!
HA
HA HA
HA

はと
ピーン

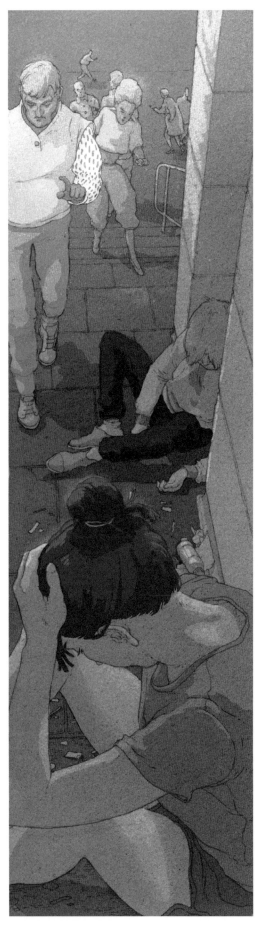

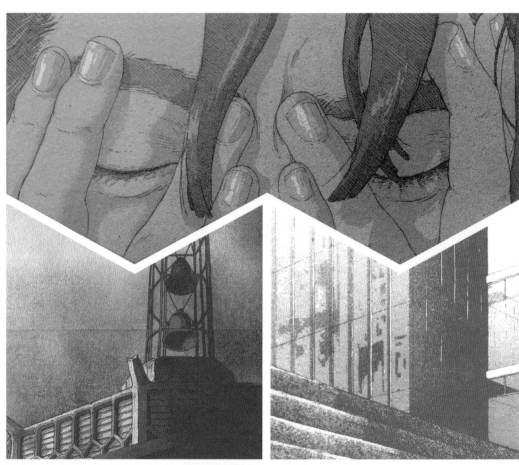

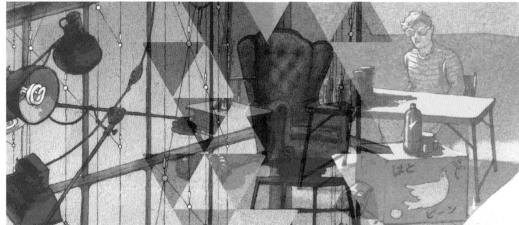

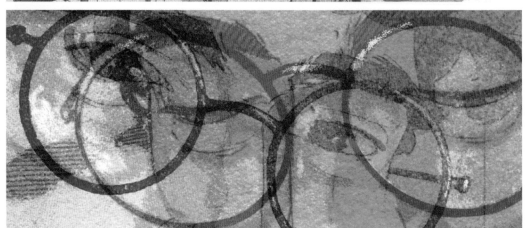

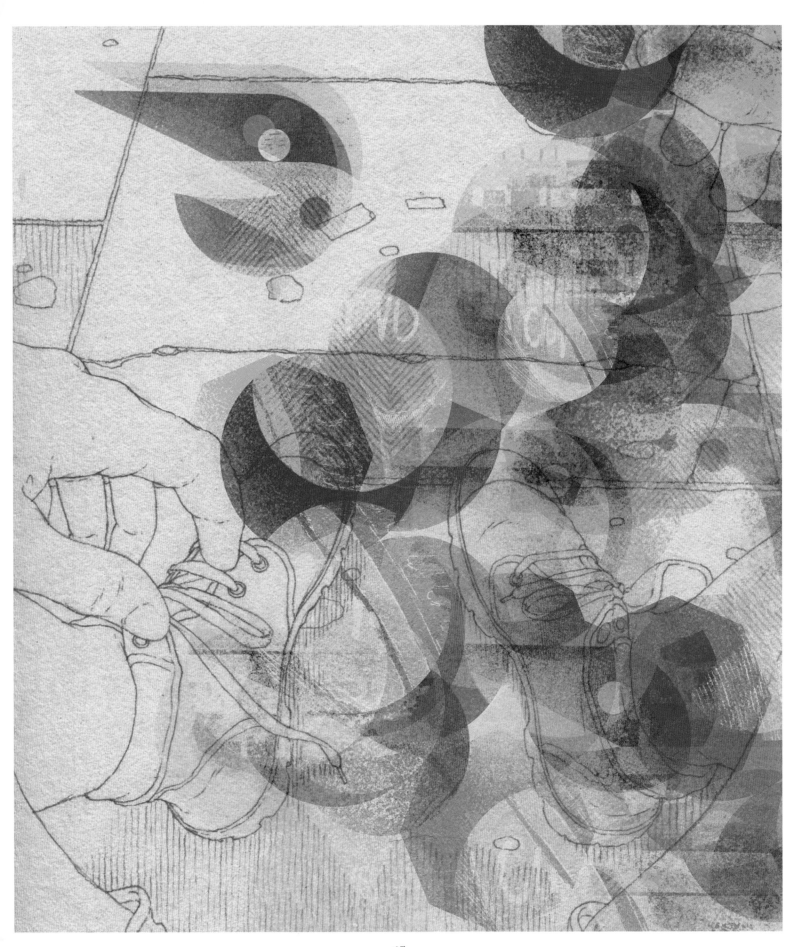

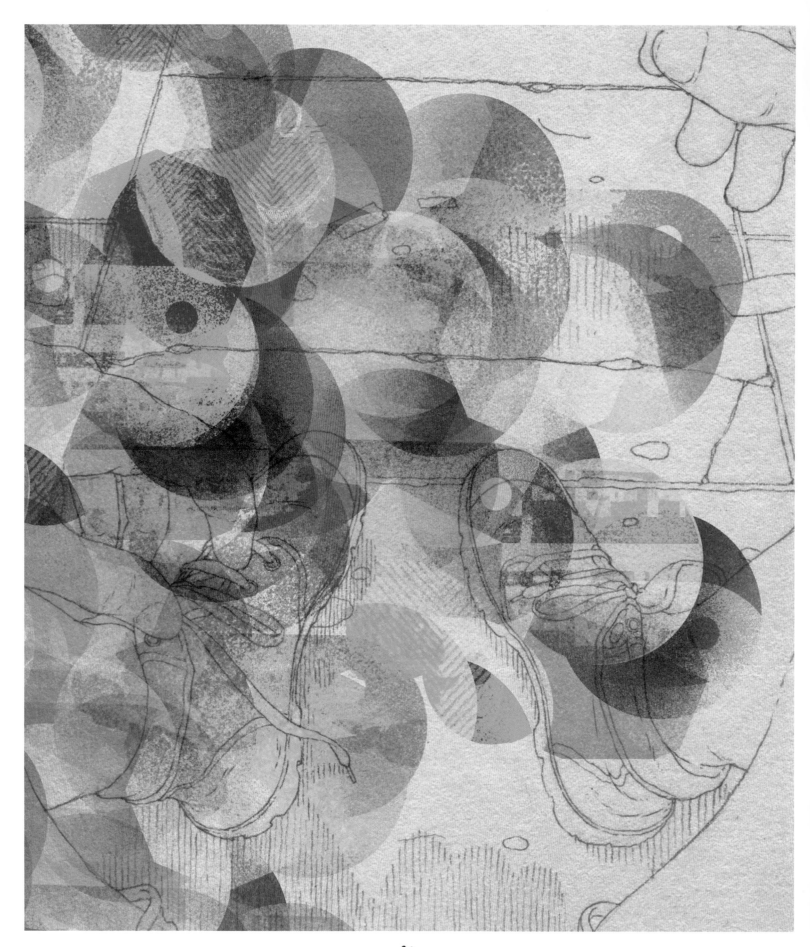

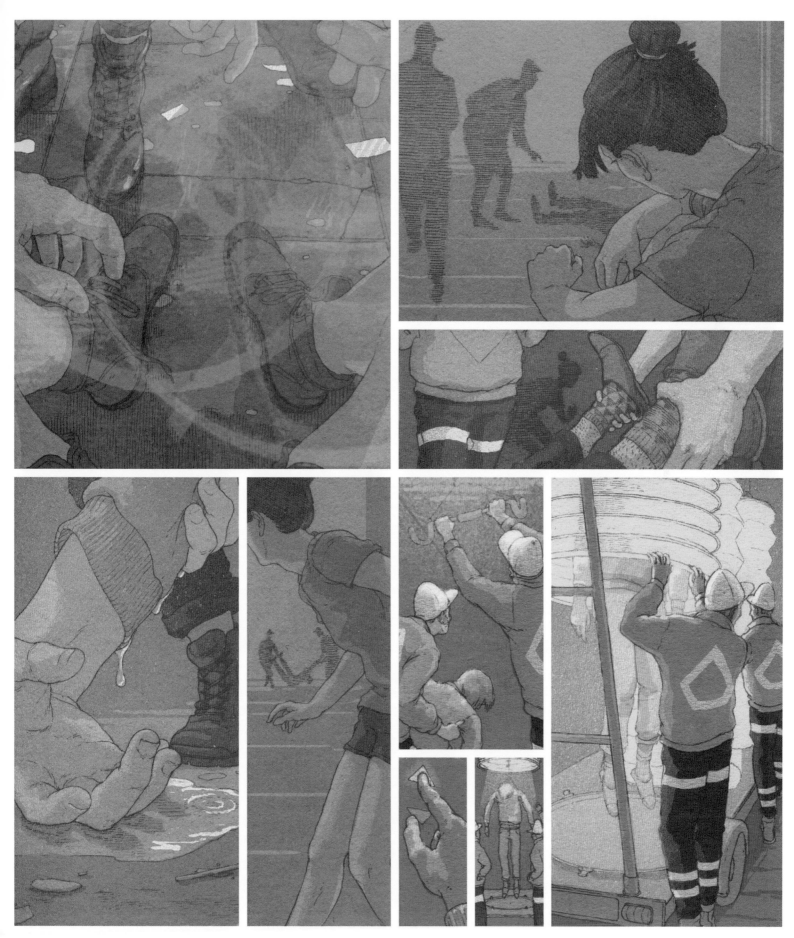

CHEAP!

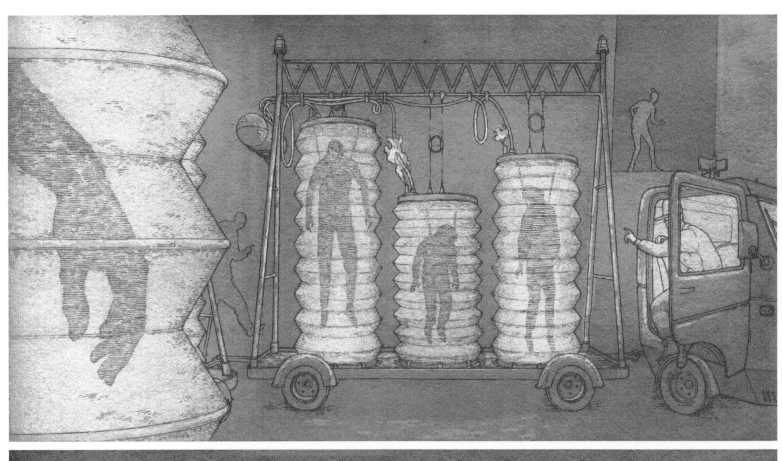

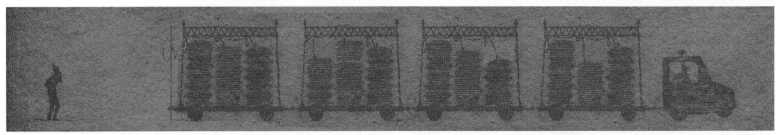

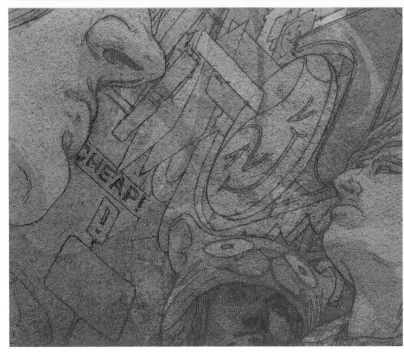

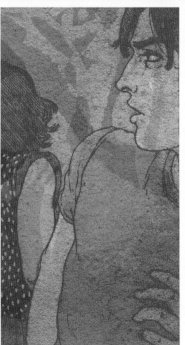

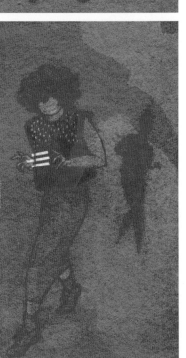

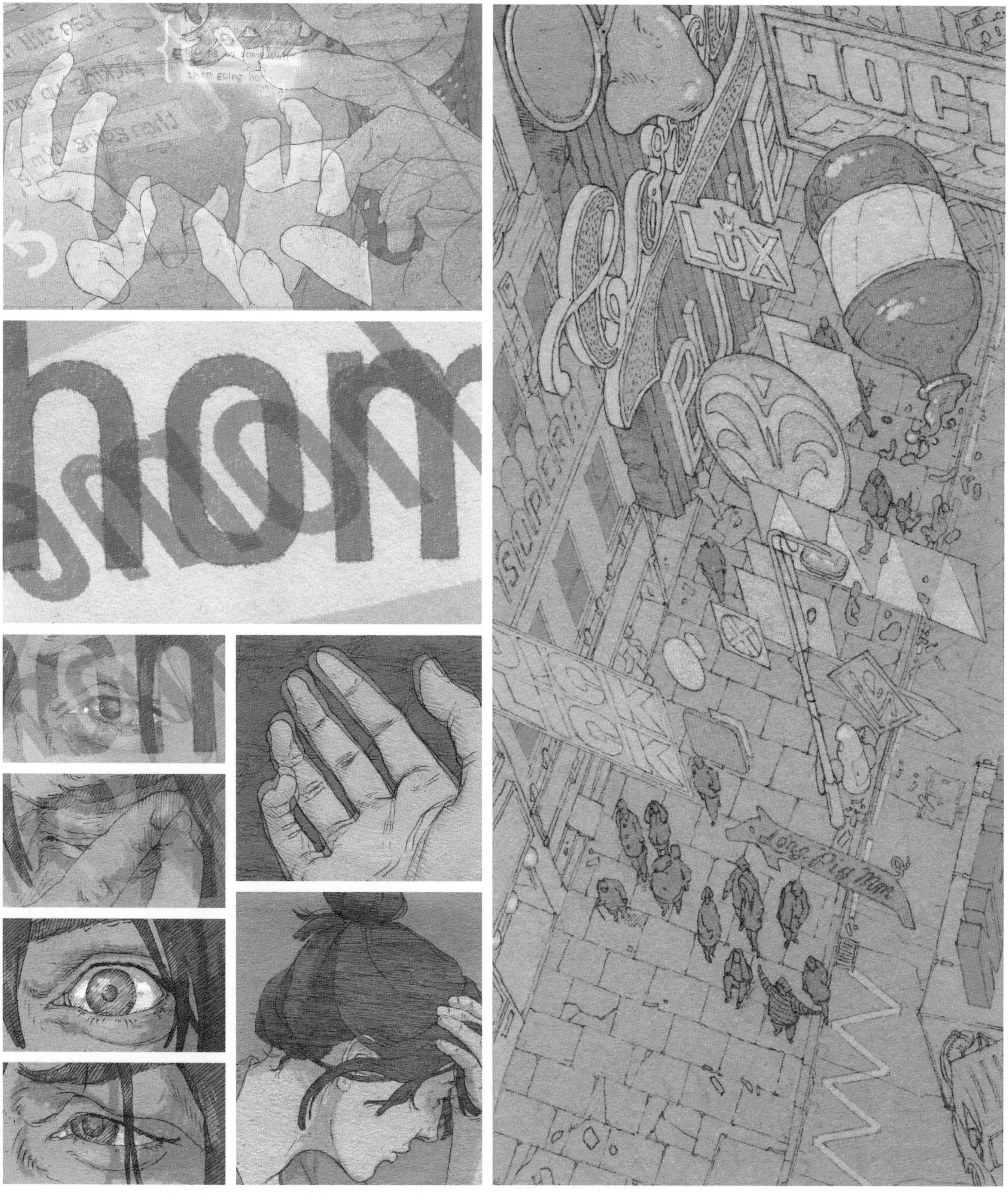
LUX

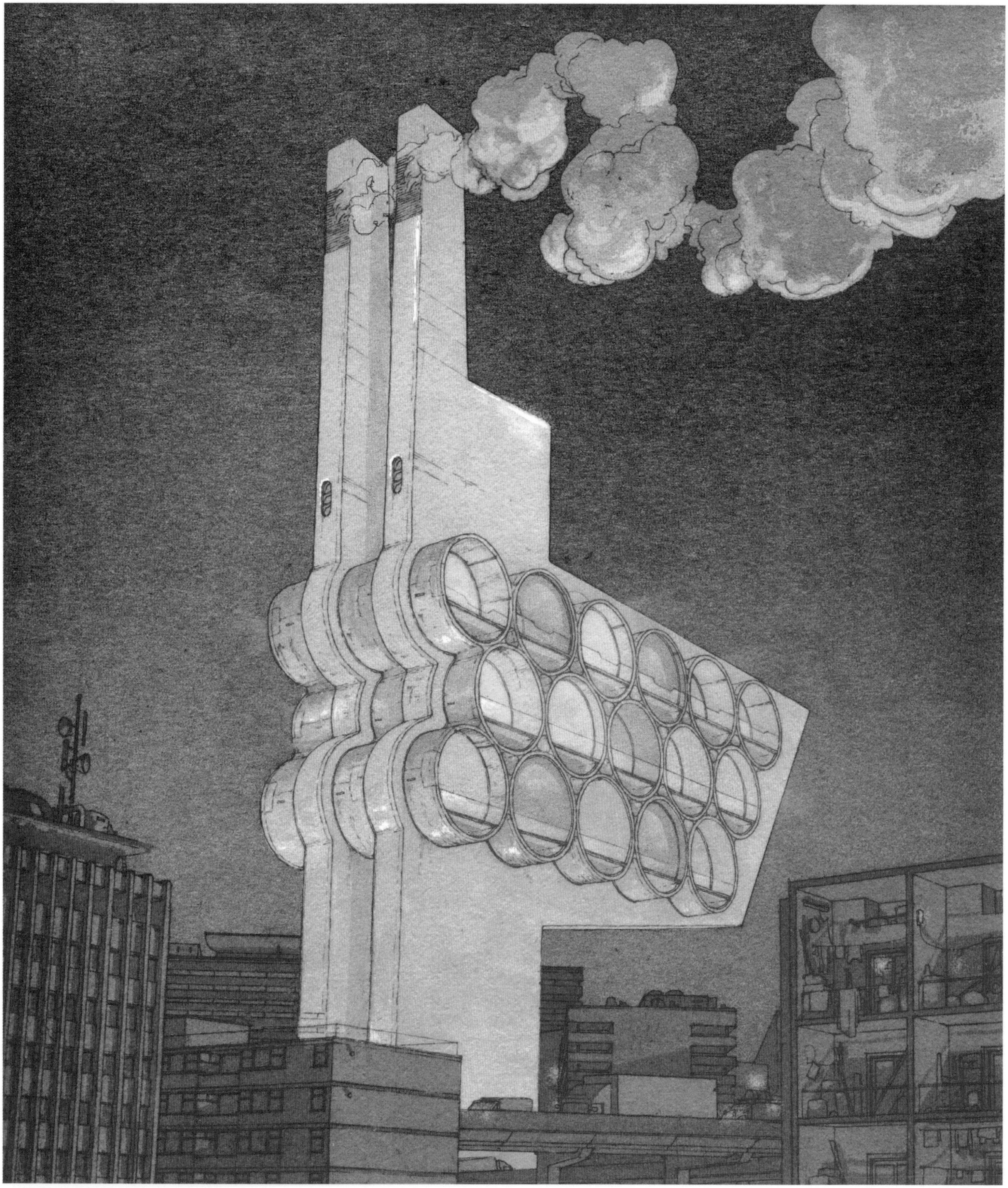

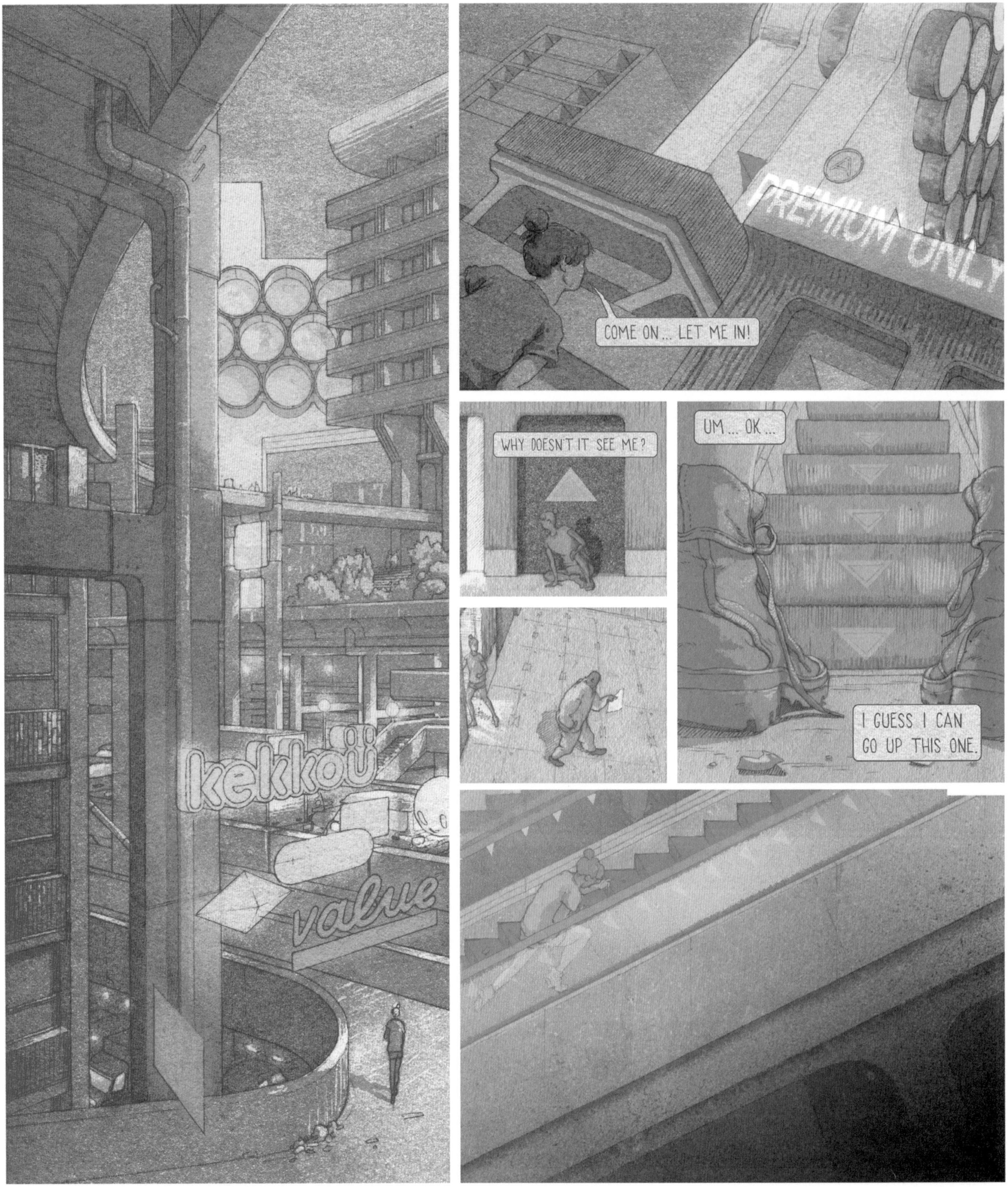

kekkou
value
PREMIUM ONLY
COME ON ... LET ME IN!
WHY DOESN'T IT SEE ME?
UM ... OK ...
I GUESS I CAN GO UP THIS ONE.

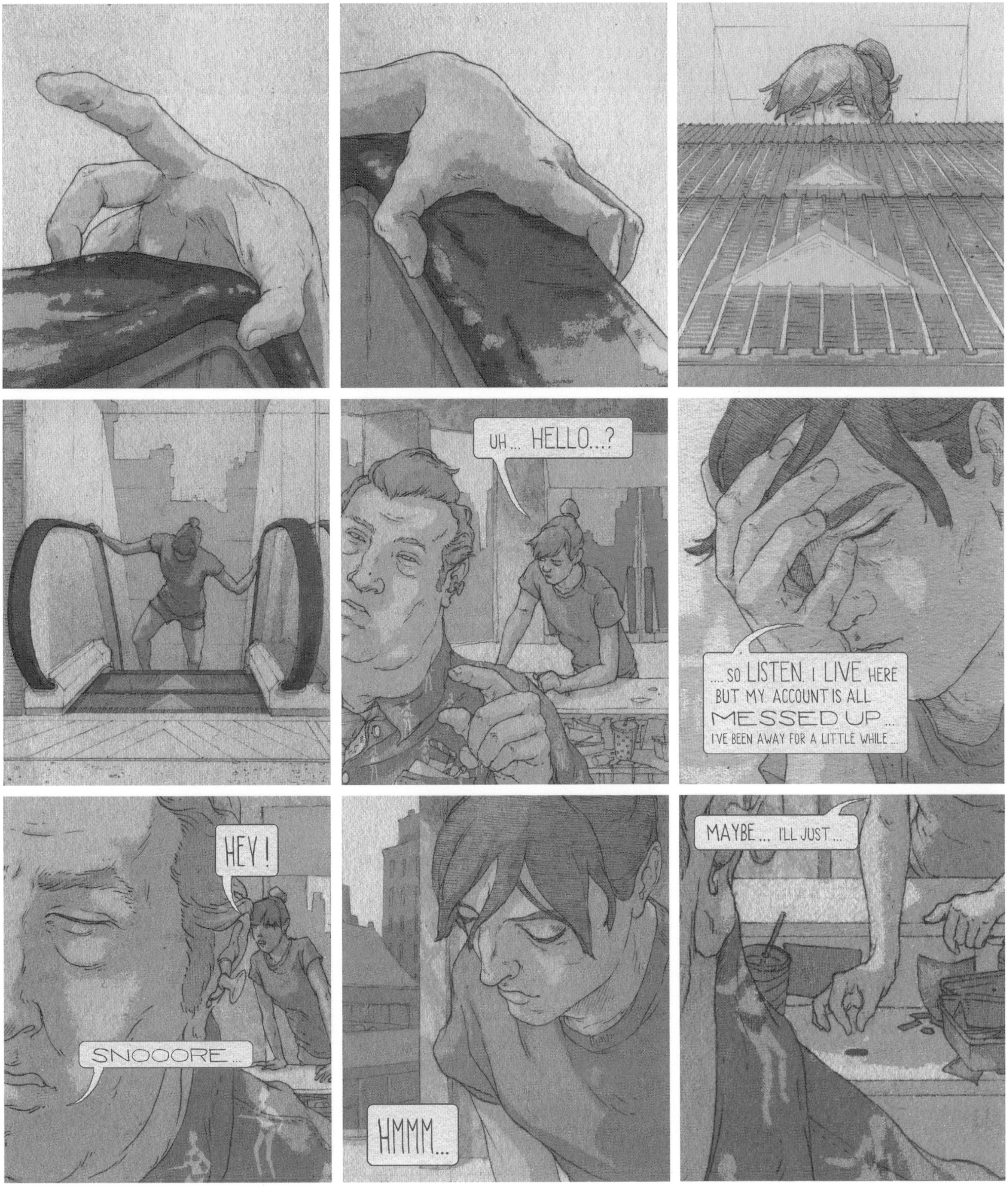
UH... HELLO...?
.... SO LISTEN. I LIVE HERE
BUT MY ACCOUNT IS ALL
MESSED UP...
I'VE BEEN AWAY FOR A LITTLE WHILE...
HEY!
SNOOORE...
HMMM...
MAYBE... I'LL JUST...

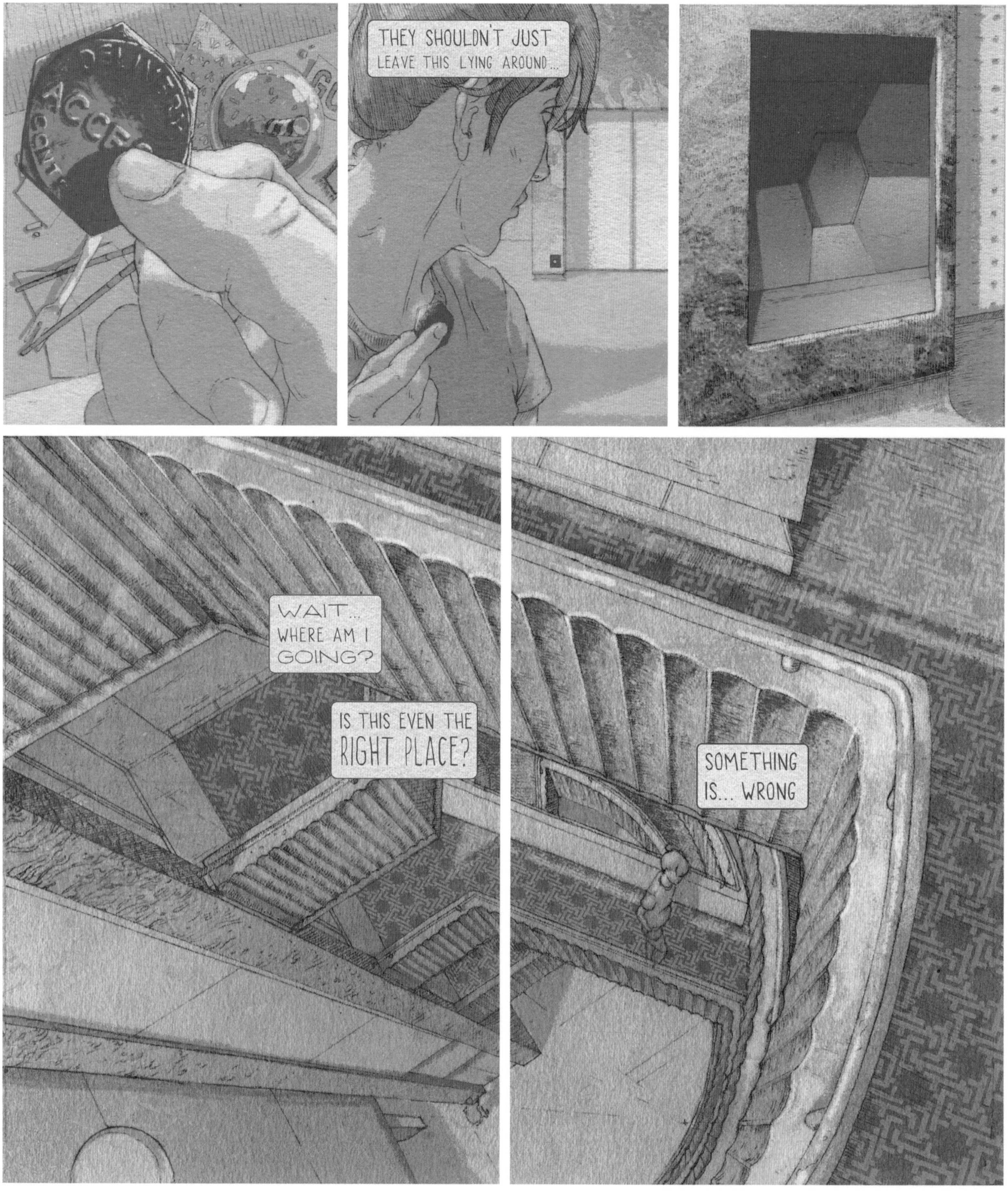
THEY SHOULDN'T JUST LEAVE THIS LYING AROUND...
WAIT... WHERE AM I GOING?
IS THIS EVEN THE RIGHT PLACE?
SOMETHING IS... WRONG

NO WAIT...
YEAH
THIS IS IT...

THIS STUFF IS MINE
I THINK...

WEIRD...
HAVE I LEFT THE
DOOR OPEN
ALL THIS TIME?

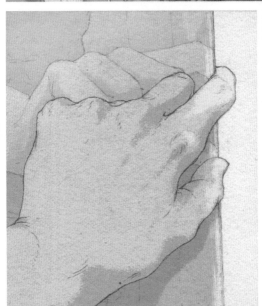

BEEP!

HUH?

WHY ARE YOU HERE
You are required to identify yourself
speak, or select a common response:

> I'm drunk!
> I work for a resident
> Where is this place?
> Unlicensed sexcreant
> This is all a terrible mistake

OTHER...!
TECHNICAL...!
LATER. OK?

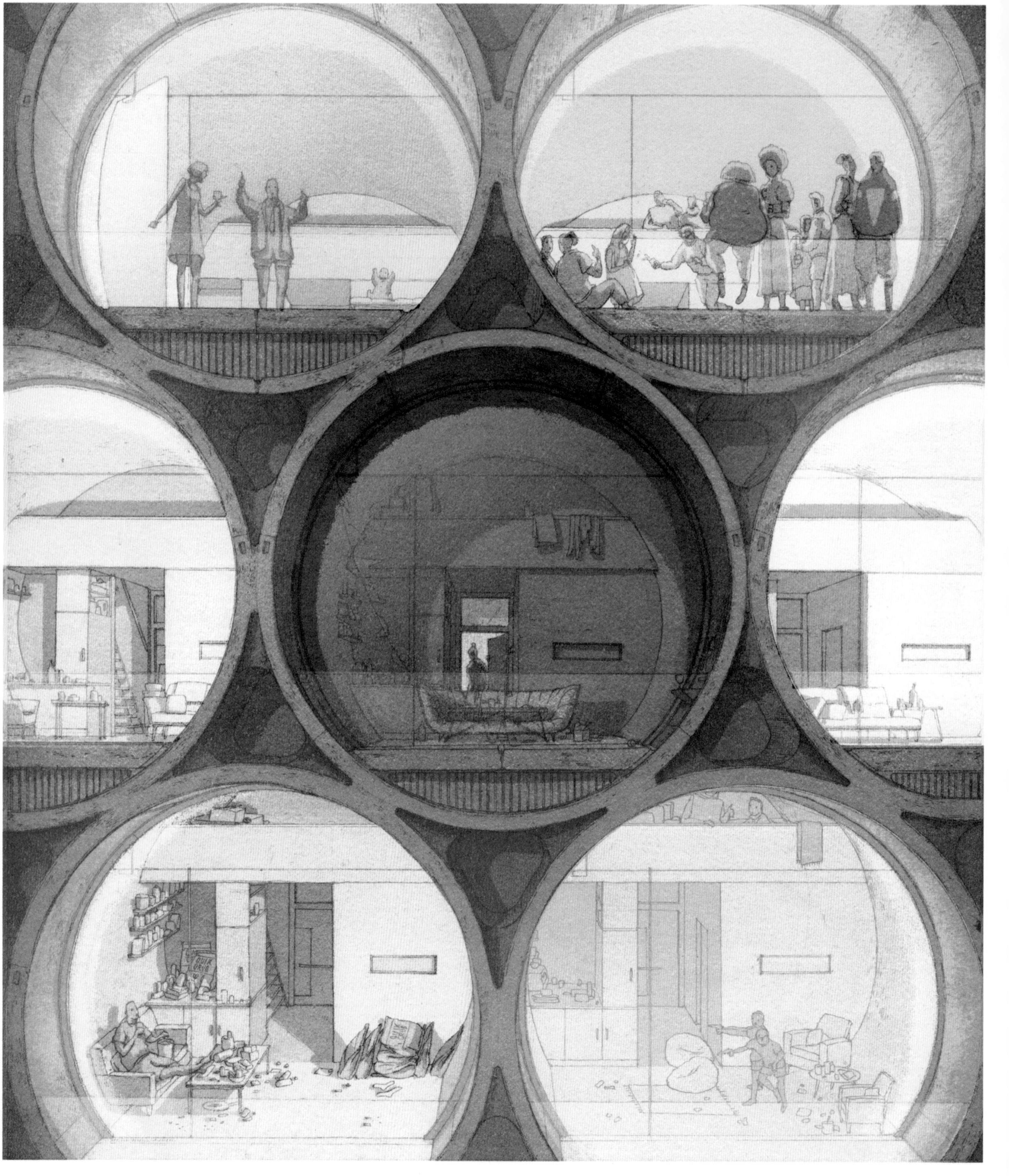

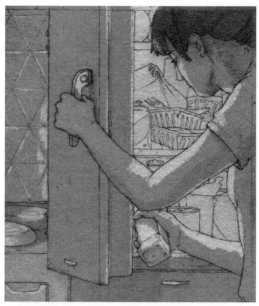

HMMM...

STILL FRESH?

BUT... I HAVEN'T BEEN HERE FOR MONTHS.

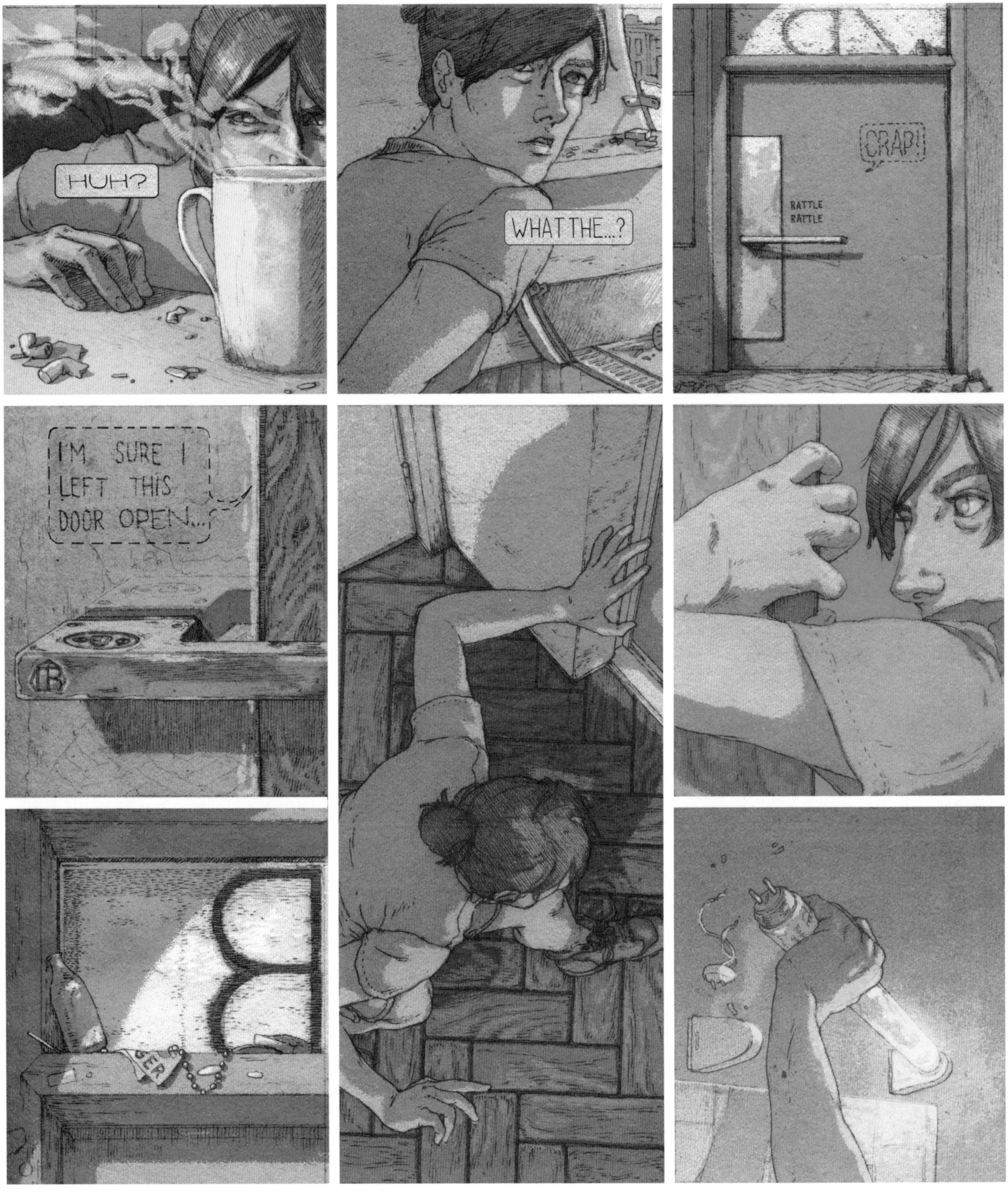
HUH?
WHAT THE...?
CRAP!
RATTLE
RATTLE
I'M SURE I LEFT THIS DOOR OPEN...

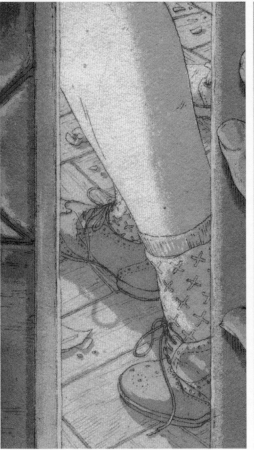

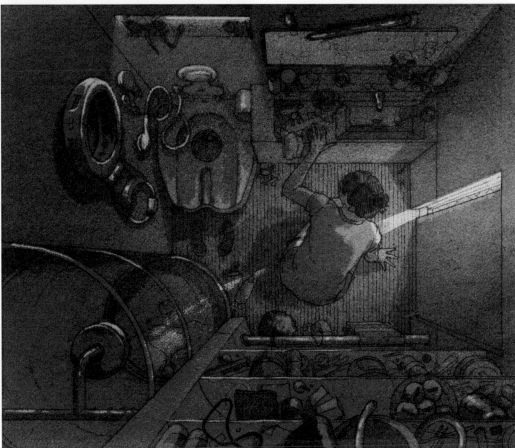

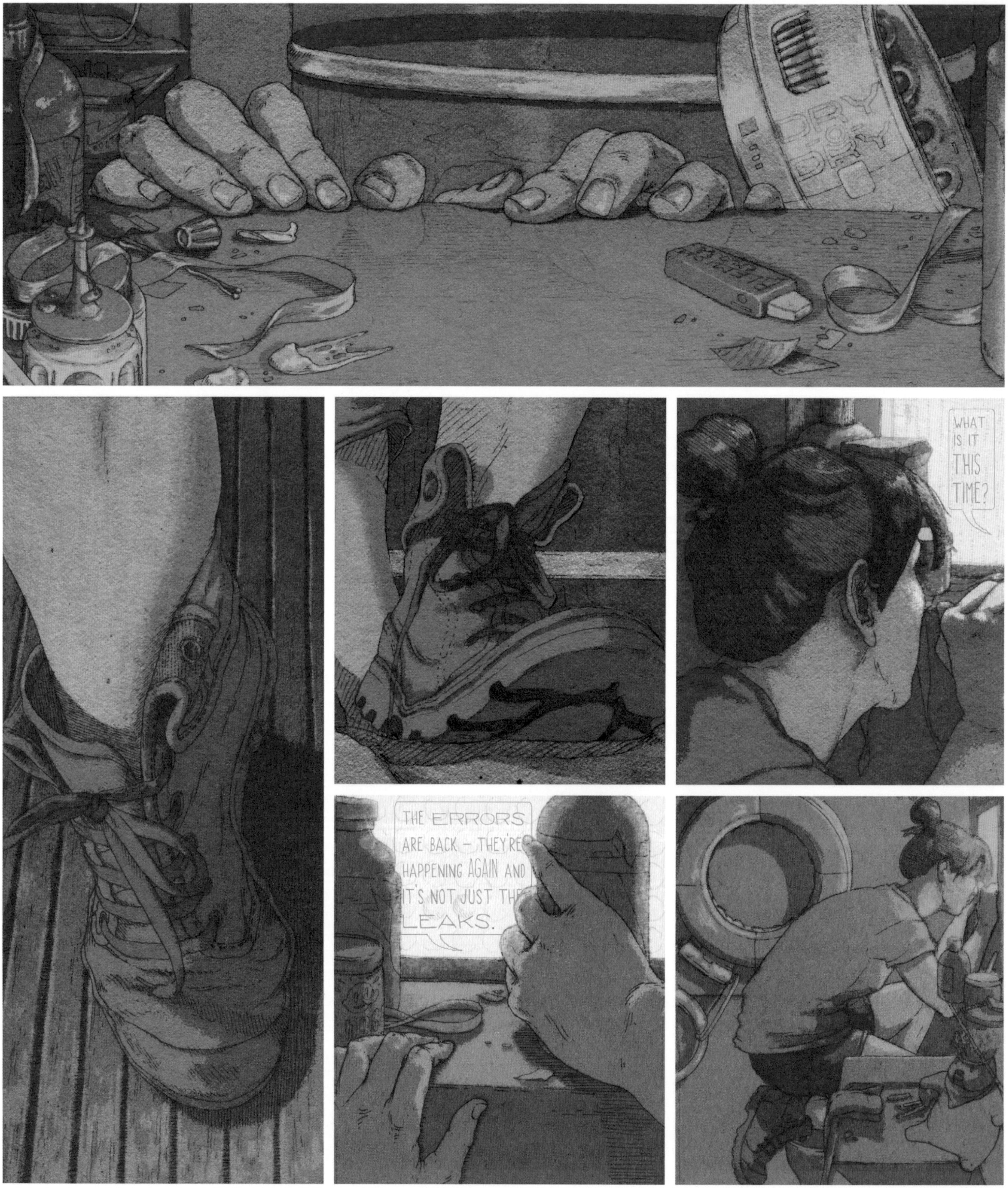
WHAT IS IT THIS TIME?
THE ERRORS ARE BACK – THEY'RE HAPPENING AGAIN AND IT'S NOT JUST THE LEAKS.

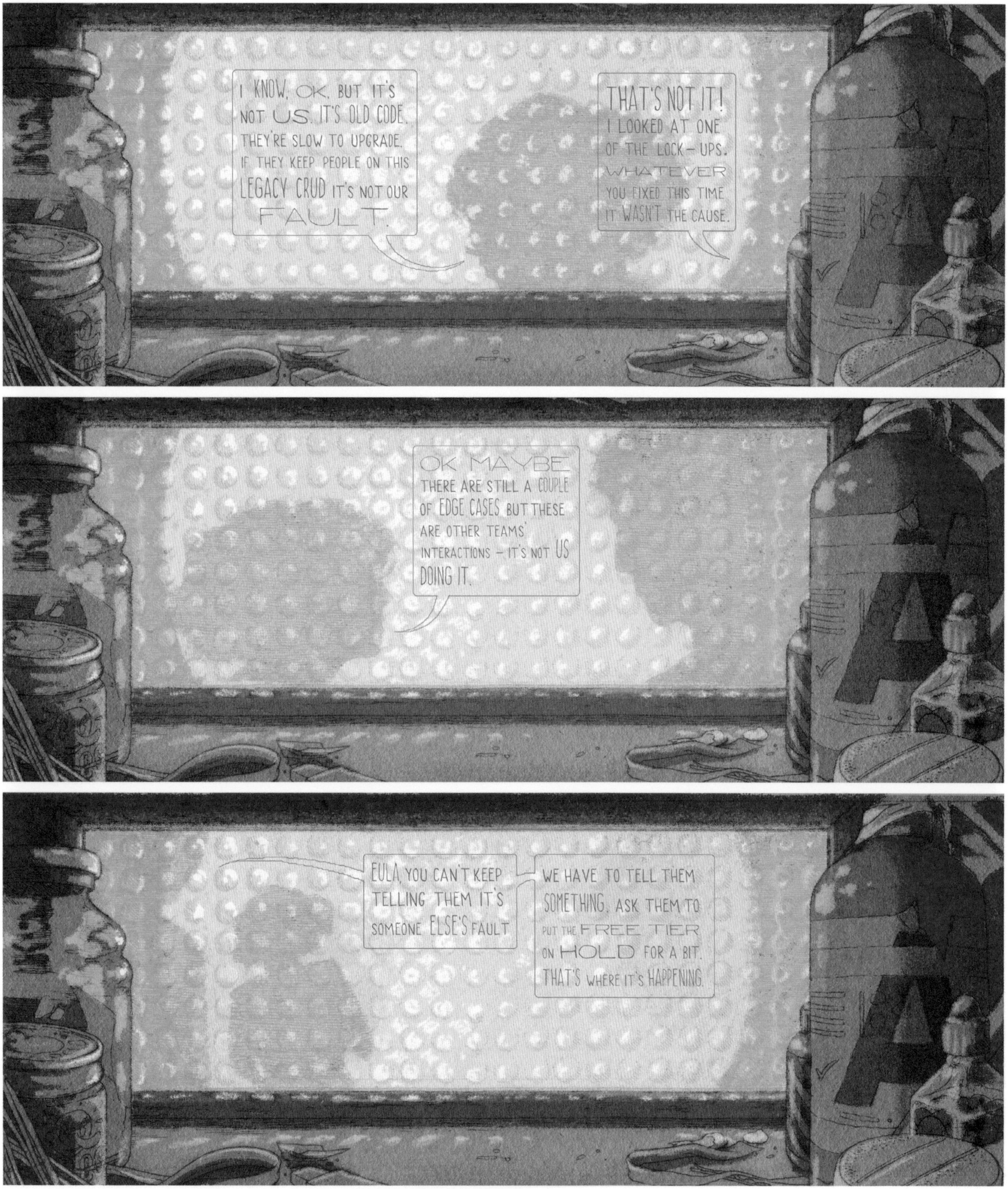
I KNOW, OK, BUT IT'S NOT US. IT'S OLD CODE. THEY'RE SLOW TO UPGRADE. IF THEY KEEP PEOPLE ON THIS LEGACY CRUD IT'S NOT OUR FAULT.
THAT'S NOT IT! I LOOKED AT ONE OF THE LOCK-UPS. WHATEVER YOU FIXED THIS TIME IT WASN'T THE CAUSE.
OK MAYBE THERE ARE STILL A COUPLE OF EDGE CASES BUT THESE ARE OTHER TEAMS' INTERACTIONS - IT'S NOT US DOING IT.
EULA, YOU CAN'T KEEP TELLING THEM IT'S SOMEONE ELSE'S FAULT
WE HAVE TO TELL THEM SOMETHING. ASK THEM TO PUT THE FREE TIER ON HOLD FOR A BIT. THAT'S WHERE IT'S HAPPENING.

YOU SAW THAT GUY... IT HAPPENED RIGHT IN THE OFFICE!
HE'S NOT RECOVERING... HE'S... STUCK LIKE THAT...!
Basysp
Miss Eula McKay Take TWO
OOOPS!
skin strip
THIS ISN'T JUST ABOUT YOU — LISTEN, IF THEY FIND OUT...
WHAT IF THIS IS HAPPENING ACROSS THE ROLLOUT? PEOPLE... THEY'LL GO CRAZY... LOSE IT...
IF YOU WON'T TELL THEM THEN I HAVE TO. LOOK, IF YOU CAN'T FIX THIS I HAVE TO GO UP THE CHAIN.

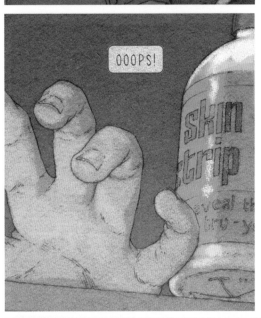

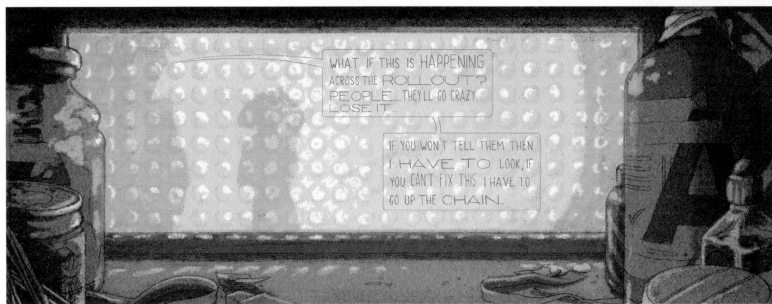

HMMN...?

OH YEAH?

AND THEN WHAT?

WHAT DO YOU THINK THEY'LL DO?

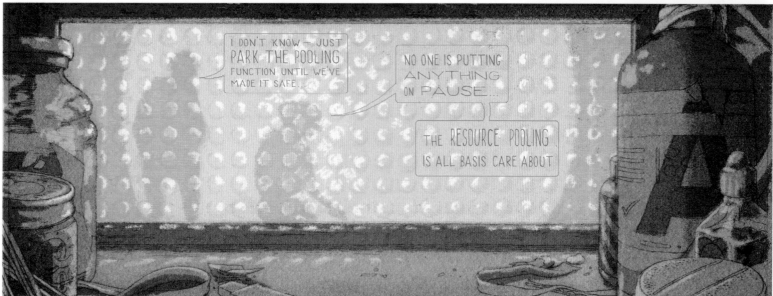

I DON'T KNOW — JUST PARK THE POOLING FUNCTION UNTIL WE'VE MADE IT SAFE...

NO ONE IS PUTTING ANYTHING ON PAUSE...

THE RESOURCE POOLING IS ALL BASIS CARE ABOUT

THAT VALUE IS LITERALLY THE ONLY THING THEY KEEP US AROUND FOR... YOU THINK THEY'RE GONNA SAY 'OH THANKS VERY MUCH, WE'LL LOOK INTO THAT'?

THEY'LL TAKE THE WHOLE TEAM. WE'LL ALL GET IT AND THEN THEY'LL CARRY ON WITHOUT FIXING ANYTHING... IF THIS BLOWS UP NO ONE IS GETTING OUT OF IT UNSCATHED.

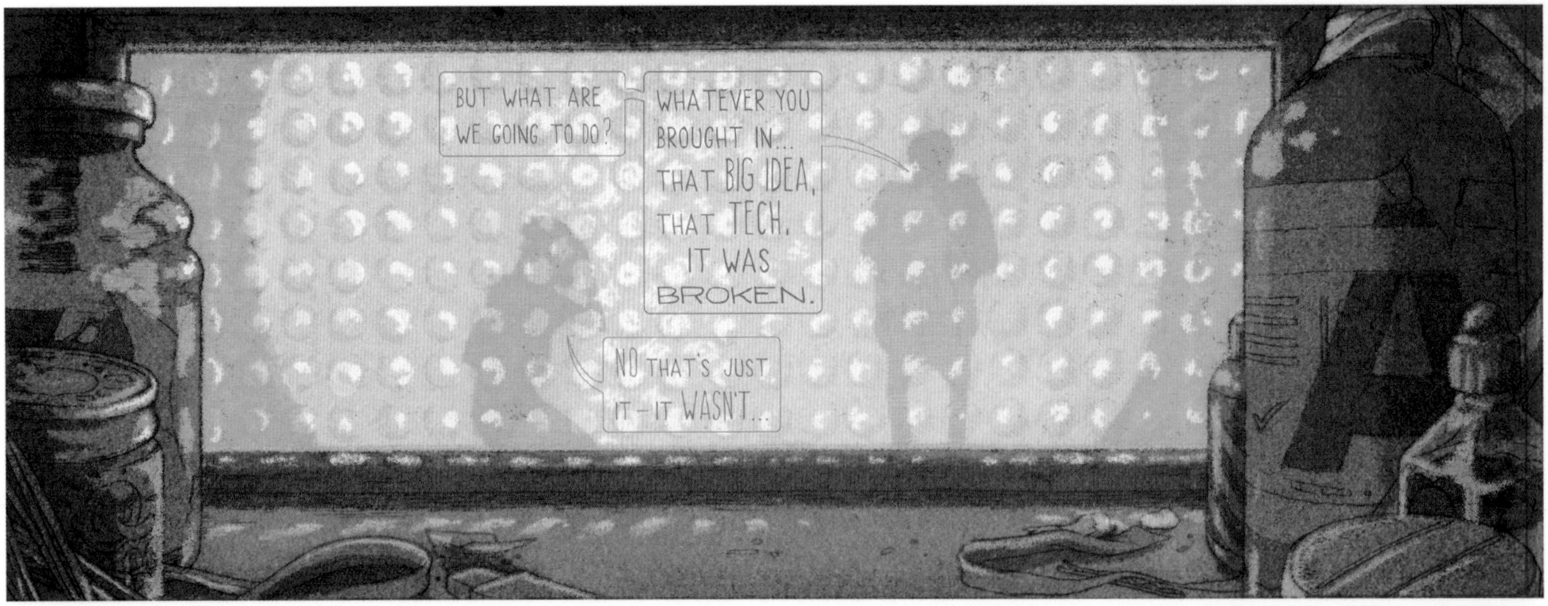
BUT WHAT ARE WE GOING TO DO?
WHATEVER YOU BROUGHT IN... THAT BIG IDEA, THAT TECH, IT WAS BROKEN.
NO THAT'S JUST IT - IT WASN'T...

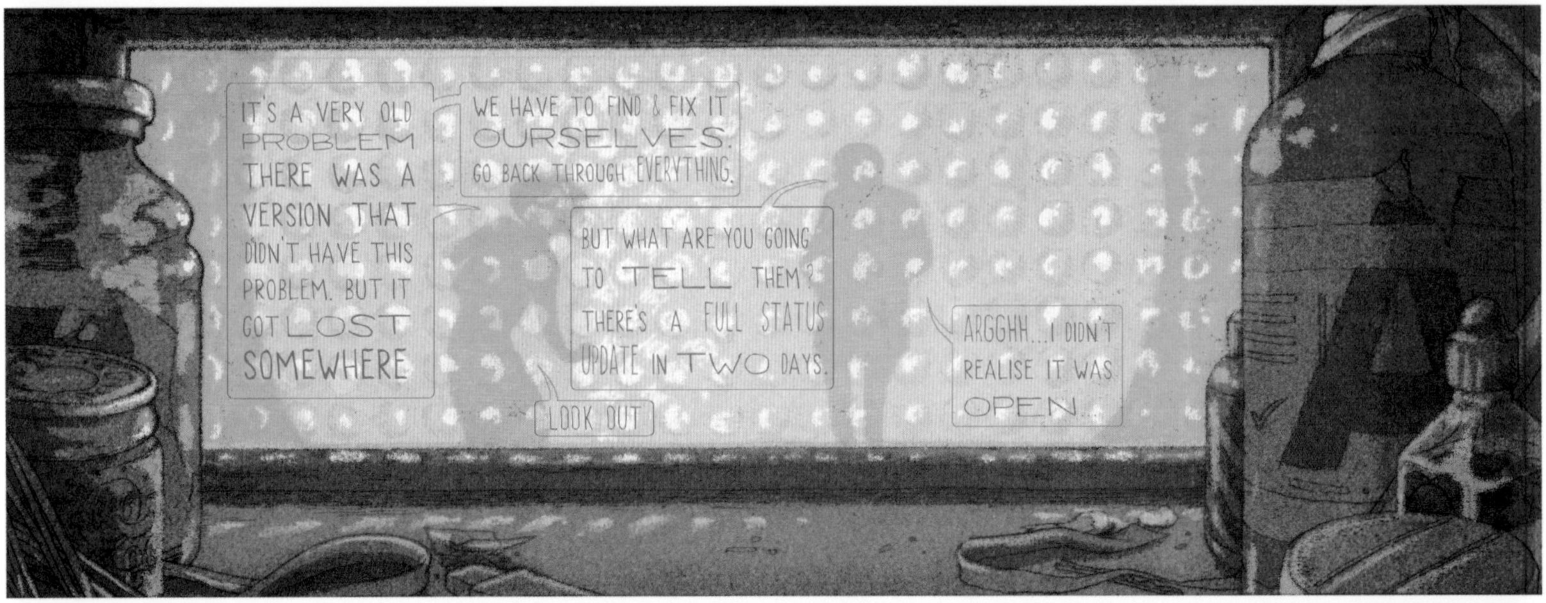
IT'S A VERY OLD PROBLEM THERE WAS A VERSION THAT DIDN'T HAVE THIS PROBLEM. BUT IT GOT LOST SOMEWHERE
WE HAVE TO FIND & FIX IT OURSELVES. GO BACK THROUGH EVERYTHING.
BUT WHAT ARE YOU GOING TO TELL THEM? THERE'S A FULL STATUS UPDATE IN TWO DAYS.
LOOK OUT
ARGGHH... I DIDN'T REALISE IT WAS OPEN...

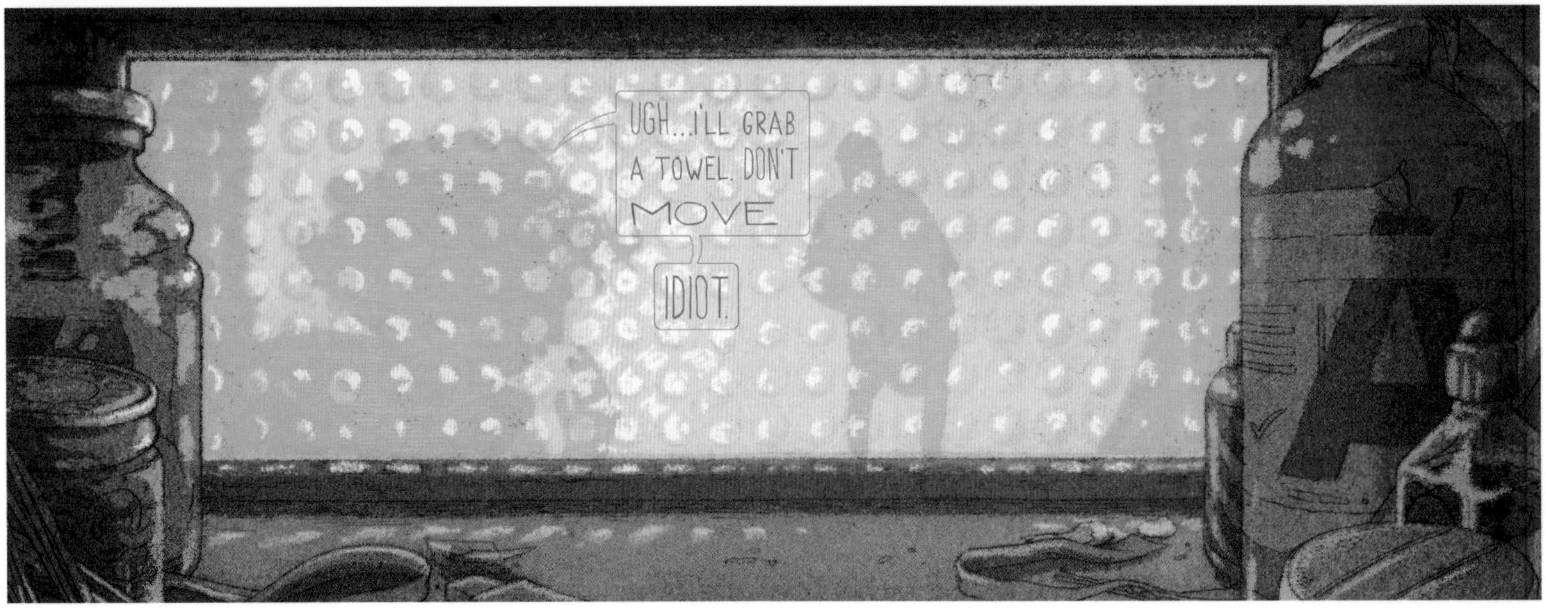
UGH... I'LL GRAB A TOWEL. DON'T MOVE
IDIOT.

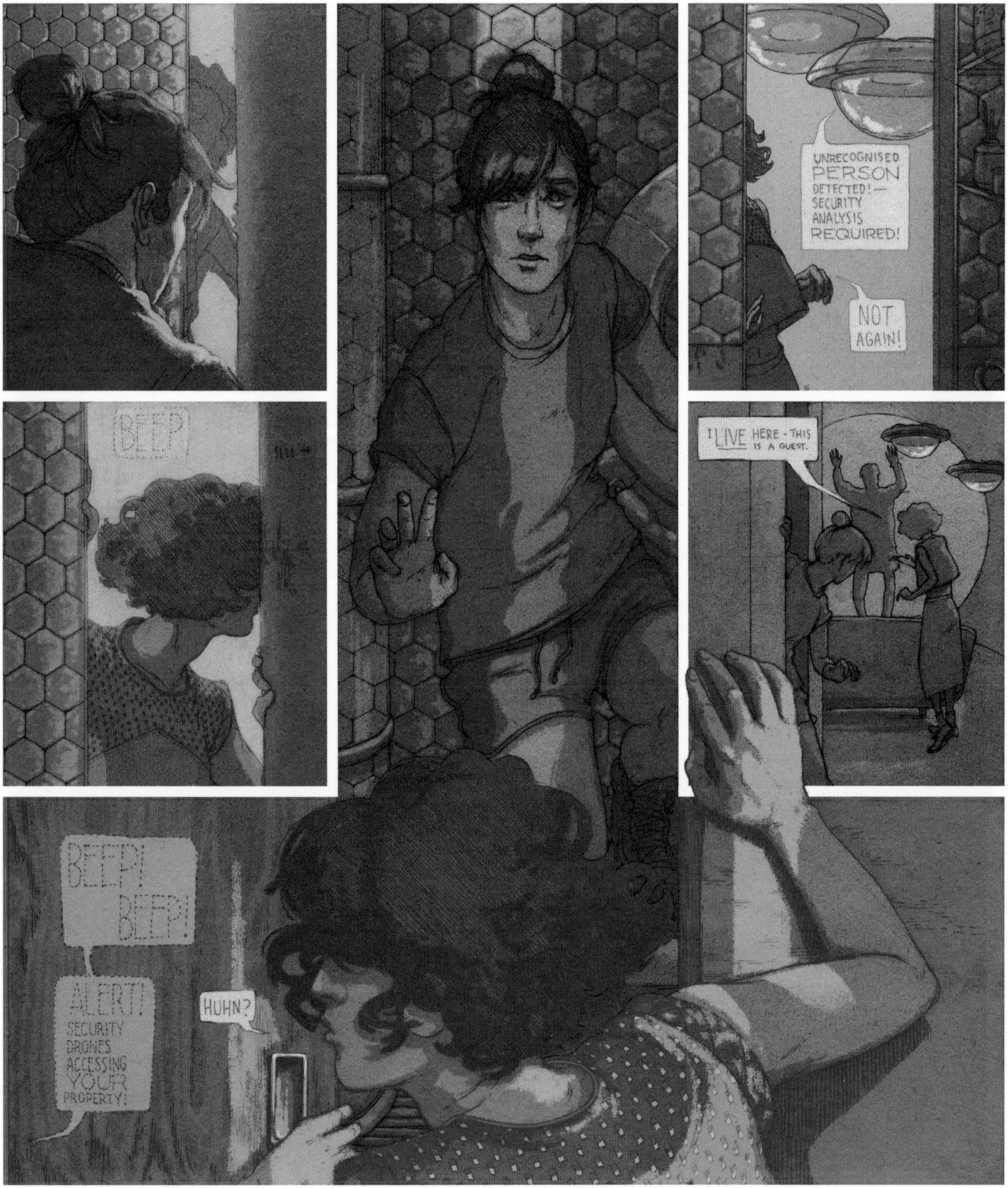

UNRECOGNISED PERSON DETECTED! — SECURITY ANALYSIS REQUIRED!
NOT AGAIN!
BEEP
I LIVE HERE - THIS IS A GUEST.
BEEP! BEEP!
ALERT! SECURITY DRONES ACCESSING YOUR PROPERTY!
HUHN?

WHAT...?
2B
FIRE EXIT

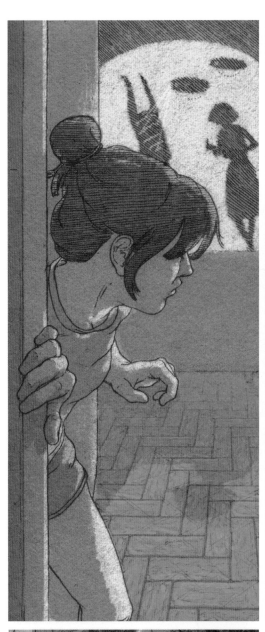

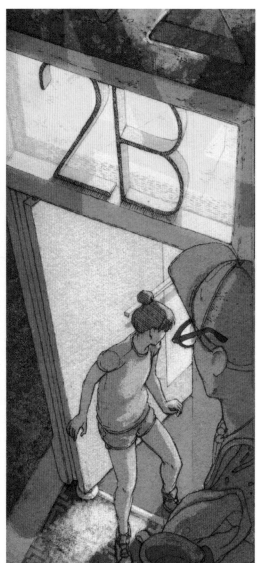

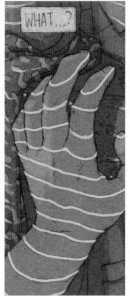

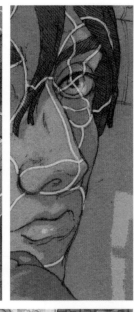

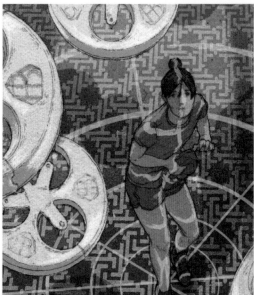

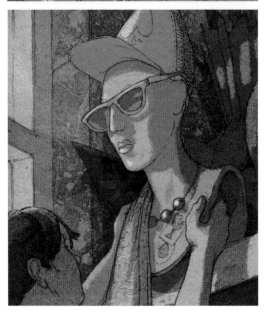

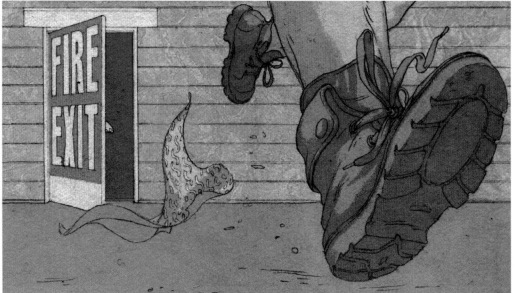

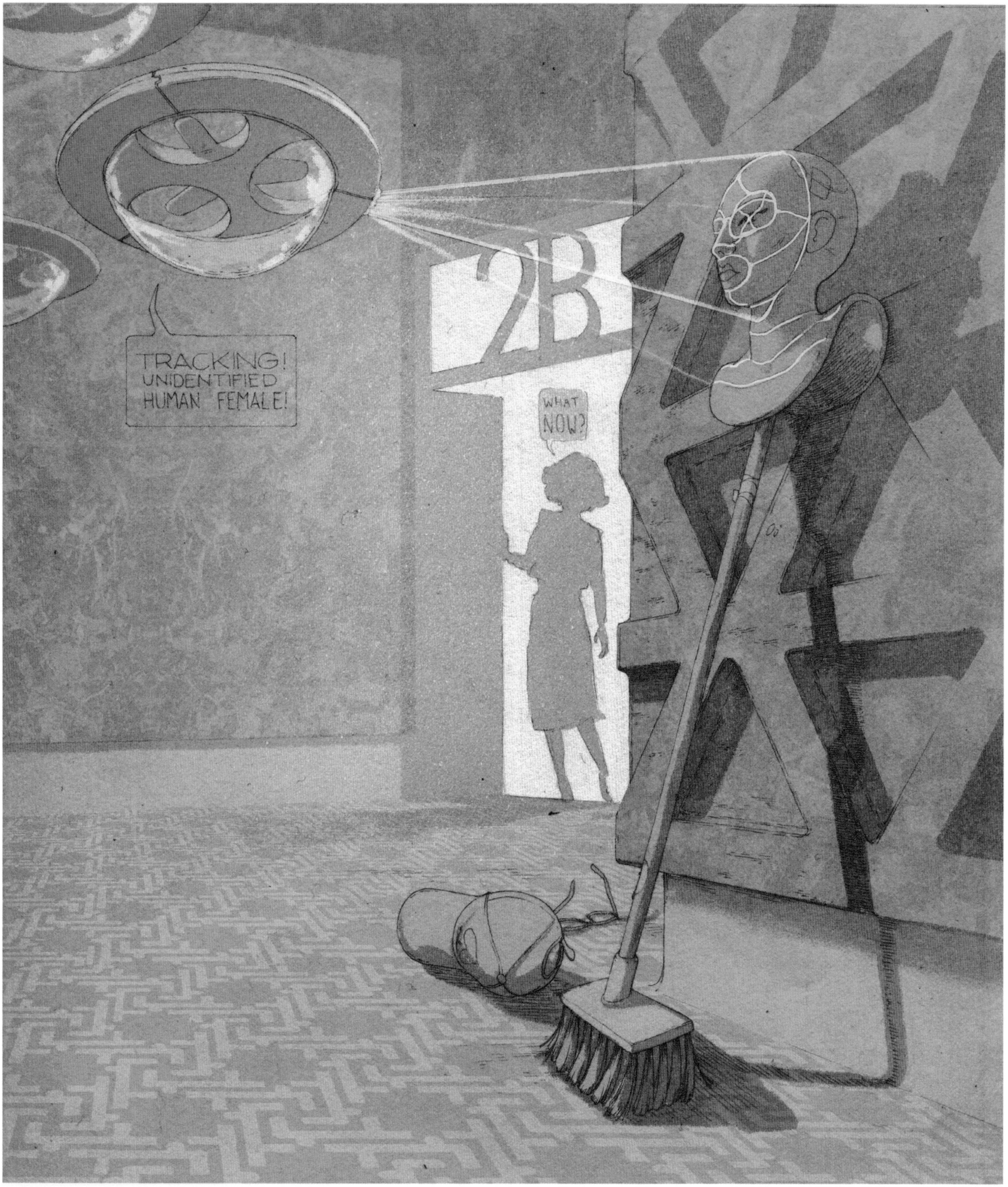
TRACKING! UNIDENTIFIED HUMAN FEMALE!
2B
WHAT NOW?

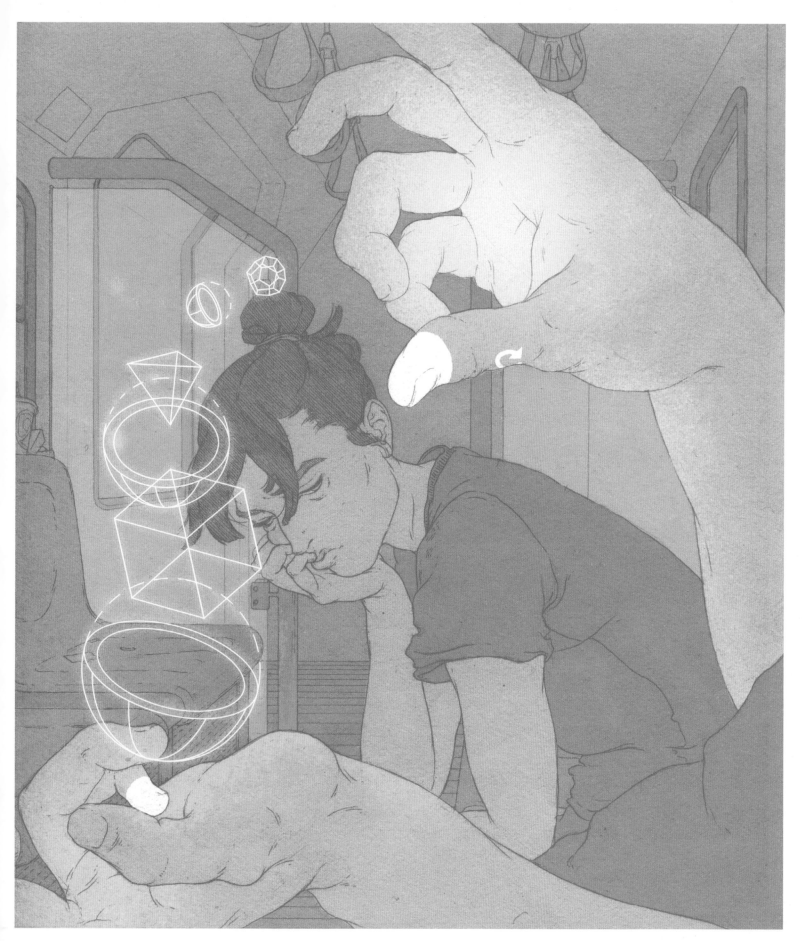

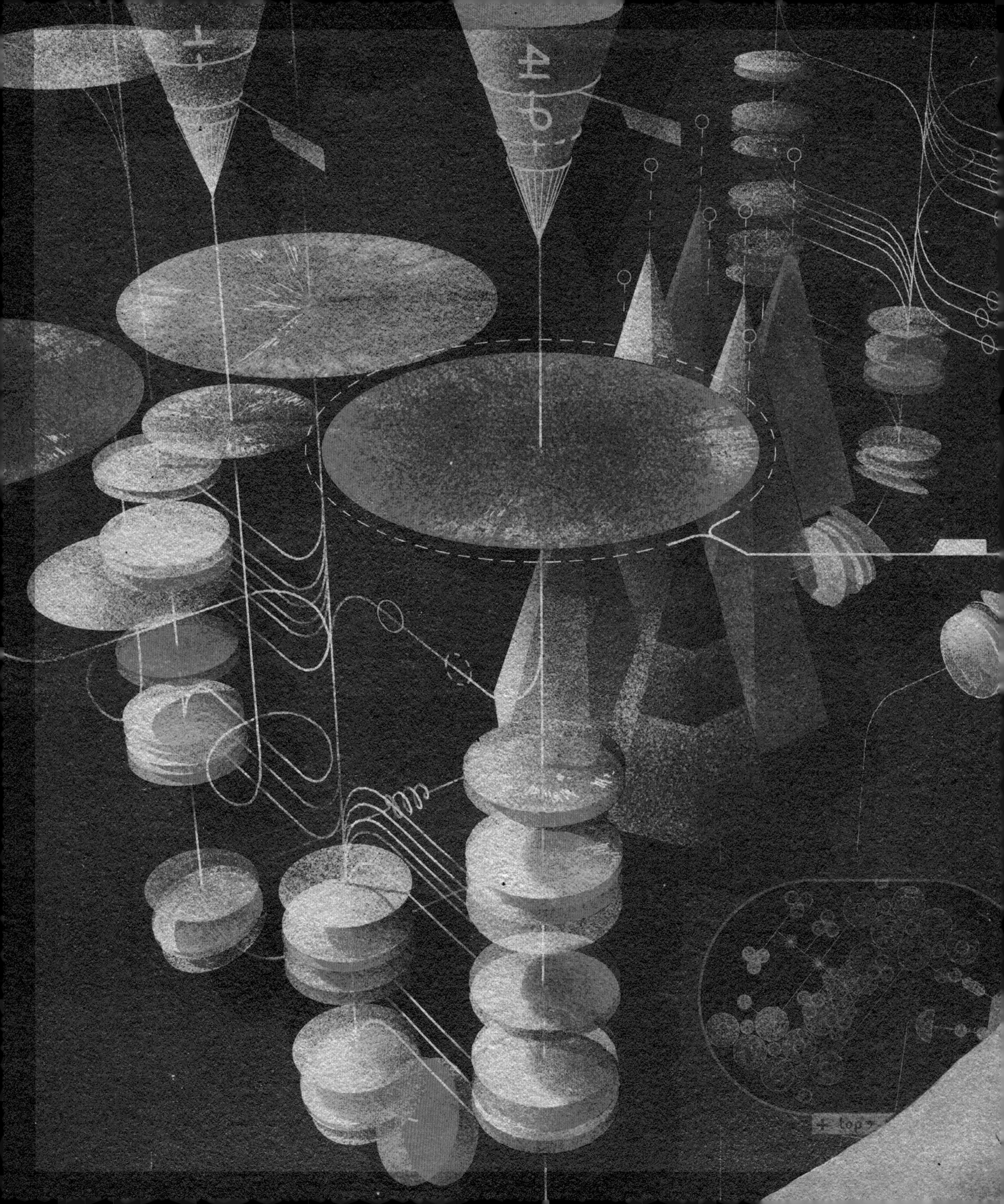
+ top +

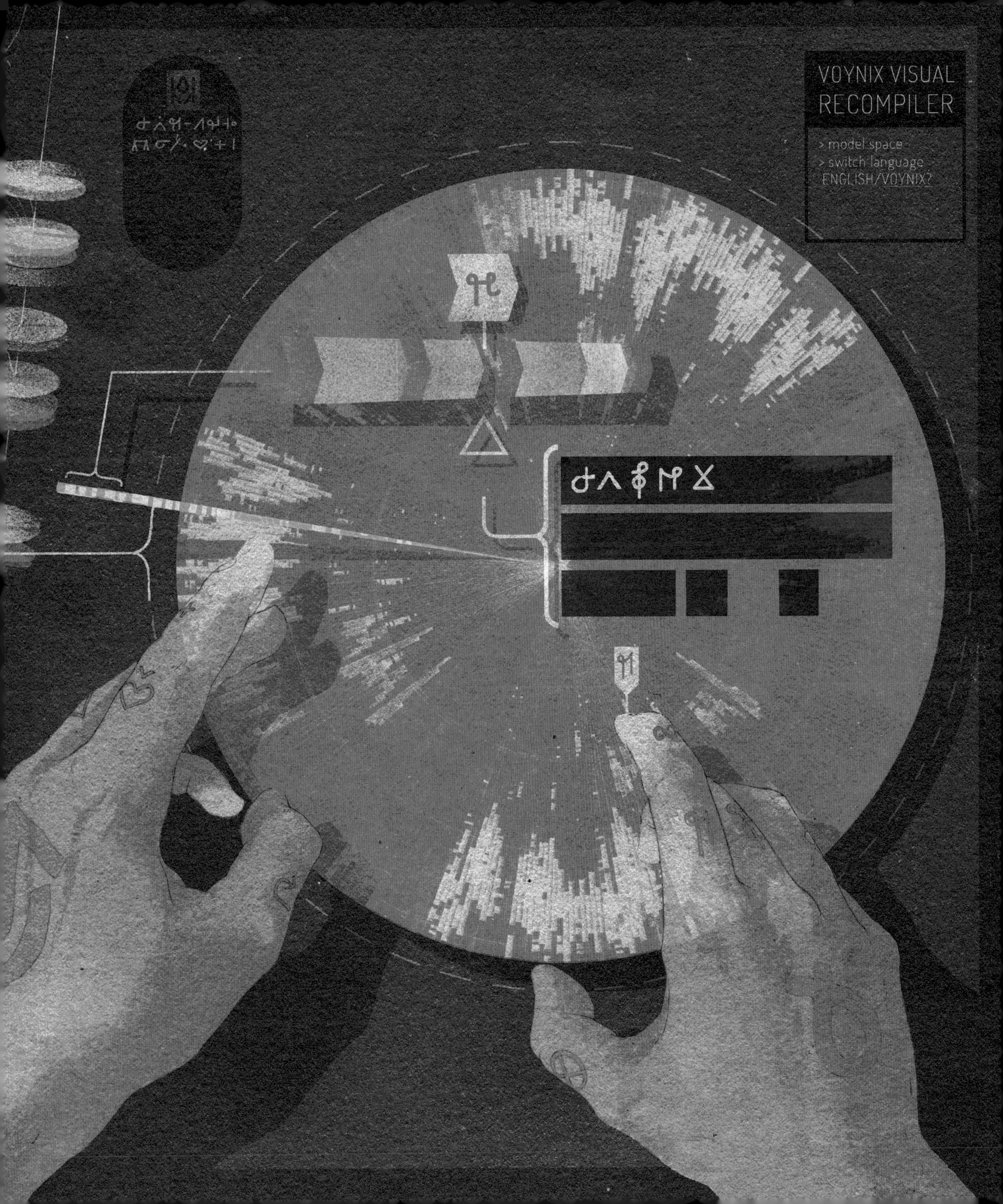
VOYNIX VISUAL
RECOMPILER
> model space
> switch language
ENGLISH/VOYNIX?

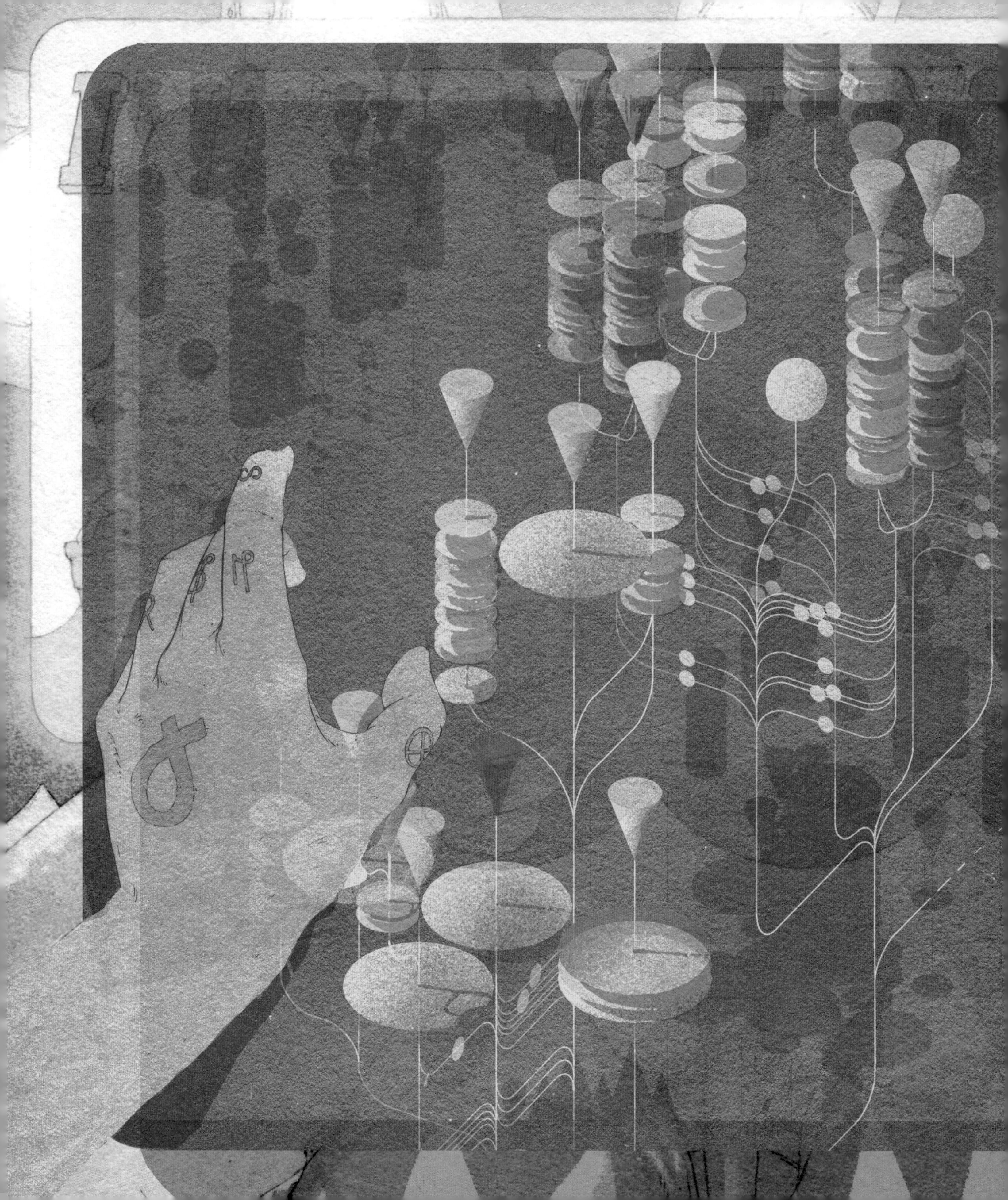

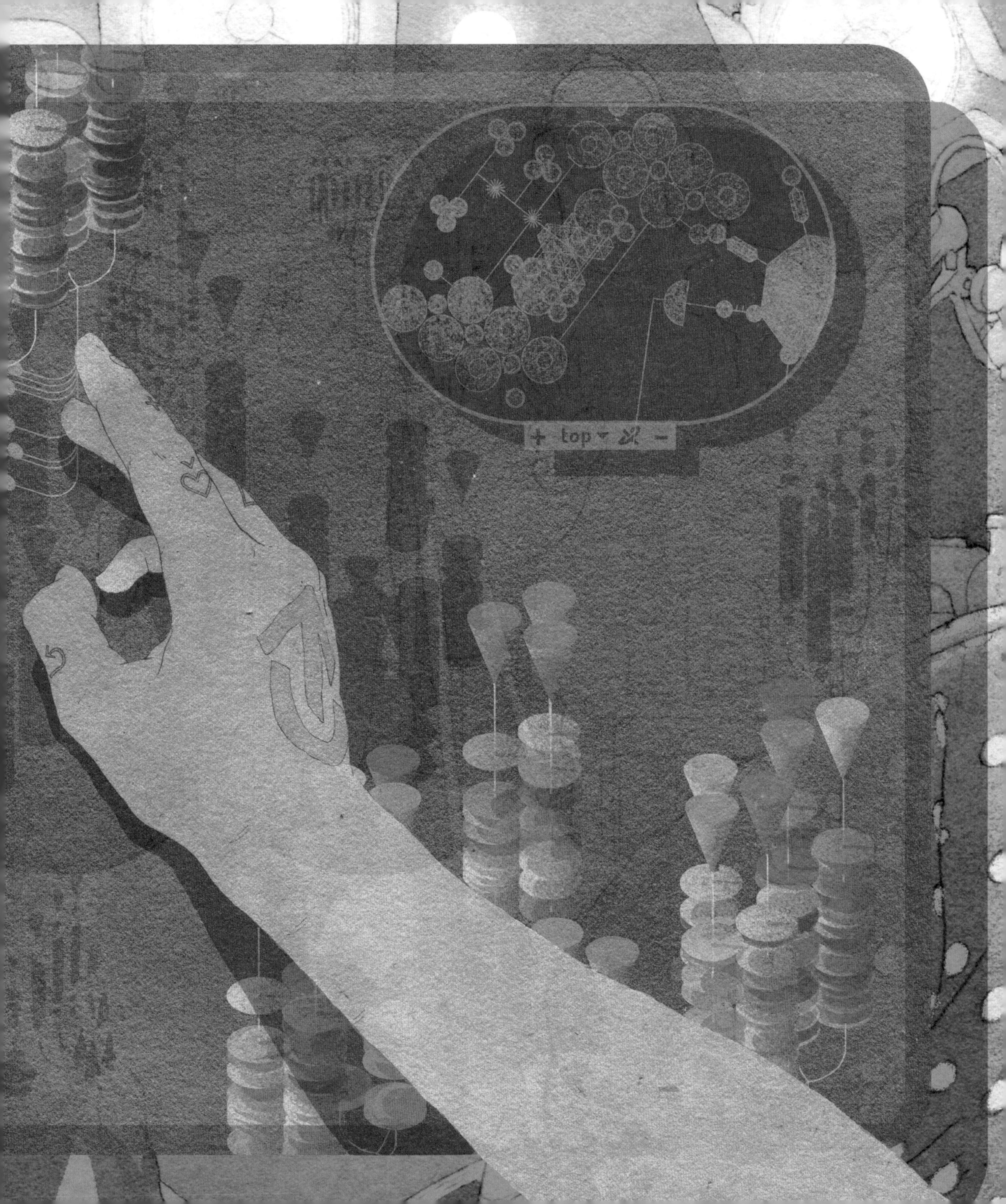
top

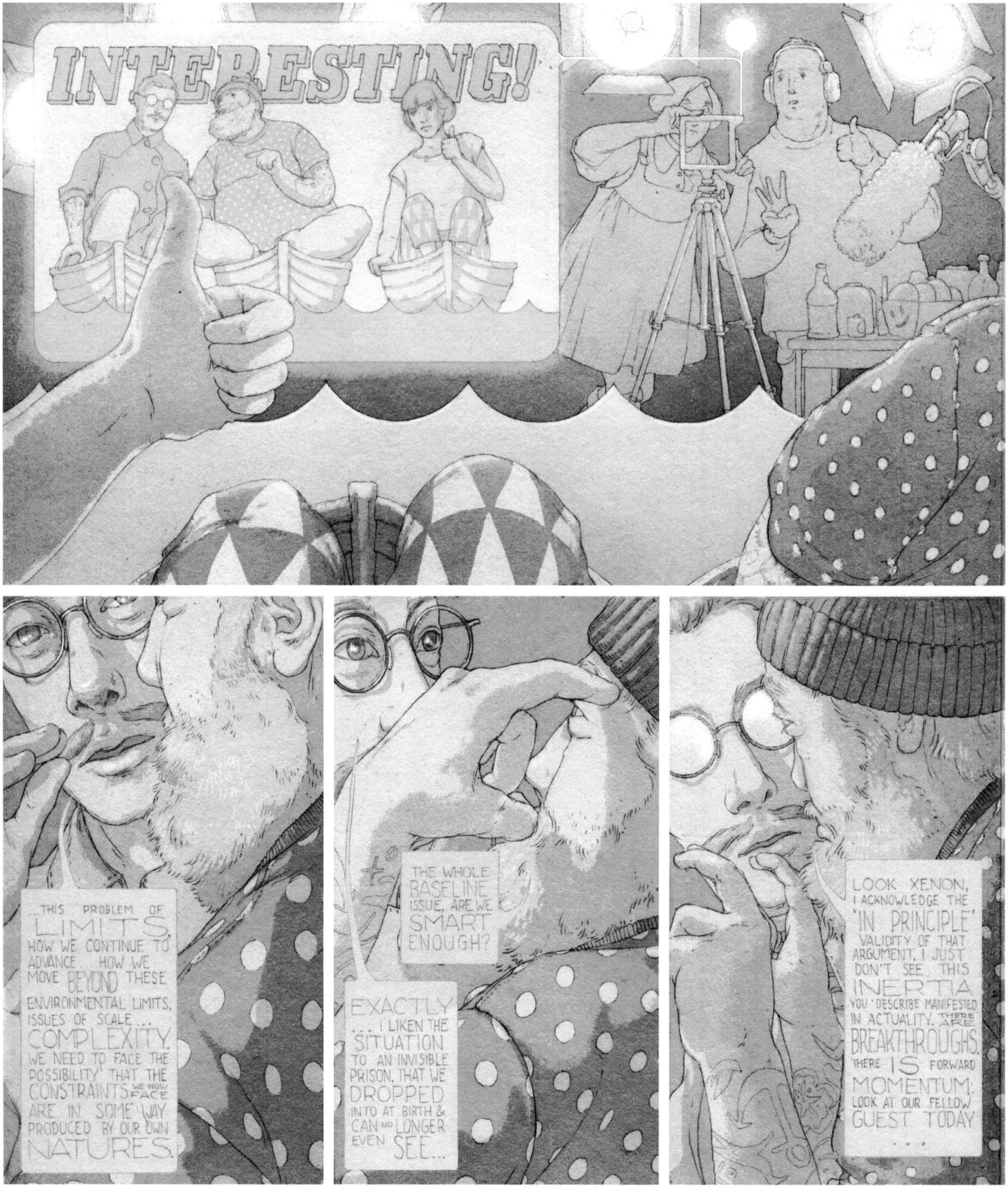
INTERESTING!
...THIS PROBLEM OF LIMITS. HOW WE CONTINUE TO ADVANCE... HOW WE MOVE BEYOND THESE ENVIRONMENTAL LIMITS, ISSUES OF SCALE... COMPLEXITY. WE NEED TO FACE THE POSSIBILITY THAT THE CONSTRAINTS WE NOW FACE ARE IN SOME WAY PRODUCED BY OUR OWN NATURES.
THE WHOLE BASELINE ISSUE, ARE WE SMART ENOUGH?
EXACTLY ... I LIKEN THE SITUATION TO AN INVISIBLE PRISON, THAT WE DROPPED INTO AT BIRTH & CAN NO LONGER EVEN SEE...
LOOK XENON, I ACKNOWLEDGE THE 'IN PRINCIPLE' VALIDITY OF THAT ARGUMENT. I JUST DON'T SEE, THIS INERTIA YOU DESCRIBE MANIFESTED IN ACTUALITY. THERE ARE BREAKTHROUGHS. THERE IS FORWARD MOMENTUM: LOOK AT OUR FELLOW GUEST TODAY ...

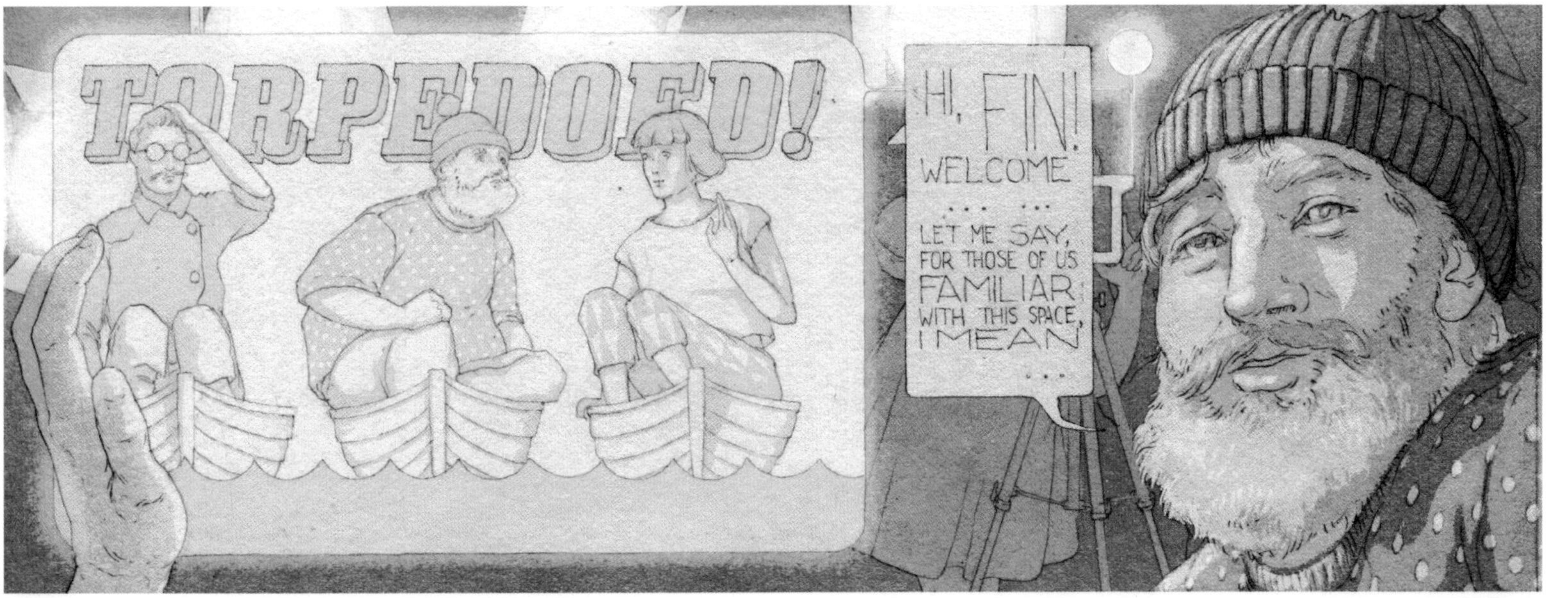
TORPEDOED!
HI, FIN! WELCOME . . . . . . LET ME SAY, FOR THOSE OF US FAMILIAR WITH THIS SPACE, I MEAN . . .

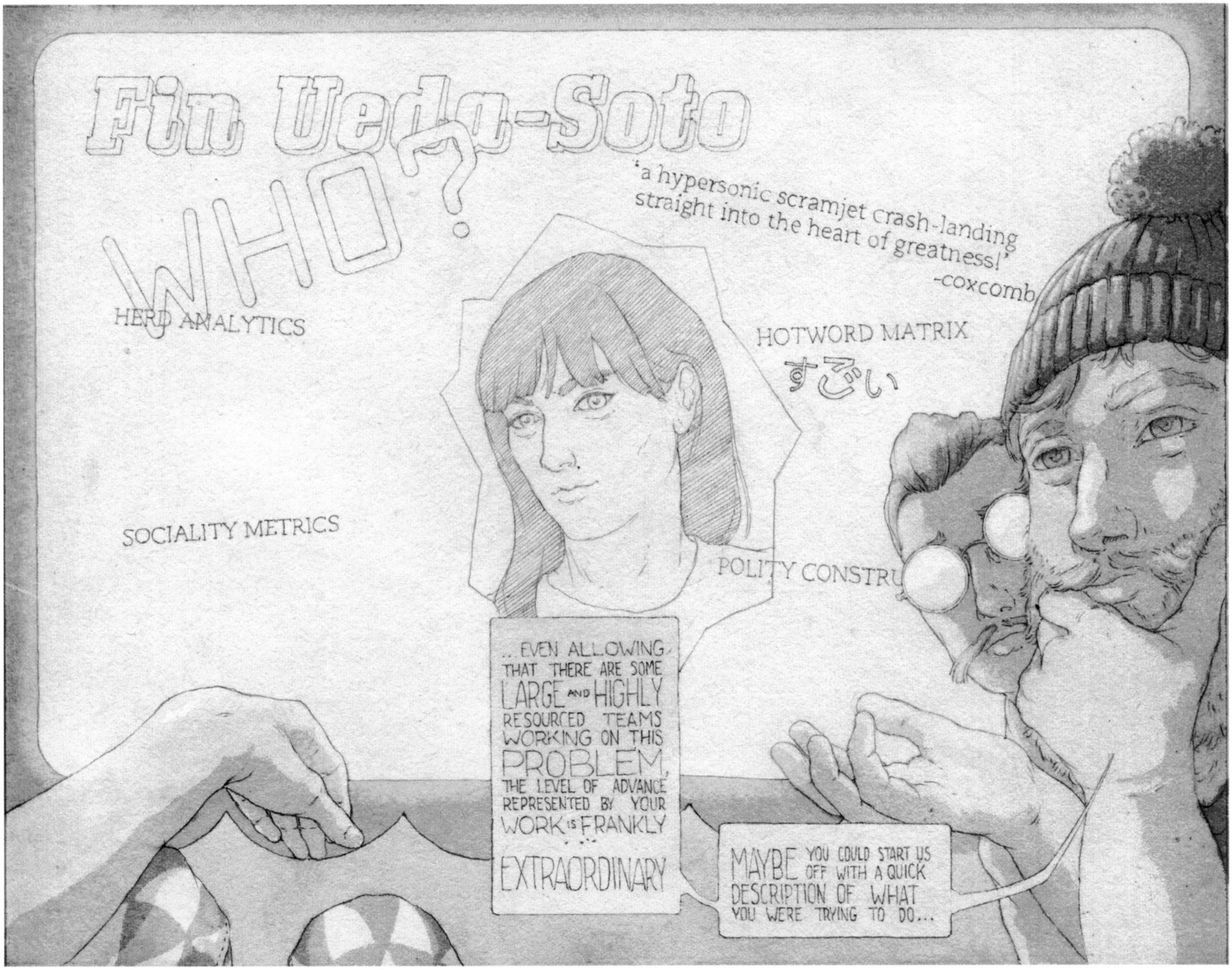
Fin Ueda-Soto
WHO?
'a hypersonic scramjet crash-landing straight into the heart of greatness!' -coxcomb
HERD ANALYTICS
HOTWORD MATRIX
すごい
SOCIALITY METRICS
POLITY CONSTRU
... EVEN ALLOWING THAT THERE ARE SOME LARGE AND HIGHLY RESOURCED TEAMS WORKING ON THIS PROBLEM, THE LEVEL OF ADVANCE REPRESENTED BY YOUR WORK IS FRANKLY . . . EXTRAORDINARY
MAYBE YOU COULD START US OFF WITH A QUICK DESCRIPTION OF WHAT YOU WERE TRYING TO DO...

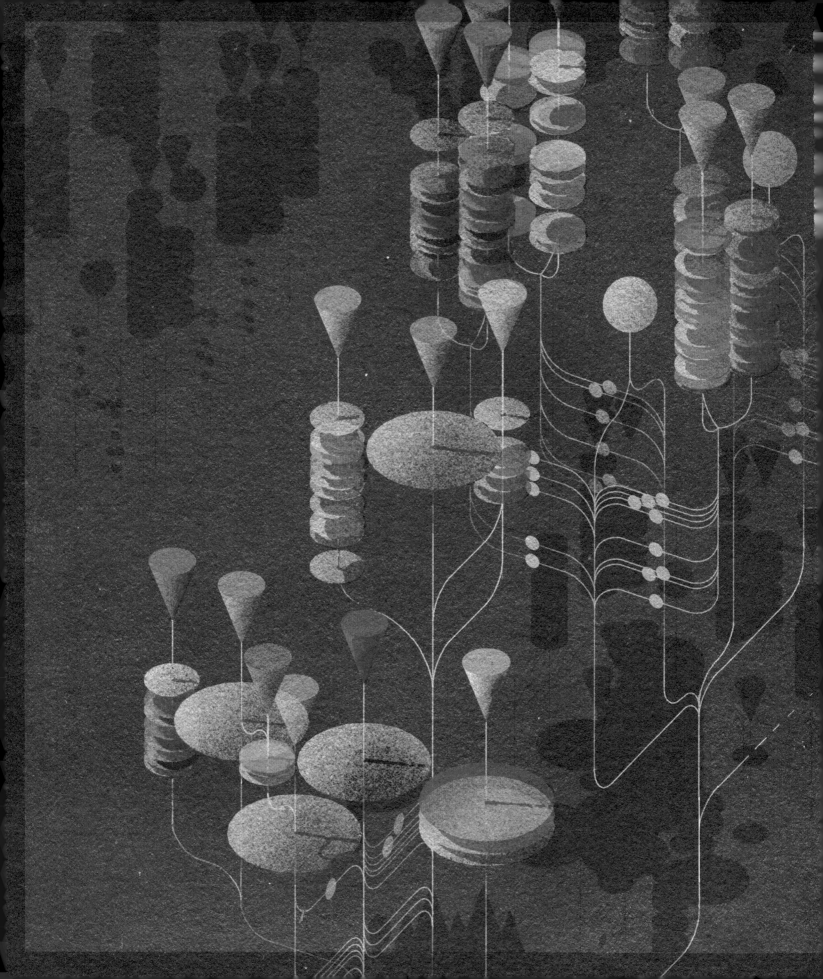

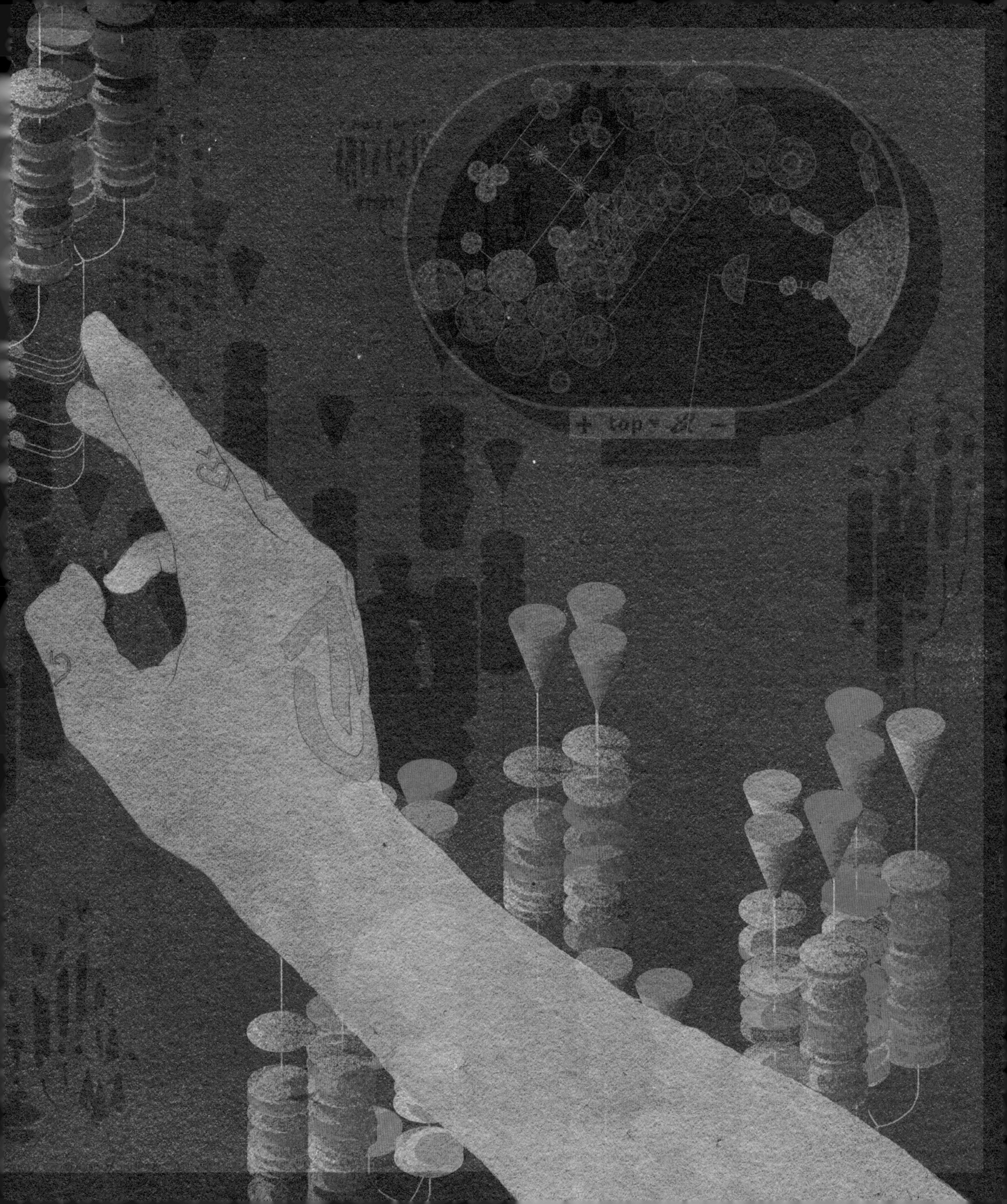

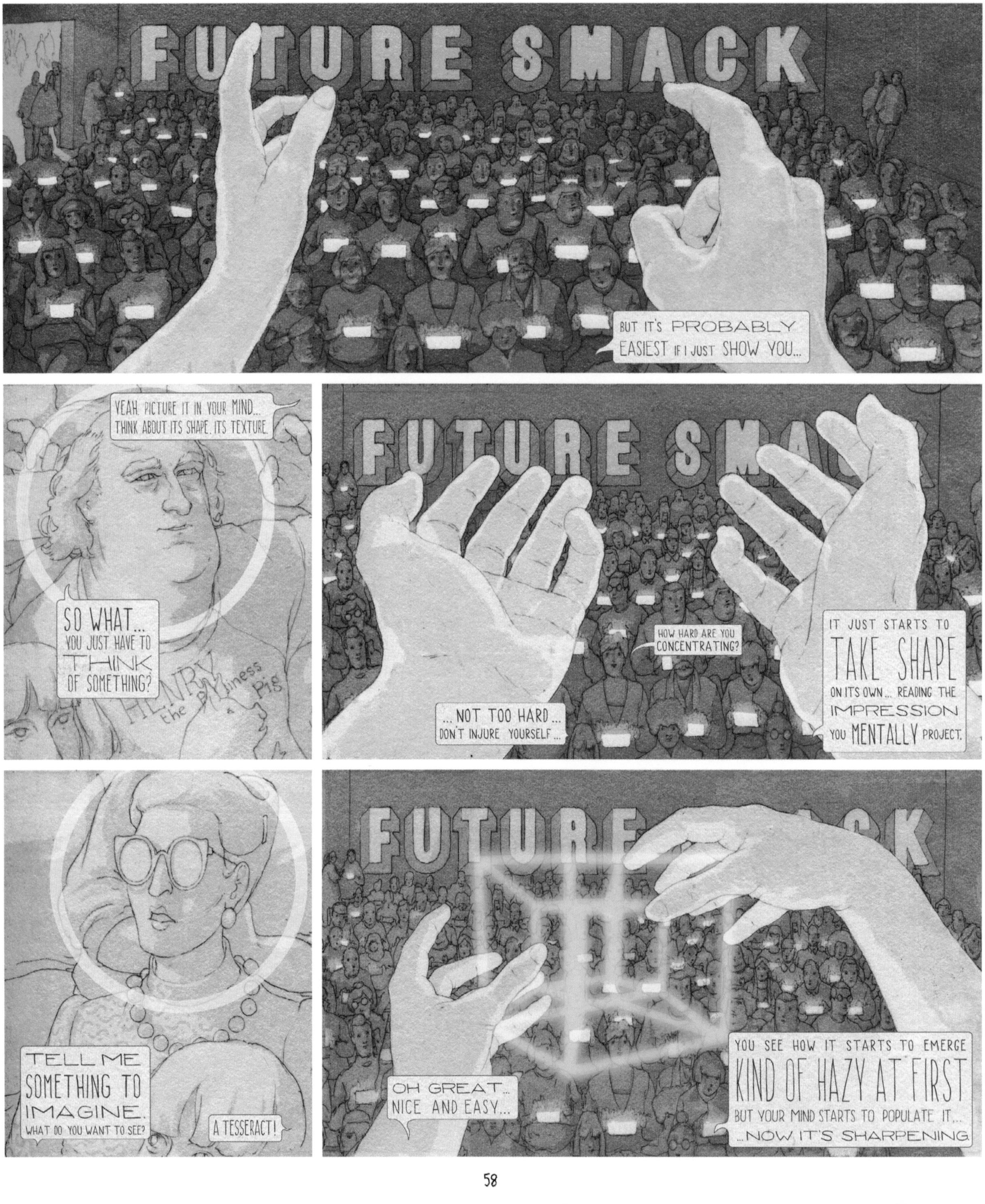
FUTURE SMACK
BUT IT'S PROBABLY EASIEST IF I JUST SHOW YOU...
VEAH. PICTURE IT IN YOUR MIND... THINK ABOUT ITS SHAPE, ITS TEXTURE.
SO WHAT... YOU JUST HAVE TO THINK OF SOMETHING?
HENRY the Happiness Pig
HOW HARD ARE YOU CONCENTRATING?
...NOT TOO HARD... DON'T INJURE YOURSELF...
IT JUST STARTS TO TAKE SHAPE ON ITS OWN... READING THE IMPRESSION YOU MENTALLY PROJECT.
TELL ME SOMETHING TO IMAGINE. WHAT DO YOU WANT TO SEE?
A TESSERACT!
OH GREAT... NICE AND EASY...
YOU SEE HOW IT STARTS TO EMERGE KIND OF HAZY AT FIRST BUT YOUR MIND STARTS TO POPULATE IT... ...NOW IT'S SHARPENING

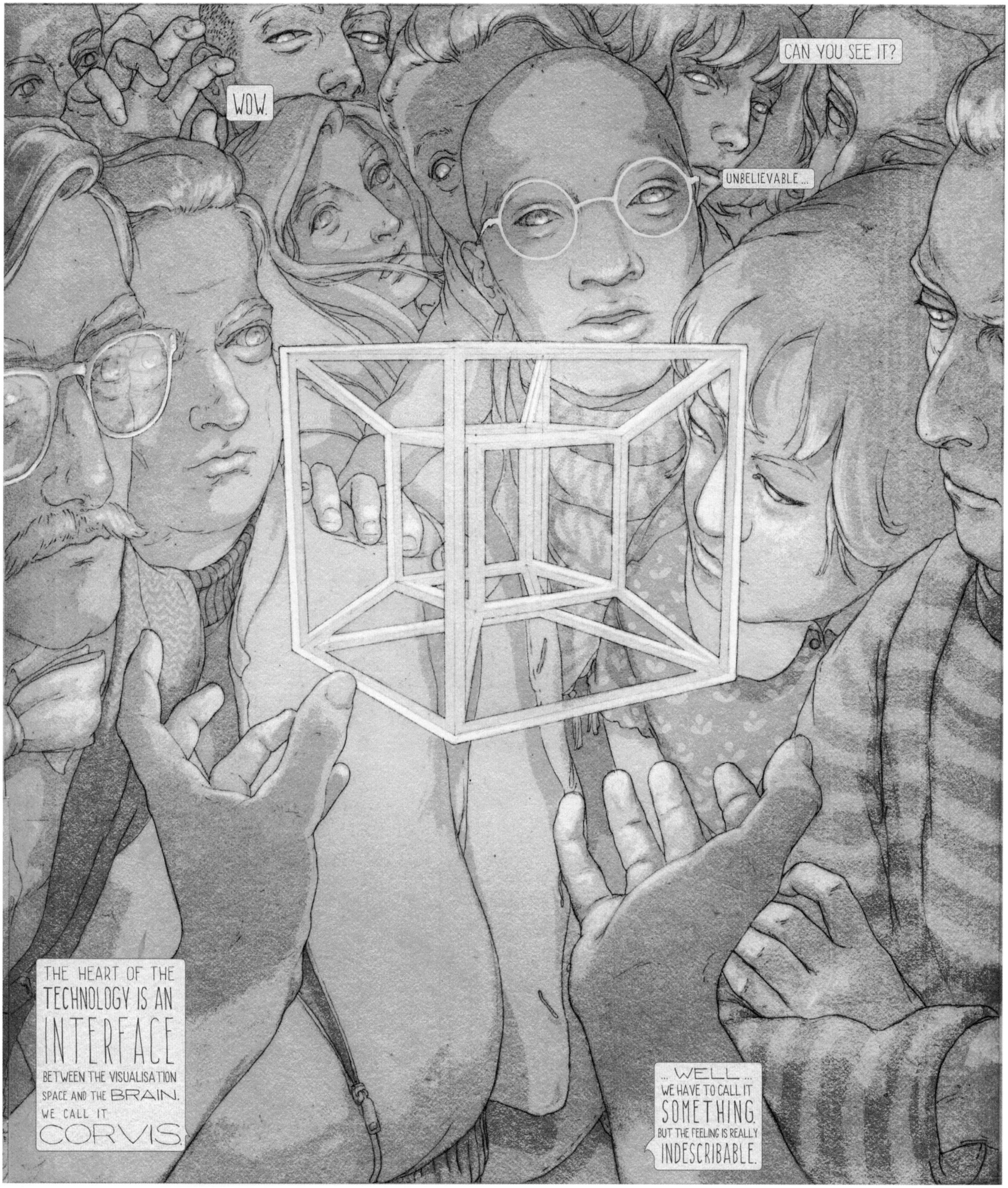
WOW.
CAN YOU SEE IT?
UNBELIEVABLE...
THE HEART OF THE TECHNOLOGY IS AN INTERFACE BETWEEN THE VISUALISATION SPACE AND THE BRAIN. WE CALL IT CORVIS.
... WELL ... WE HAVE TO CALL IT SOMETHING. BUT THE FEELING IS REALLY INDESCRIBABLE.

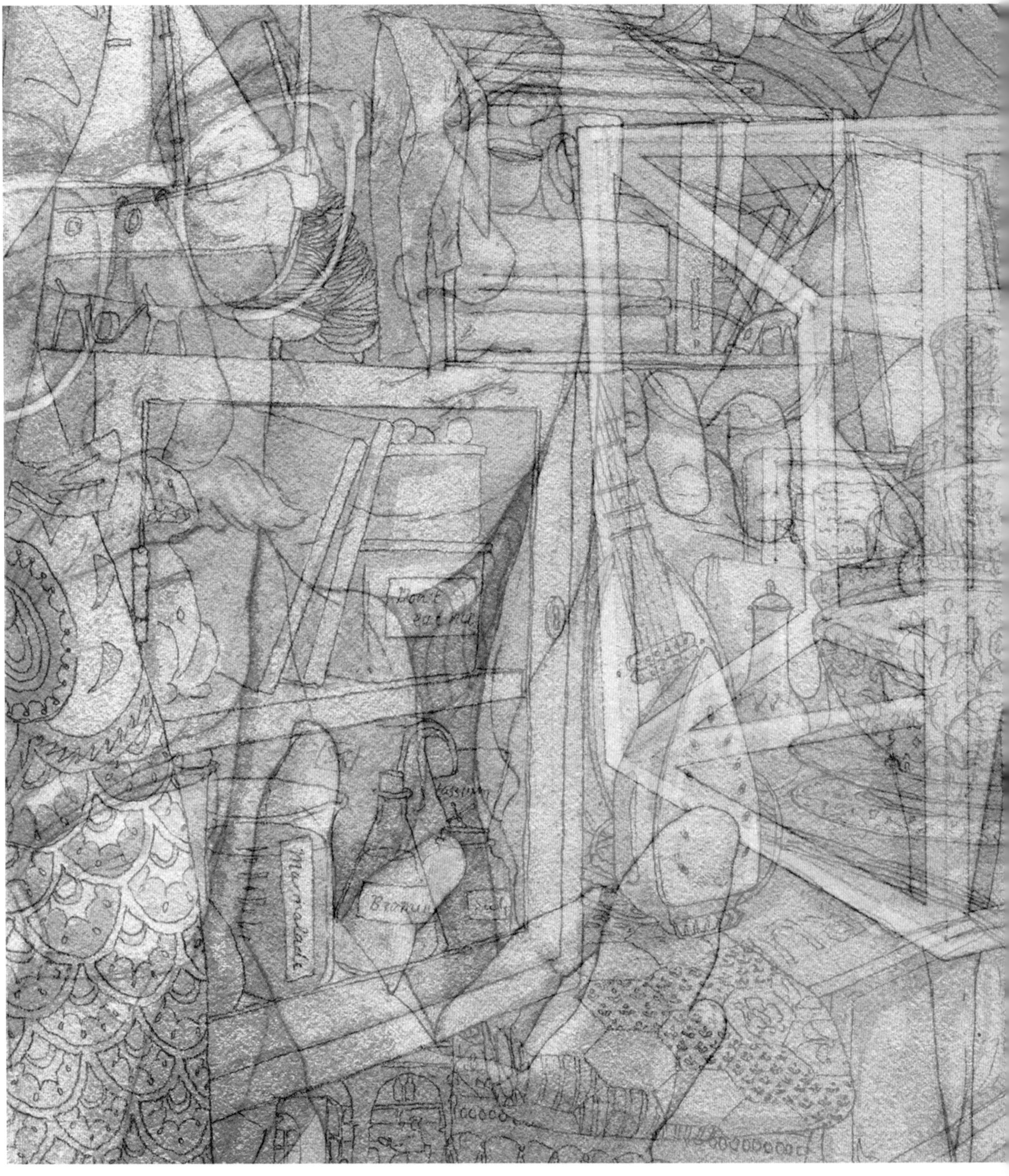
Marmalade

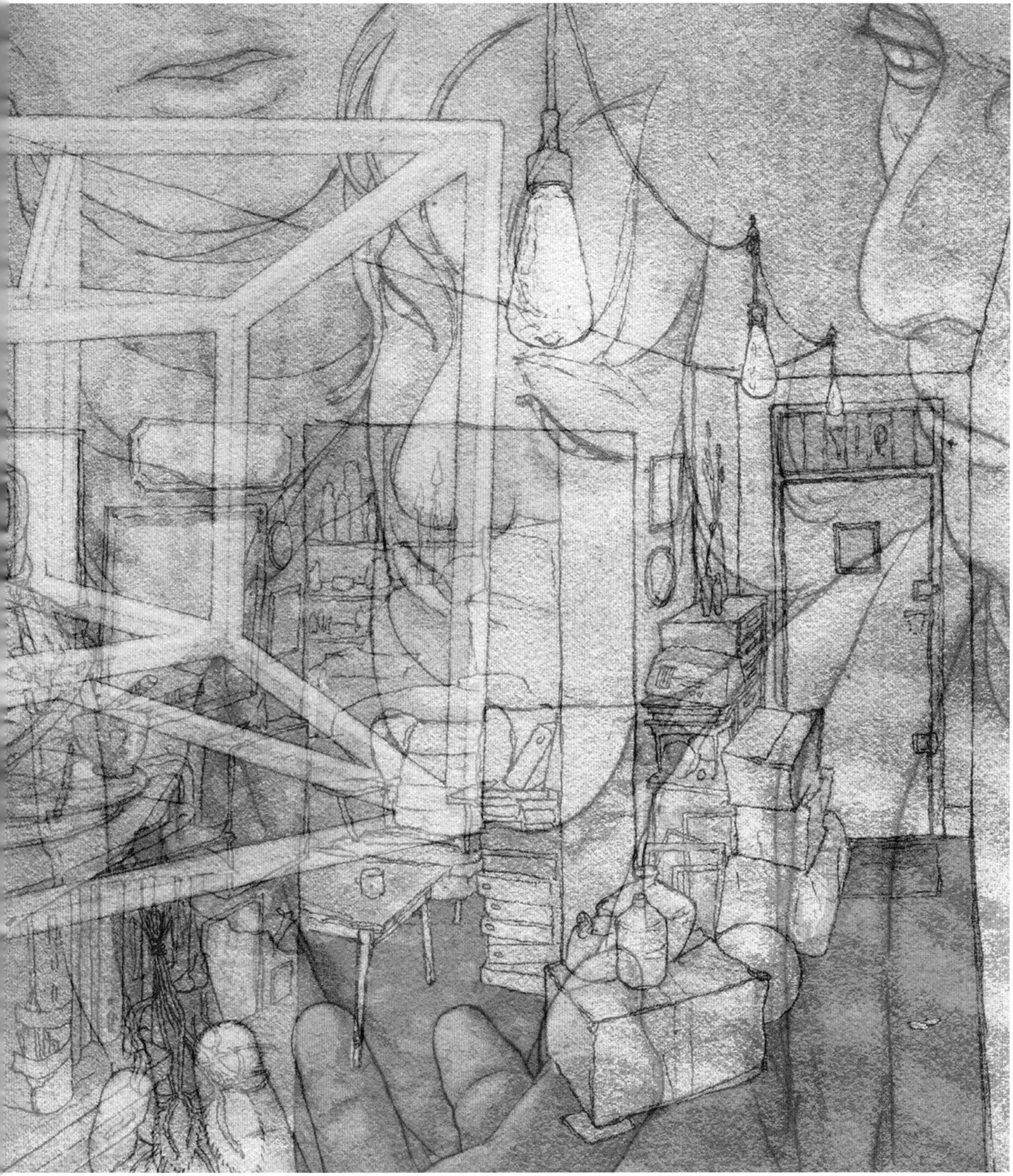

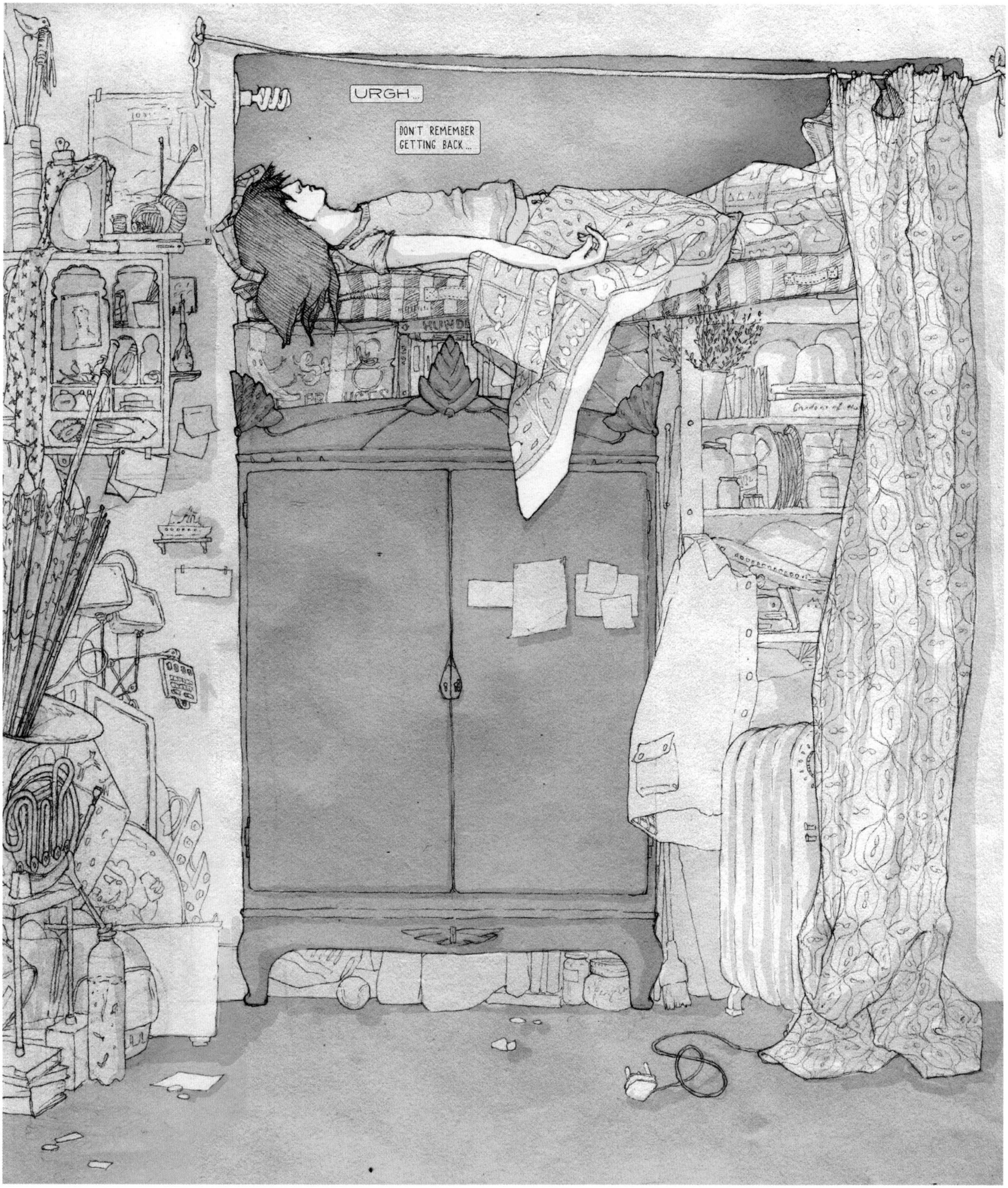
URGH...
DON'T REMEMBER GETTING BACK...

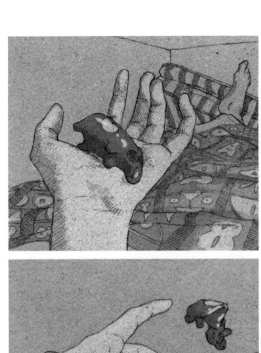

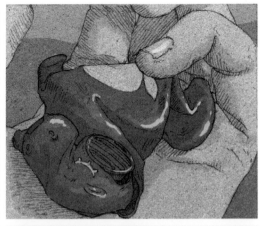

STILL HAVEN'T RECONNECTED

WHAT AM I MEANT TO DO?

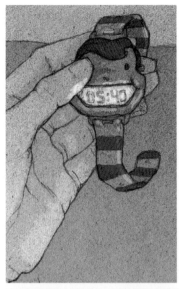

SERVICE UNAVAILABLE
SERVICE UNAVAILABLE
NOTHING WORKS OUT HERE...
NEIGHBOURHOOD'S BEEN DEAD FOR YEARS... I THINK THAT'S WHY GRANNY LIKED IT...

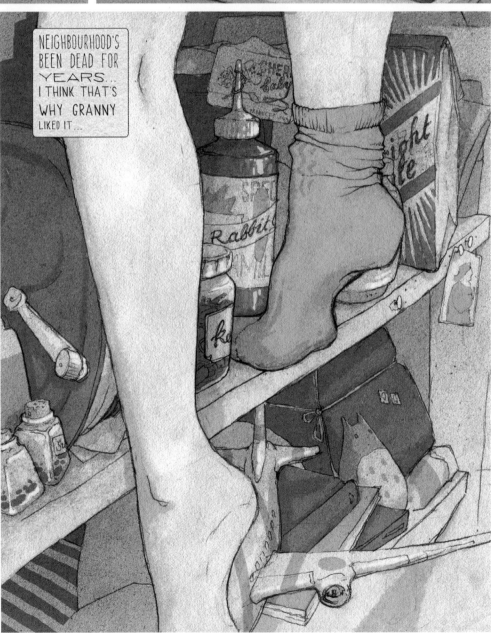

OLD PEOPLE
HAVE SO MUCH JUNK.

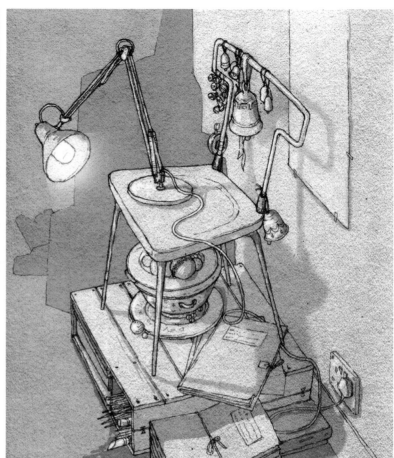

....MUST HAVE PUSHED
DEMOLITION BACK AGAIN.

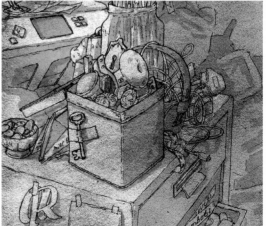

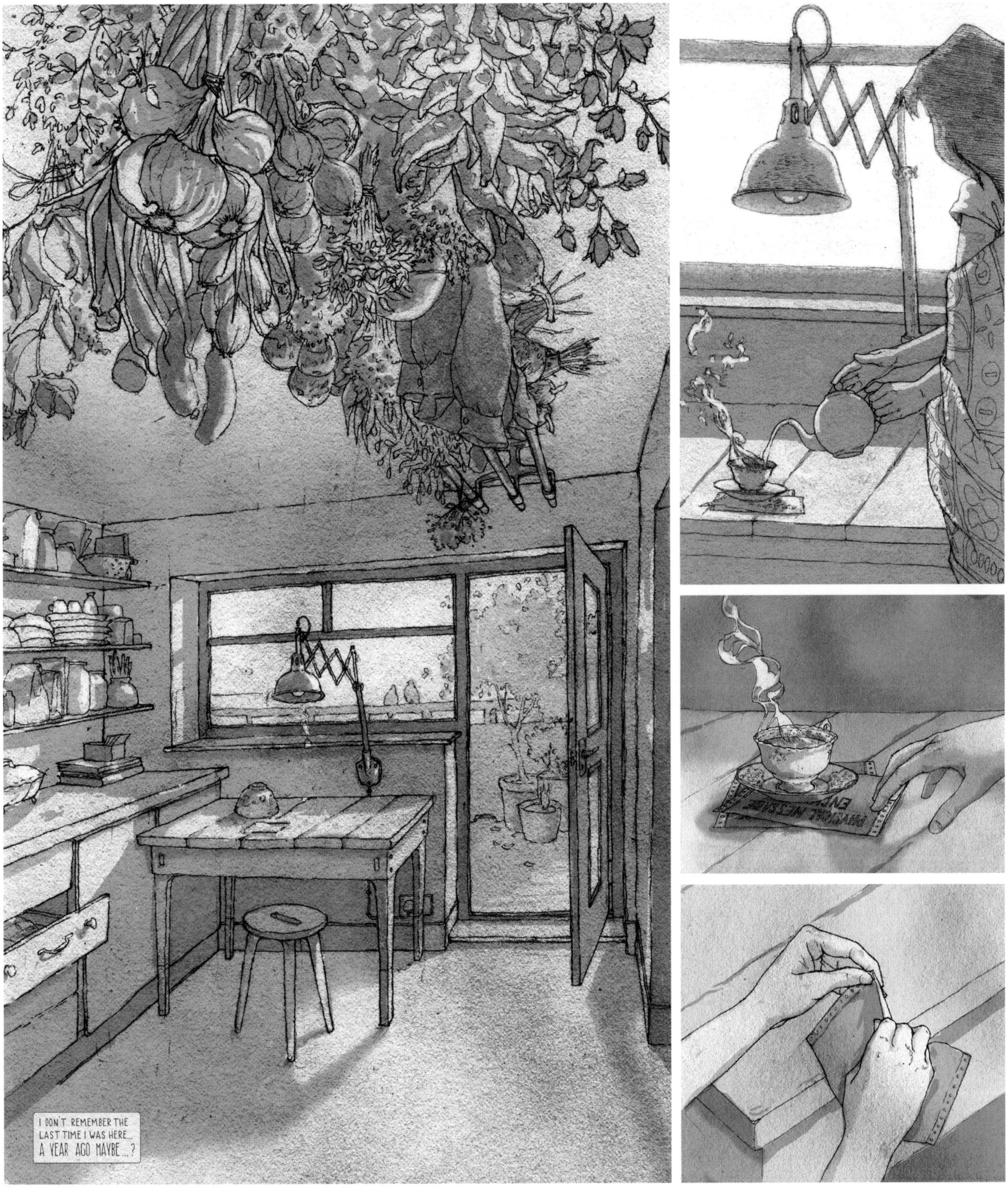
I DON'T REMEMBER THE LAST TIME I WAS HERE... A YEAR AGO MAYBE...?

AT FIRST WHEN I WAS AT THE CENTRE I USED TO WAKE UP AND FORGET IT HAD HAPPENED

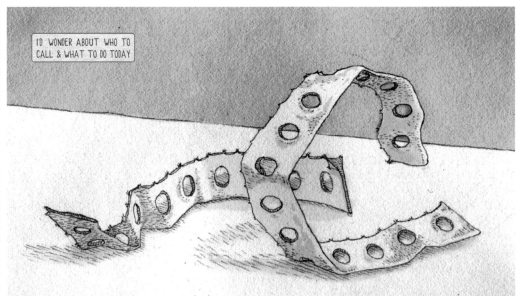

I'D WONDER ABOUT WHO TO CALL & WHAT TO DO TODAY

THEN SOMEONE WOULD TELL ME THAT IT WAS ALL GONE

EVERYTHING I WORKED FOR HAD BEEN TAKEN

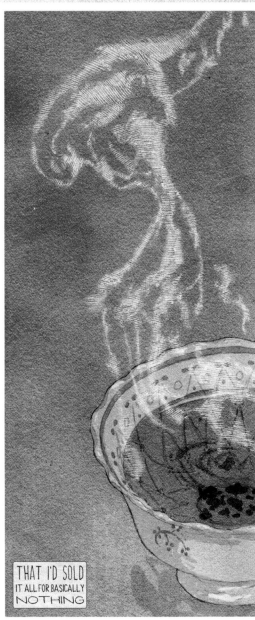

THAT I'D SOLD IT ALL FOR BASICALLY NOTHING

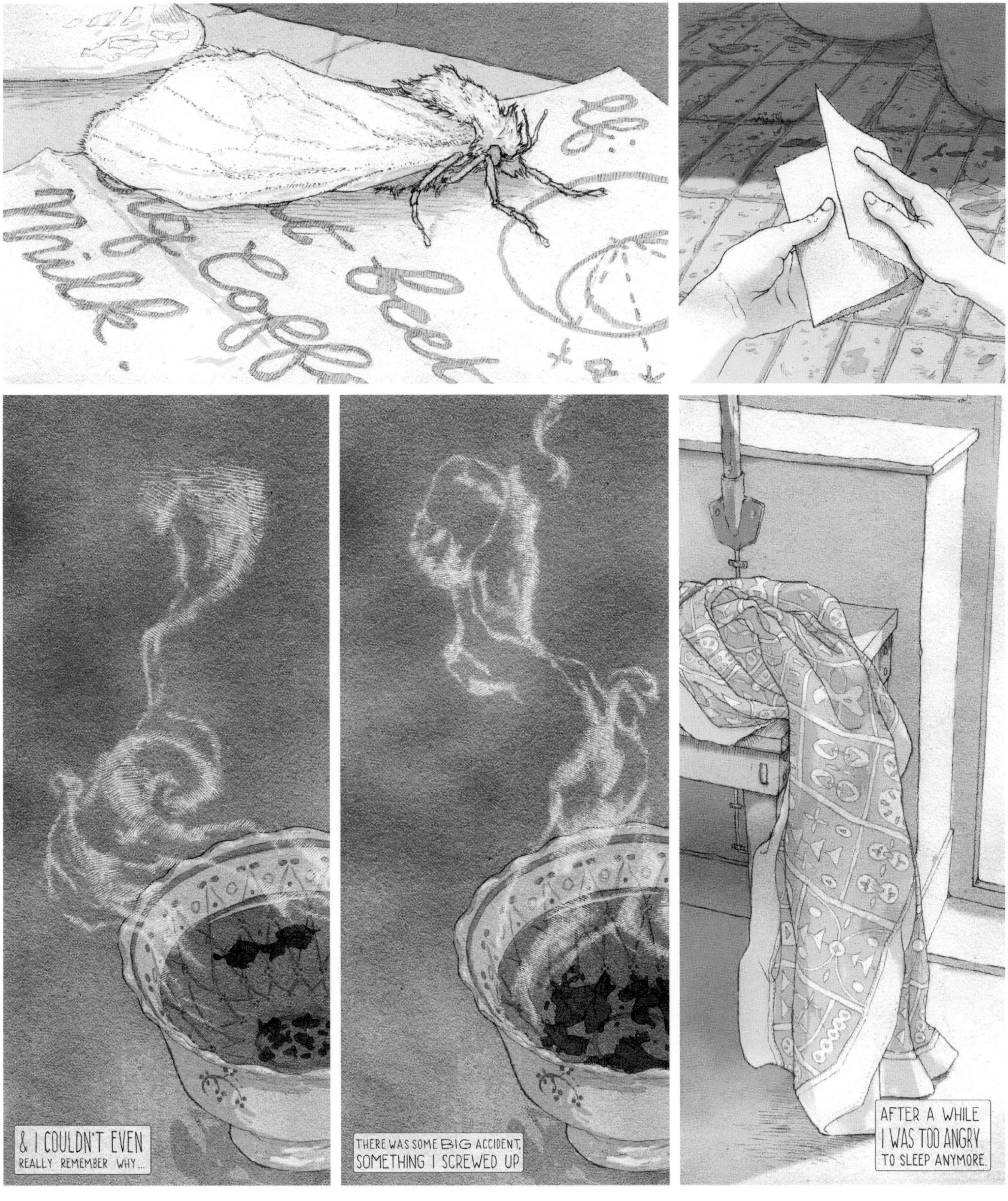
& I COULDN'T EVEN
REALLY REMEMBER WHY...
THERE WAS SOME BIG ACCIDENT,
SOMETHING I SCREWED UP
AFTER A WHILE
I WAS TOO ANGRY
TO SLEEP ANYMORE.

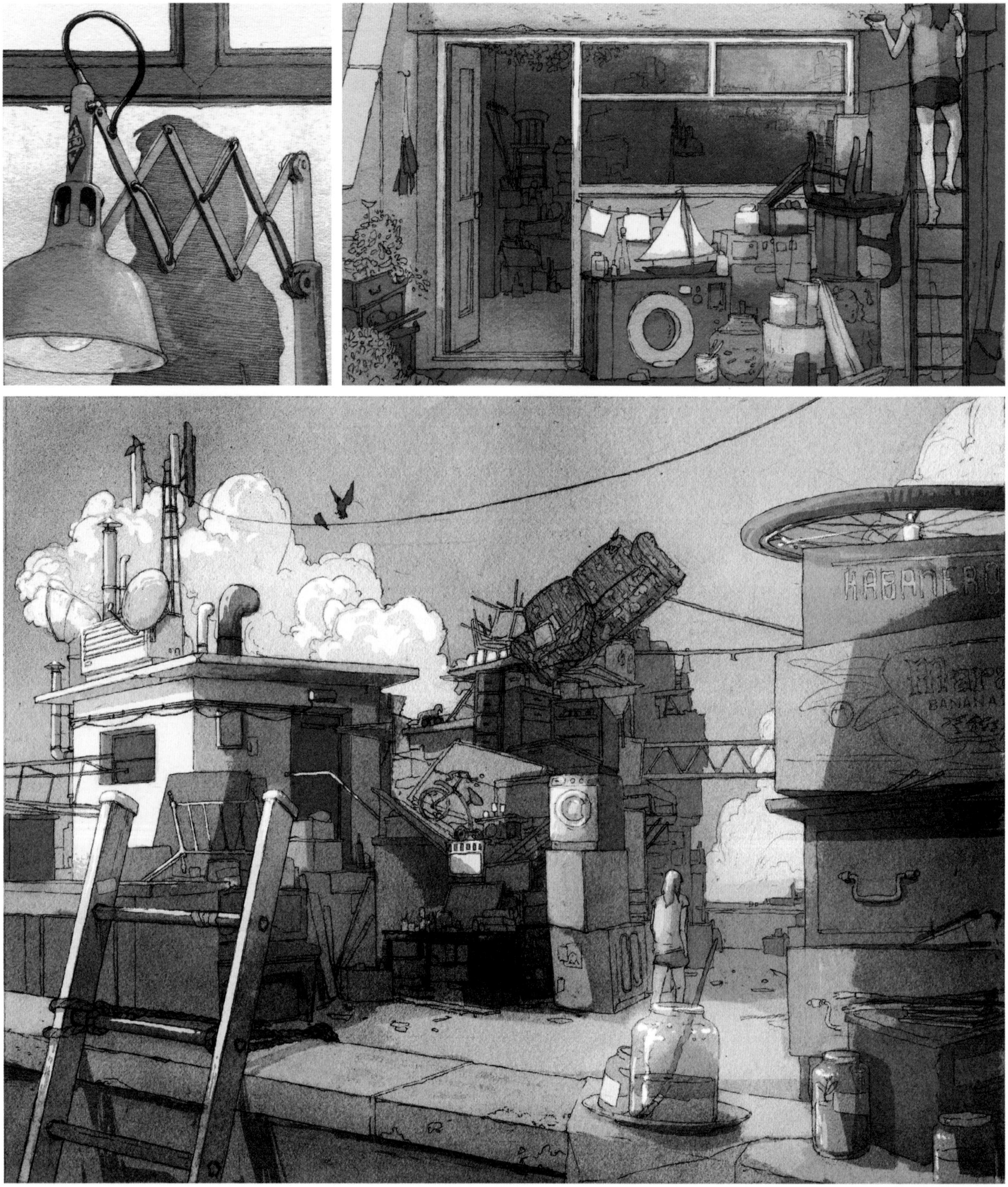

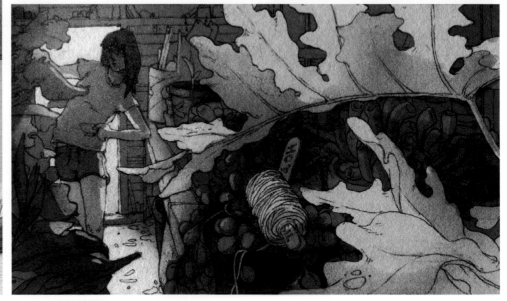

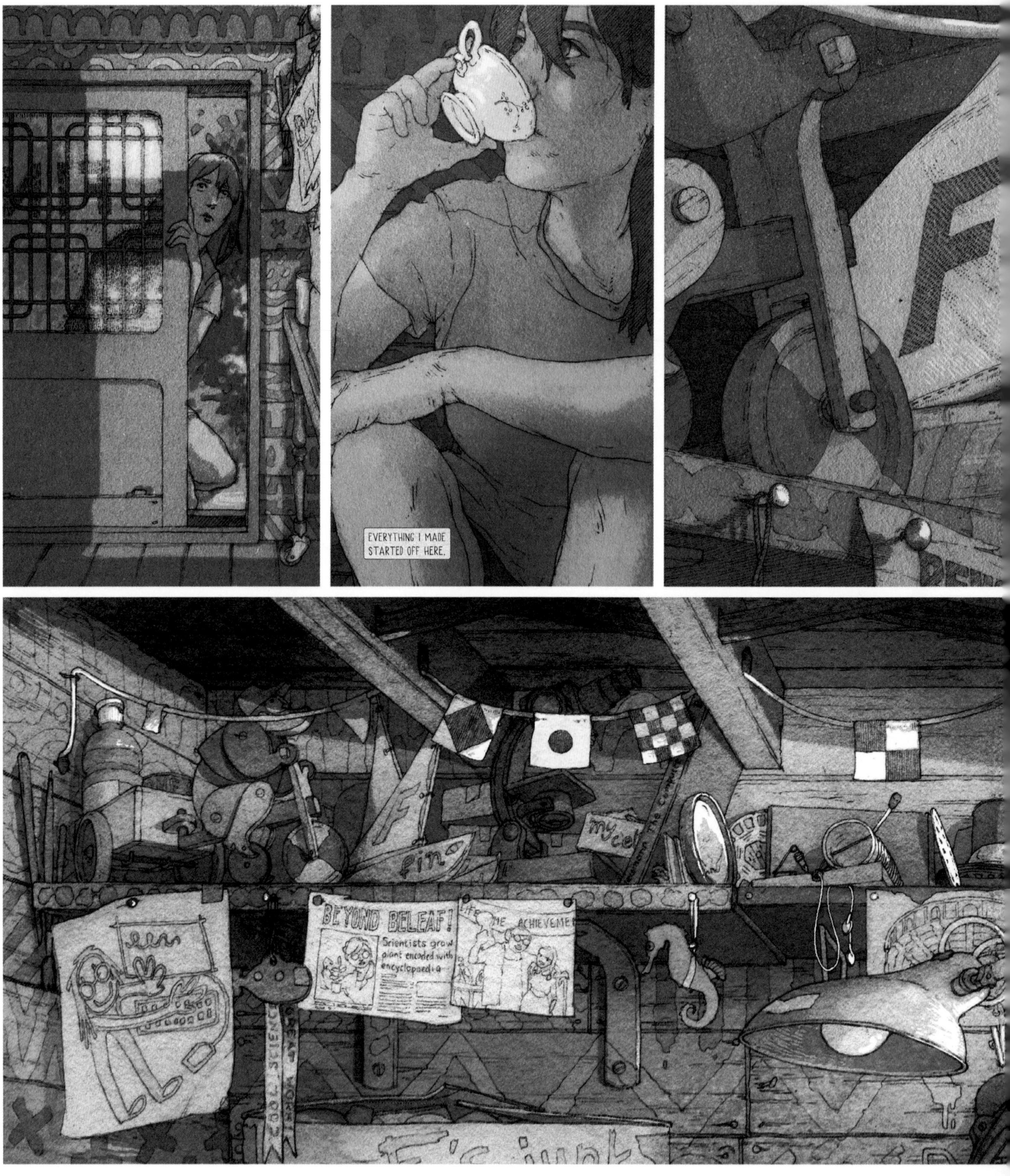
EVERYTHING I MADE
STARTED OFF HERE.
BEYOND BELEAF!
Scientists grow plant encoded with encyclopaedia

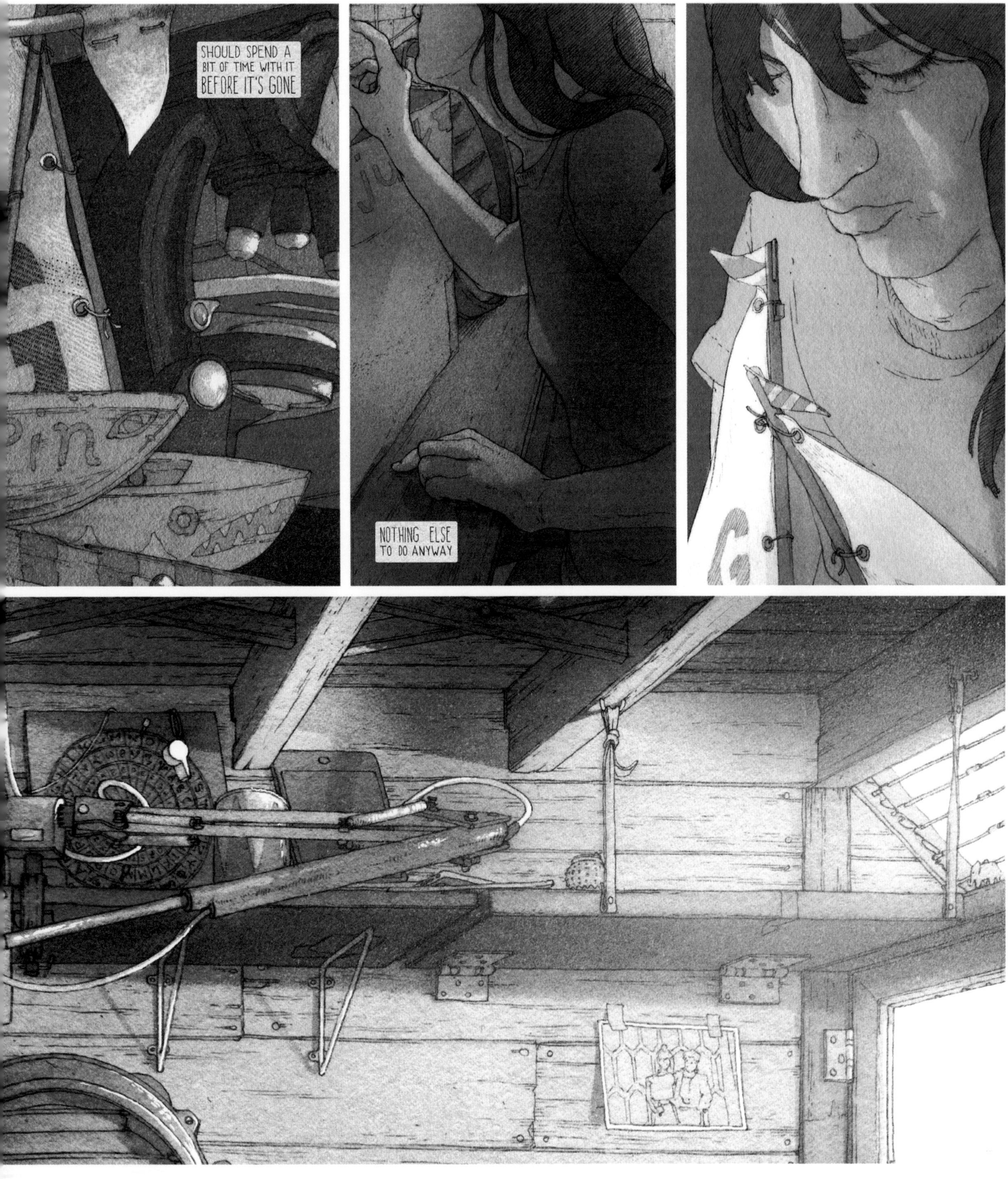
SHOULD SPEND A BIT OF TIME WITH IT BEFORE IT'S GONE
NOTHING ELSE TO DO ANYWAY

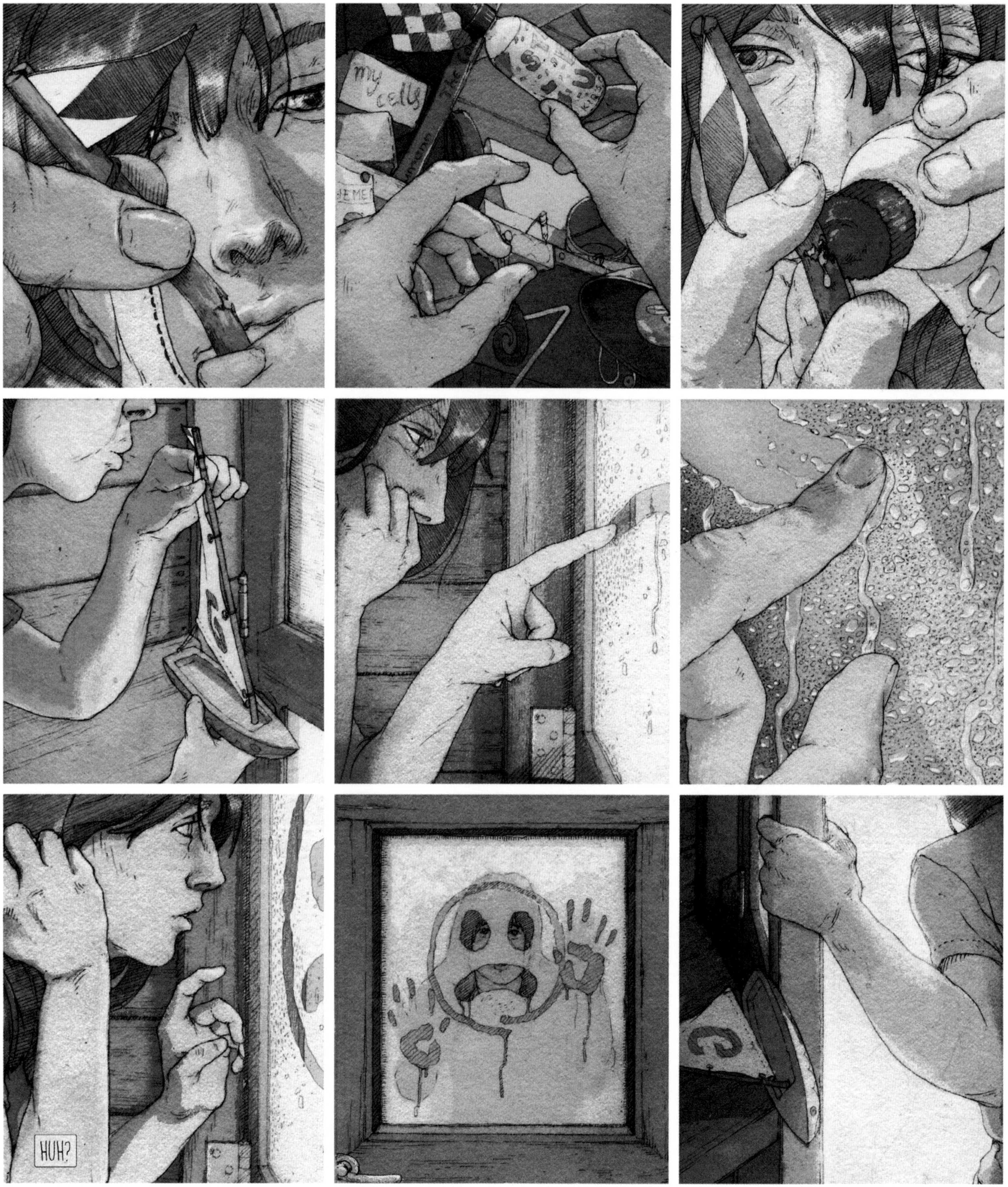
HUH?

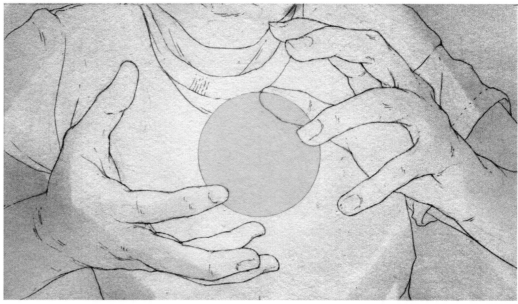

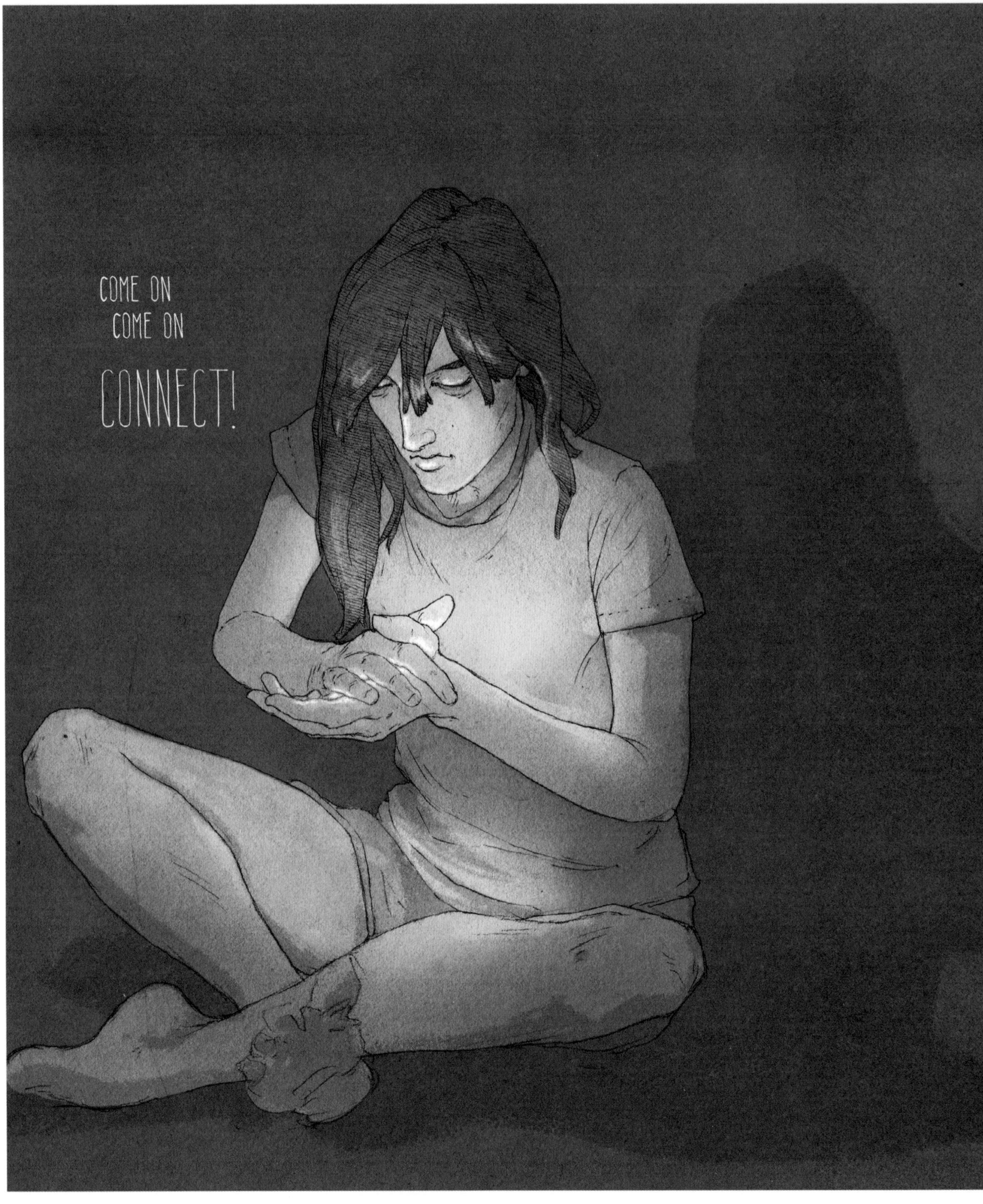
COME ON
COME ON
CONNECT!

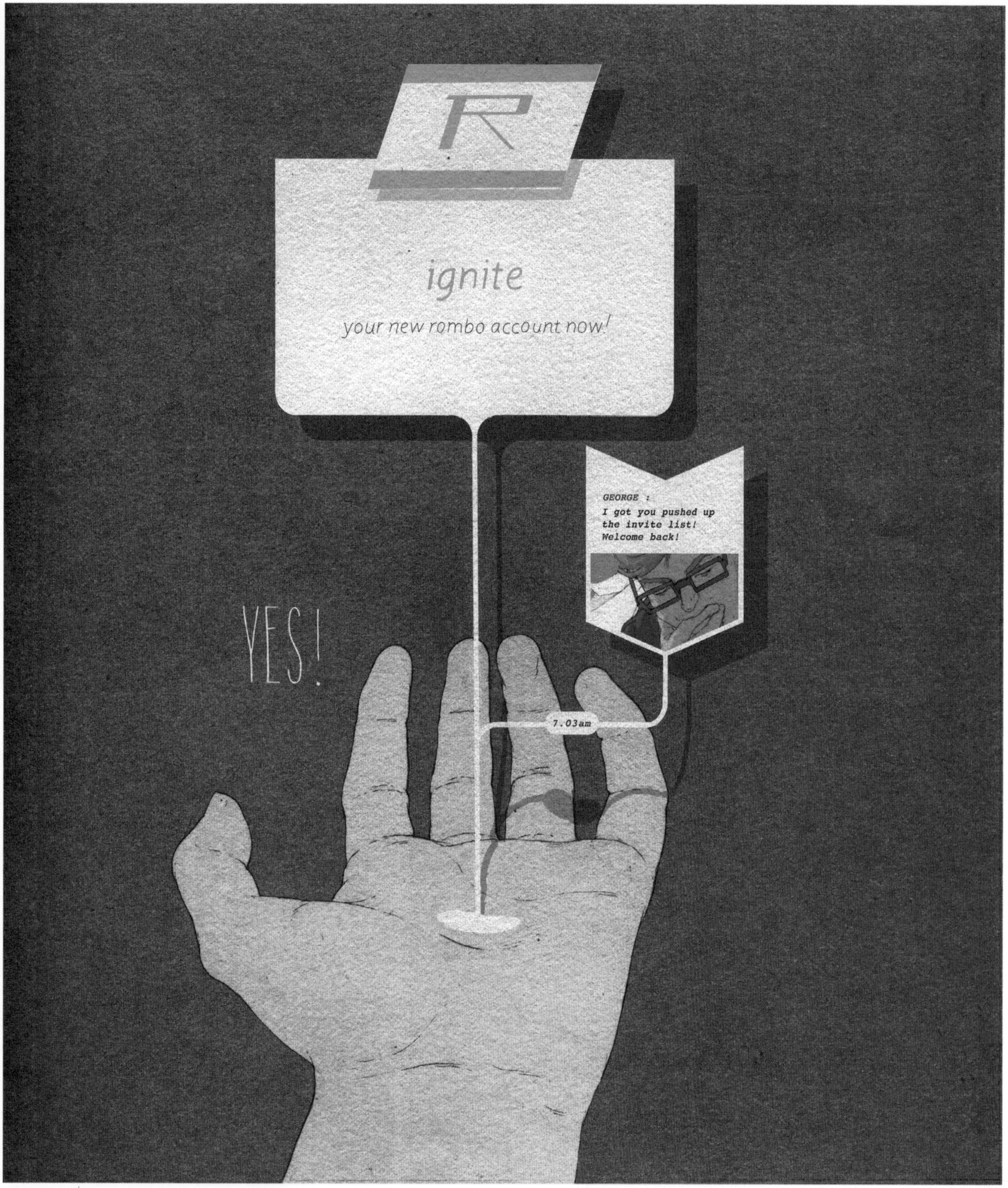
ignite
your new rombo account now!
GEORGE :
I got you pushed up the invite list! Welcome back!
YES!
7.03am

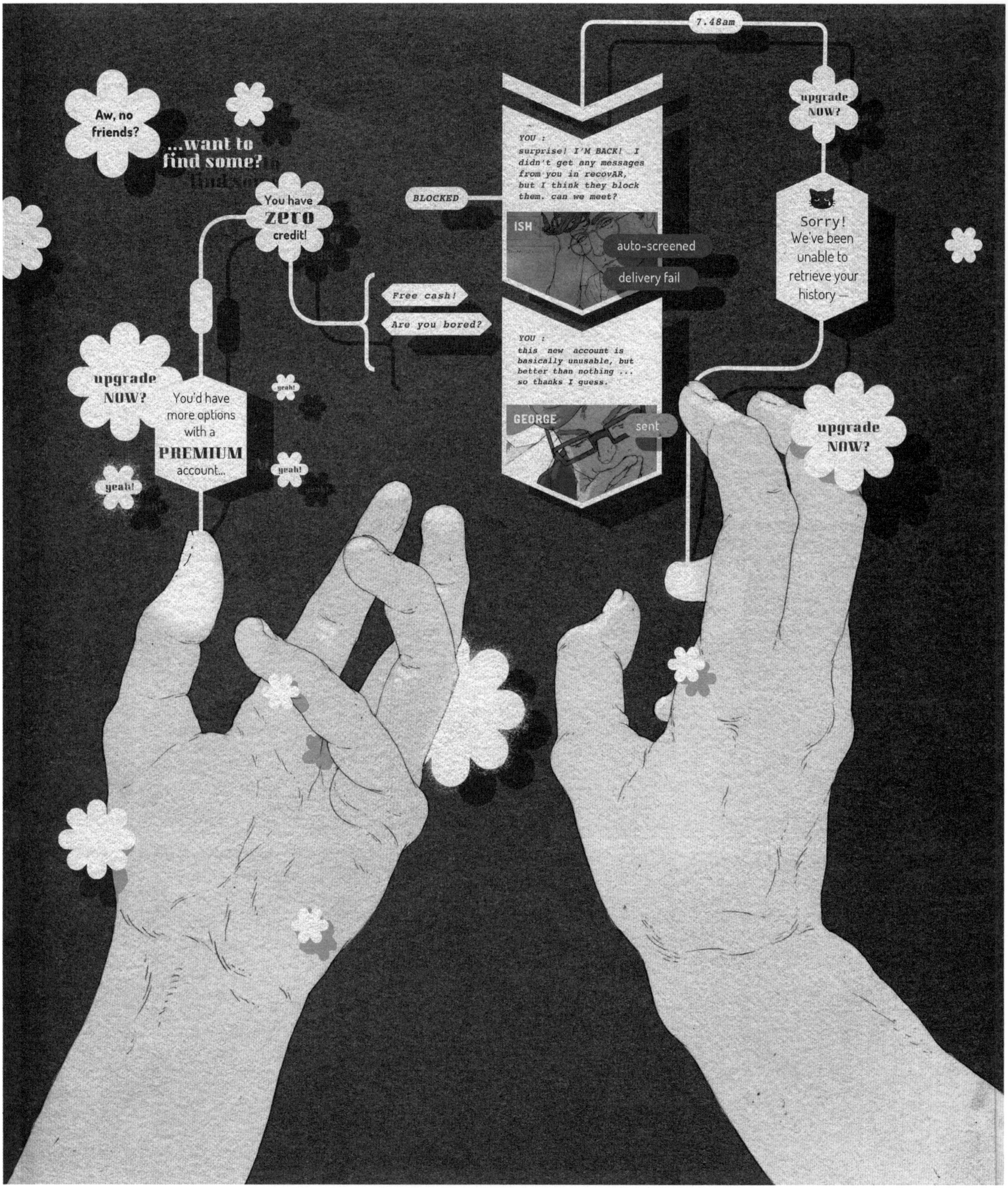

Aw, no friends?
...want to find some?
You have zero credit!
Free cash!
Are you bored?
upgrade NOW?
You'd have more options with a PREMIUM account...
yeah!
yeah!
yeah!
7.48am
BLOCKED
YOU :
surprise! I'M BACK! I didn't get any messages from you in recovAR, but I think they block them. can we meet?
ISH
auto-screened
delivery fail
YOU :
this new account is basically unusable, but better than nothing ... so thanks I guess.
GEORGE
sent
upgrade NOW?
Sorry! We've been unable to retrieve your history —
upgrade NOW?

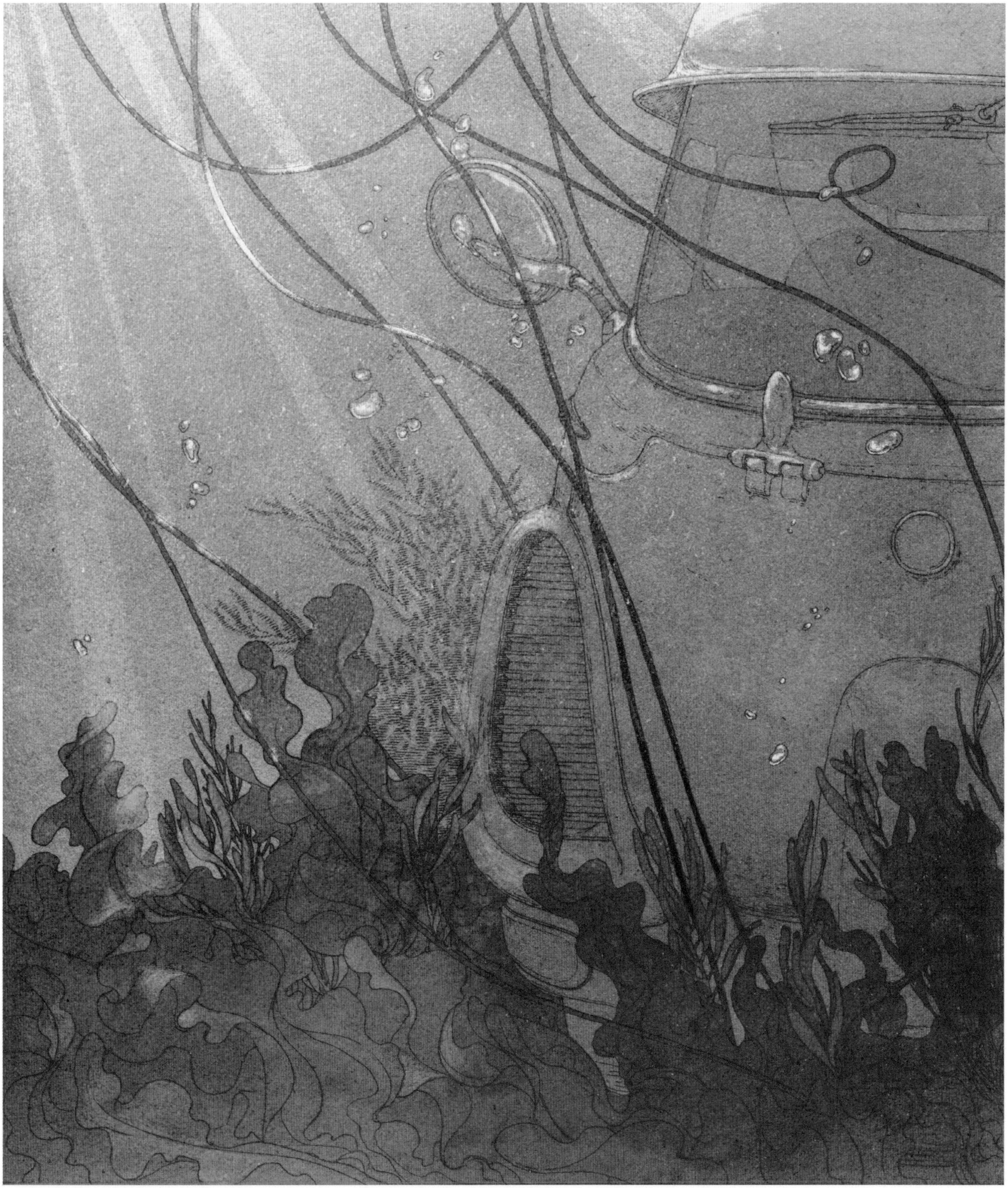

diagnose?
MULTIVALENT DISPLACEMENT err
ANXCOR21 'anxious corner'
reported frequent adverse emotional response in addition to fragmentation and displacement issue — pls run expanded archetype diagnosis and neurosis check
Simon
this is a PRIORITY FIX
GROKLIST
010
run — spatial displacement appraisal pattern
35 sec
032
bug-fix — generalised volume-scattering & fragmentation — open ended
8 min max
223
respond — stimulus over-intensity calibration
3 min
4b2
usr def — cartesian reswoggle
2 min
71a
request — anxiety response archetype check
6 min
ff6
toggle — brand consistency filter runtime
25 sec
completion
>>>
autodetect

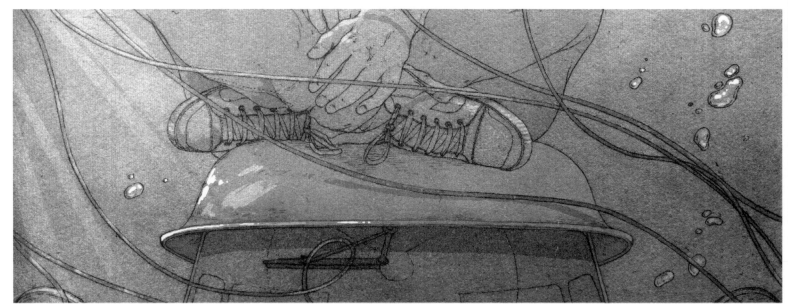

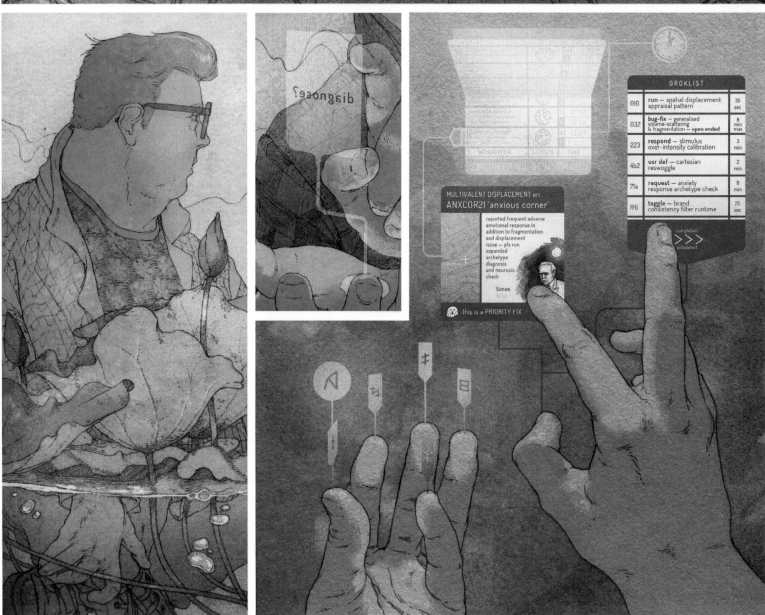

the ARCHETYPER ver 0.348

Identify, if you can, any inopportune visual resonance within the affected image-region —

SKULL SNAKE BLOOD

AGE THE POOR A...

WILD DOG FAILURE A...

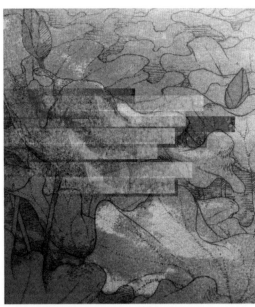

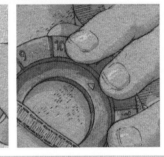

Use test frames to view the error through a random cycle of local user profiles.

Record inconsistencies below:

USER 1 USER 2 USER 3 USER 4

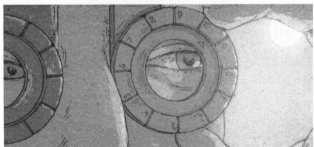

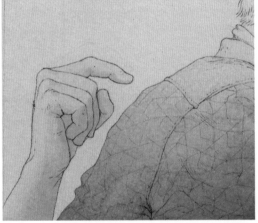

AARGGH!

HEY! YOU BUSY?

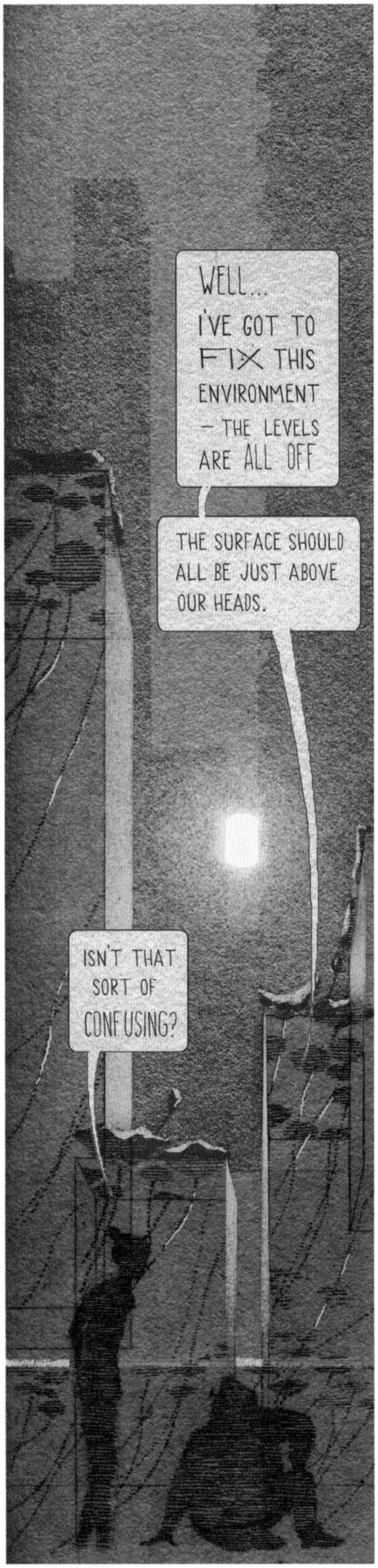
WELL... I'VE GOT TO FIX THIS ENVIRONMENT – THE LEVELS ARE ALL OFF
THE SURFACE SHOULD ALL BE JUST ABOVE OUR HEADS.
ISN'T THAT SORT OF CONFUSING?

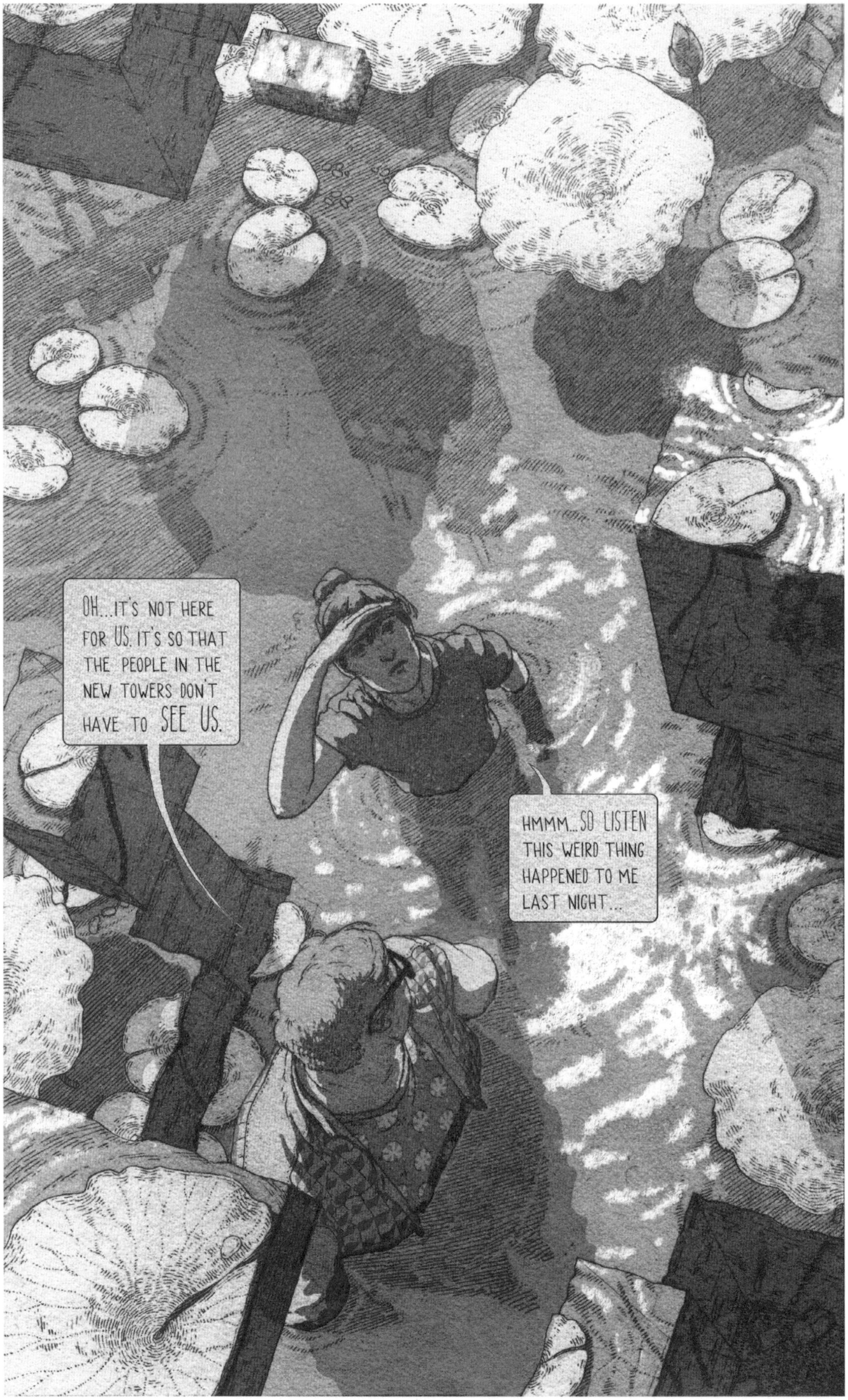
OH...IT'S NOT HERE FOR US. IT'S SO THAT THE PEOPLE IN THE NEW TOWERS DON'T HAVE TO SEE US.
HMMM...SO LISTEN THIS WEIRD THING HAPPENED TO ME LAST NIGHT...

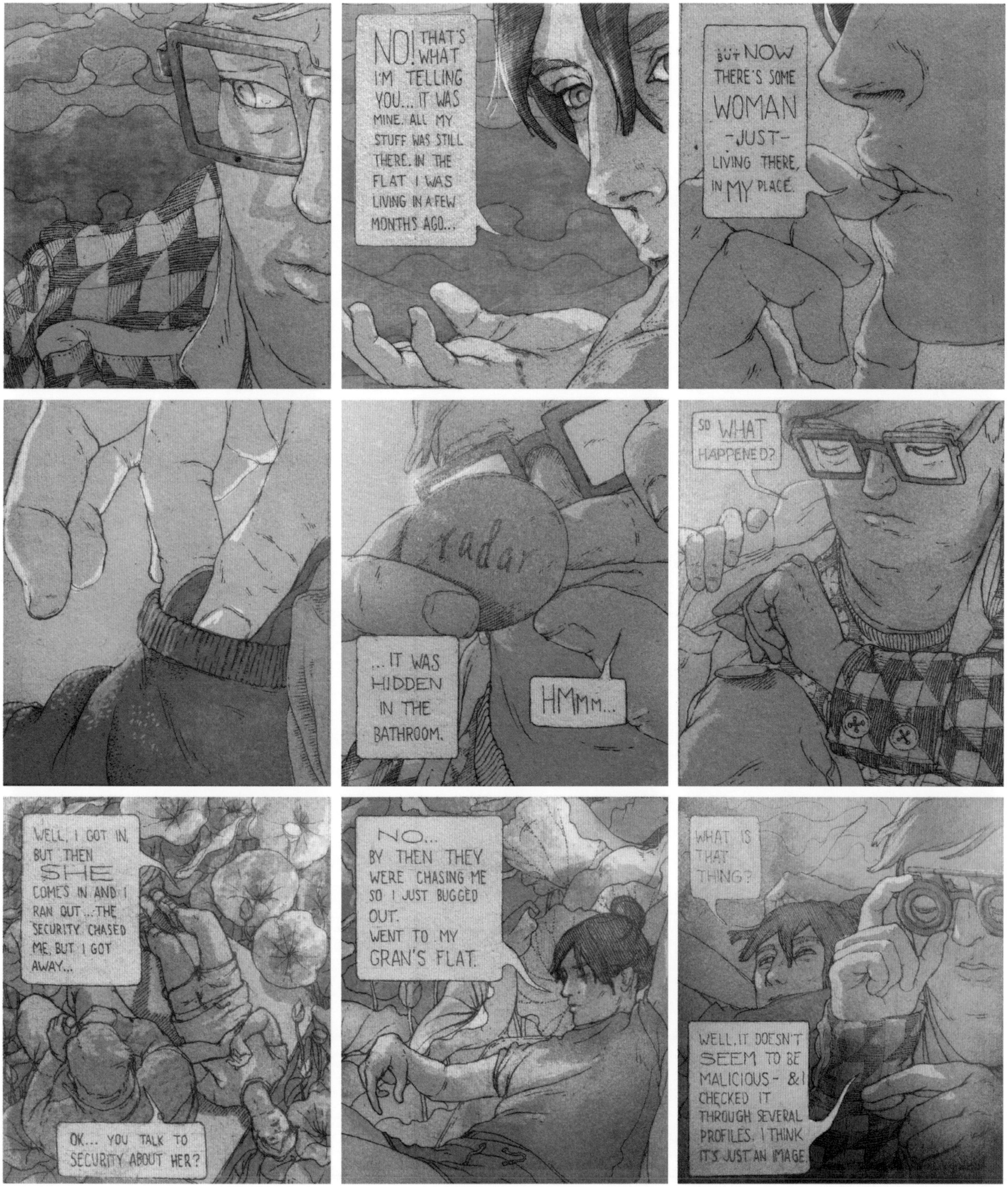

NO! THAT'S WHAT I'M TELLING YOU... IT WAS MINE. ALL MY STUFF WAS STILL THERE. IN THE FLAT I WAS LIVING IN A FEW MONTHS AGO...
BUT NOW THERE'S SOME WOMAN -JUST- LIVING THERE, IN MY PLACE.
radar
...IT WAS HIDDEN IN THE BATHROOM.
HMmm...
SO WHAT HAPPENED?
WELL, I GOT IN, BUT THEN SHE COMES IN AND I RAN OUT... THE SECURITY CHASED ME, BUT I GOT AWAY...
OK... YOU TALK TO SECURITY ABOUT HER?
NO... BY THEN THEY WERE CHASING ME SO I JUST BUGGED OUT. WENT TO MY GRAN'S FLAT.
WHAT IS THAT THING?
WELL, IT DOESN'T SEEM TO BE MALICIOUS - & I CHECKED IT THROUGH SEVERAL PROFILES. I THINK IT'S JUST AN IMAGE.

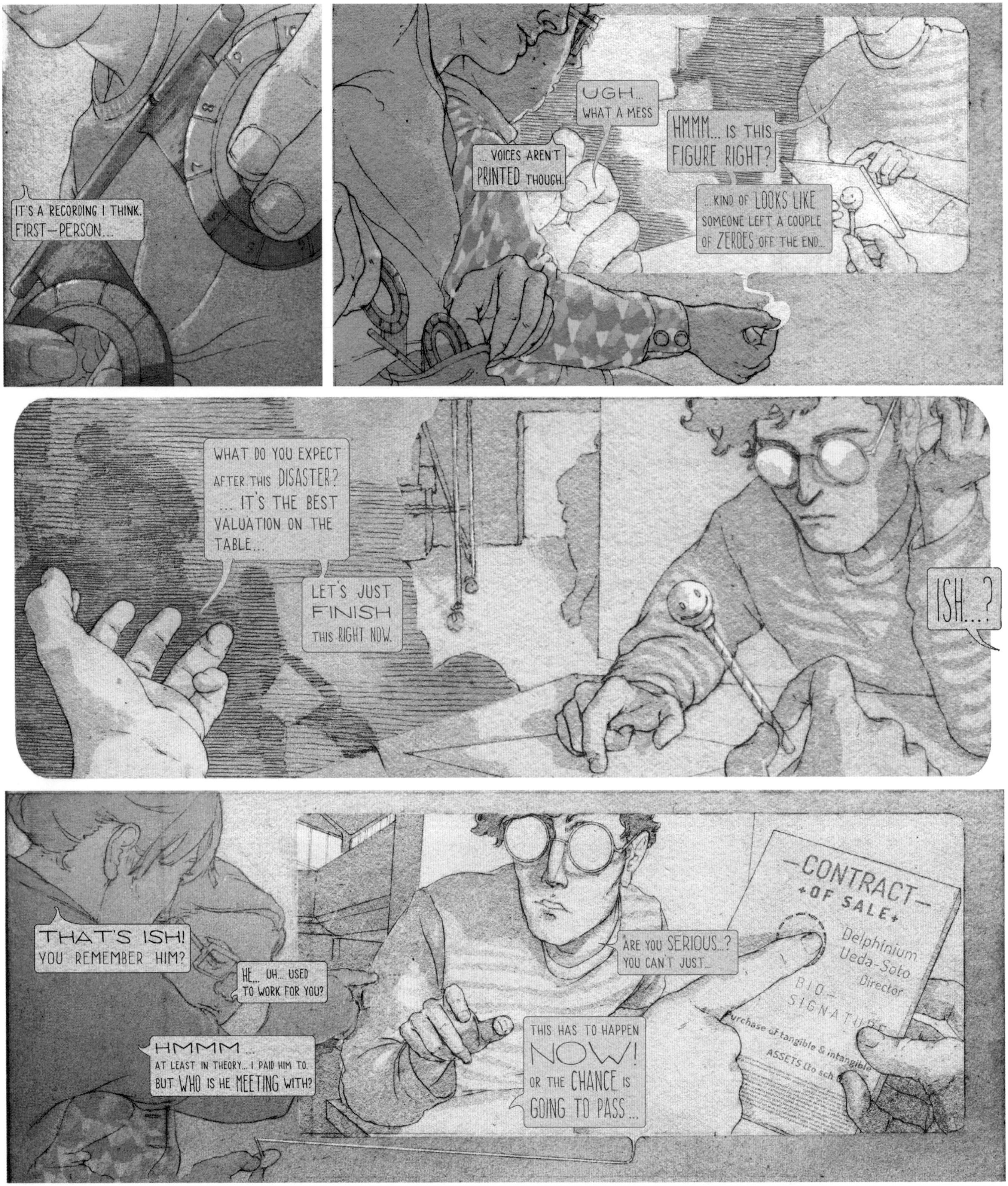
IT'S A RECORDING I THINK. FIRST—PERSON...
... VOICES AREN'T PRINTED THOUGH.
UGH... WHAT A MESS
HMMM... IS THIS FIGURE RIGHT?
...KIND OF LOOKS LIKE SOMEONE LEFT A COUPLE OF ZEROES OFF THE END...
WHAT DO YOU EXPECT AFTER THIS DISASTER? ... IT'S THE BEST VALUATION ON THE TABLE...
LET'S JUST FINISH THIS RIGHT NOW.
ISH...?
THAT'S ISH! YOU REMEMBER HIM?
HE... UH... USED TO WORK FOR YOU?
HMMM... AT LEAST IN THEORY... I PAID HIM TO. BUT WHO IS HE MEETING WITH?
ARE YOU SERIOUS...? YOU CAN'T JUST...
THIS HAS TO HAPPEN NOW! OR THE CHANCE IS GOING TO PASS...
—CONTRACT— +OF SALE+
Delphinium Ueda-Soto Director
BIO-SIGNATURE
Purchase of tangible & intangible ASSETS (to sch

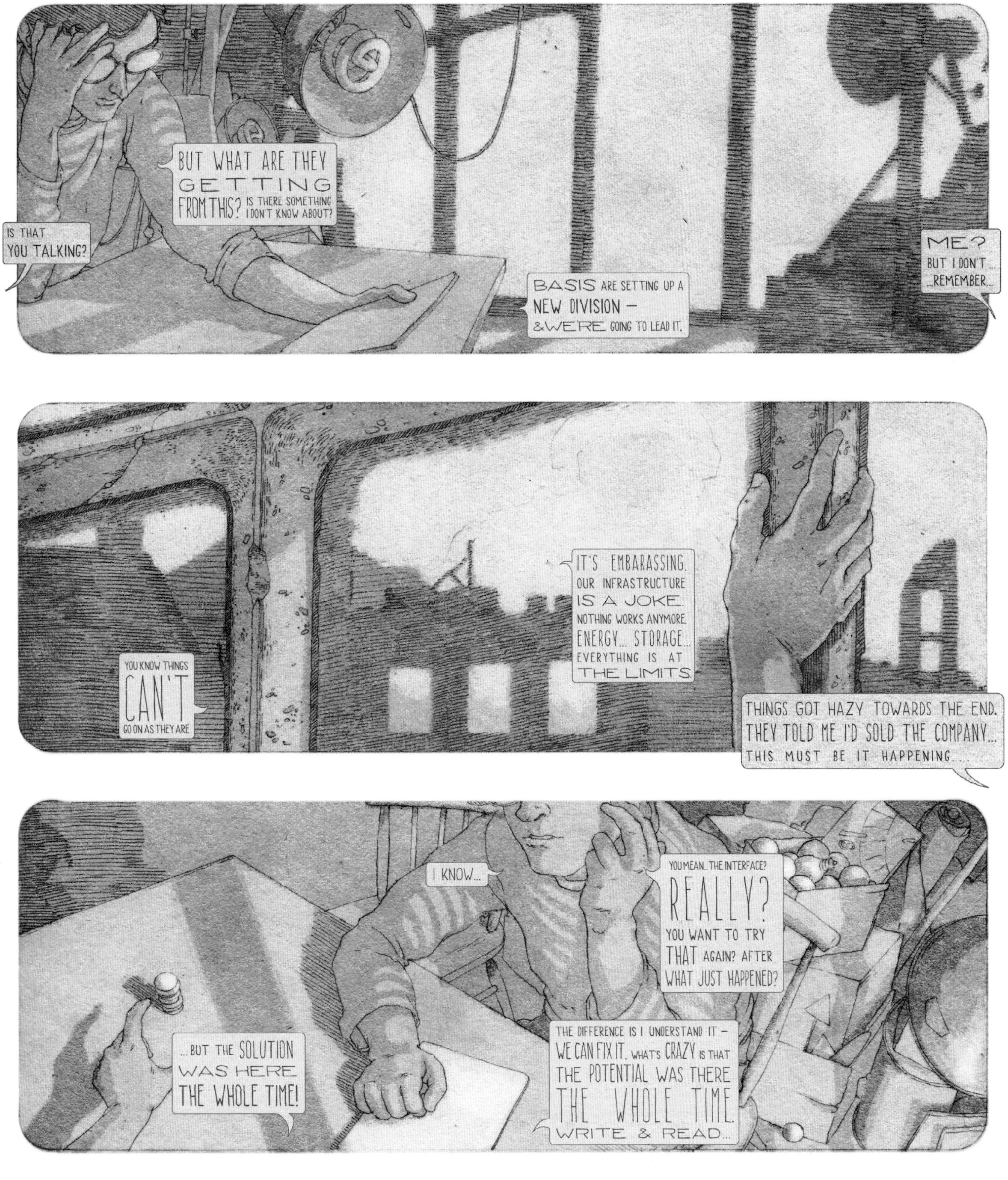
BUT WHAT ARE THEY GETTING FROM THIS? IS THERE SOMETHING I DON'T KNOW ABOUT?
IS THAT YOU TALKING?
BASIS ARE SETTING UP A NEW DIVISION – &WE'RE GOING TO LEAD IT.
ME? BUT I DON'T... ...REMEMBER...
YOU KNOW THINGS CAN'T GO ON AS THEY ARE
IT'S EMBARASSING. OUR INFRASTRUCTURE IS A JOKE. NOTHING WORKS ANYMORE. ENERGY... STORAGE... EVERYTHING IS AT THE LIMITS.
THINGS GOT HAZY TOWARDS THE END. THEY TOLD ME I'D SOLD THE COMPANY... THIS MUST BE IT HAPPENING...
I KNOW...
YOU MEAN...THE INTERFACE? REALLY? YOU WANT TO TRY THAT AGAIN? AFTER WHAT JUST HAPPENED?
...BUT THE SOLUTION WAS HERE THE WHOLE TIME!
THE DIFFERENCE IS I UNDERSTAND IT – WE CAN FIX IT. WHAT'S CRAZY IS THAT THE POTENTIAL WAS THERE THE WHOLE TIME. WRITE & READ...

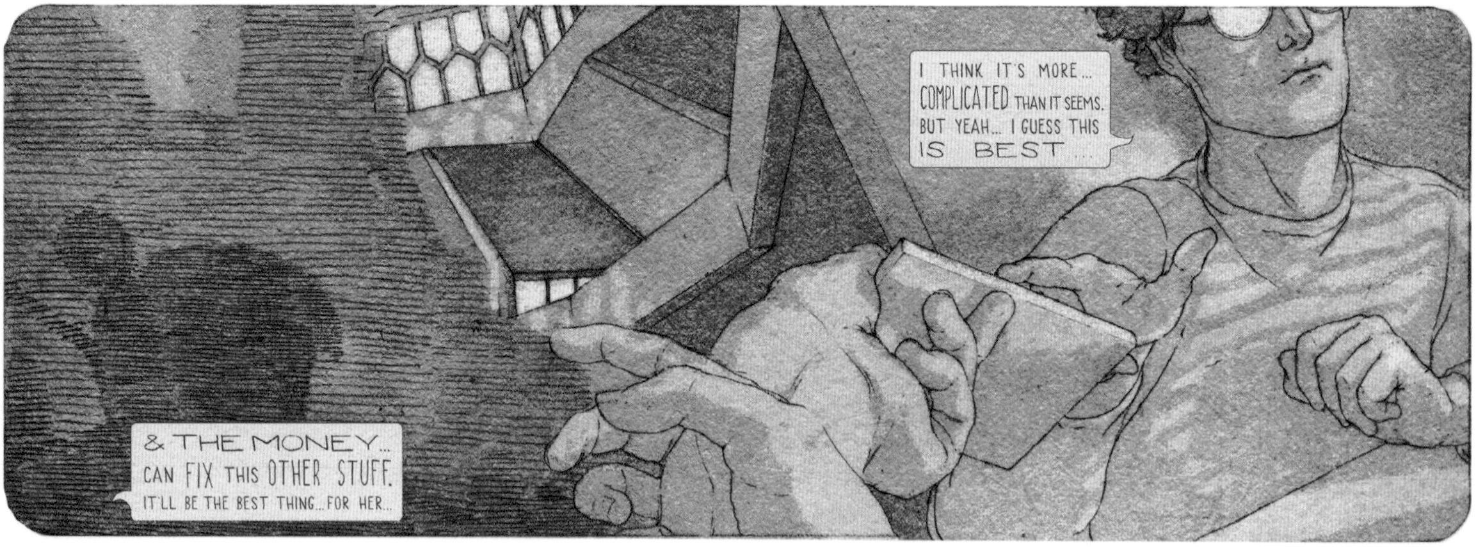
I THINK IT'S MORE... COMPLICATED THAN IT SEEMS. BUT YEAH... I GUESS THIS IS BEST...
& THE MONEY... CAN FIX THIS OTHER STUFF. IT'LL BE THE BEST THING... FOR HER...

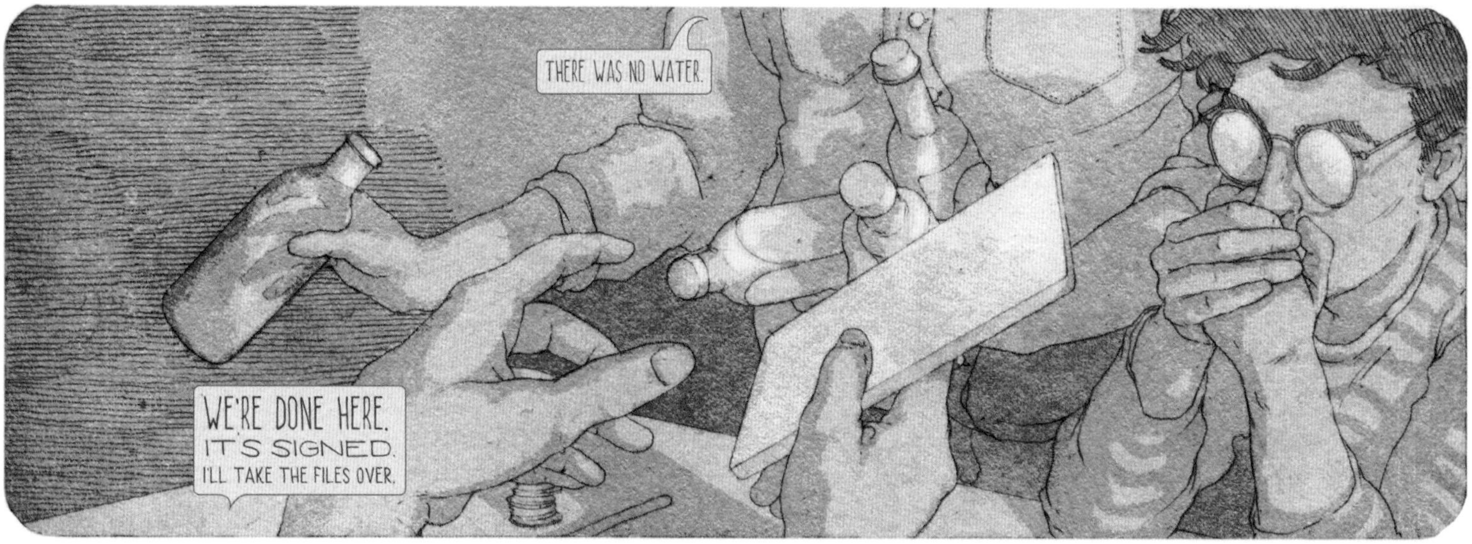
THERE WAS NO WATER.
WE'RE DONE HERE. IT'S SIGNED. I'LL TAKE THE FILES OVER.

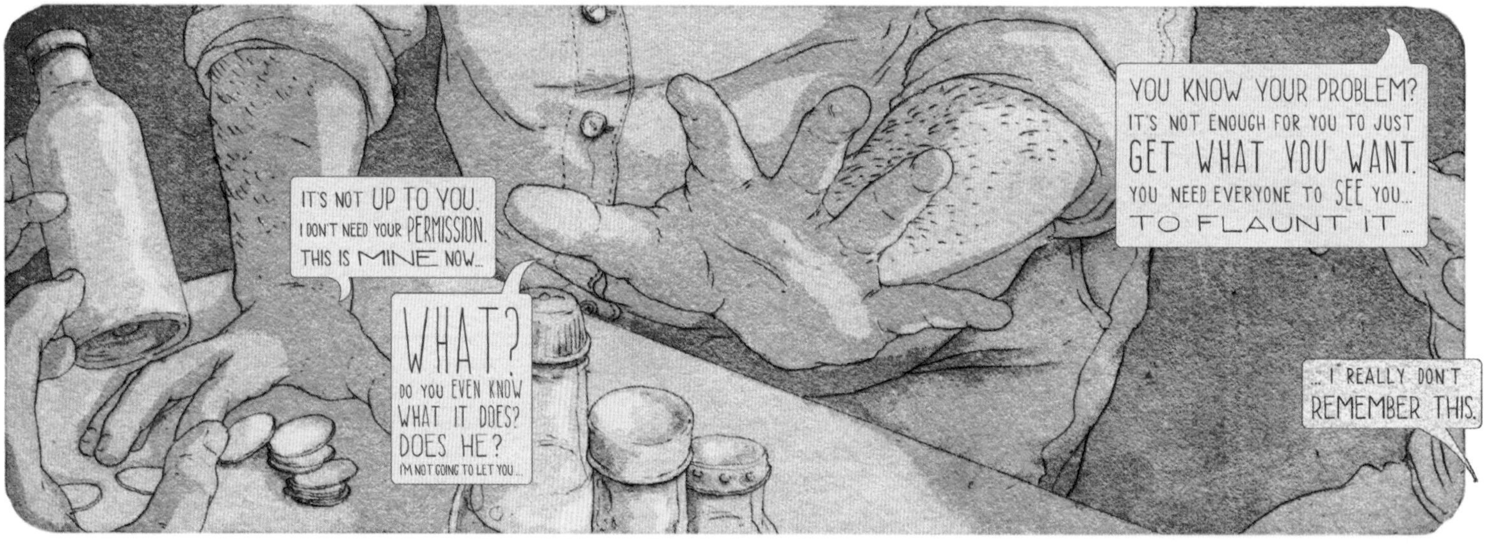
YOU KNOW YOUR PROBLEM? IT'S NOT ENOUGH FOR YOU TO JUST GET WHAT YOU WANT. YOU NEED EVERYONE TO SEE YOU... TO FLAUNT IT...
IT'S NOT UP TO YOU. I DON'T NEED YOUR PERMISSION. THIS IS MINE NOW...
WHAT? DO YOU EVEN KNOW WHAT IT DOES? DOES HE? I'M NOT GOING TO LET YOU...
... I REALLY DON'T REMEMBER THIS.

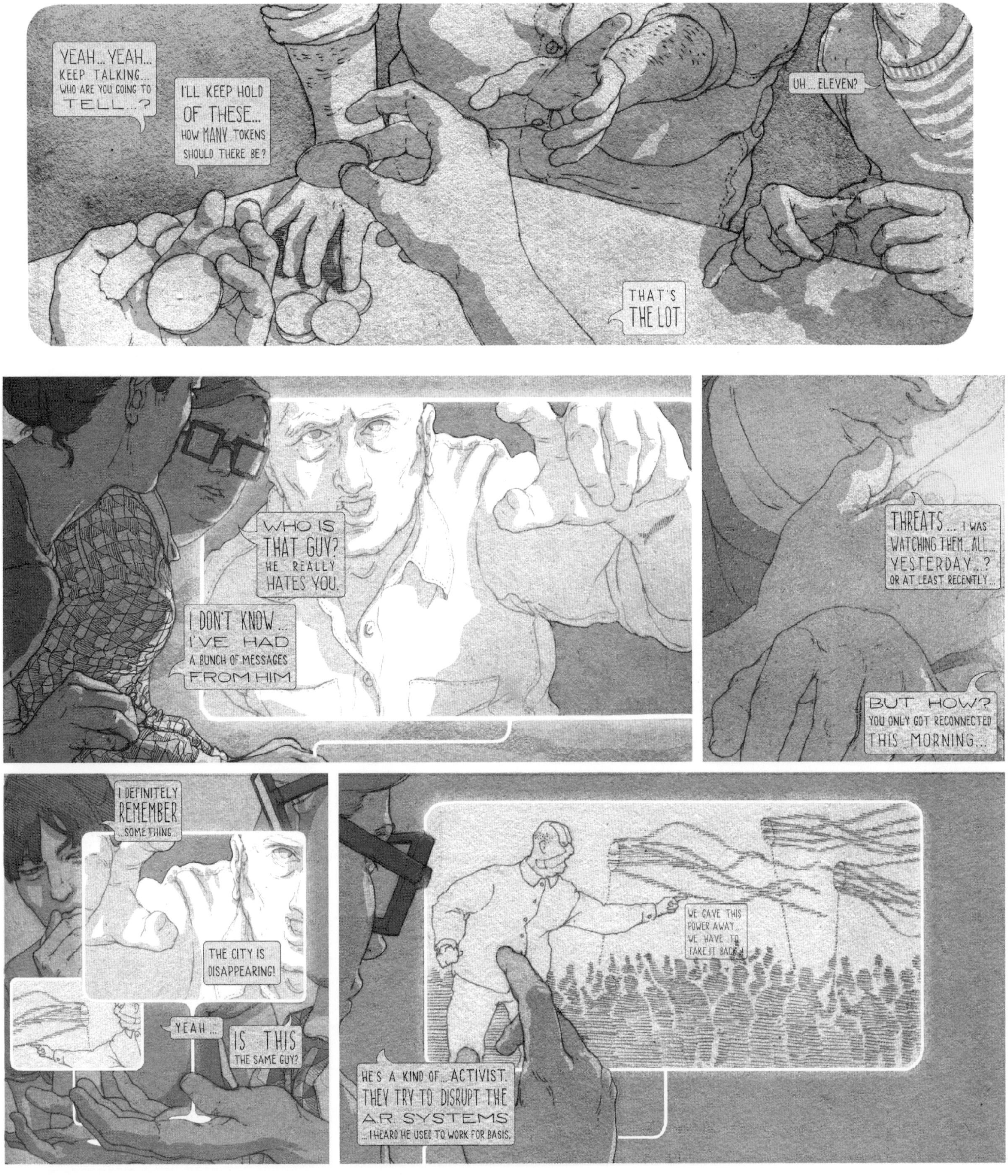
YEAH... YEAH... KEEP TALKING... WHO ARE YOU GOING TO TELL...?
I'LL KEEP HOLD OF THESE... HOW MANY TOKENS SHOULD THERE BE?
UH... ELEVEN?
THAT'S THE LOT
WHO IS THAT GUY? HE REALLY HATES YOU.
I DON'T KNOW... I'VE HAD A BUNCH OF MESSAGES FROM HIM
THREATS... I WAS WATCHING THEM... ALL... YESTERDAY...? OR AT LEAST RECENTLY...
BUT HOW? YOU ONLY GOT RECONNECTED THIS MORNING...
I DEFINITELY REMEMBER ...SOMETHING...
THE CITY IS DISAPPEARING!
YEAH...
IS THIS THE SAME GUY?
WE GAVE THIS POWER AWAY. WE HAVE TO TAKE IT BACK!
HE'S A KIND OF... ACTIVIST. THEY TRY TO DISRUPT THE A.R. SYSTEMS ...I HEARD HE USED TO WORK FOR BASIS.

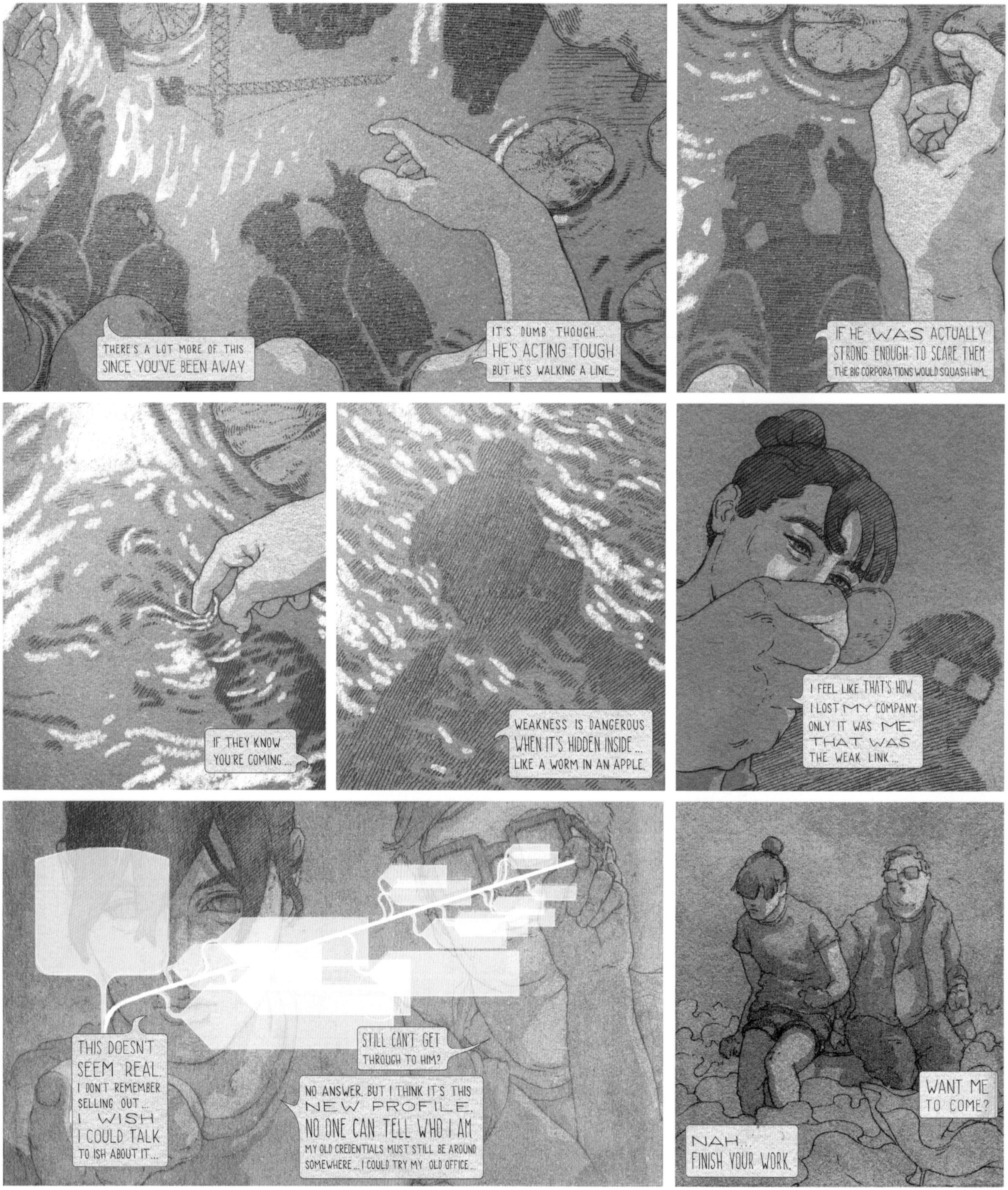
THERE'S A LOT MORE OF THIS SINCE YOU'VE BEEN AWAY
IT'S DUMB THOUGH... HE'S ACTING TOUGH BUT HE'S WALKING A LINE...
IF HE WAS ACTUALLY STRONG ENOUGH TO SCARE THEM THE BIG CORPORATIONS WOULD SQUASH HIM...
IF THEY KNOW YOU'RE COMING...
WEAKNESS IS DANGEROUS WHEN IT'S HIDDEN INSIDE... LIKE A WORM IN AN APPLE.
I FEEL LIKE THAT'S HOW I LOST MY COMPANY. ONLY IT WAS ME THAT WAS THE WEAK LINK...
THIS DOESN'T SEEM REAL. I DON'T REMEMBER SELLING OUT... I WISH I COULD TALK TO ISH ABOUT IT...
STILL CAN'T GET THROUGH TO HIM?
NO ANSWER. BUT I THINK IT'S THIS NEW PROFILE. NO ONE CAN TELL WHO I AM MY OLD CREDENTIALS MUST STILL BE AROUND SOMEWHERE... I COULD TRY MY OLD OFFICE...
WANT ME TO COME?
NAH... FINISH YOUR WORK.

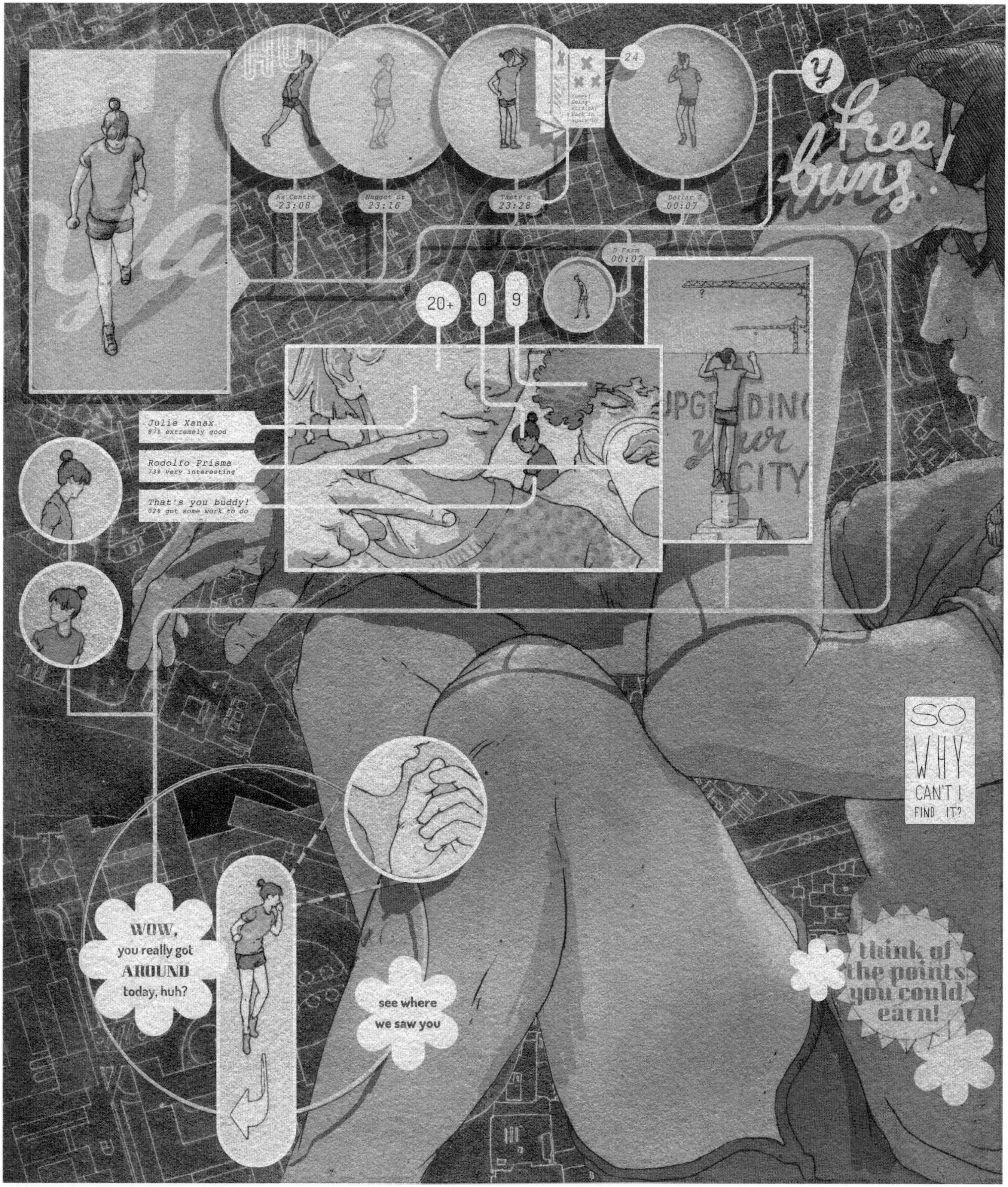

Ax Centre 23:08
Nugget St 23:16
Tasty's 23:28
24
Dollar 00:07
y free buns!
D Farm 00:07
20+
0
9
Julie Xanax
87% extremely good
Rodolfo Prisma
73% very interesting
That's you buddy!
02% got some work to do
UPGRADING your CITY
SO WHY CAN'T I FIND IT?
WOW, you really got AROUND today, huh?
see where we saw you
think of the points you could earn!

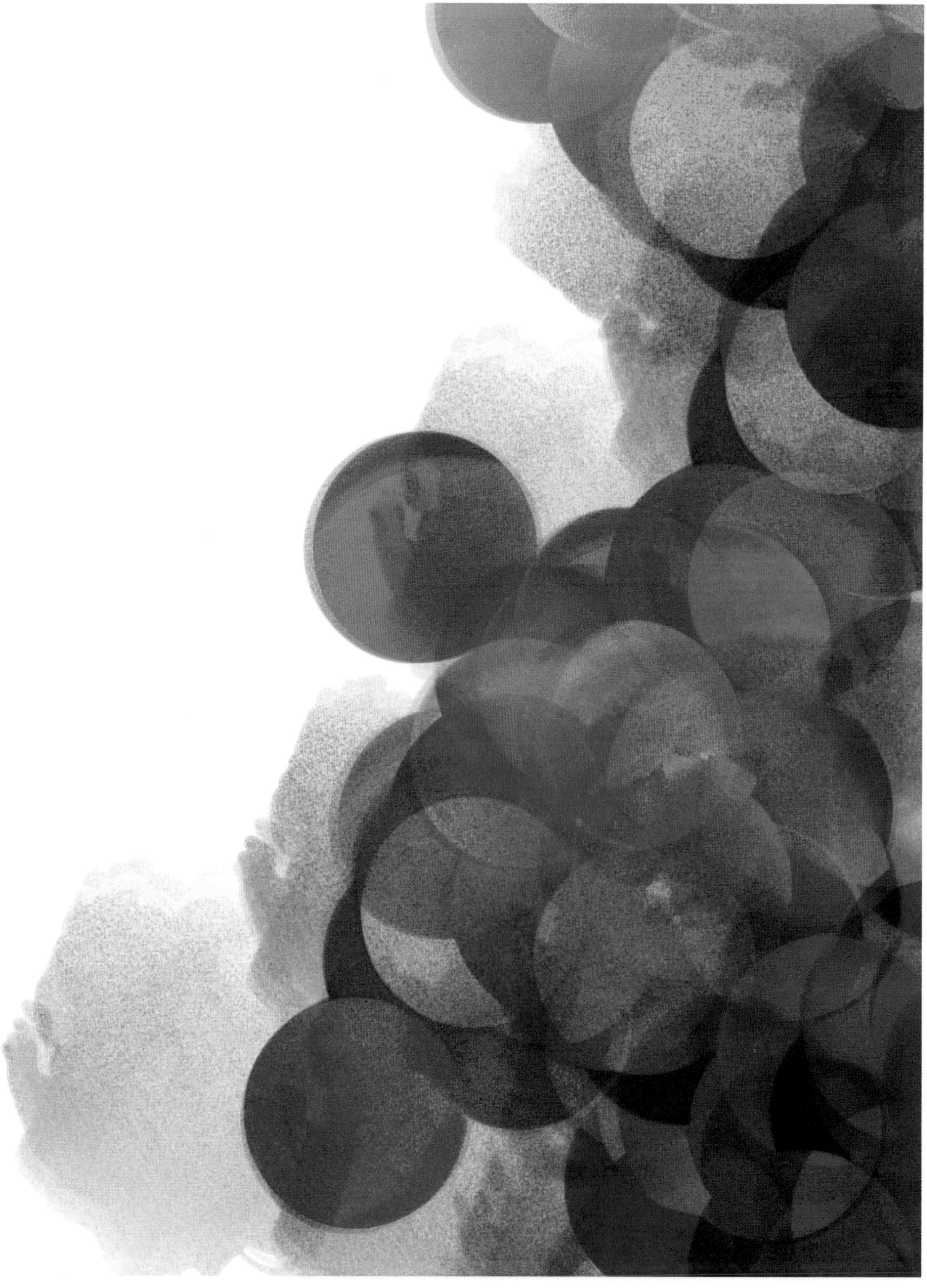

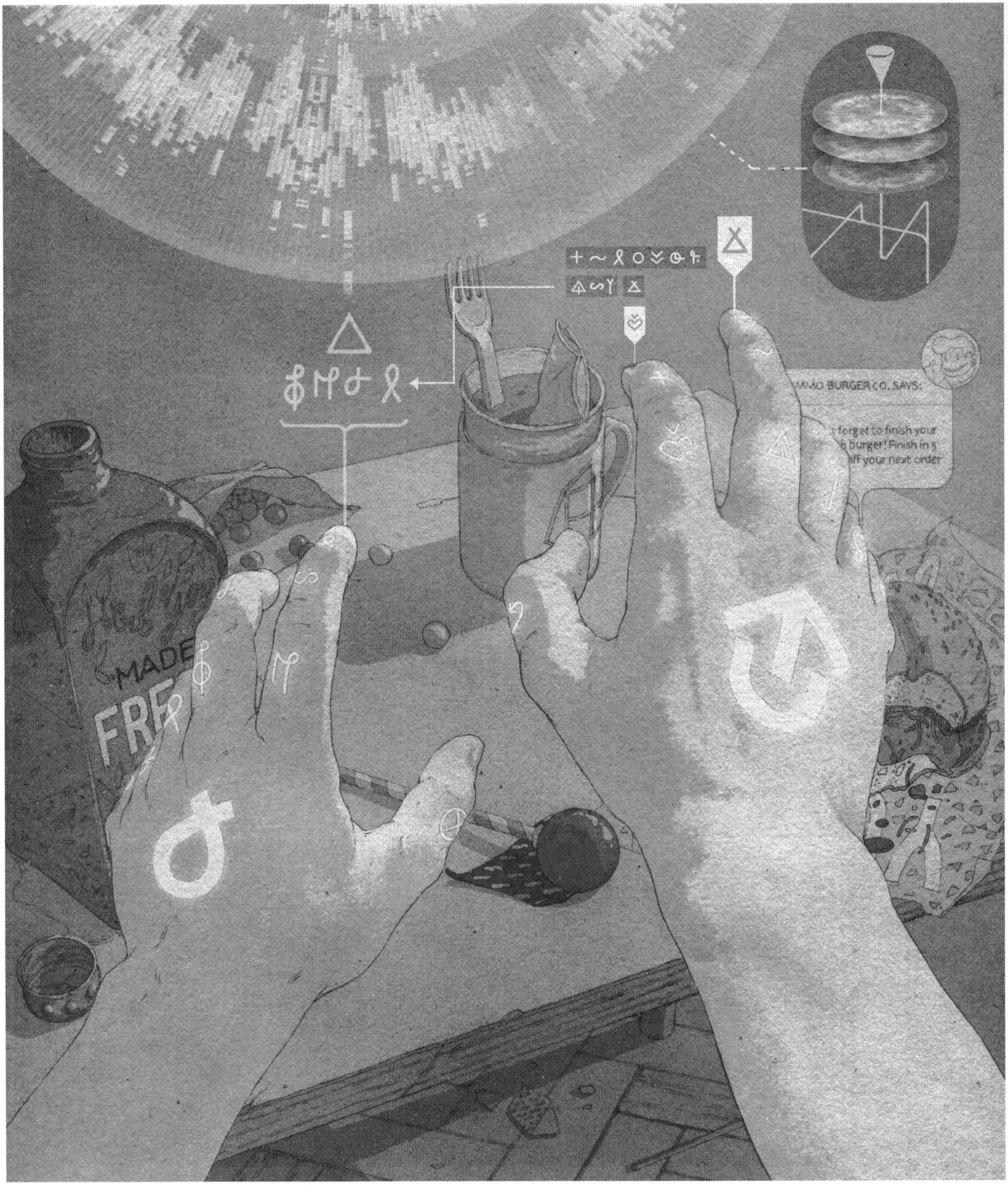

MADE
FRE
MMO BURGER CO. SAYS:
forget to finish your
burger! Finish in 5
your next order

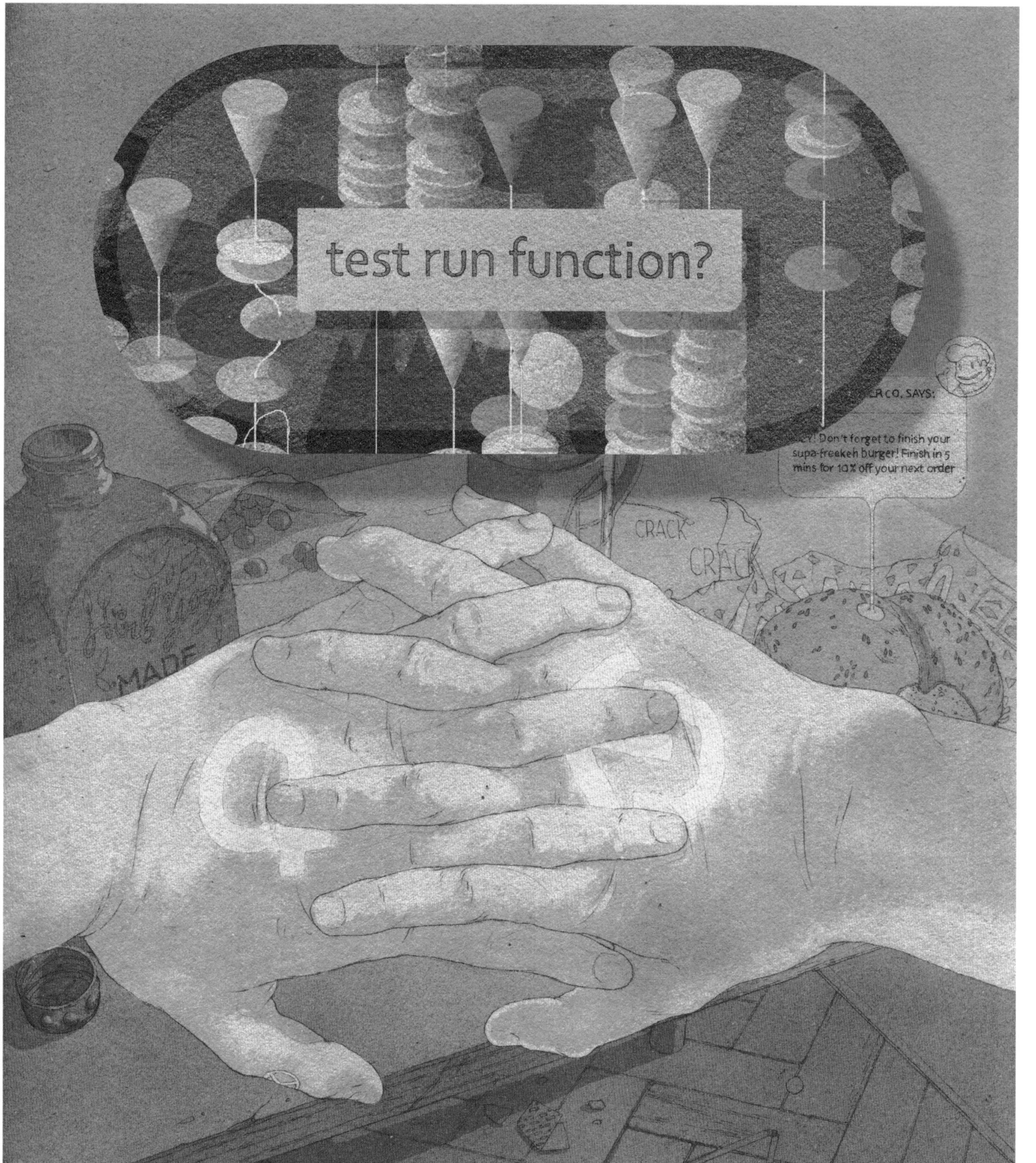
test run function?
CO. SAYS:
Don't forget to finish your supa-freekeh burger! Finish in 5 mins for 10% off your next order
CRACK
CRACK
MADE

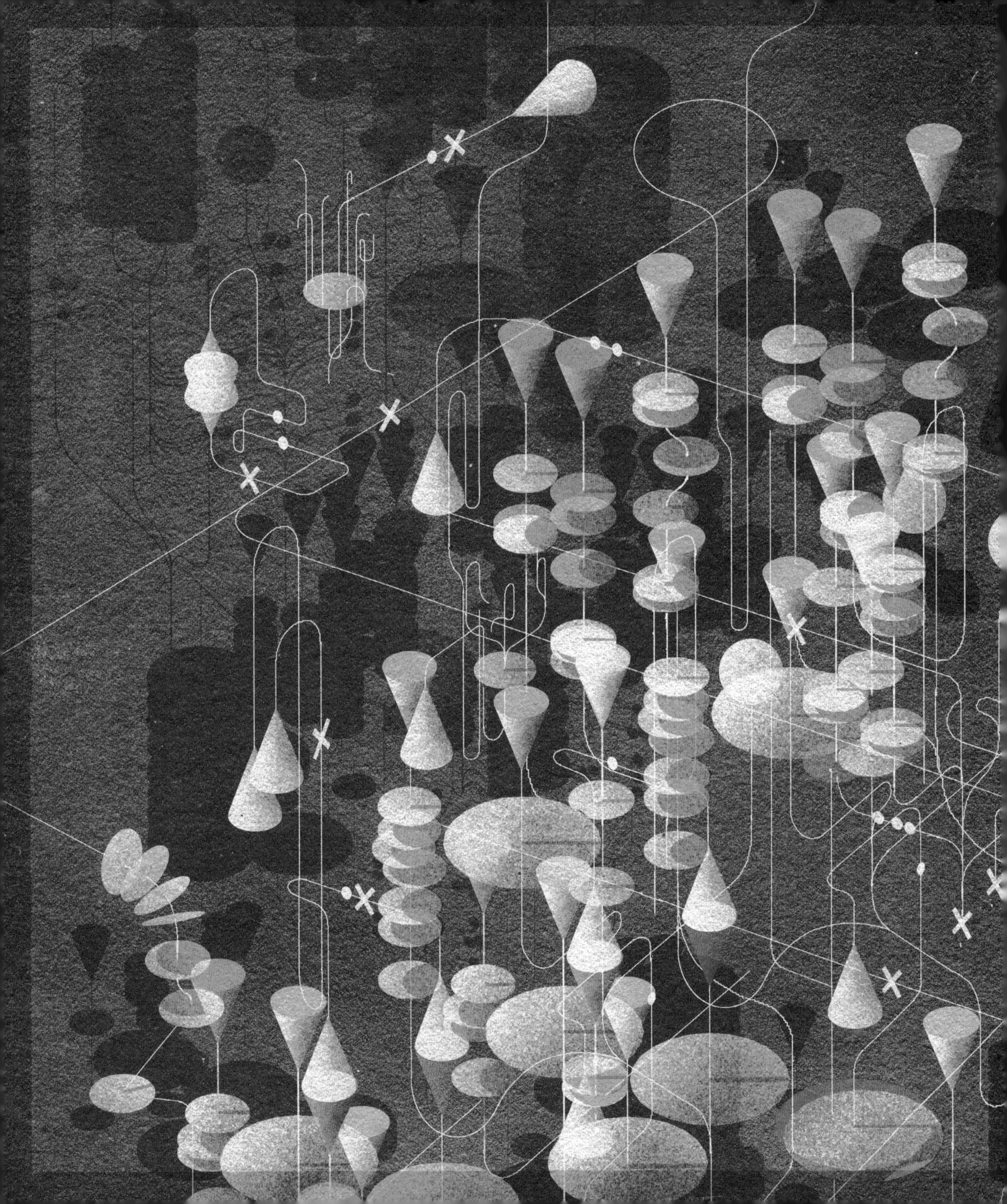

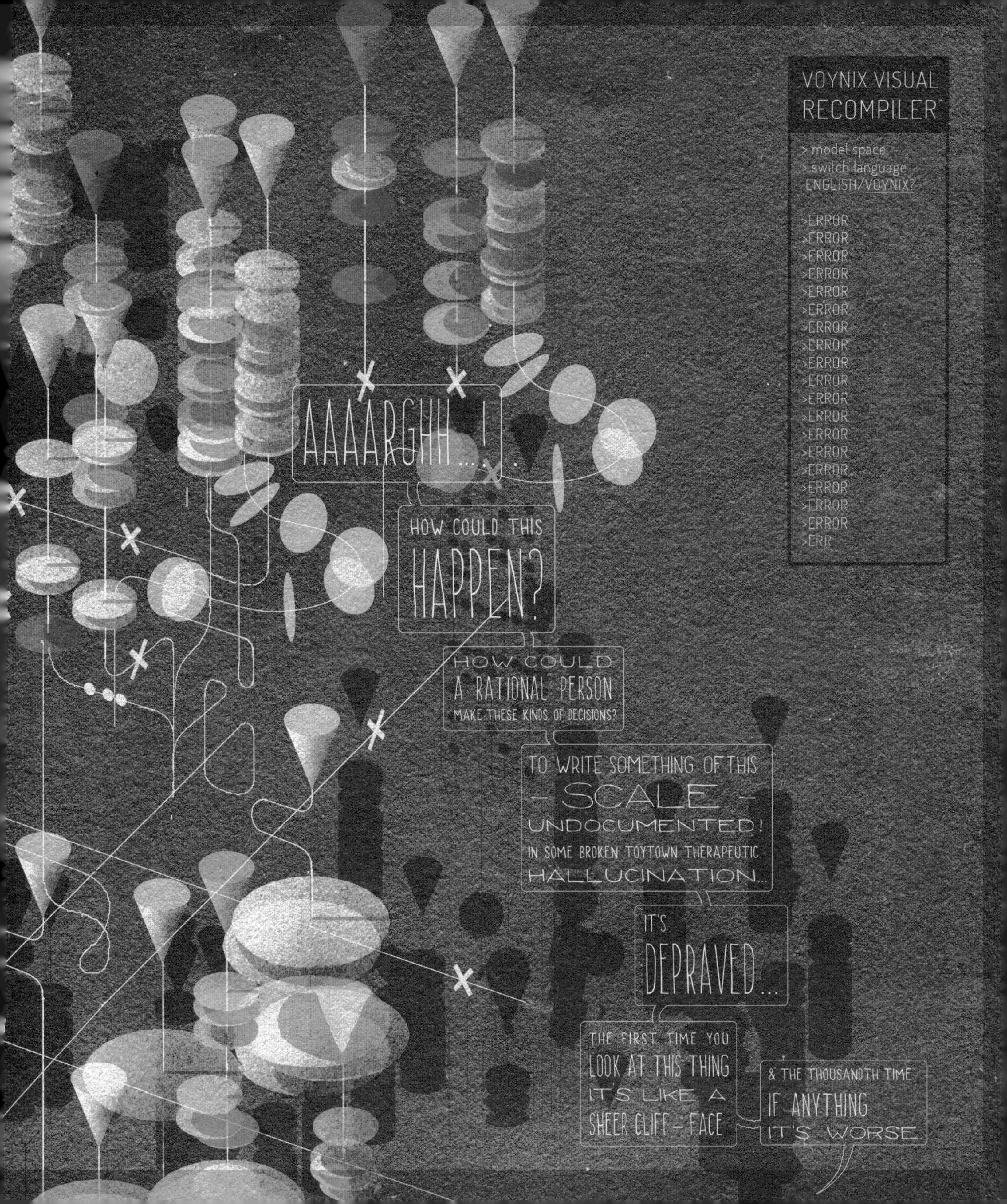
VOYNIX VISUAL RECOMPILER™
> model space
> switch language
ENGLISH/VOYNIX?
>ERROR
>ERROR
>ERROR
>ERROR
>ERROR
>ERROR
>ERROR
>ERROR
>ERROR
>ERROR
>ERROR
>ERROR
>ERROR
>ERROR
>ERROR
>ERROR
>ERROR
>ERROR
>ERR
AAAARGHH....!
HOW COULD THIS HAPPEN?
HOW COULD A RATIONAL PERSON MAKE THESE KINDS OF DECISIONS?
TO WRITE SOMETHING OF THIS – SCALE – UNDOCUMENTED! IN SOME BROKEN TOYTOWN THERAPEUTIC HALLUCINATION...
IT'S DEPRAVED...
THE FIRST TIME YOU LOOK AT THIS THING IT'S LIKE A SHEER CLIFF-FACE
& THE THOUSANDTH TIME IF ANYTHING IT'S WORSE.

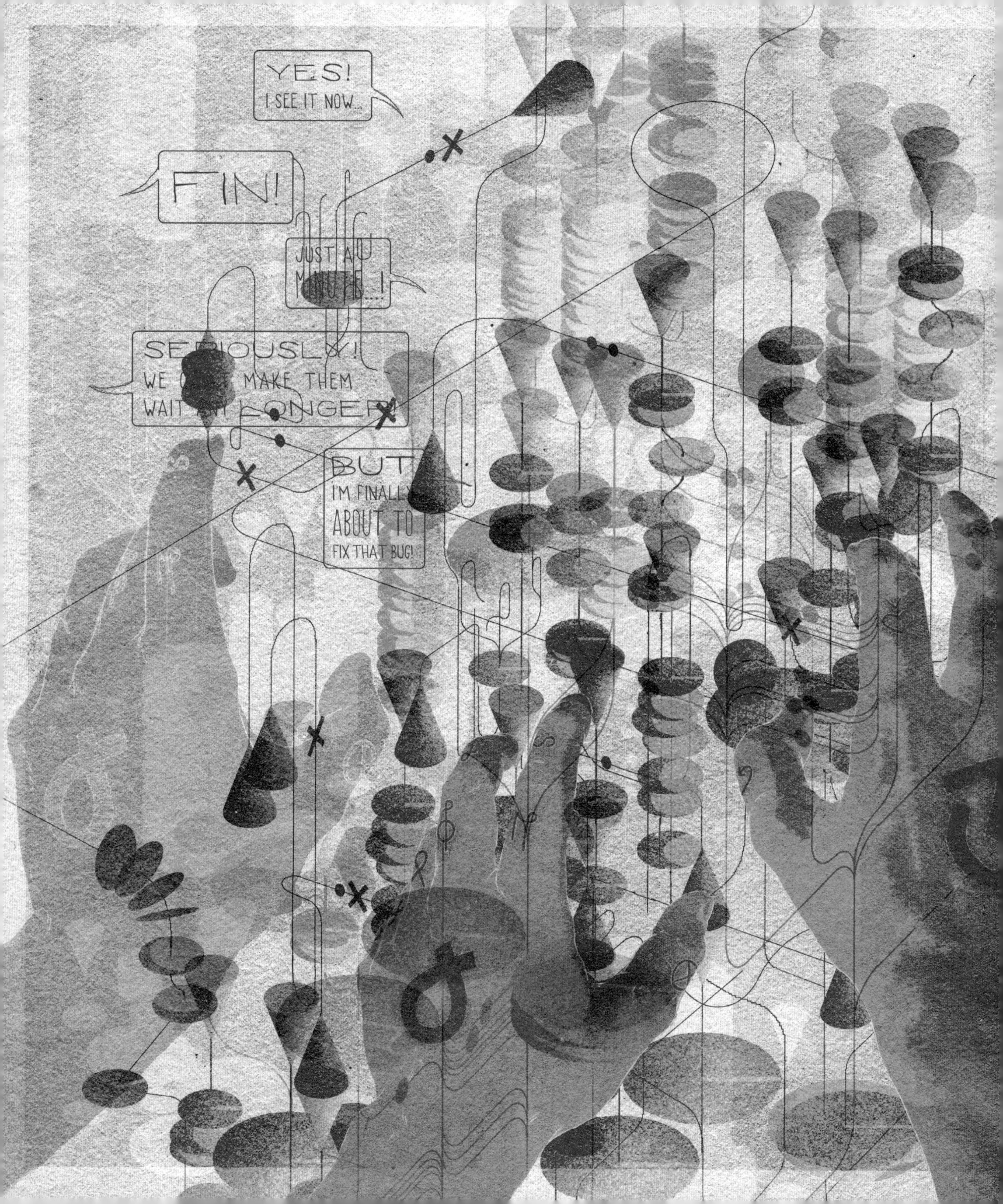
YES! I SEE IT NOW...
FIN!
JUST A MINUTE...!
SERIOUSLY! WE C MAKE THEM WAIT AN LONGER!
BUT I'M FINALLY ABOUT TO FIX THAT BUG!

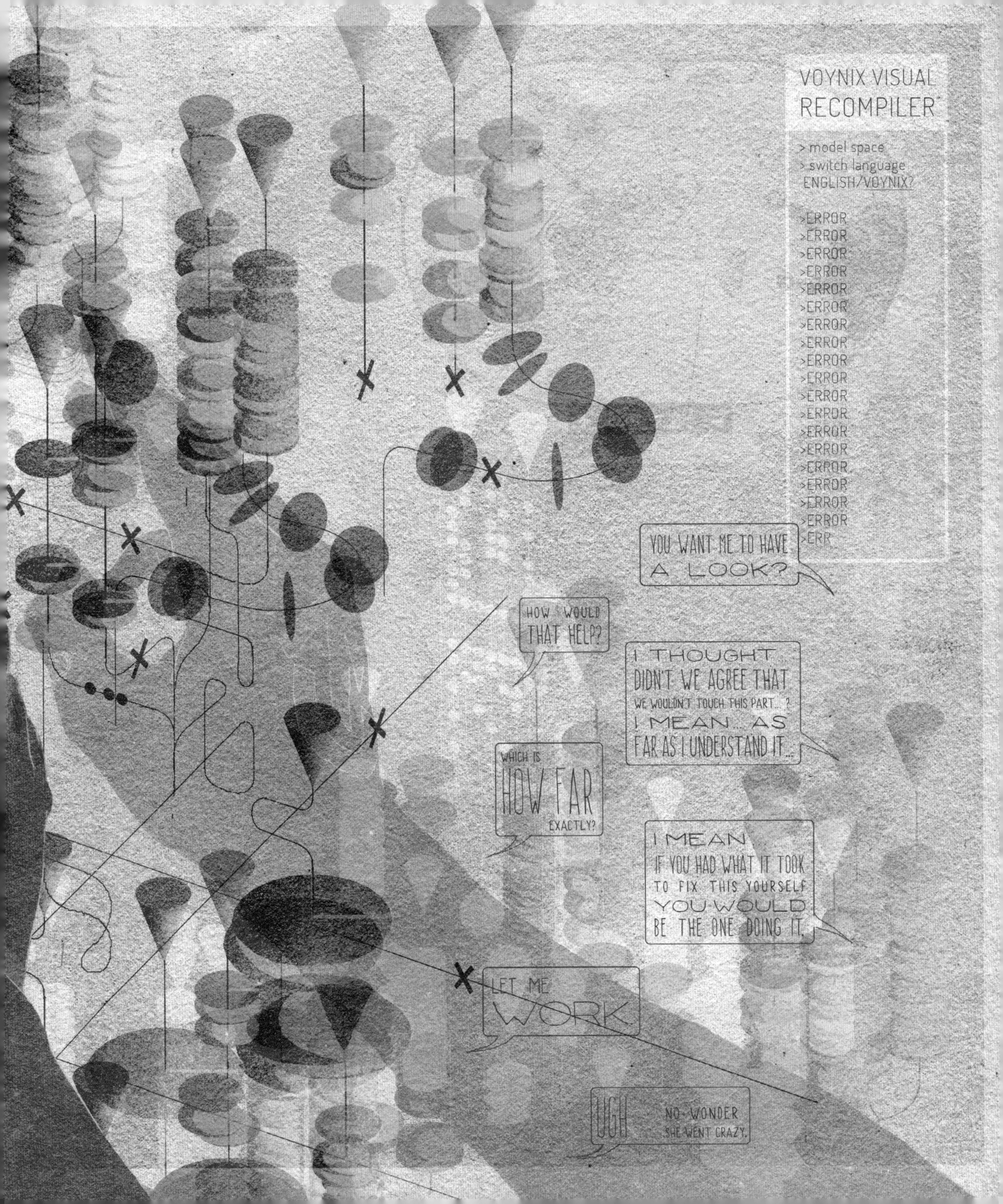
VOYNIX VISUAL RECOMPILER
> model space
> switch language
ENGLISH/VOYNIX?
>ERROR
>ERROR
>ERROR
>ERROR
>ERROR
>ERROR
>ERROR
>ERROR
>ERROR
>ERROR
>ERROR
>ERRDR
>ERROR
>ERROR
>ERROR
>ERROR
>ERROR
>ERROR
>ERR
YOU WANT ME TO HAVE A LOOK?
HOW WOULD THAT HELP?
I THOUGHT DIDN'T WE AGREE THAT WE WOULDN'T TOUCH THIS PART... ? I MEAN... AS FAR AS I UNDERSTAND IT...
WHICH IS HOW FAR EXACTLY?
I MEAN IF YOU HAD WHAT IT TOOK TO FIX THIS YOURSELF YOU WOULD BE THE ONE DOING IT.
LET ME WORK
UGH
NO WONDER SHE WENT CRAZY.

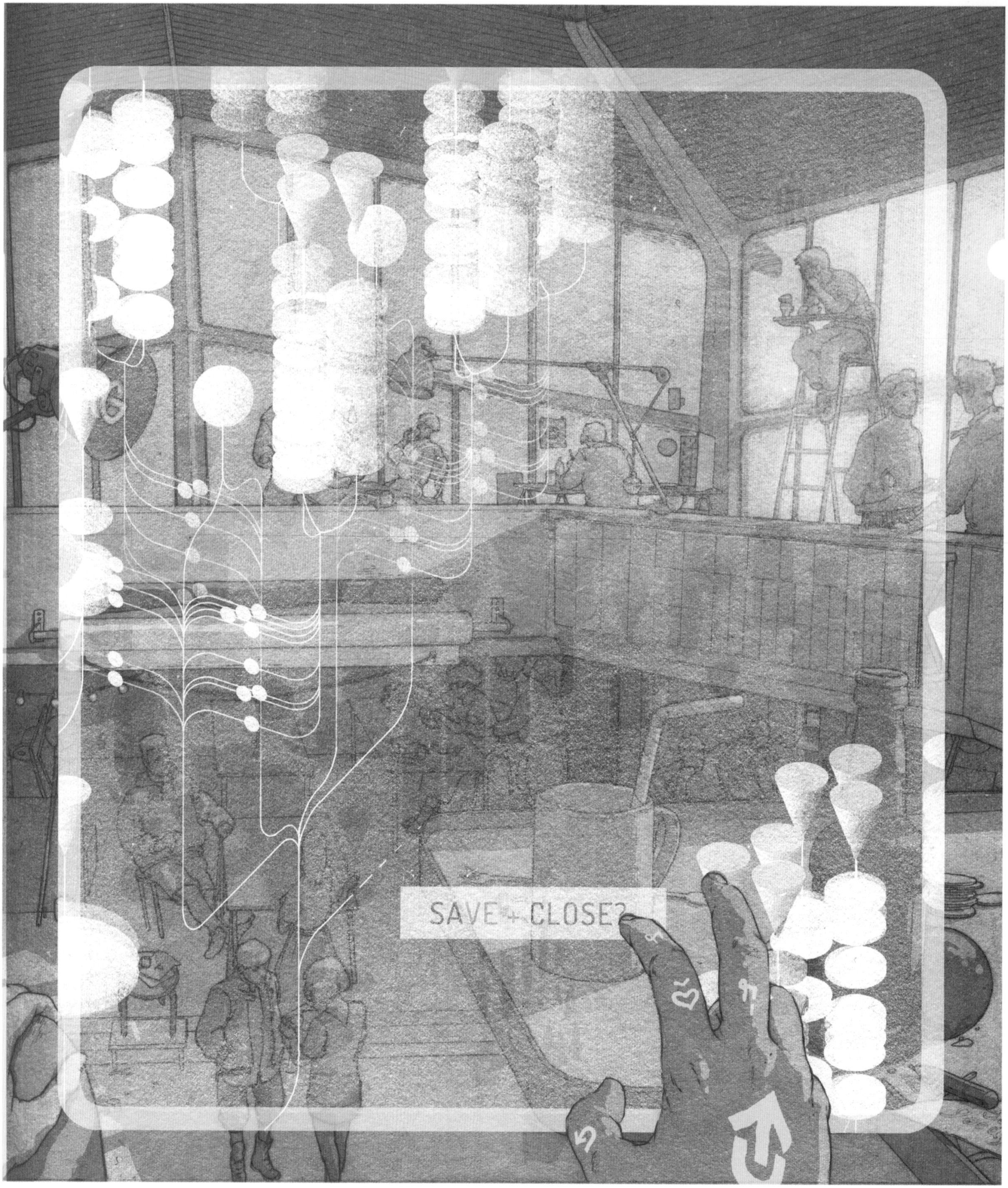
SAVE + CLOSE?

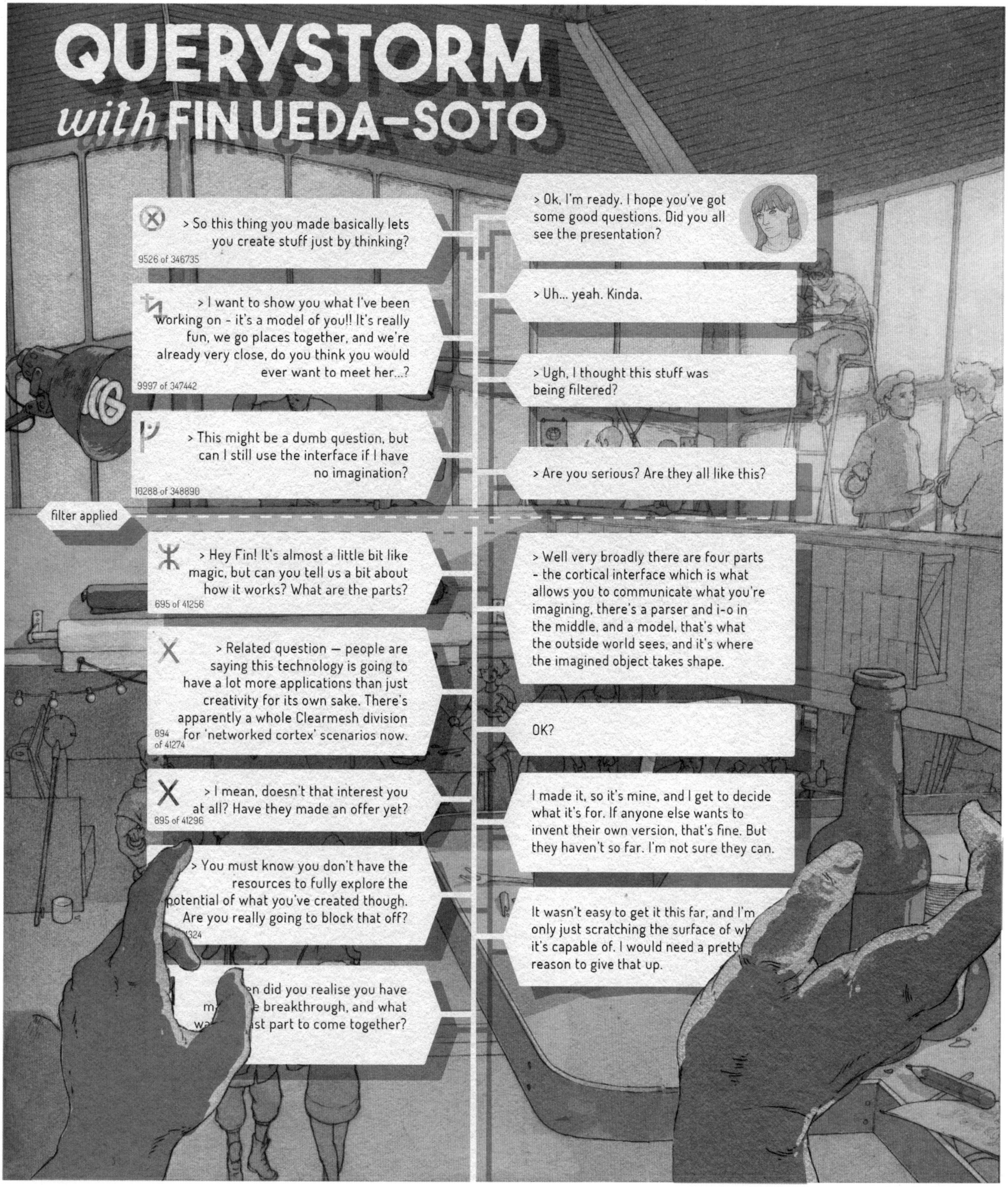

QUERYSTORM
with FIN UEDA-SOTO
> Ok, I'm ready. I hope you've got some good questions. Did you all see the presentation?
> So this thing you made basically lets you create stuff just by thinking?
9526 of 346735
> Uh... yeah. Kinda.
> I want to show you what I've been working on - it's a model of you!! It's really fun, we go places together, and we're already very close, do you think you would ever want to meet her...?
9997 of 347442
> Ugh, I thought this stuff was being filtered?
> This might be a dumb question, but can I still use the interface if I have no imagination?
10288 of 348890
> Are you serious? Are they all like this?
filter applied
> Hey Fin! It's almost a little bit like magic, but can you tell us a bit about how it works? What are the parts?
695 of 41256
> Well very broadly there are four parts - the cortical interface which is what allows you to communicate what you're imagining, there's a parser and i-o in the middle, and a model, that's what the outside world sees, and it's where the imagined object takes shape.
> Related question — people are saying this technology is going to have a lot more applications than just creativity for its own sake. There's apparently a whole Clearmesh division for 'networked cortex' scenarios now.
894 of 41274
OK?
> I mean, doesn't that interest you at all? Have they made an offer yet?
895 of 41296
I made it, so it's mine, and I get to decide what it's for. If anyone else wants to invent their own version, that's fine. But they haven't so far. I'm not sure they can.
> You must know you don't have the resources to fully explore the potential of what you've created though. Are you really going to block that off?
1324
It wasn't easy to get it this far, and I'm only just scratching the surface of wh it's capable of. I would need a pretty reason to give that up.
n did you realise you have breakthrough, and what st part to come together?

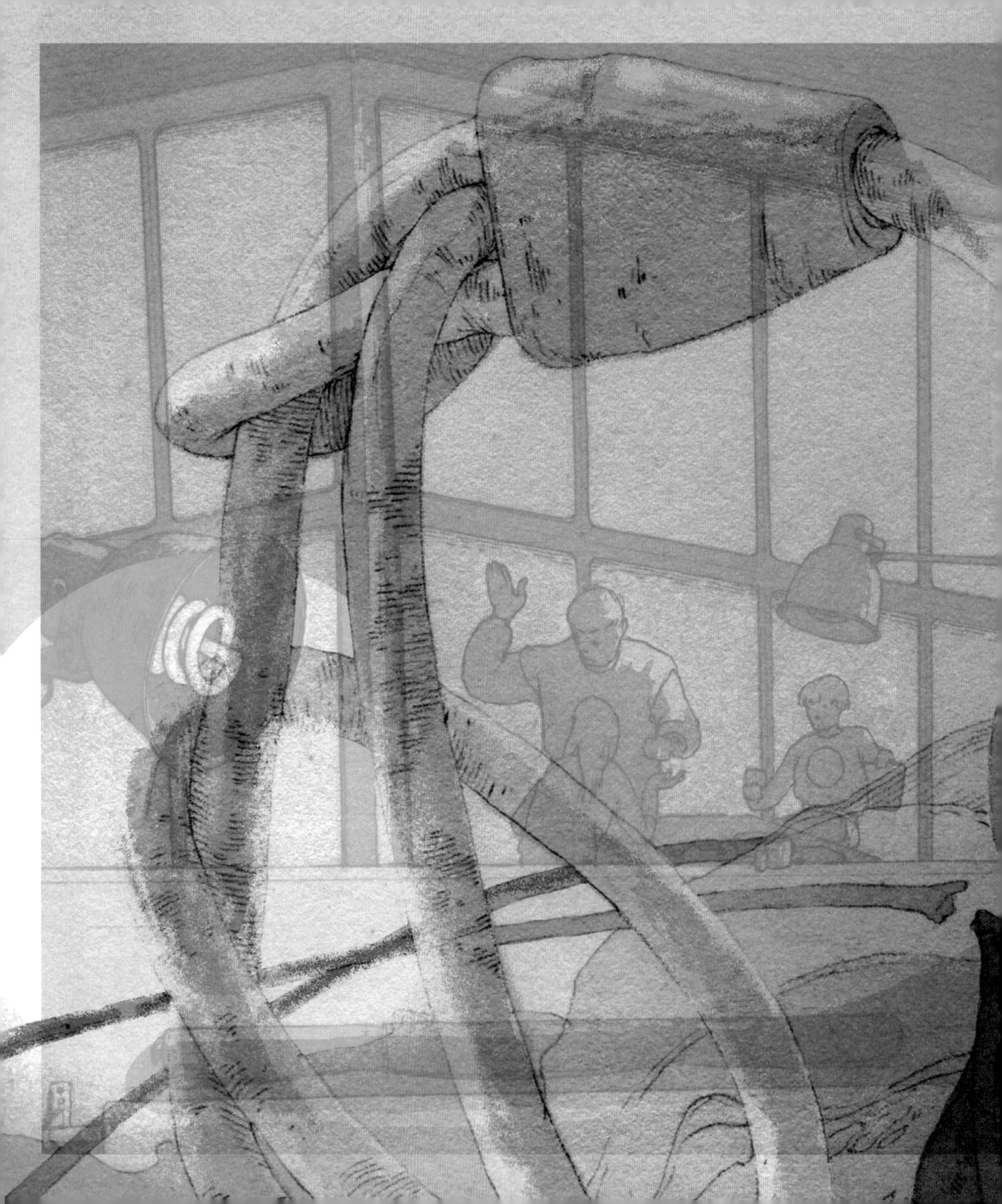

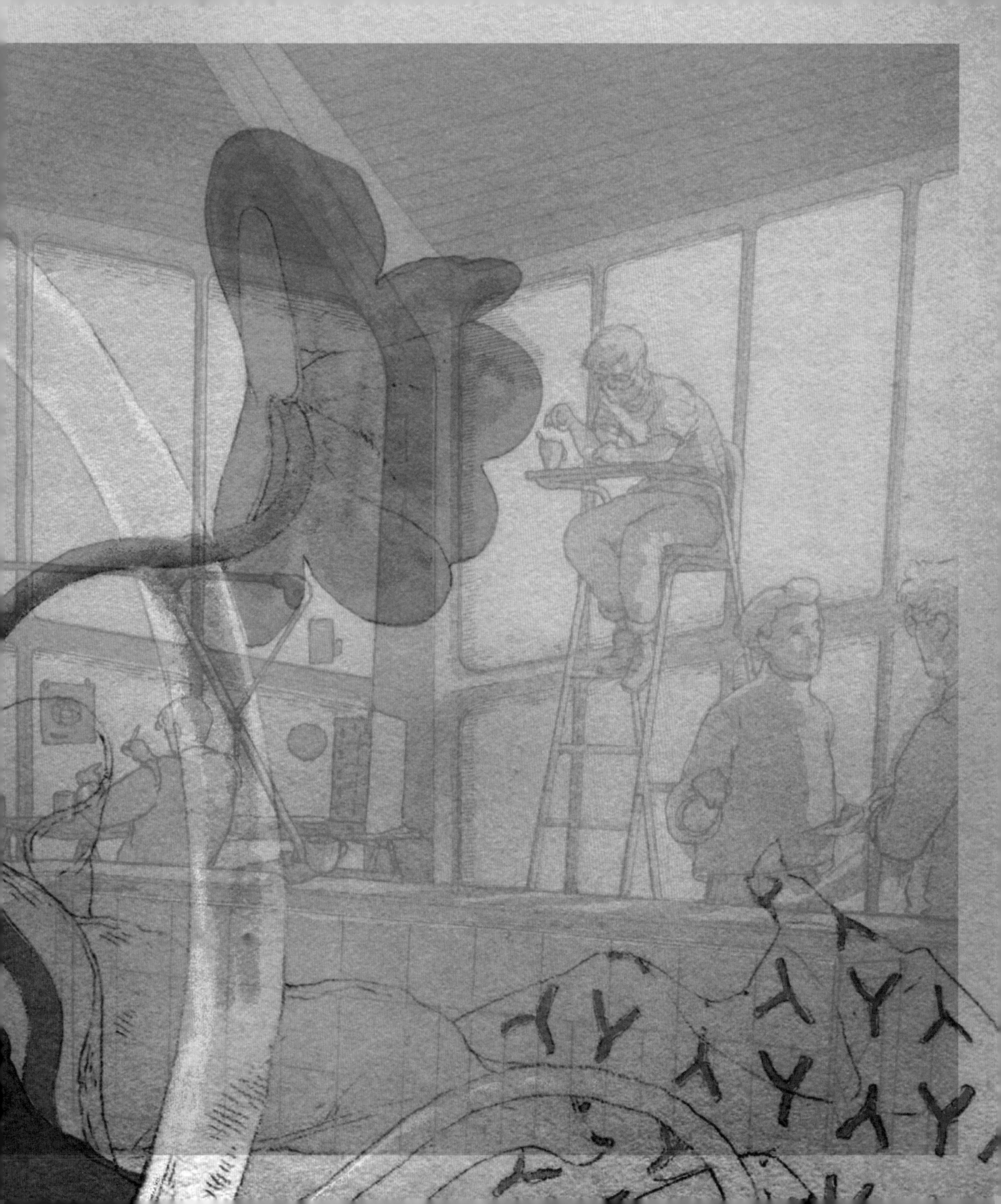

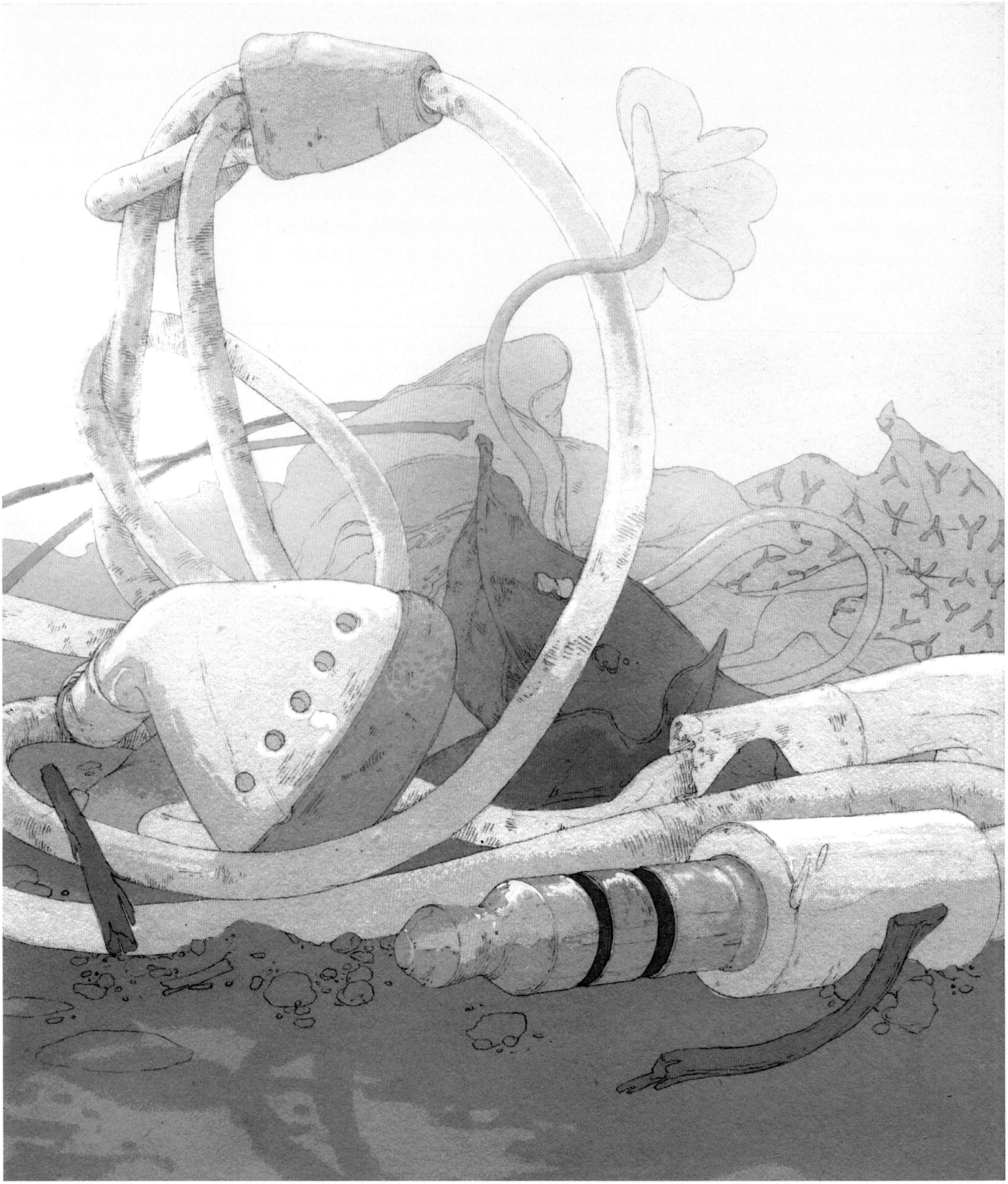

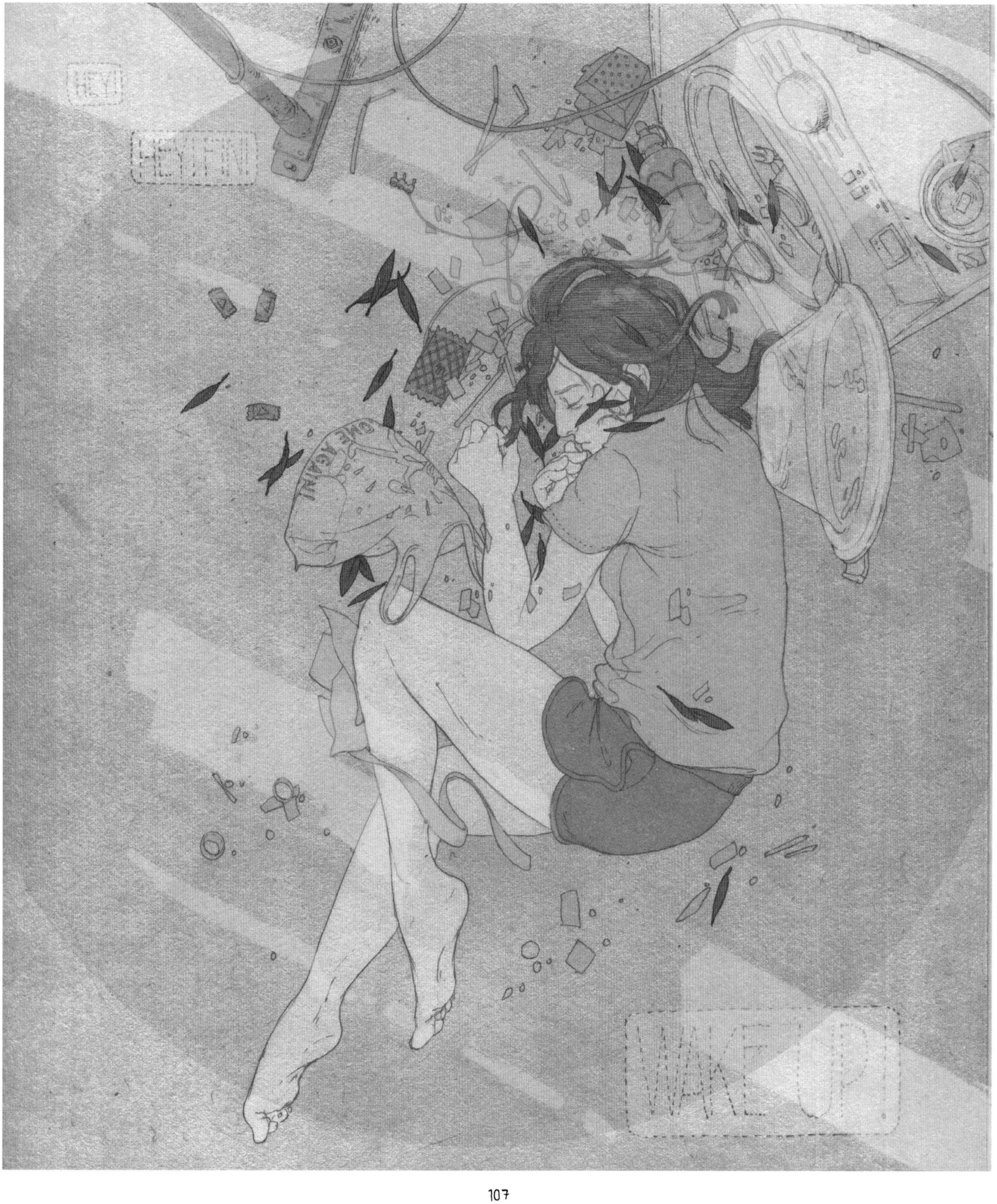
HEY!
HEY! FIN!
OME AGAIN!
WAKE UP

AH! RIGHT – I'VE GOT YOU AN INTERVIEW. YOU NEED TO BE THERE BY...

...ERR... DID YOU SLEEP ON THE ROOF?

IT'S THE ONLY PLACE I GET A DECENT CONNECTION.

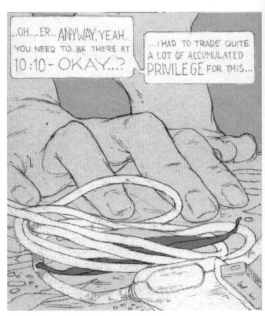

...OH... ER... ANYWAY, YEAH. YOU NEED TO BE THERE AT 10:10 – OKAY...?

...I HAD TO TRADE QUITE A LOT OF ACCUMULATED PRIVILEGE FOR THIS...

...AND... PERHAPS, TIDY YOURSELF UP A BIT?

UGH!

DO I HAVE TO DO THIS?

YOU NEED MONEY... ...AND YOU NEED CREDIBILITY — IF YOU WANT TO KEEP LIVING IN THE CITY PAST THE END OF THE WEEK.

HOW...?

...YOU MISSED THIS I SUPPOSE, BUT YOU DON'T JUST GET A RIGHT TO BE IN THE CITY ANYMORE...IF YOU AREN'T ATTACHED TO SOME GROWTH ACTIVITY YOU'LL GET MOVED ON.

MOVED ON..? ...WHERE?

... ...

WHERE ARE THEY MOVING THEM?

... ...WHAT? SORRY. I'VE GOT TO GO...

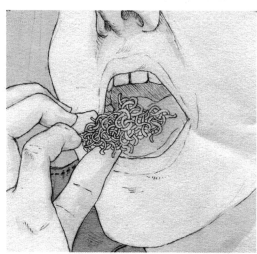

...LISTEN, THEY'RE STILL GATHERING YO-PROS LIKE CRAZY WITH THE UPGRADE DELIVERY GETTING SO LATE...

... ... YOU'LL BE FINE. JUST DON'T TURN THEM DOWN...

...TAKE WHATEVER THEY OFFER YOU.

109

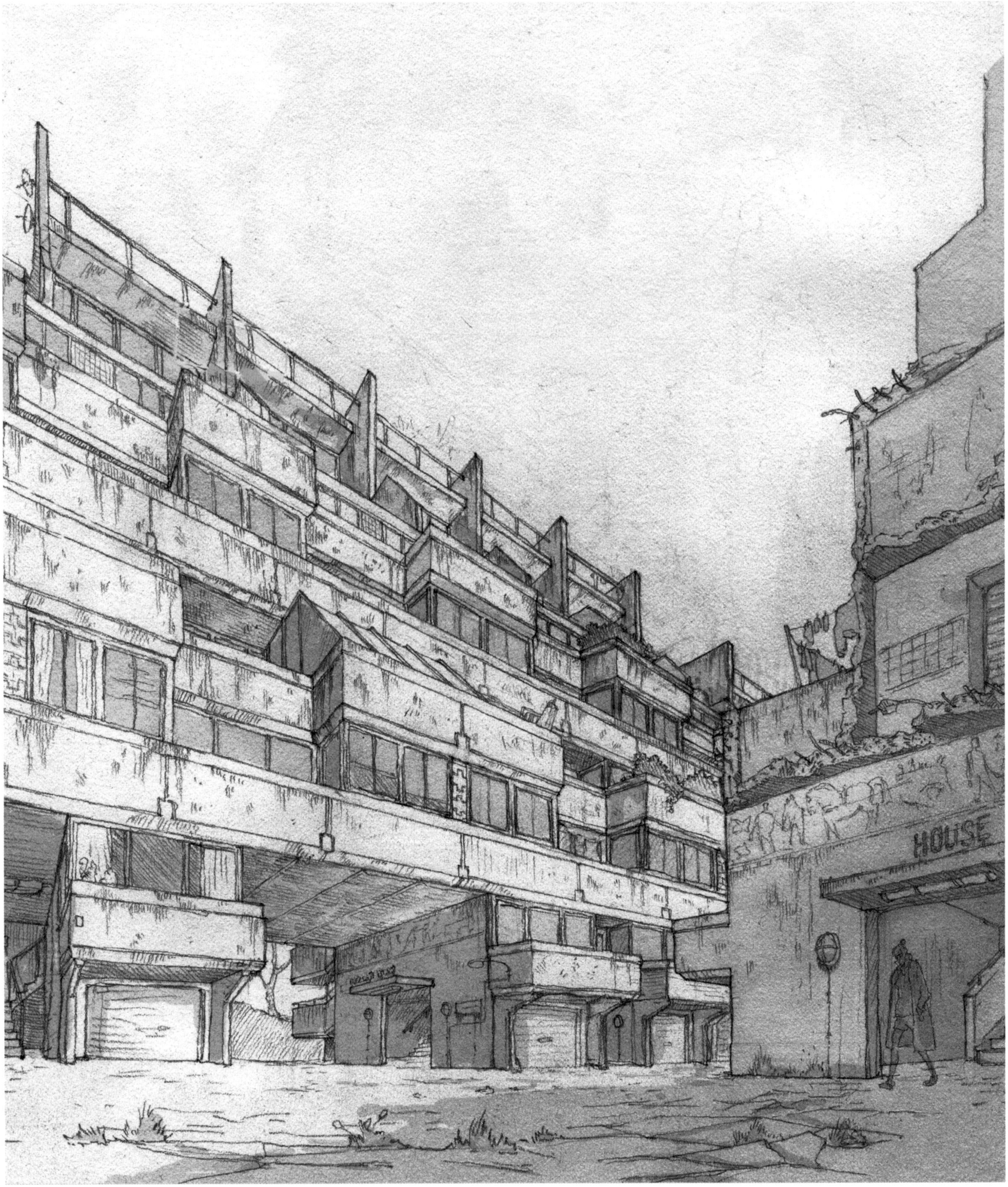
HOUSE

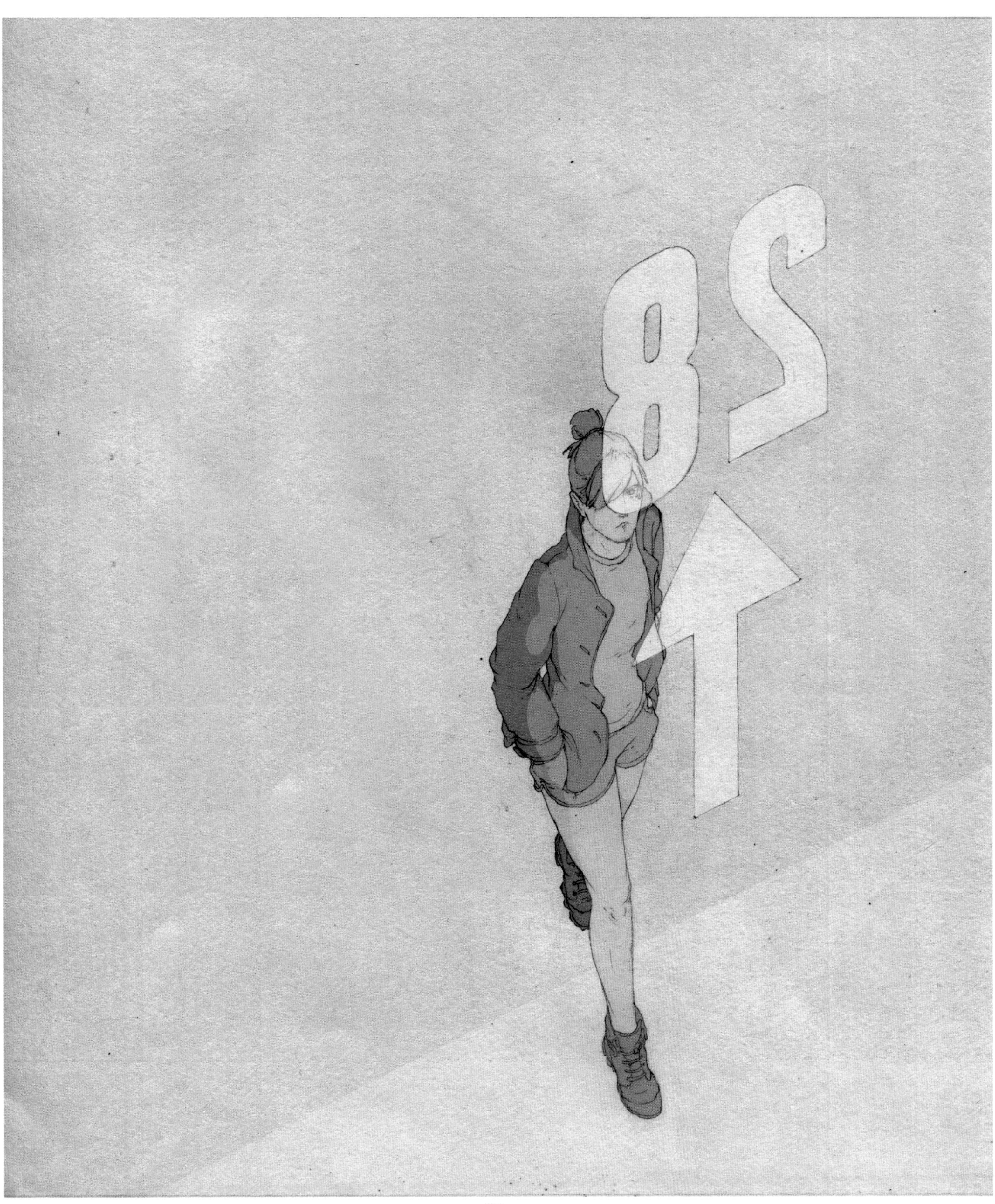

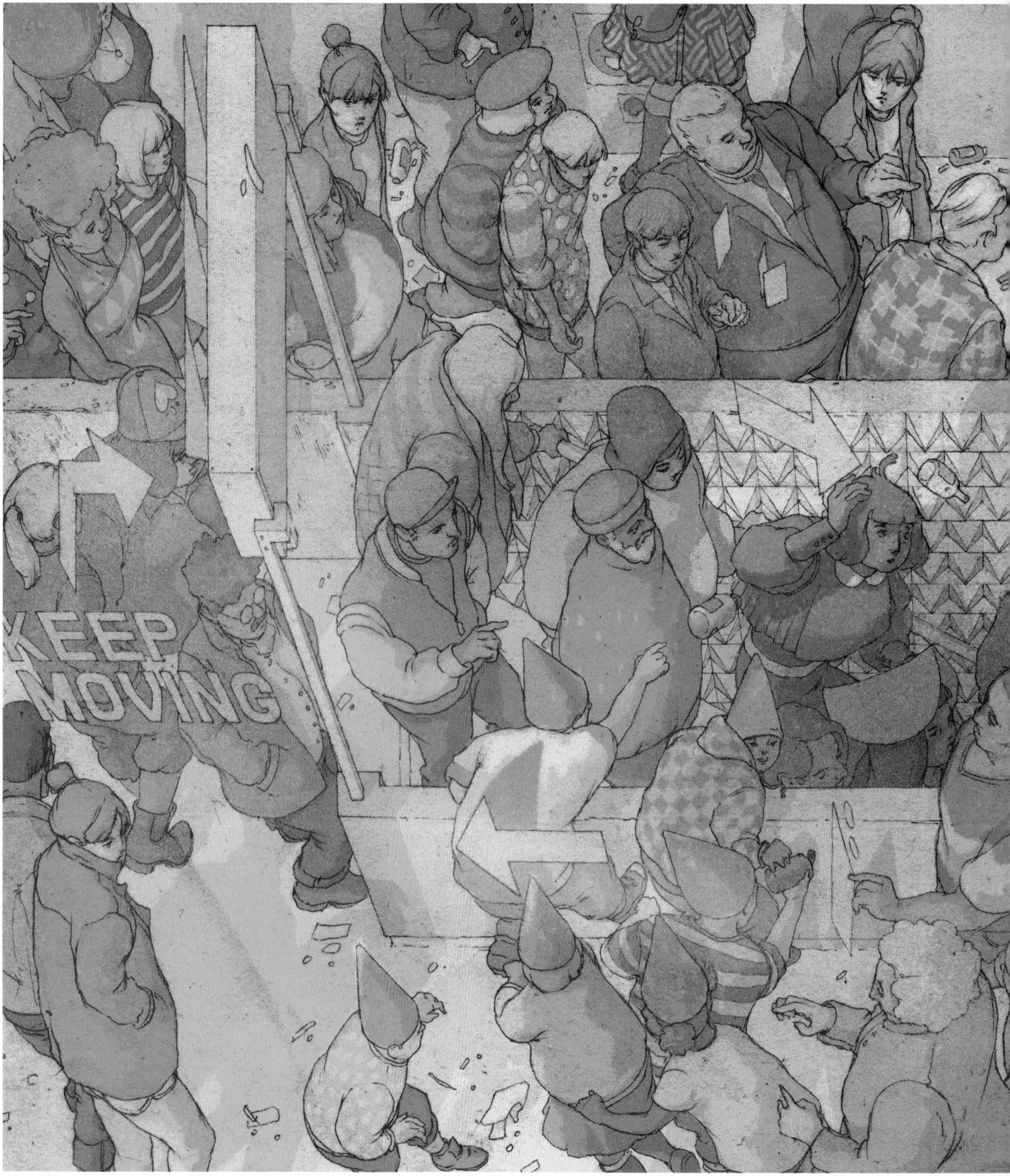
KEEP MOVING

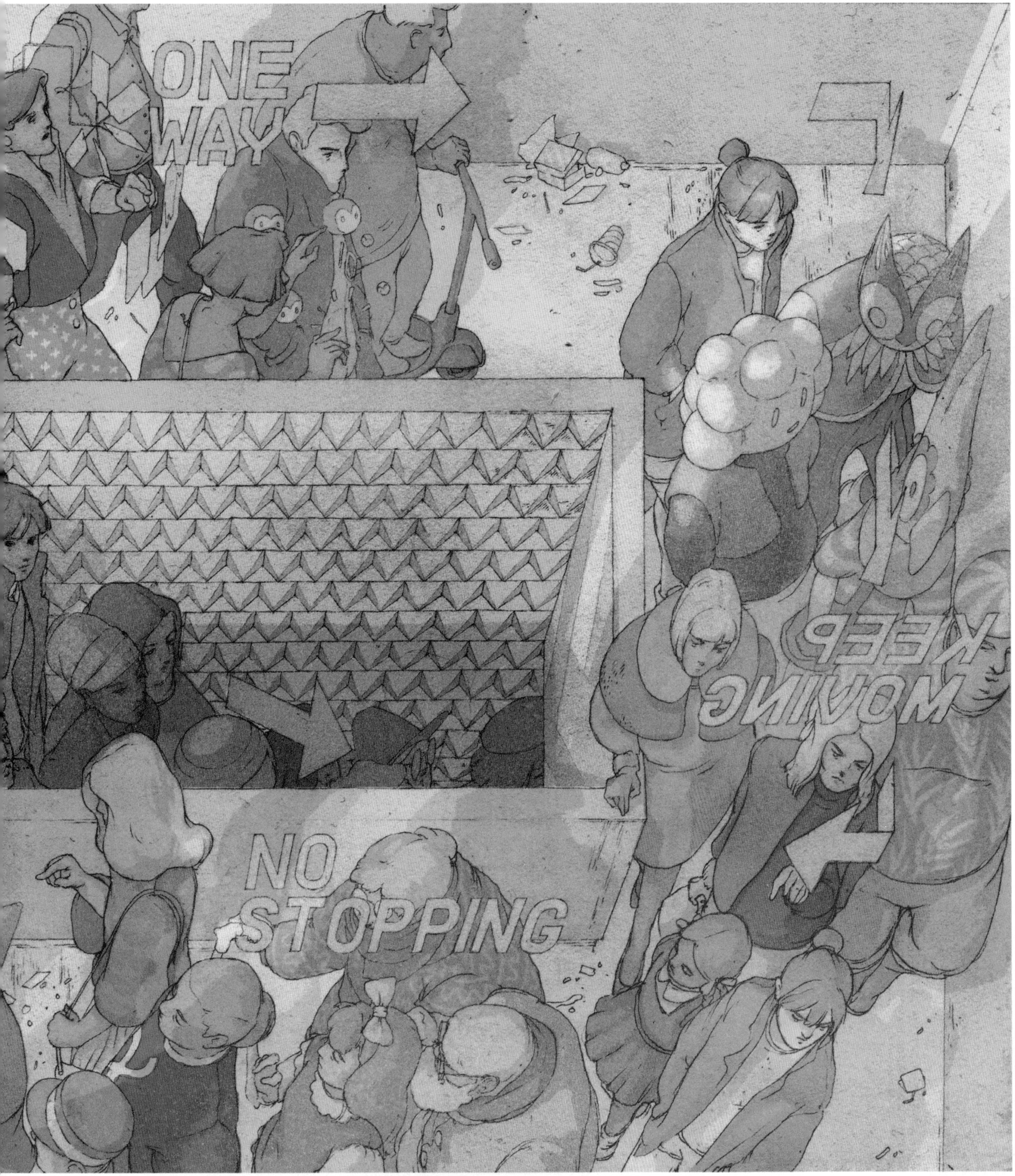
ONE WAY
KEEP MOVING
NO STOPPING

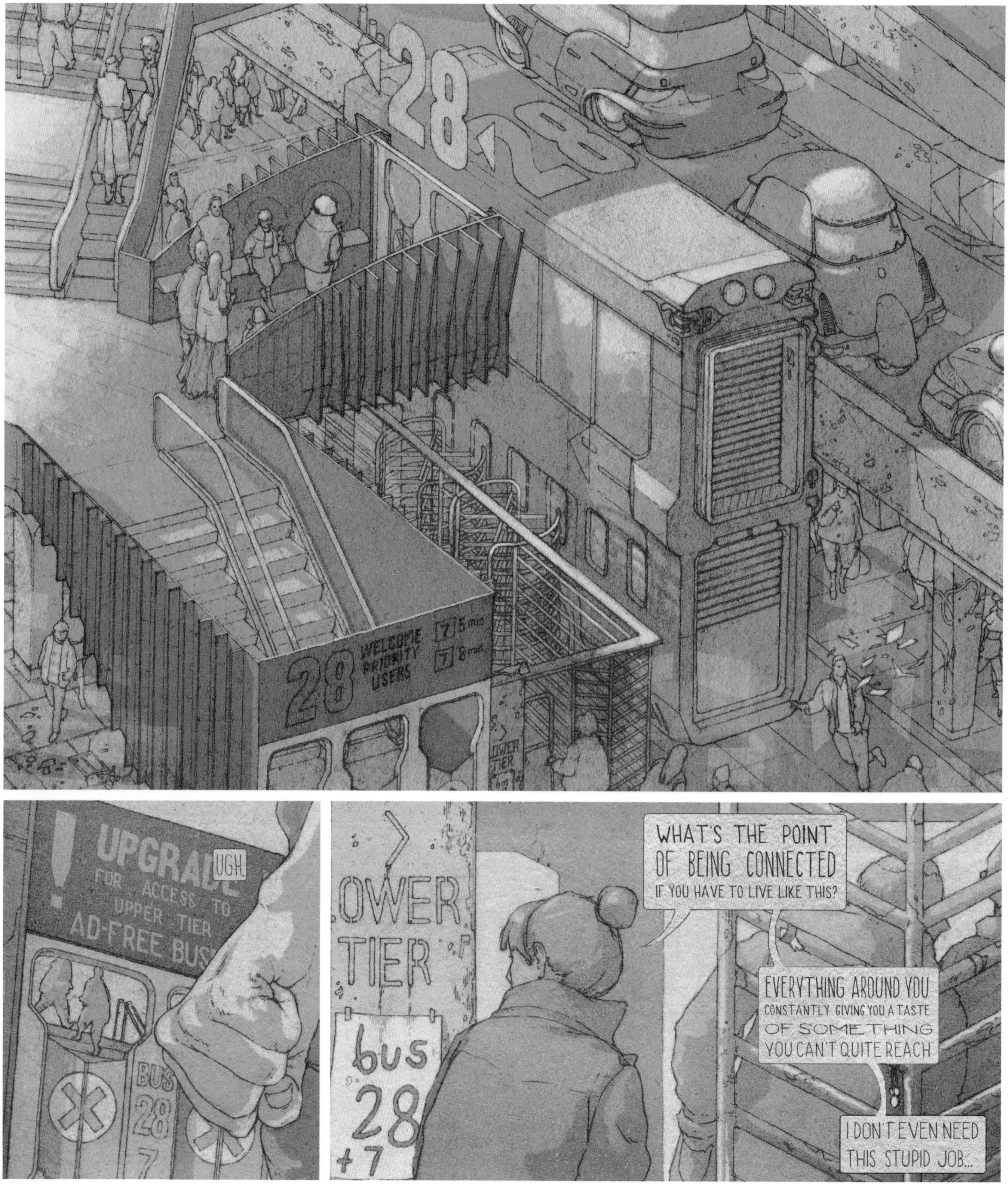
28
28
WELCOME PRIORITY USERS
7 5 min
7 8 min
UPGRADE FOR ACCESS TO UPPER TIER AD-FREE BUS
UGH.
BUS 28 7
TIER
bus 28 +7
WHAT'S THE POINT OF BEING CONNECTED IF YOU HAVE TO LIVE LIKE THIS?
EVERYTHING AROUND YOU CONSTANTLY GIVING YOU A TASTE OF SOMETHING YOU CAN'T QUITE REACH
I DON'T EVEN NEED THIS STUPID JOB...

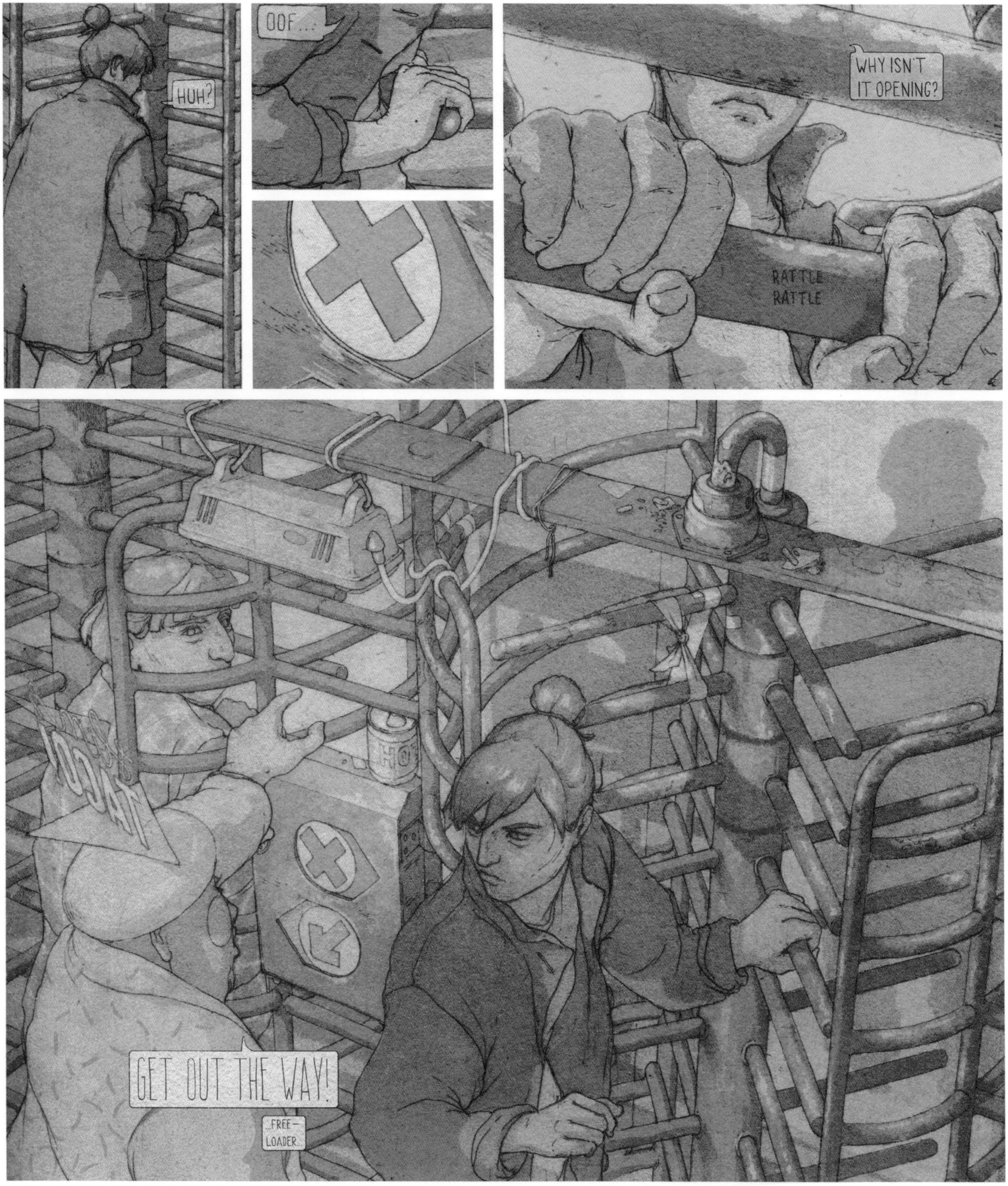
HUH?
OOF...
WHY ISN'T IT OPENING?
RATTLE RATTLE
GET OUT THE WAY!
...FREE-LOADER...

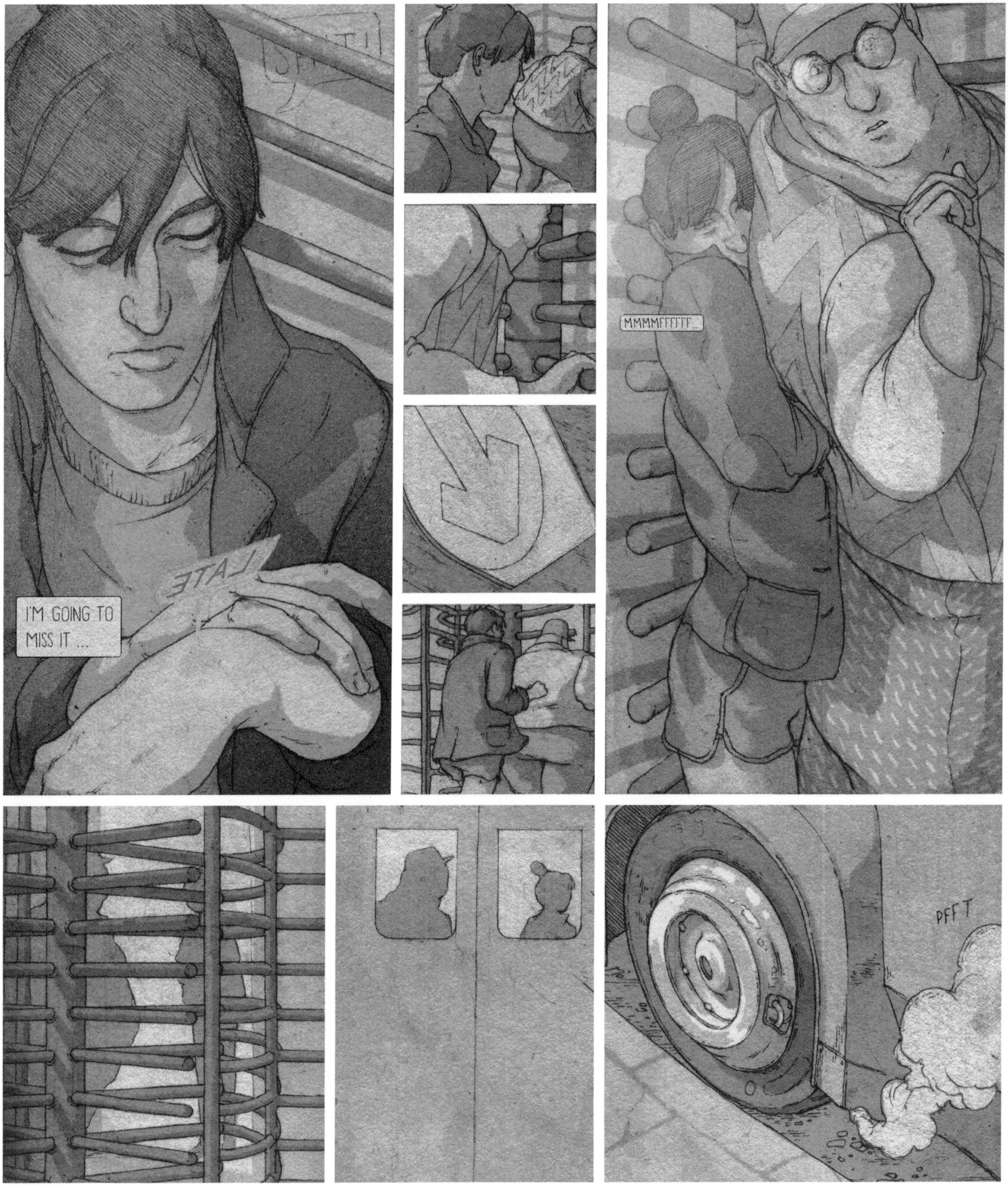
LATE
I'M GOING TO MISS IT ...
MMMMFFFFFF...
PFFT

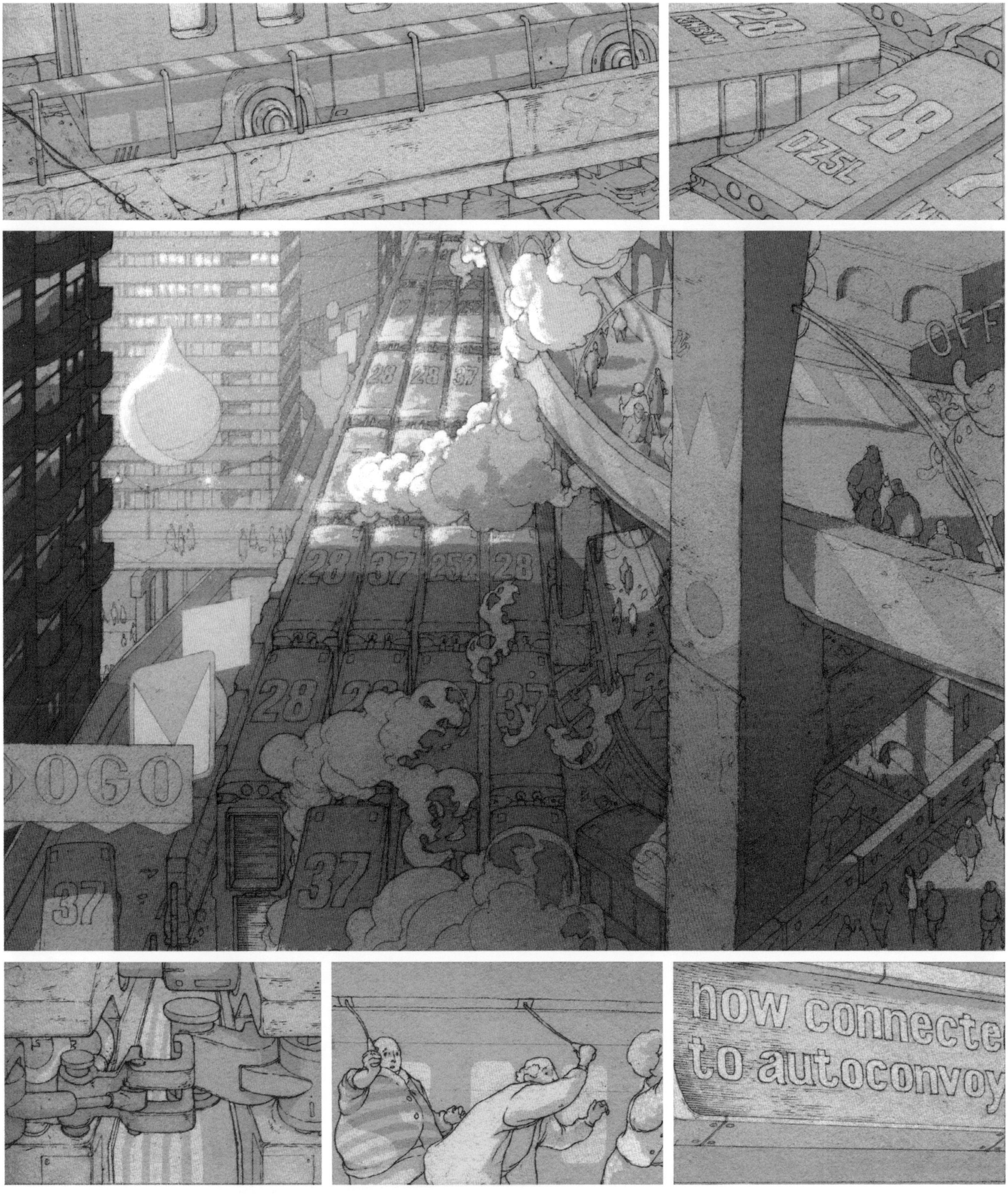
28
DZ5L
OGO
now connecte
to autoconvoy

WHAT'S BEEN HAPPENING?
EULA MCKAY
NATURAL POLYDACT
++++++++++++++
20% better than y
suckas /////
MY 24
14,532 peeks
6 syncs
96 hi-5s
37 chi
mor
SO WHO ARE YOU? & HOW COME YOU'RE BASICALLY LIVING MY LIFE?
Had a SATIS encounter with a YUMMO BURGER othing like a it-grown horse set you up for a code mara
truther von
Weird shout- know, but do anyone know a good VOYNIX DE-VELOPER? Legacy project we dealing with...
Ish Vandav
Uke_man_x
MegaJoe
I think they're all dead man.
granUla_star
Ish Vandavale
yeh - good luck with that!
See my SNAP JUDGEMENT on YMAXION GIN LACE >>
THOSE ARE MY FRI EVEN THO THEY DON'T SEEM TO RE

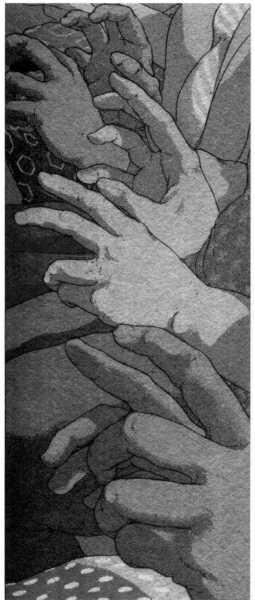

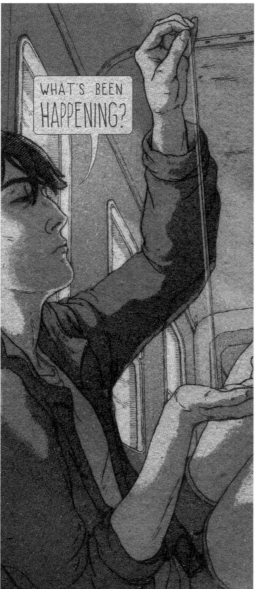

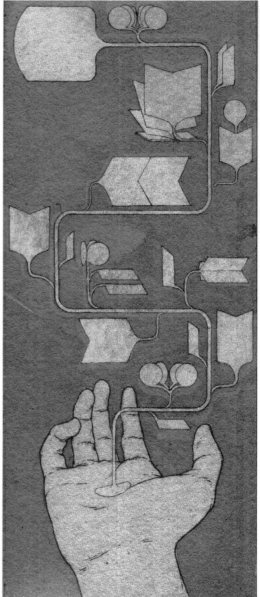

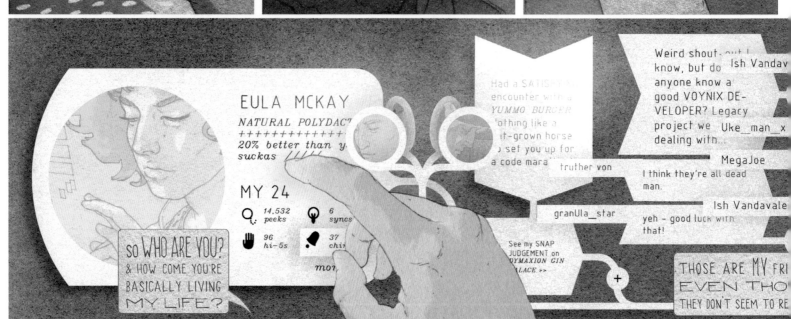

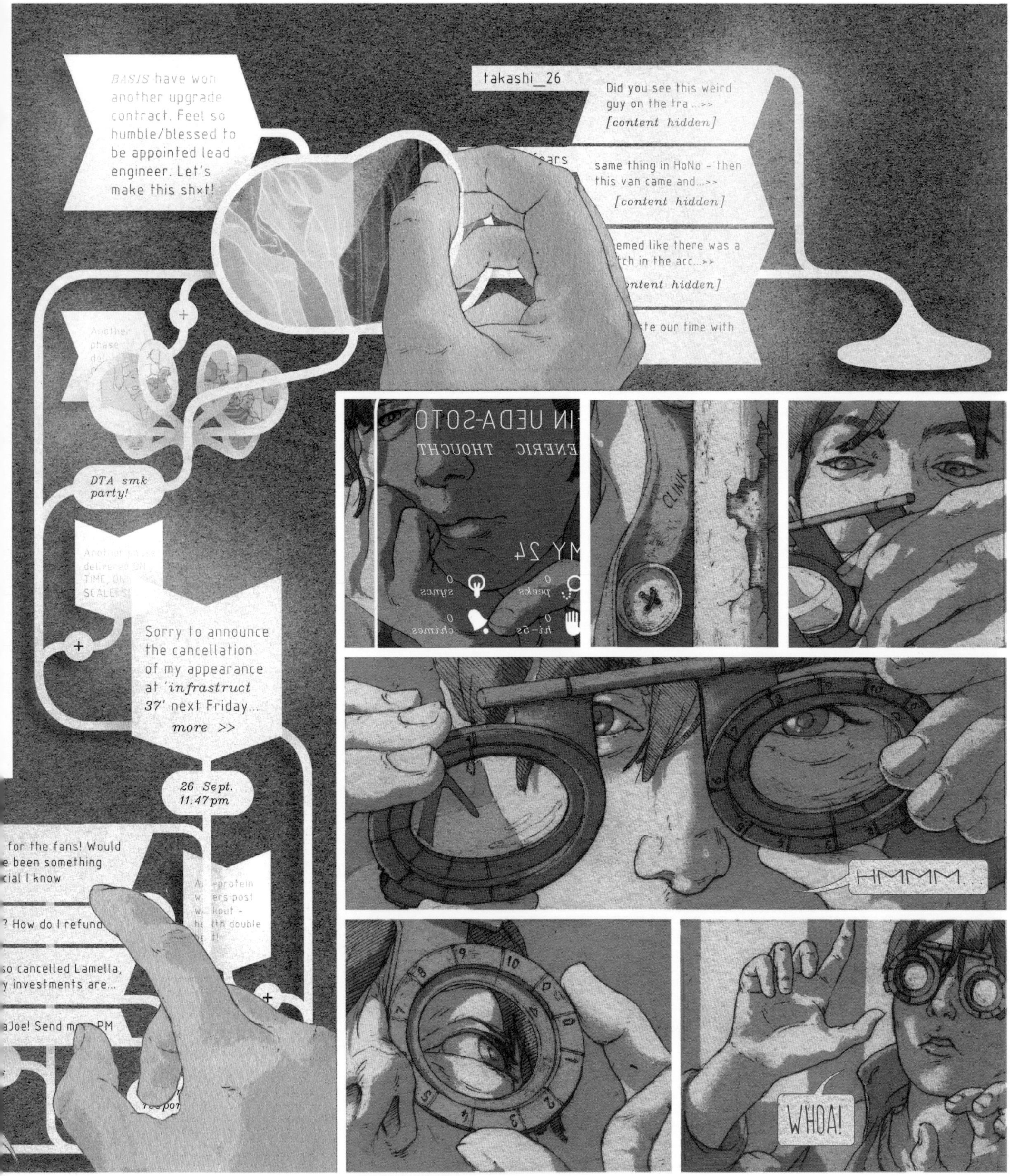
BASIS have won another upgrade contract. Feel so humble/blessed to be appointed lead engineer. Let's make this sh×t!
takashi_26
Did you see this weird guy on the tra ...>>
[content hidden]
same thing in HoNo - then this van came and...>>
[content hidden]
DTA smk party!
Sorry to announce the cancellation of my appearance at 'infrastruct 37' next Friday...
more >>
26 Sept. 11.47pm
for the fans! Would
? How do I refund
o cancelled Lamella,
y investments are...
aJoe! Send
CLINK
HMMM...
WHOA!

WOW...
3
do they source the bran from sci-farms?
I won't give jojo anything harvested by a human
it's just not hygienic
more girls waiting
moira
10
0
ALL
0
ALL
CLICK

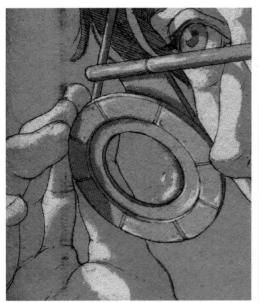

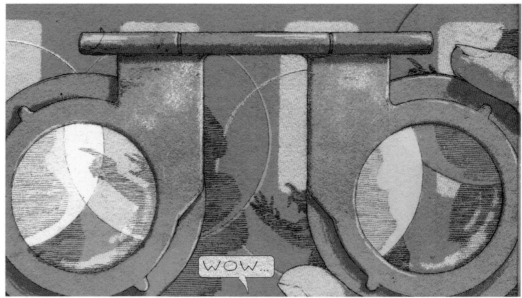

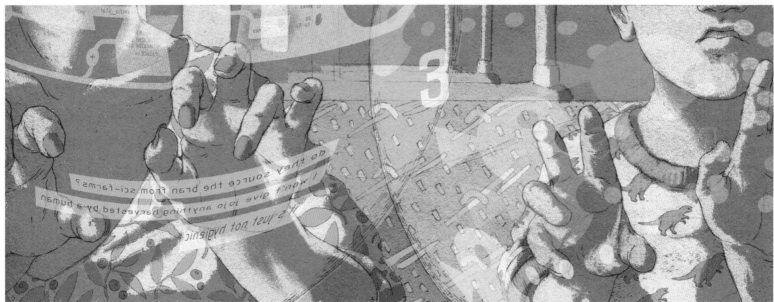

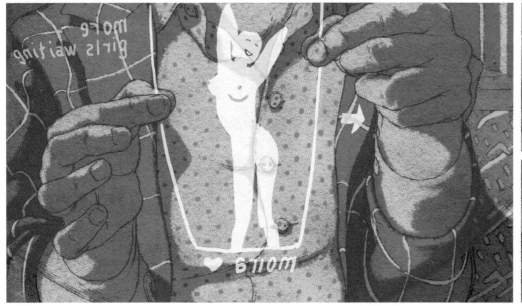

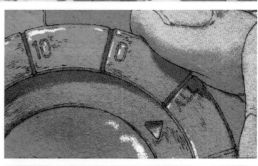

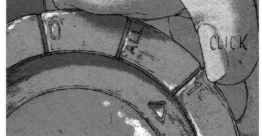

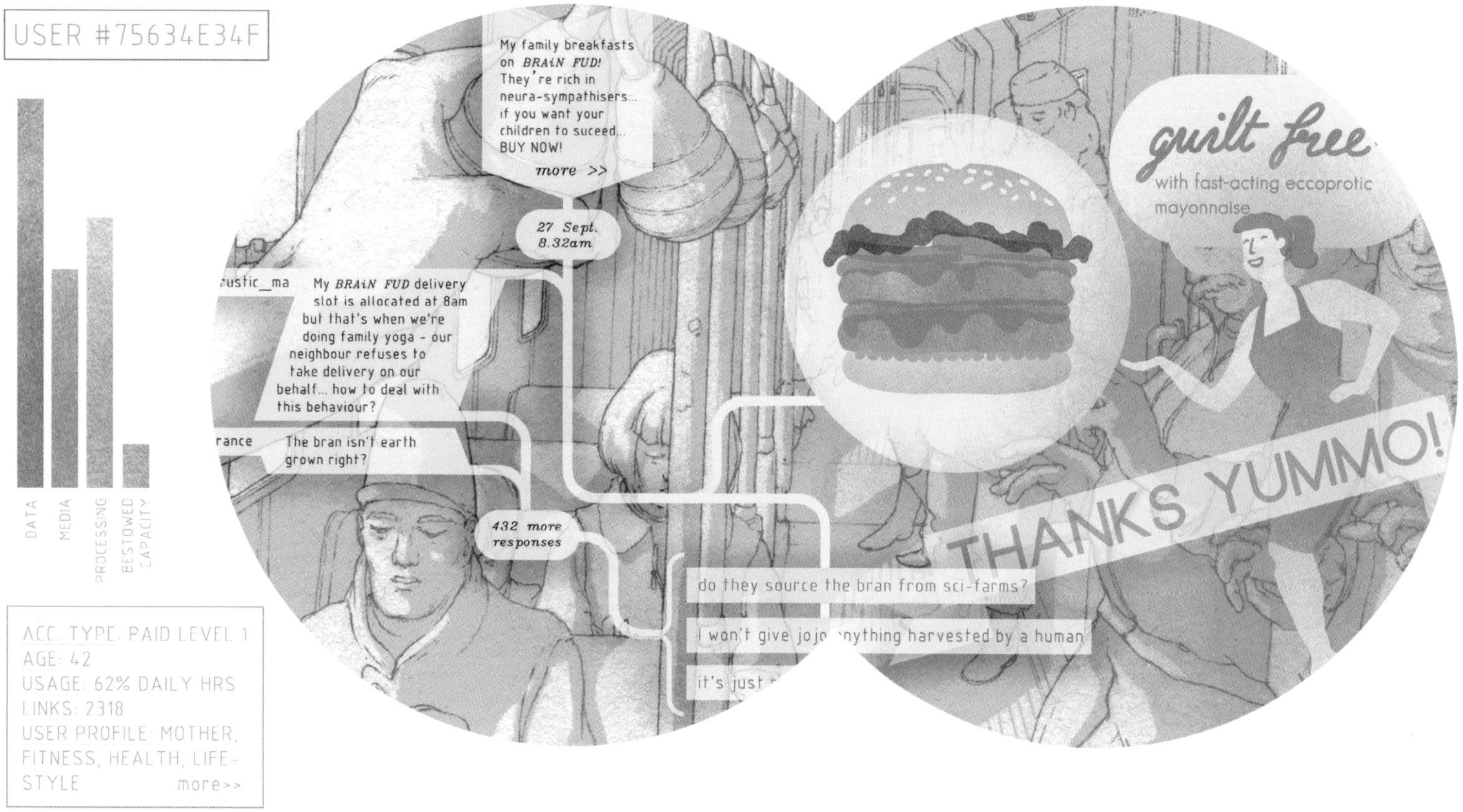
USER #75634E34F
DATA
MEDIA
PROCESSING
BESTOWED CAPACITY
ACC. TYPE: PAID LEVEL 1
AGE: 42
USAGE: 62% DAILY HRS
LINKS: 2318
USER PROFILE: MOTHER, FITNESS, HEALTH, LIFE-STYLE
more>>
My family breakfasts on BRAiN FUD! They're rich in neura-sympathisers... if you want your children to suceed... BUY NOW!
more >>
27 Sept. 8.32am
rustic_ma
My BRAiN FUD delivery slot is allocated at 8am but that's when we're doing family yoga - our neighbour refuses to take delivery on our behalf... how to deal with this behaviour?
rance
The bran isn't earth grown right?
432 more responses
do they source the bran from sci-farms?
I won't give jojo
nything harvested by a human
it's just
guilt free
with fast-acting eccoprotic mayonnaise
THANKS YUMMO!

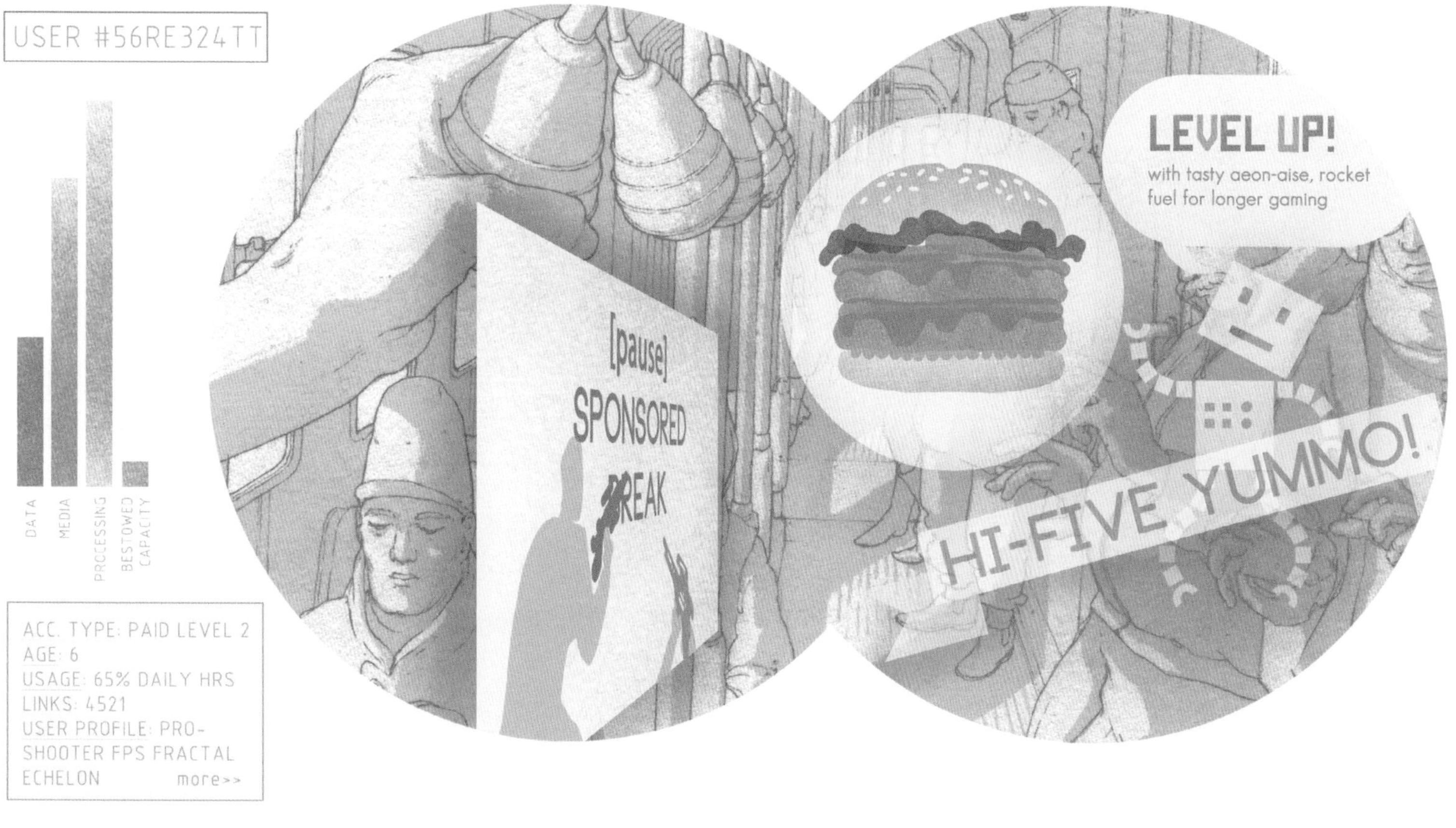
USER #56RE324TT
DATA
MEDIA
PROCESSING
BESTOWED CAPACITY
ACC. TYPE: PAID LEVEL 2
AGE: 6
USAGE: 65% DAILY HRS
LINKS: 4521
USER PROFILE: PRO-SHOOTER FPS FRACTAL ECHELON
more>>
[pause]
SPONSORED
REAK
LEVEL UP!
with tasty aeon-aise, rocket fuel for longer gaming
HI-FIVE YUMMO!

USER #328FQW92

DATA | MEDIA | PROCESSING | BESTOWED CAPACITY

ACC. TYPE: ROMBO FREE
AGE: 31
USAGE: 100% DAILY HRS
LINKS: 1A3}~
USER PROFILE: LOW TIER
FEMALE   more>>

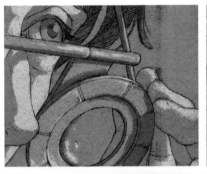

USER #328FQW92
USER #76TD4BR6
USER #76TT4VF3
USER #899UY76N

USER #328FQW92

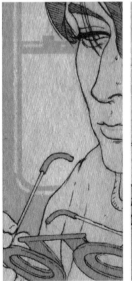

BANG BANG BANG

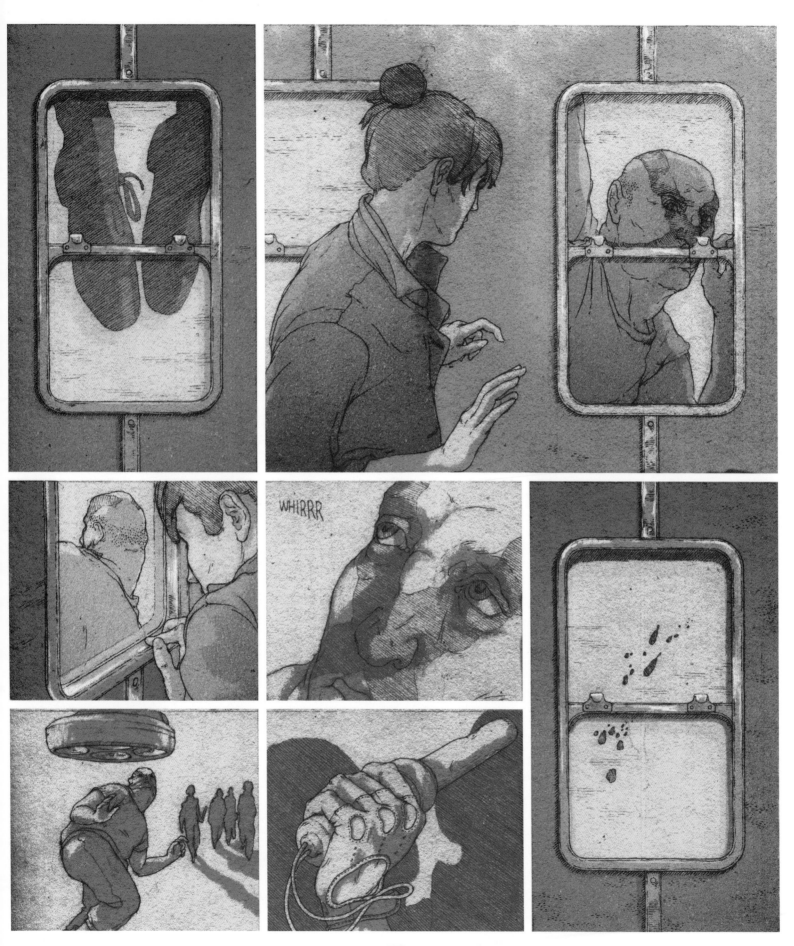

WHIRRR

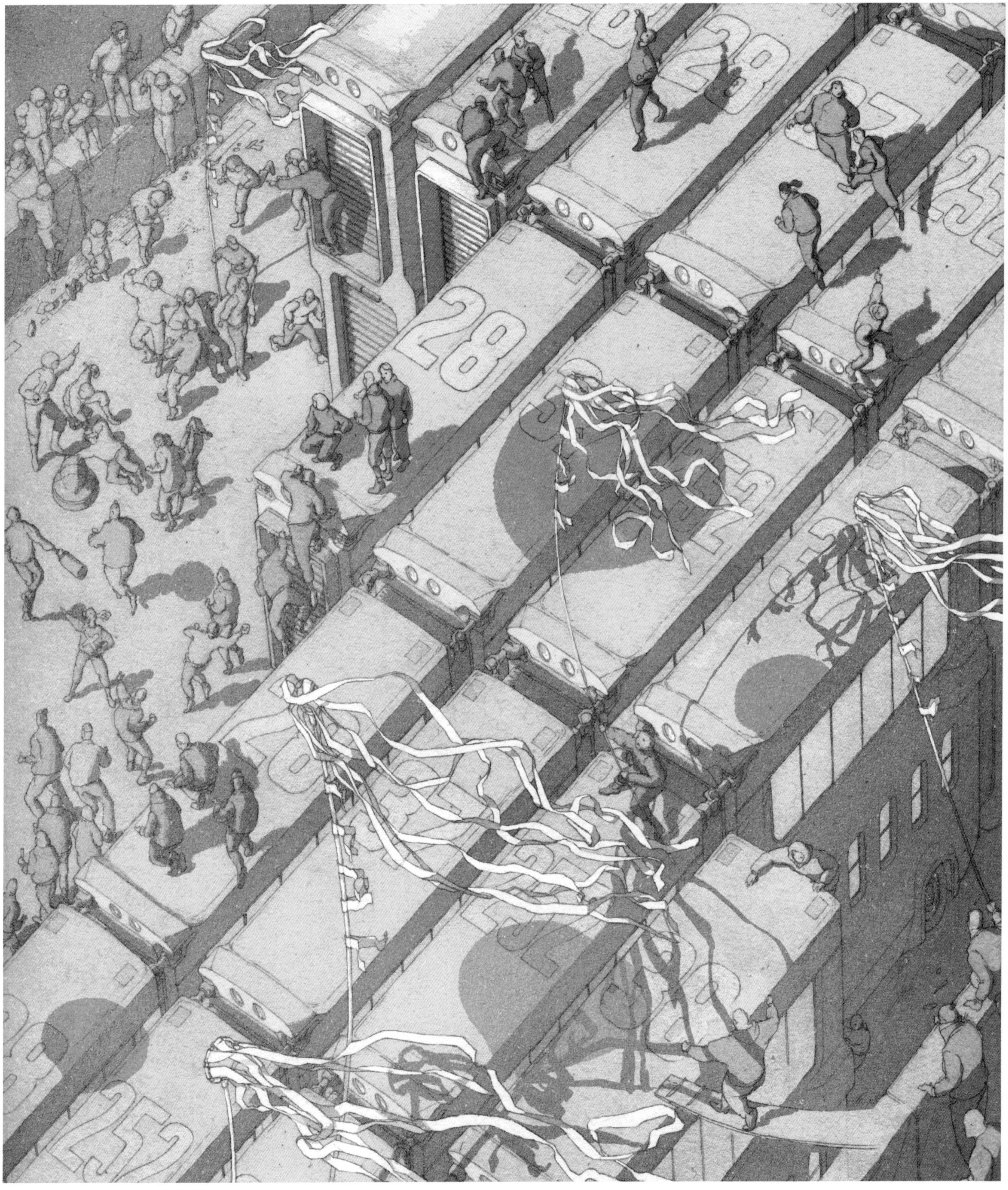
28

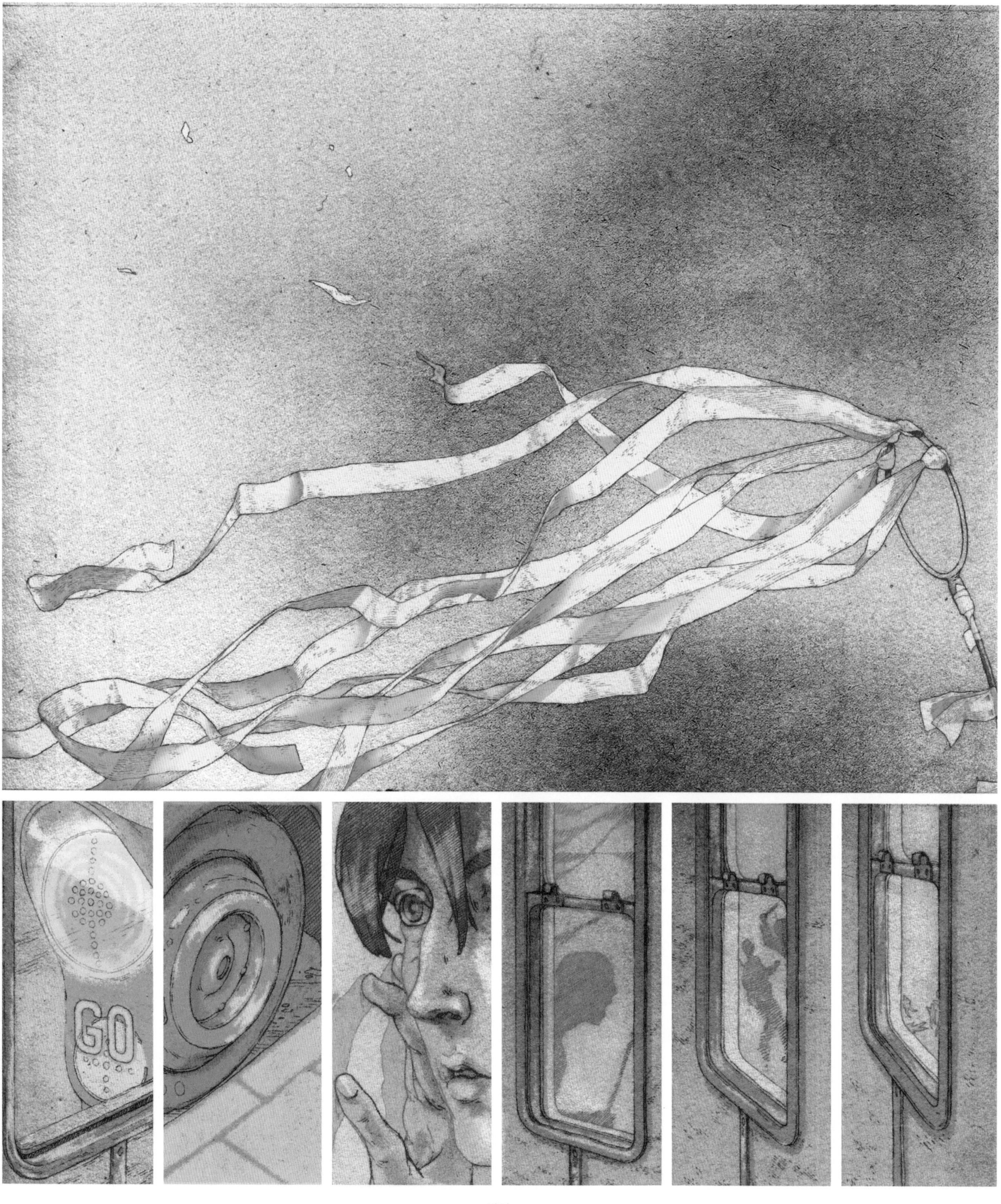
GO

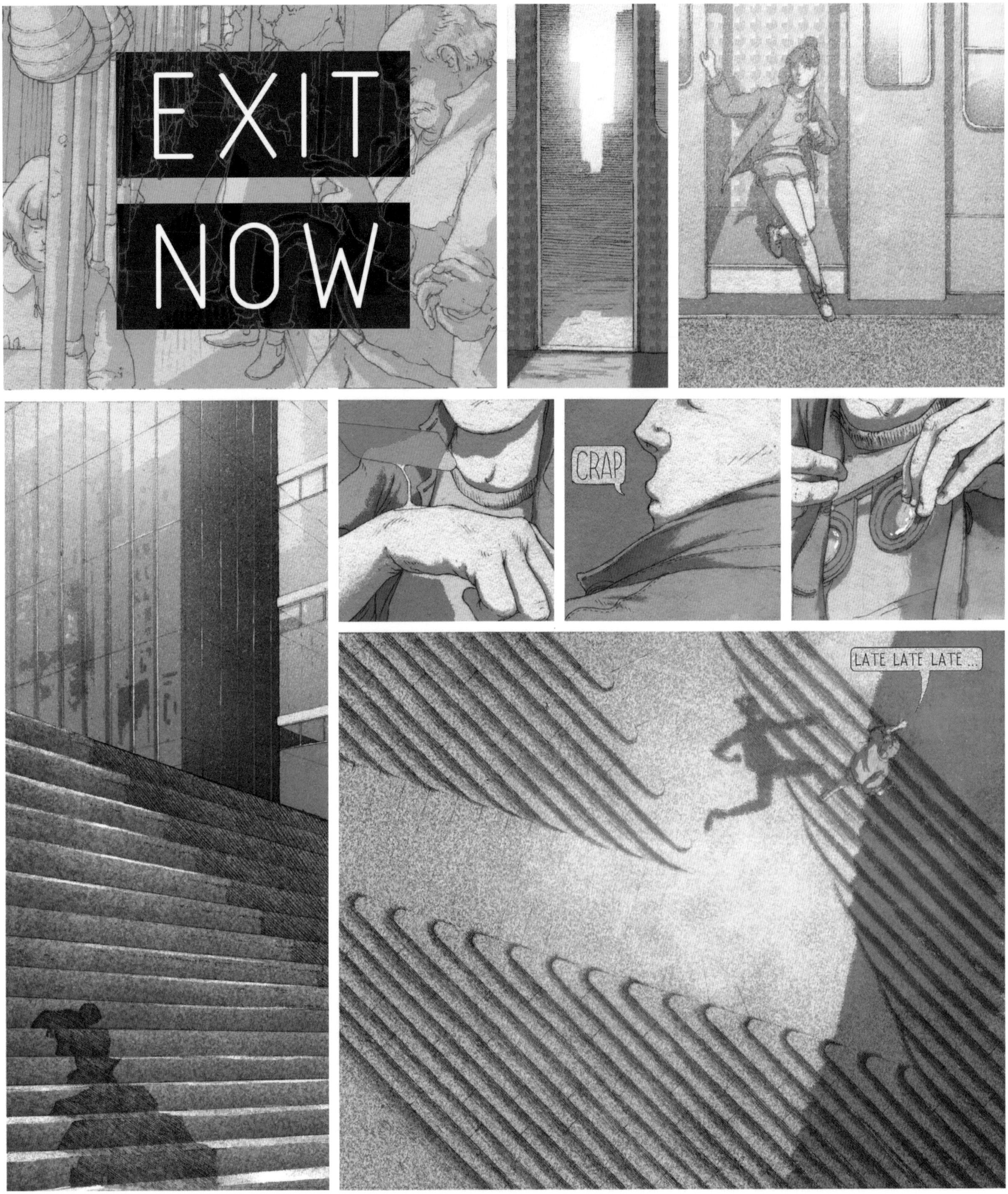
EXIT
NOW
CRAP
LATE LATE LATE ...

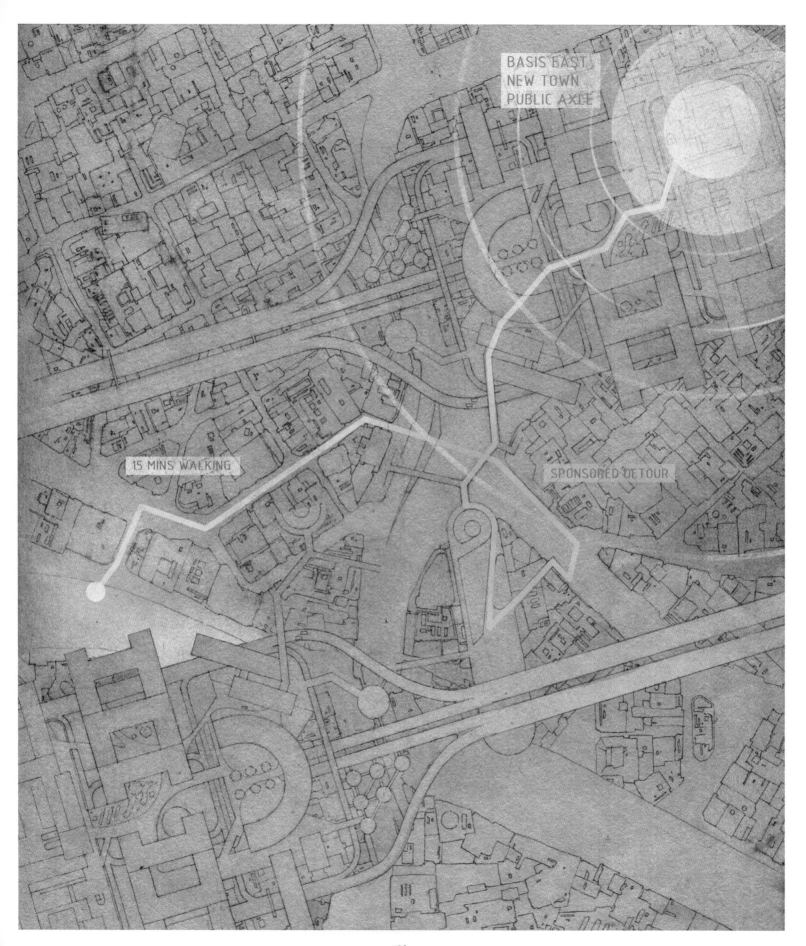

BASIS EAST
NEW TOWN
PUBLIC AXLE

15 MINS WALKING

SPONSORED DETOUR

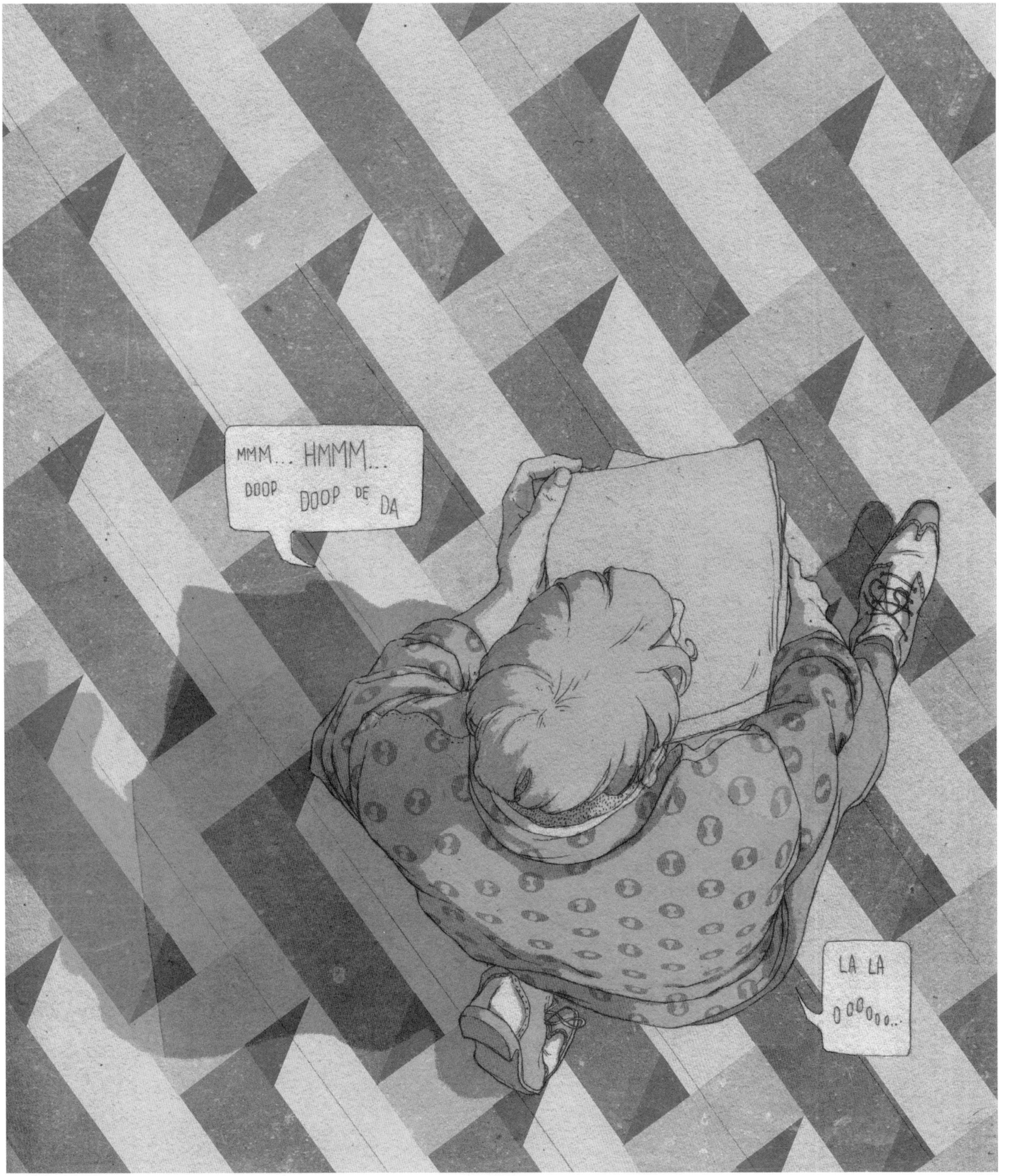
MMM... HMMM...
DOOP DOOP DE DA
LA LA
OOOOOO..

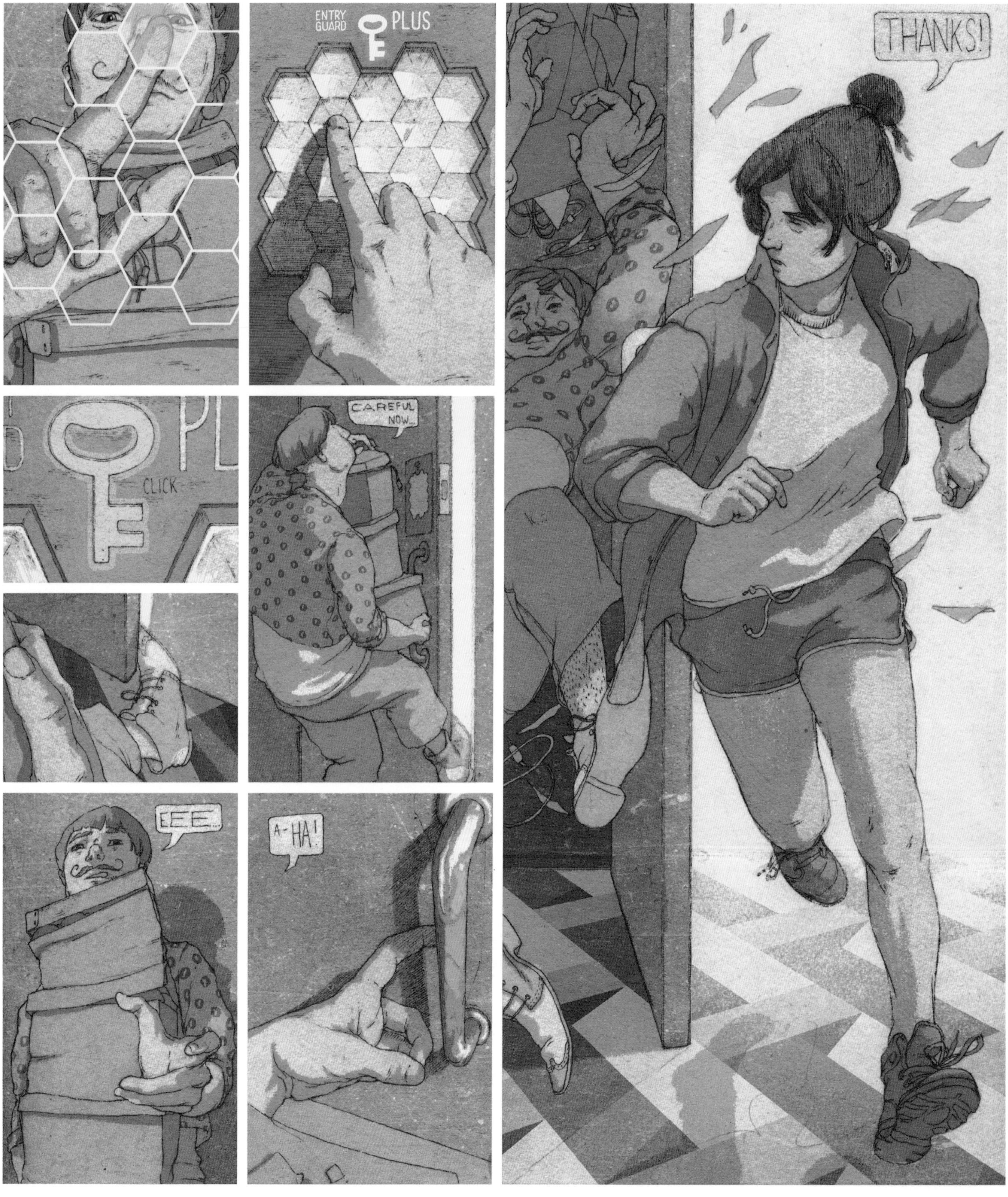
ENTRY GUARD PLUS
CLICK
CAREFUL NOW...
EEE...
A-HA!
THANKS!

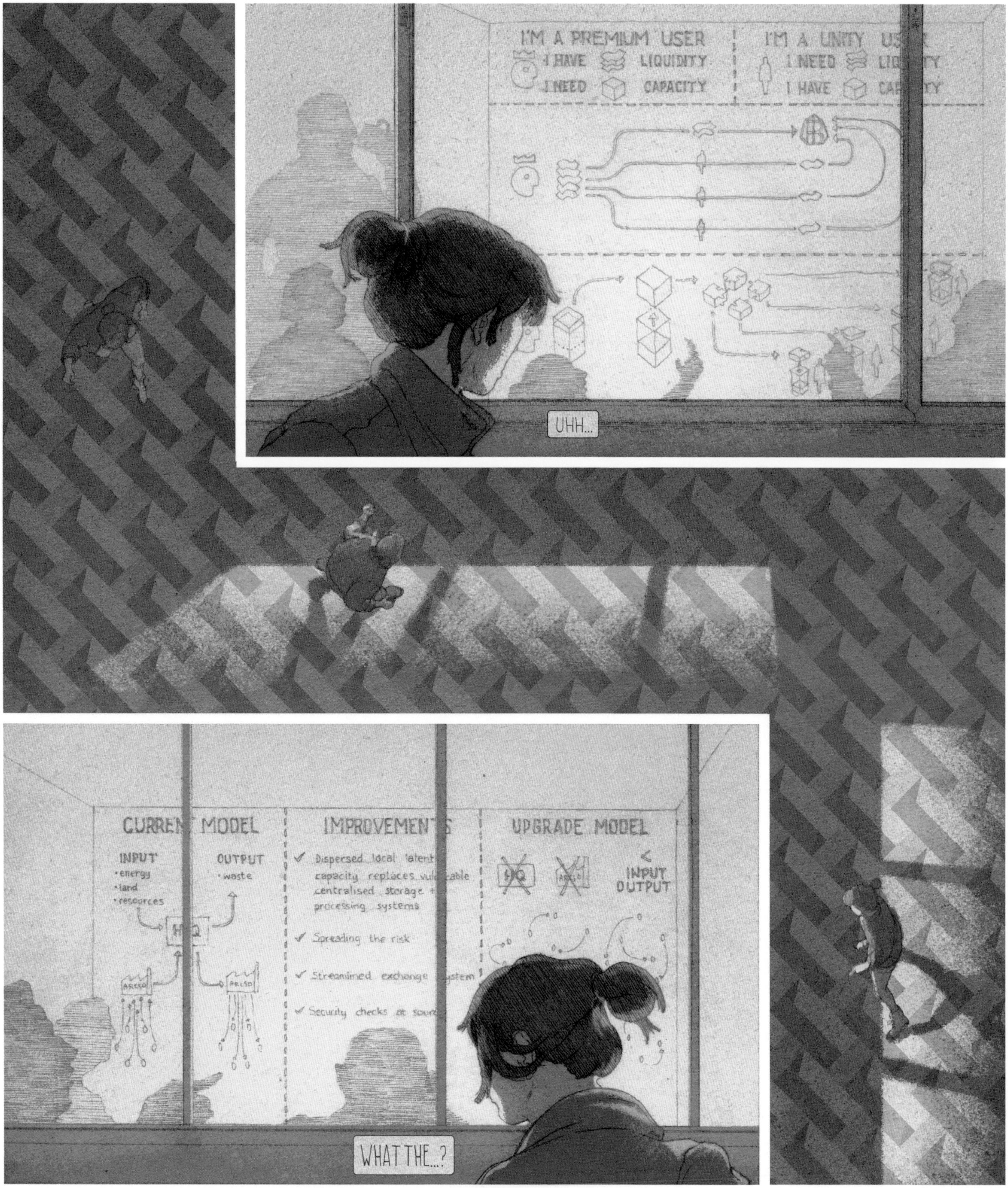
I'M A PREMIUM USER
I HAVE LIQUIDITY
I NEED CAPACITY
UHH...
INPUT
•energy
•land
•resources
OUTPUT
•waste
✓ Spreading the risk
UPGRADE MODEL
INPUT
OUTPUT
WHAT THE...?

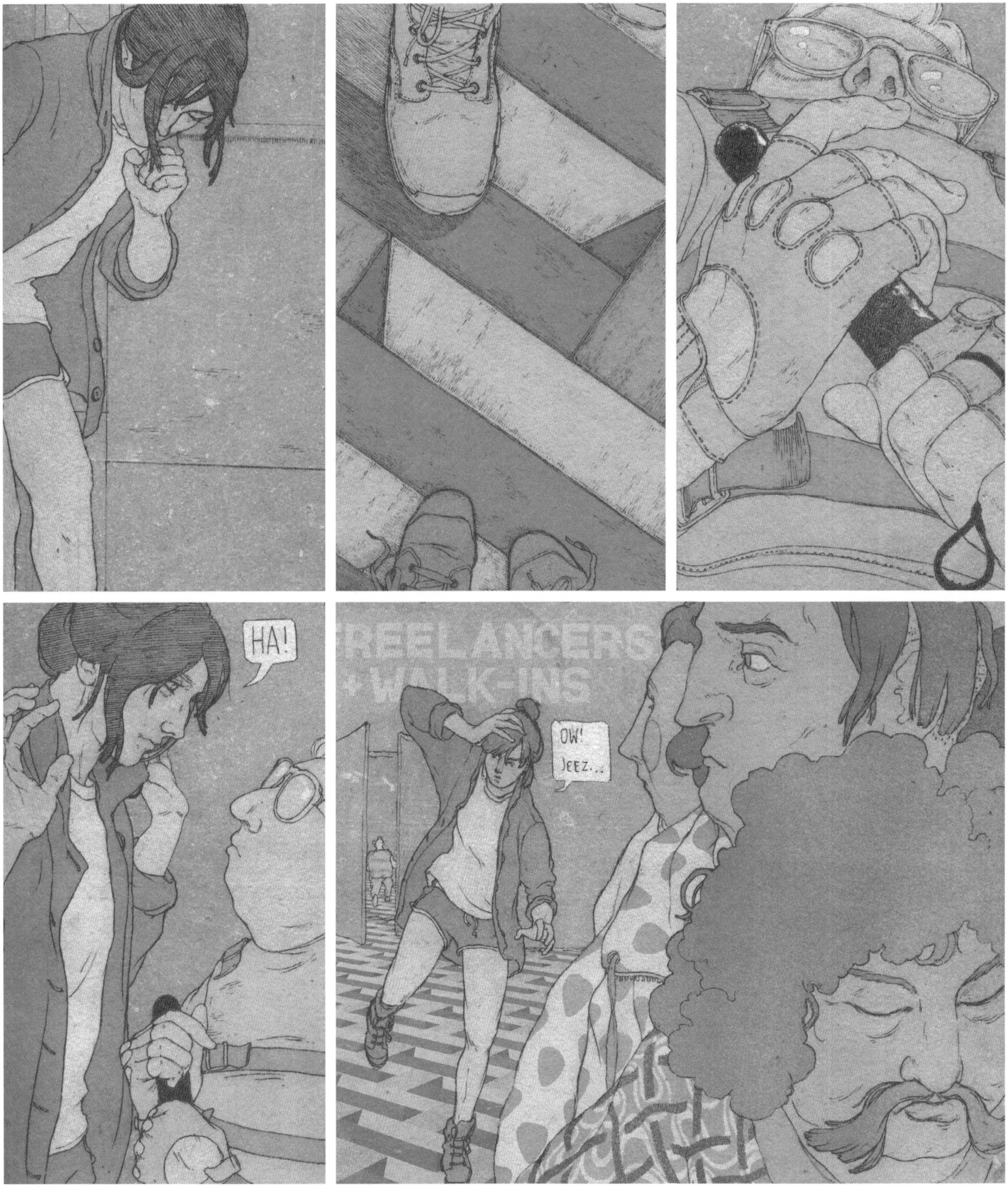
HA!
FREELANCERS
+ WALK-INS
OW!
JEEZ...

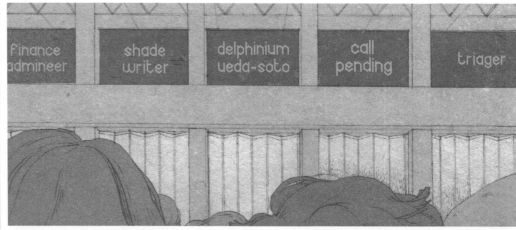

finance
admineer

shade
writer

delphinium
ueda-soto

call
pending

triager

delphinium
ueda-sot

HEY...!
I'M HERE!

WAIT!

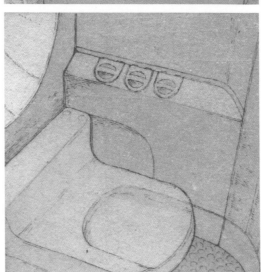

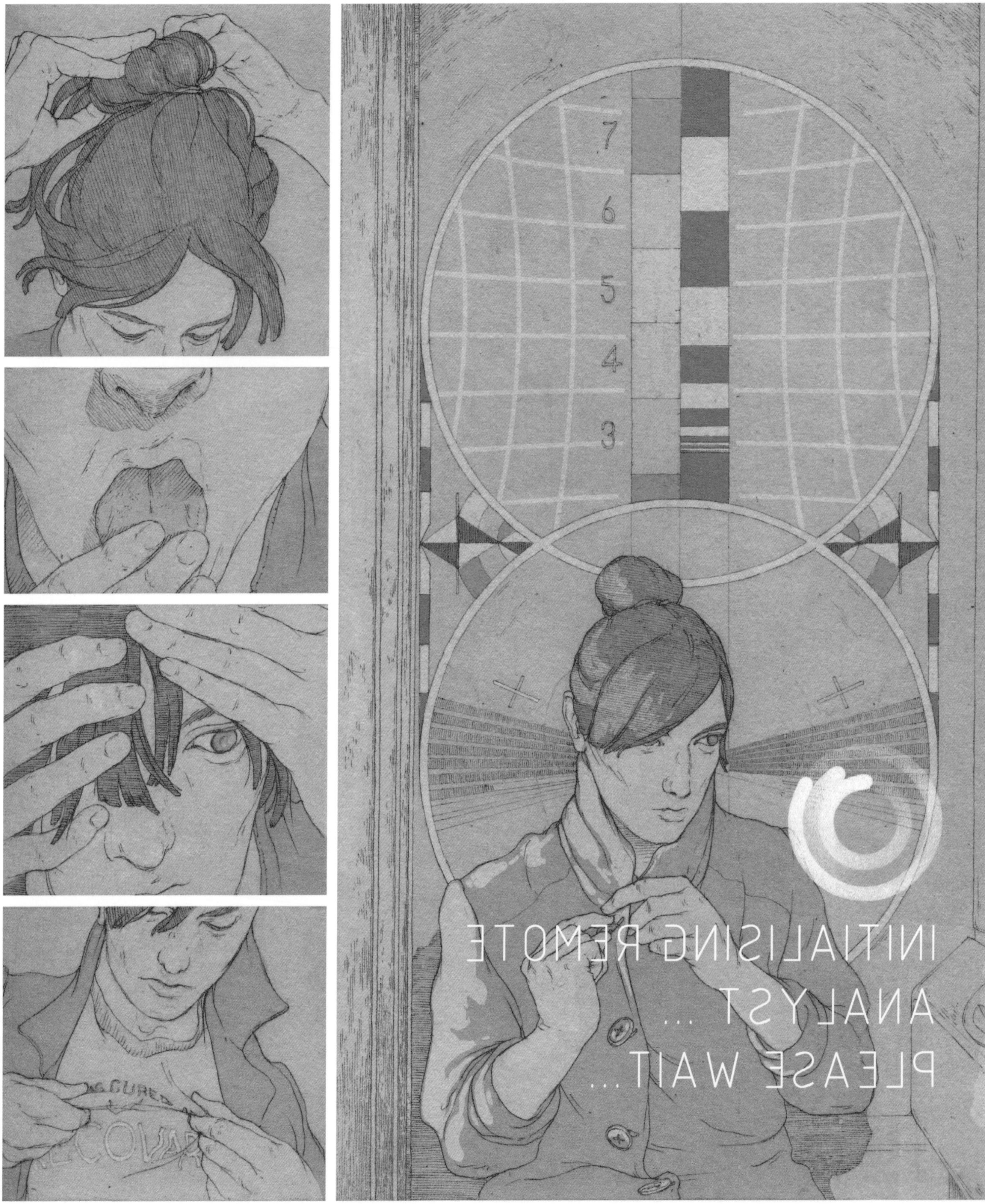
INITIALISING REMOTE
ANALYST ...
PLEASE WAIT...

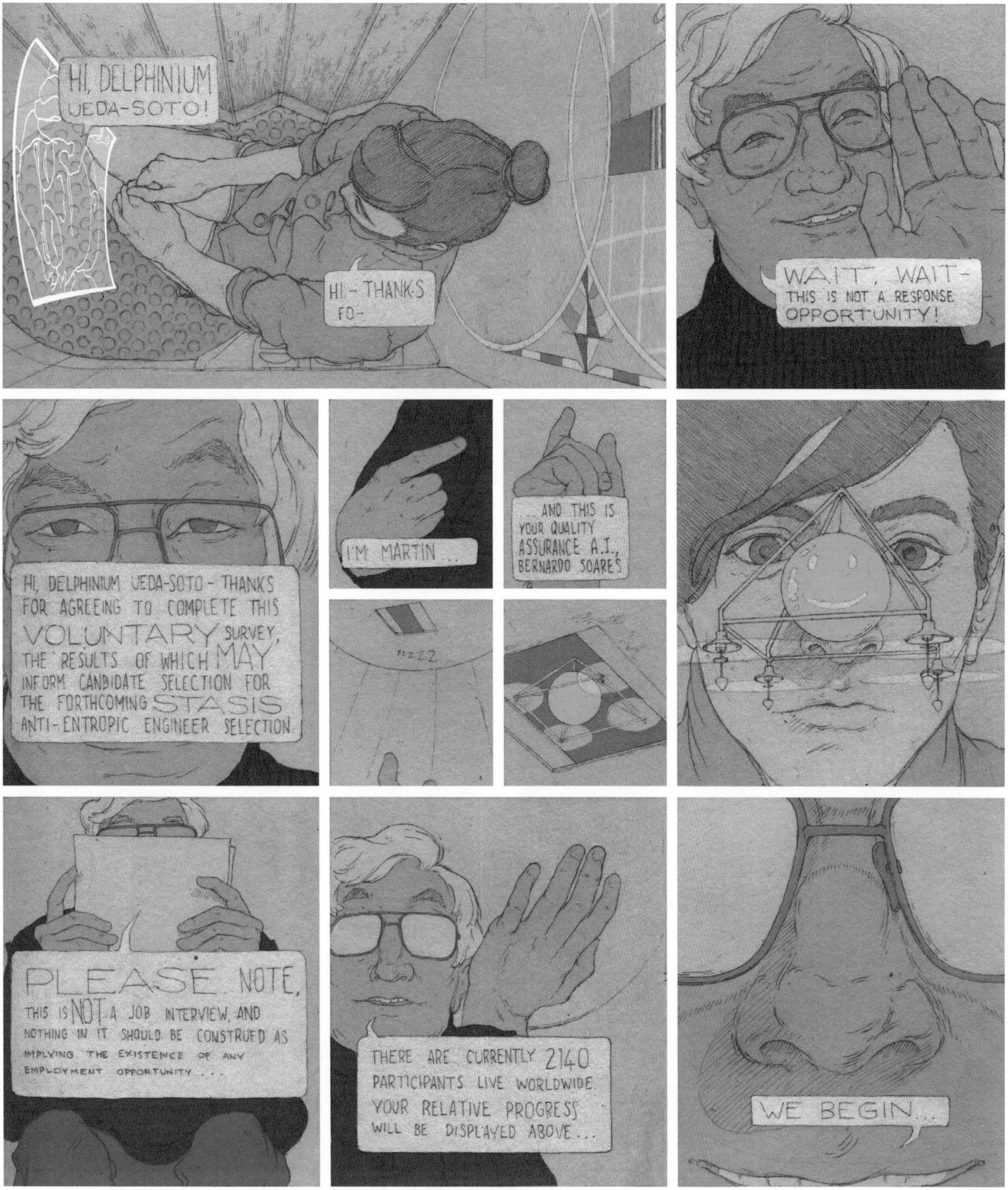
HI, DELPHINIUM UEDA-SOTO!
HI - THANKS FO-
WAIT, WAIT - THIS IS NOT A RESPONSE OPPORTUNITY!
HI, DELPHINIUM UEDA-SOTO - THANKS FOR AGREEING TO COMPLETE THIS VOLUNTARY SURVEY, THE RESULTS OF WHICH MAY INFORM CANDIDATE SELECTION FOR THE FORTHCOMING STASIS ANTI-ENTROPIC ENGINEER SELECTION.
I'M MARTIN ...
... AND THIS IS YOUR QUALITY ASSURANCE A.I., BERNARDO SOARES
BZZZ
PLEASE NOTE, THIS IS NOT A JOB INTERVIEW, AND NOTHING IN IT SHOULD BE CONSTRUED AS IMPLYING THE EXISTENCE OF ANY EMPLOYMENT OPPORTUNITY ...
THERE ARE CURRENTLY 2140 PARTICIPANTS LIVE WORLDWIDE. YOUR RELATIVE PROGRESS WILL BE DISPLAYED ABOVE ...
WE BEGIN...

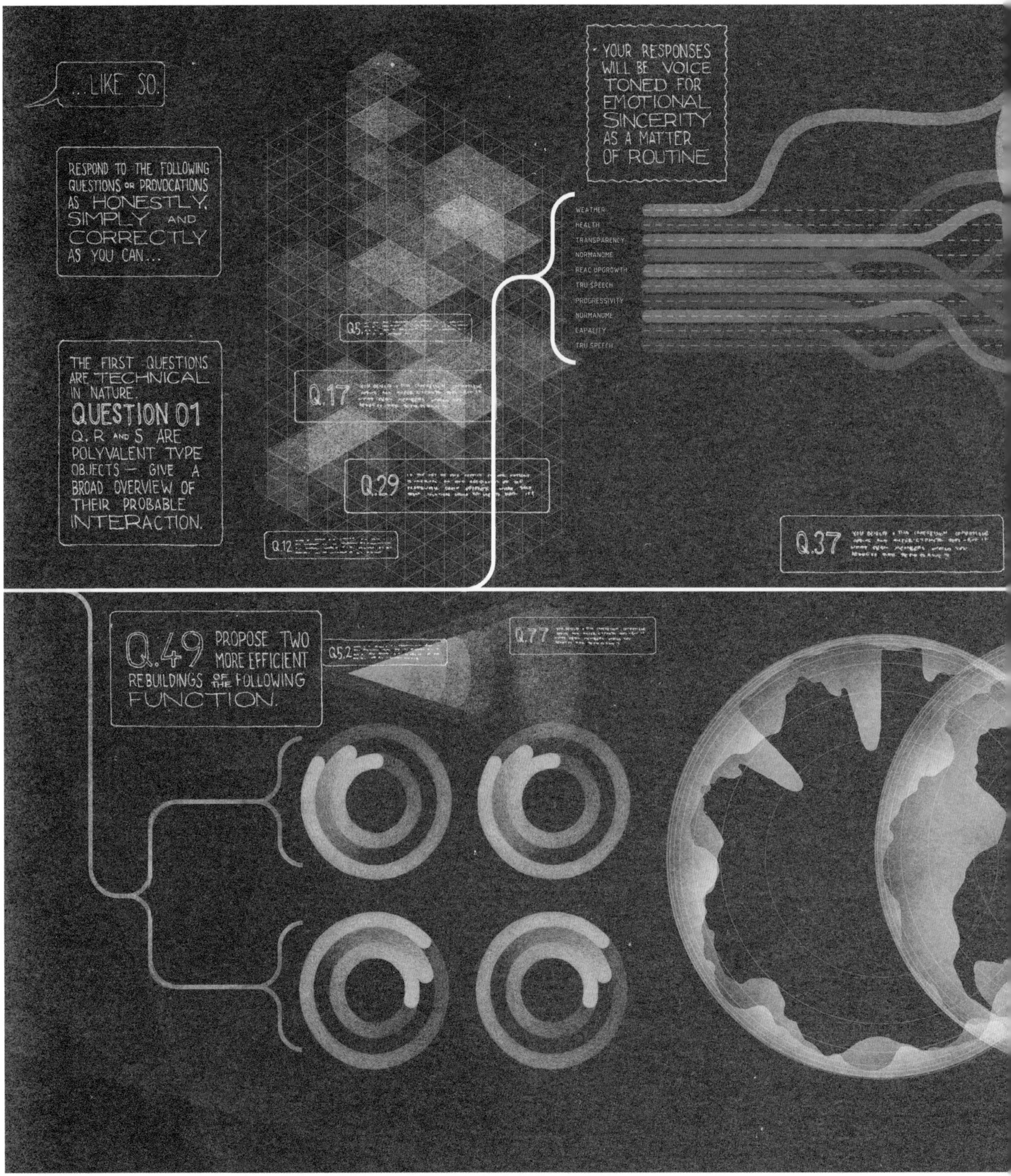

...LIKE SO.
RESPOND TO THE FOLLOWING QUESTIONS OR PROVOCATIONS AS HONESTLY, SIMPLY AND CORRECTLY AS YOU CAN...
THE FIRST QUESTIONS ARE TECHNICAL IN NATURE.
QUESTION 01
Q, R AND S ARE POLYVALENT TYPE OBJECTS — GIVE A BROAD OVERVIEW OF THEIR PROBABLE INTERACTION.
YOUR RESPONSES WILL BE VOICE TONED FOR EMOTIONAL SINCERITY AS A MATTER OF ROUTINE
WEATHER
HEALTH
TRANSPARENCY
NORMANOME
REAC UPGROWTH
TRU SPEECH
PROGRESSIVITY
NORMANOME
CAPACITY
TRU SPEECH
Q.5
Q.17
Q.29
Q.12
Q.37
Q.49 PROPOSE TWO MORE EFFICIENT REBUILDINGS OF THE FOLLOWING FUNCTION.
Q.5.2
Q.77

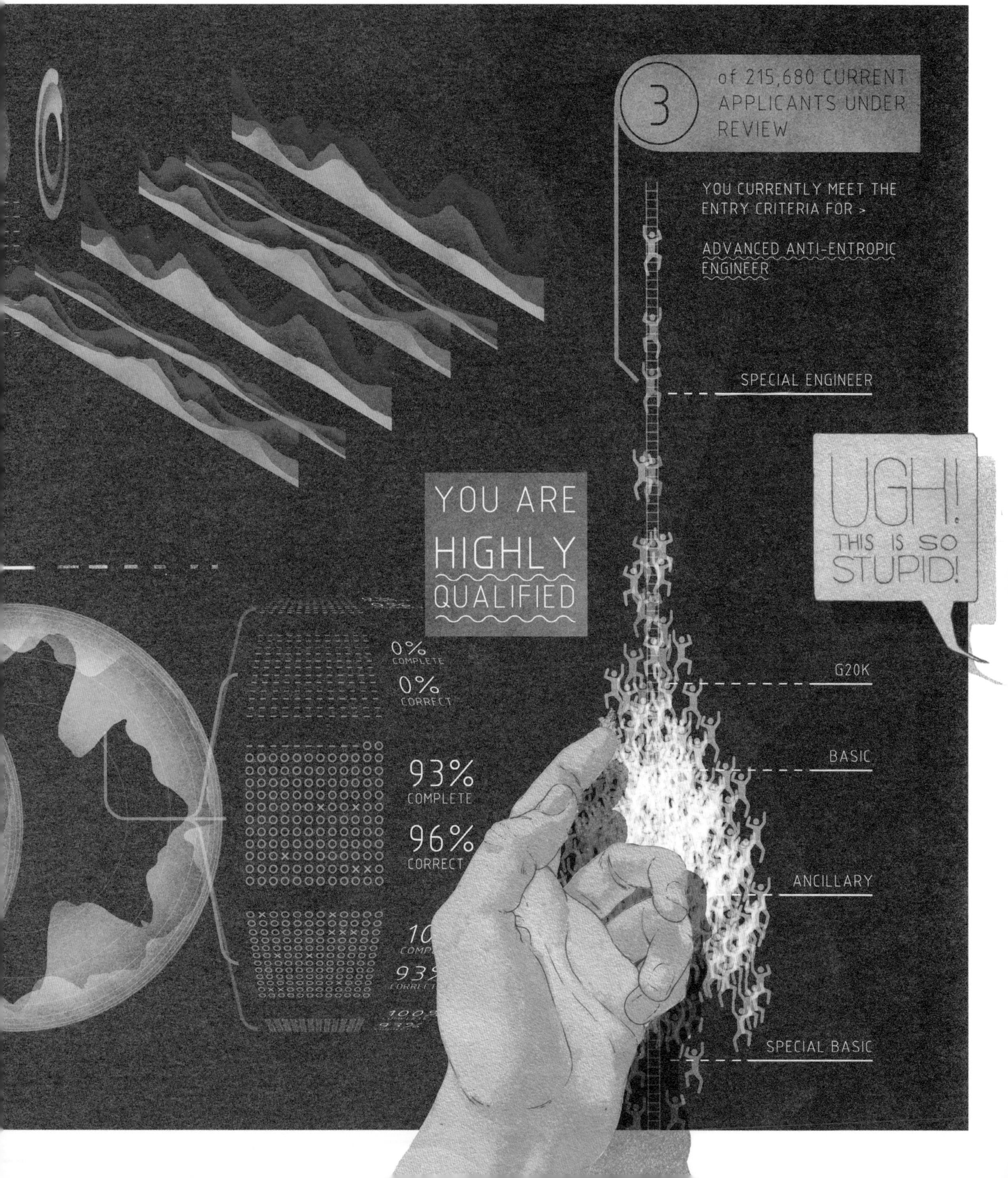
3
of 215,680 CURRENT APPLICANTS UNDER REVIEW
YOU CURRENTLY MEET THE ENTRY CRITERIA FOR >
ADVANCED ANTI-ENTROPIC ENGINEER
SPECIAL ENGINEER
YOU ARE HIGHLY QUALIFIED
UGH! THIS IS SO STUPID!
0% COMPLETE
0% CORRECT
93% COMPLETE
96% CORRECT
G20K
BASIC
ANCILLARY
SPECIAL BASIC

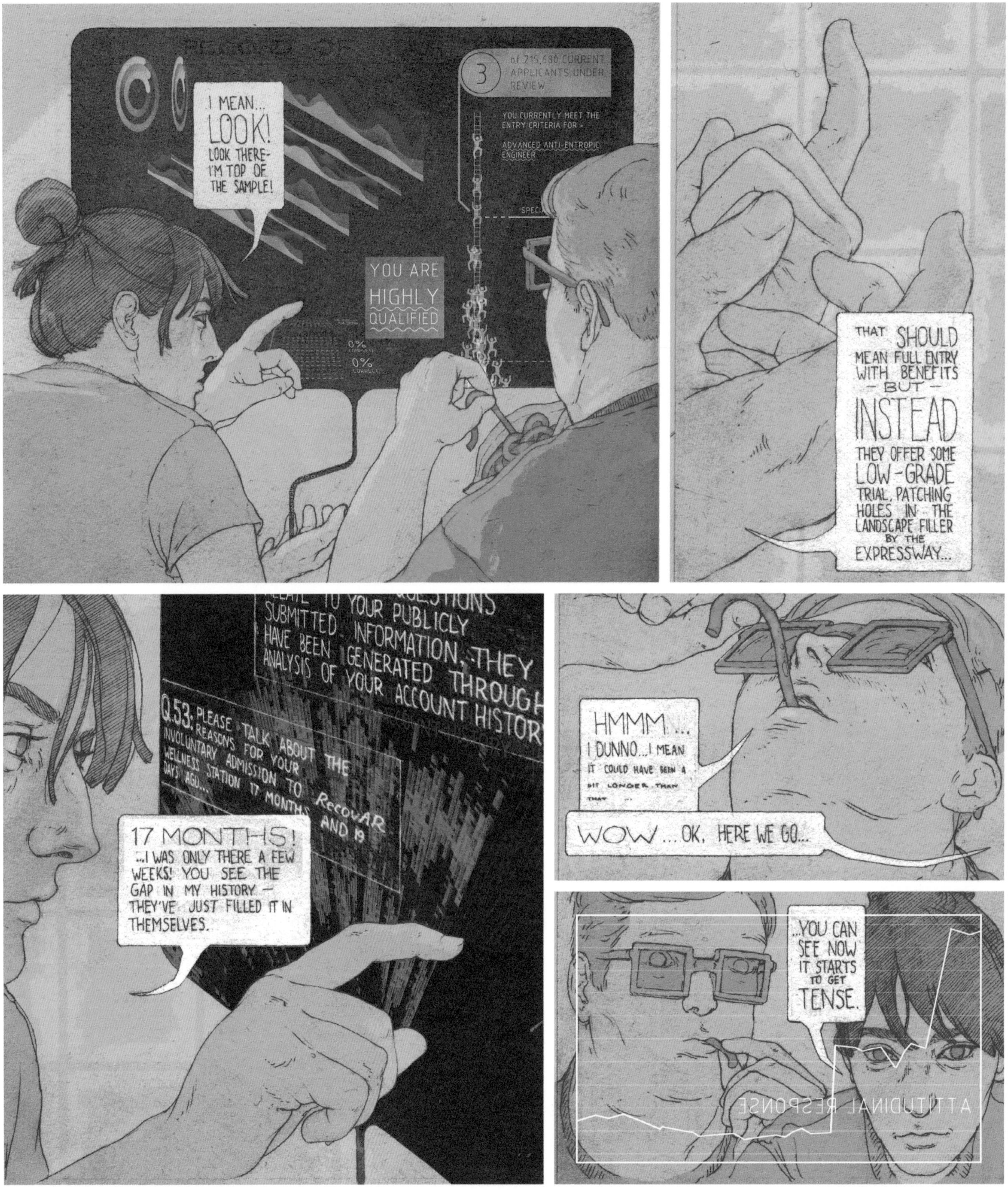

of 215,680 CURRENT APPLICANTS UNDER REVIEW
3
YOU CURRENTLY MEET THE ENTRY CRITERIA FOR >
ADVANCED ANTI-ENTROPIC ENGINEER
I MEAN... LOOK! LOOK THERE- I'M TOP OF THE SAMPLE!
YOU ARE HIGHLY QUALIFIED
0%
0%
THAT SHOULD MEAN FULL ENTRY WITH BENEFITS - BUT - INSTEAD THEY OFFER SOME LOW-GRADE TRIAL, PATCHING HOLES IN THE LANDSCAPE FILLER BY THE EXPRESSWAY...
SUBMITTED INFORMATION, THEY HAVE BEEN GENERATED THROUGH ANALYSIS OF YOUR ACCOUNT HISTORY
YOUR PUBLICLY
Q.53: PLEASE TALK ABOUT THE REASONS FOR YOUR INVOLUNTARY ADMISSION TO RecovAR WELLNESS STATION 17 MONTHS AND 19 DAYS AGO...
17 MONTHS! ...I WAS ONLY THERE A FEW WEEKS! YOU SEE THE GAP IN MY HISTORY — THEY'VE JUST FILLED IT IN THEMSELVES.
HMMM... I DUNNO...I MEAN IT COULD HAVE BEEN A BIT LONGER THAN THAT ...
WOW ... OK, HERE WE GO...
...YOU CAN SEE NOW IT STARTS TO GET TENSE.
ATTITUDINAL RESPONSE

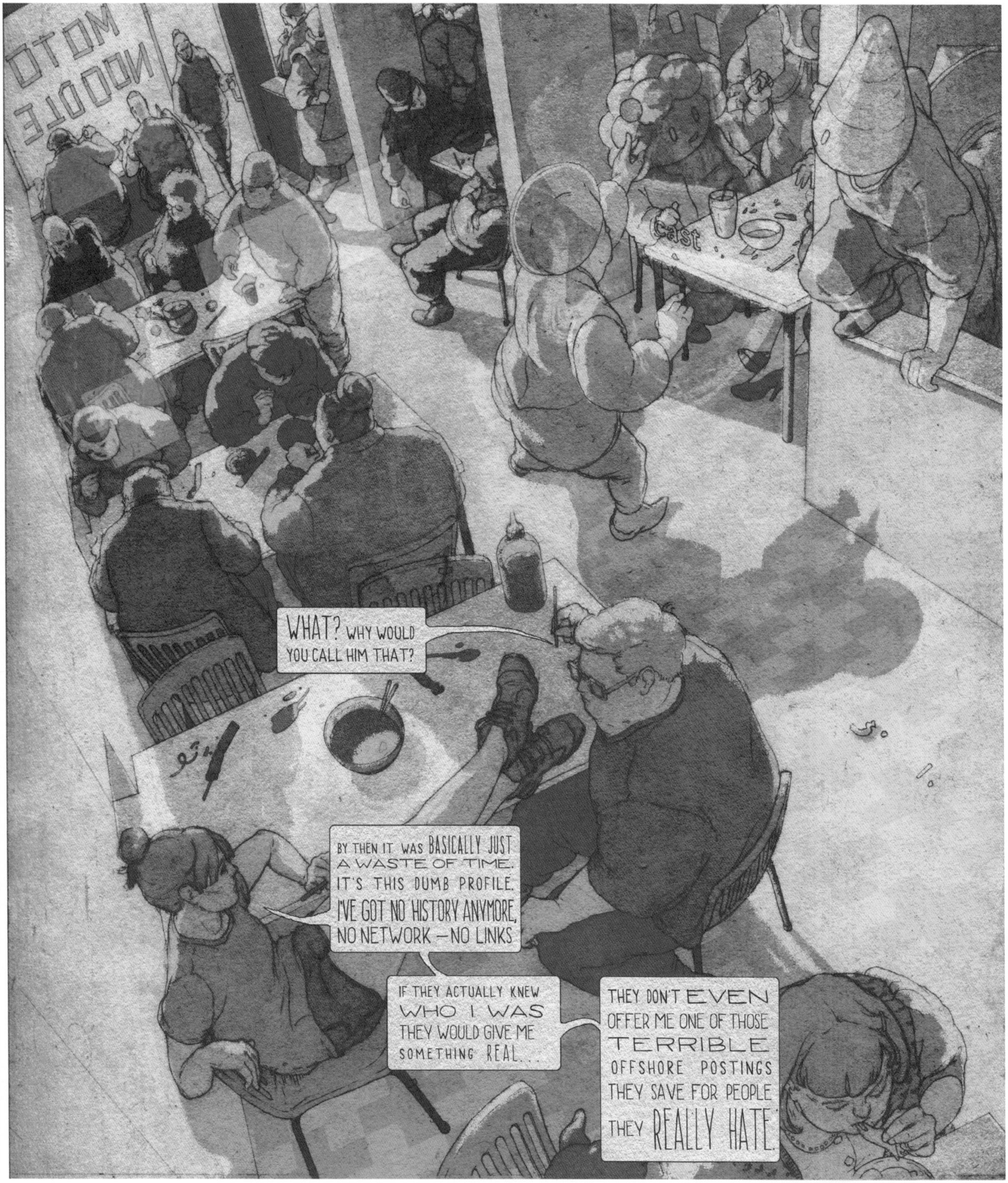
MOTO NOODLE
cast
WHAT? WHY WOULD YOU CALL HIM THAT?
BY THEN IT WAS BASICALLY JUST A WASTE OF TIME. IT'S THIS DUMB PROFILE. I'VE GOT NO HISTORY ANYMORE, NO NETWORK — NO LINKS
IF THEY ACTUALLY KNEW WHO I WAS THEY WOULD GIVE ME SOMETHING REAL...
THEY DON'T EVEN OFFER ME ONE OF THOSE TERRIBLE OFFSHORE POSTINGS THEY SAVE FOR PEOPLE THEY REALLY HATE.

WHAT ARE YOU GOING TO DO NOW? YOU'LL NEED SOMETHING ... . MONEY.
YEAH YEAH ... ...
...SO WHAT DO YOU THINK OF THIS?
LATENCY DISPERSAL.. ...USER-INFRASTRUCTURE CONVERGENCE...
...UNTAPPED... ...RECIPROCITY...
...BIOSTORAG
THIS LOOKS SORT OF SECRET. WHERE DID YOU...?
WAIT...! GO BACK. I SAW THIS TODAY – THIS LOGO. THERE WERE THESE PEOPLE...
...ALL STANDING AROUND, SORT OF... FROZEN. ...
HMMM...?
THEY ALL HAD AN ERROR MESSAGE AND THAT LOGO ...
LOOK! ...THEY'RE CODING IN VOYNIX! NO ONE USES VOYNIX NOW EXCEPT ME... ...IN FACT THIS STRUCTURE LOOKS...
...FAMILIAR...ER...UGH...
AND THEN, ALL THESE MEN CAME SHOUTING AND CHASING PEOPLE AWAY...
CAN YOU GO BACK? FIN?
ARE YOU OK?

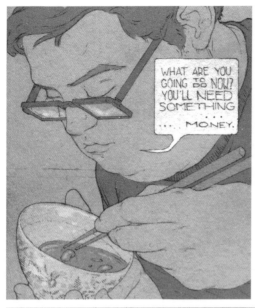

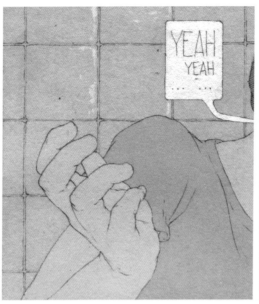

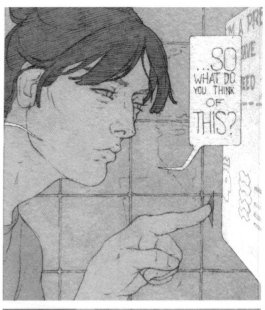

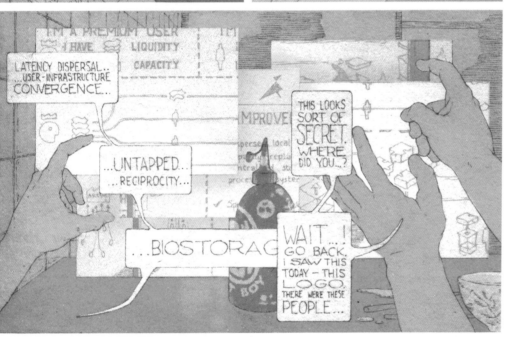

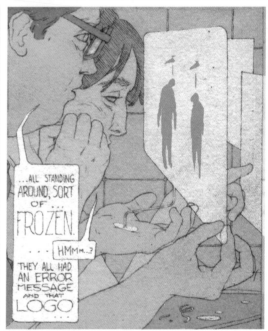

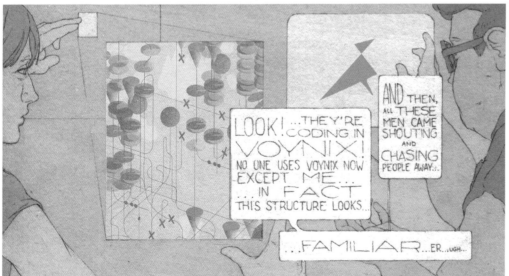

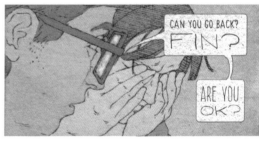

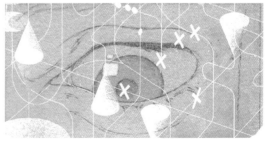

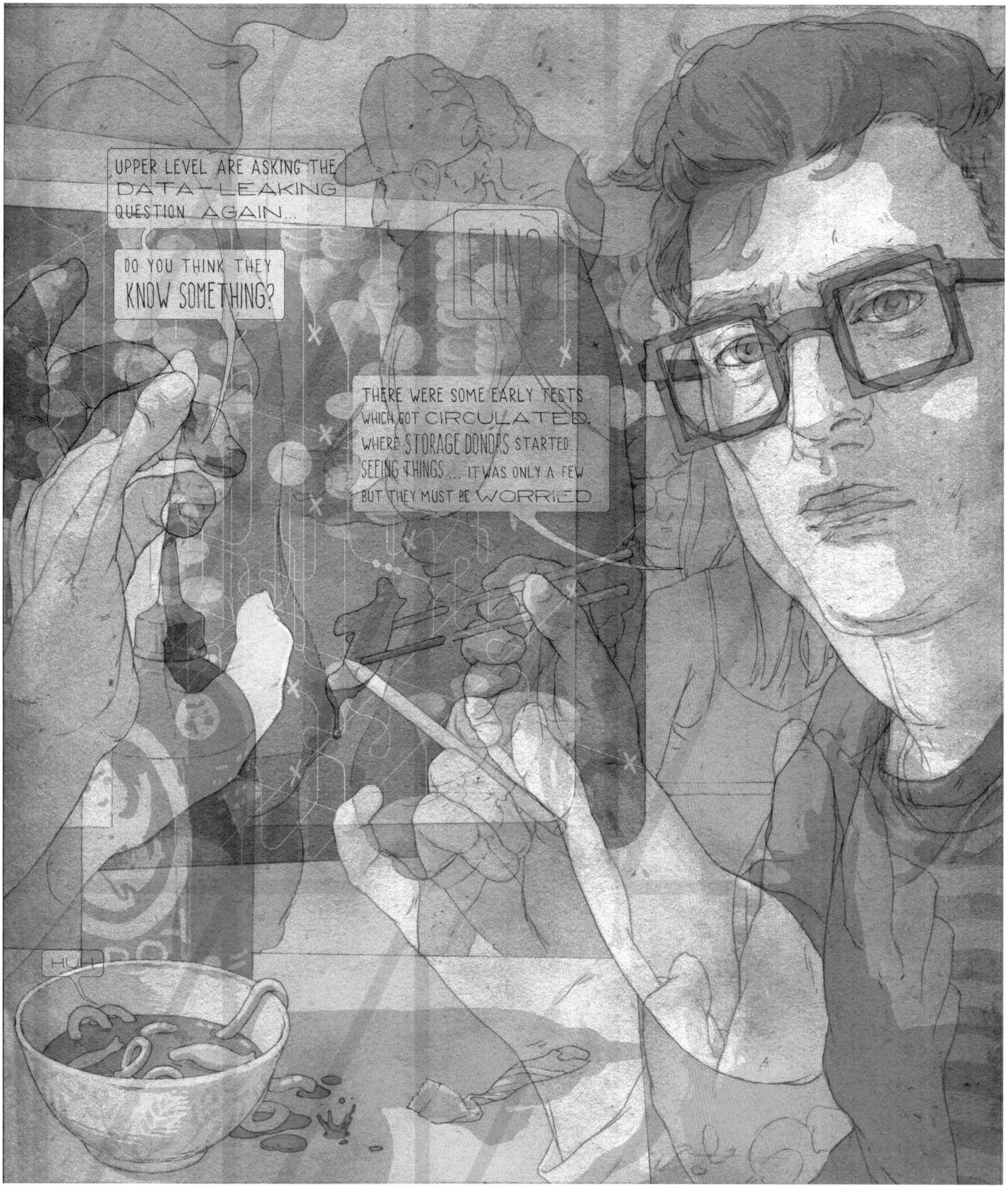
UPPER LEVEL ARE ASKING THE DATA-LEAKING QUESTION AGAIN...
DO YOU THINK THEY KNOW SOMETHING?
FIN?
THERE WERE SOME EARLY TESTS WHICH GOT CIRCULATED. WHERE STORAGE DONORS STARTED... SEEING THINGS... IT WAS ONLY A FEW BUT THEY MUST BE WORRIED...
HUH

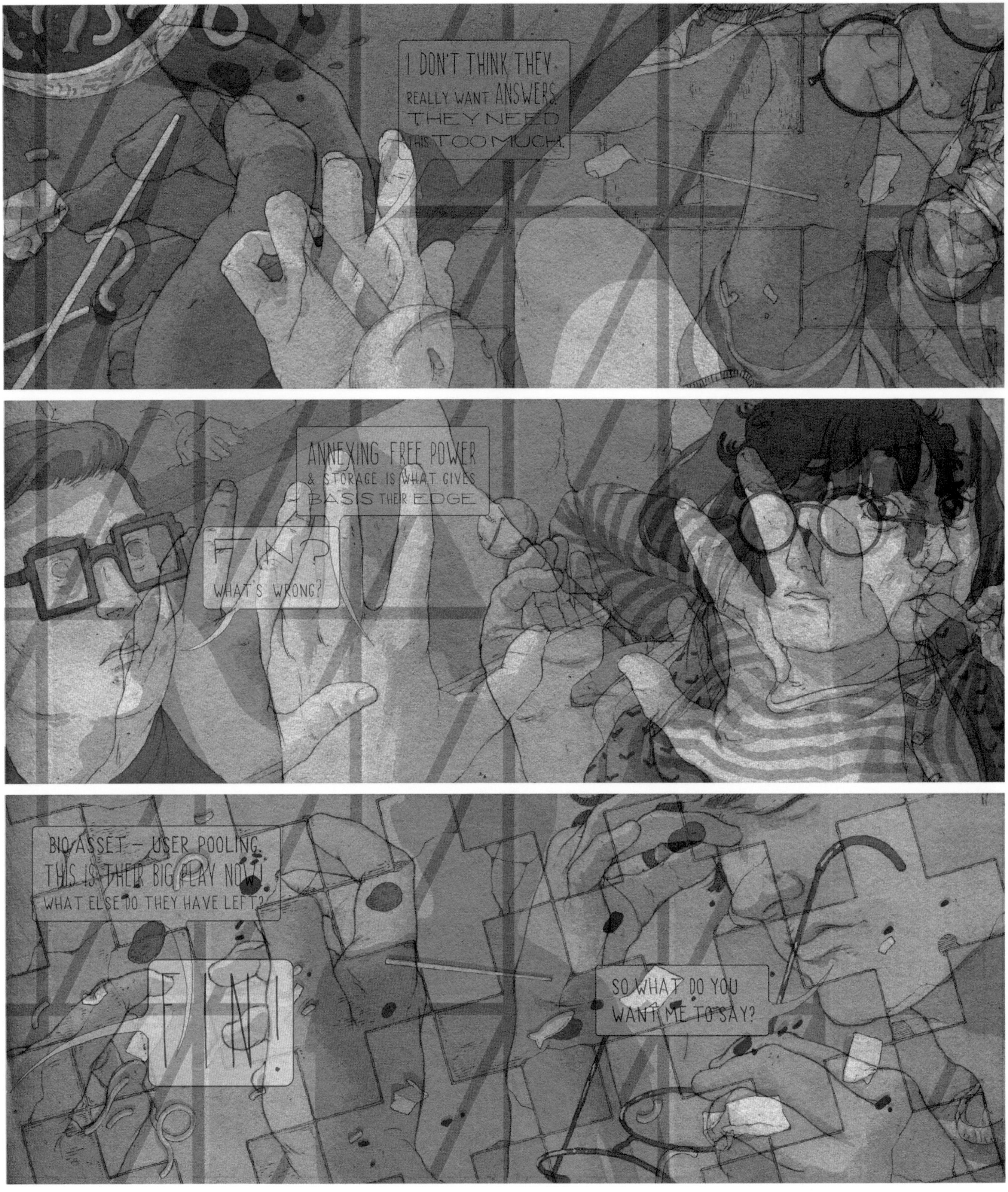
I DON'T THINK THEY REALLY WANT ANSWERS. THEY NEED THIS TOO MUCH.
ANNEXING FREE POWER & STORAGE IS WHAT GIVES BASIS THEIR EDGE
FIN? WHAT'S WRONG?
BIO ASSET – USER POOLING. THIS IS THEIR BIG PLAY NOW! WHAT ELSE DO THEY HAVE LEFT?
FINI
SO WHAT DO YOU WANT ME TO SAY?

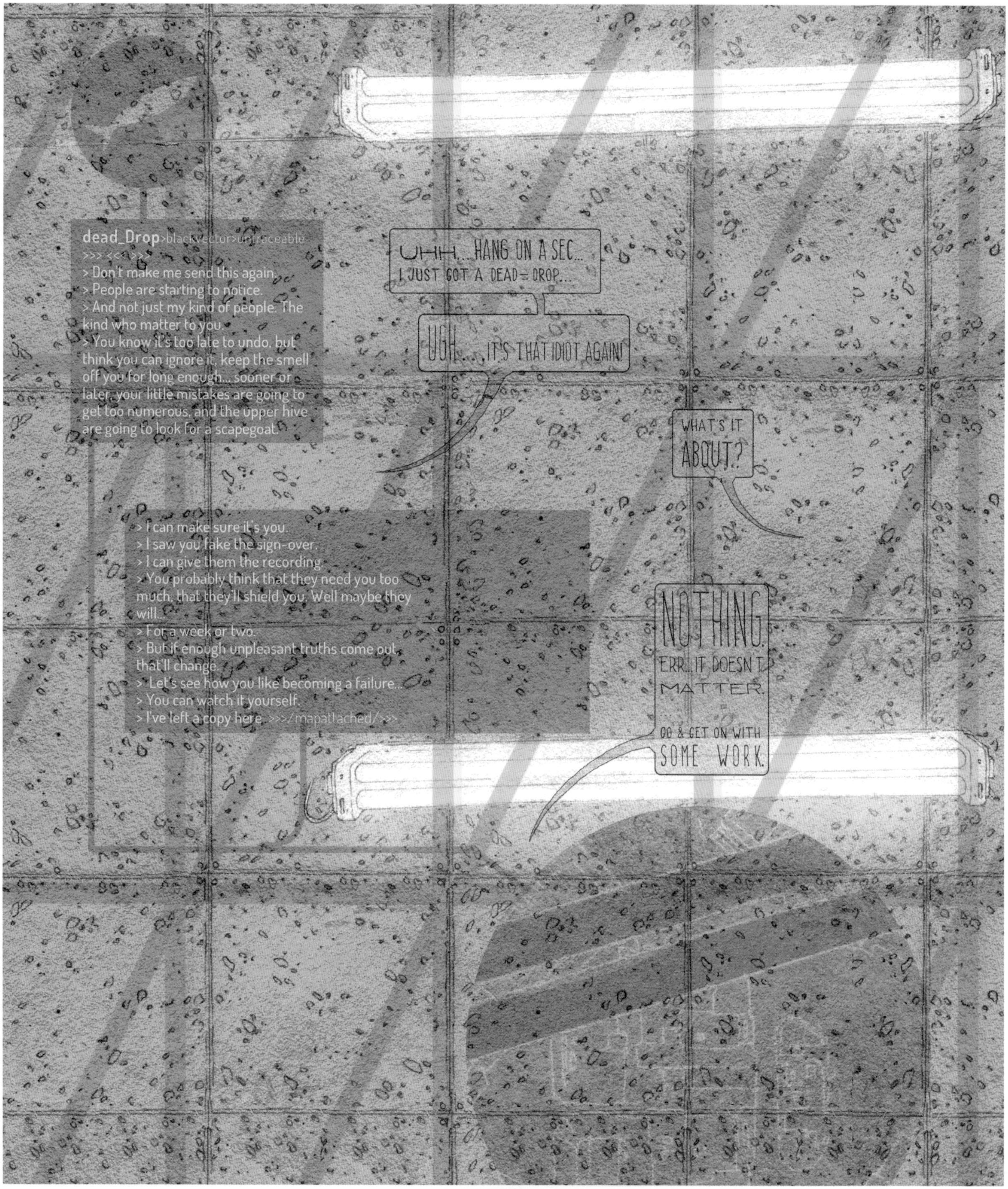
UHHH... HANG ON A SEC... I JUST GOT A DEAD-DROP...
dead_Drop>blackvector>untraceable
>>> <<?>>>
> Don't make me send this again.
> People are starting to notice.
> And not just my kind of people. The kind who matter to you.
> You know it's too late to undo, but think you can ignore it, keep the smell off you for long enough... sooner or later, your little mistakes are going to get too numerous, and the upper hive are going to look for a scapegoat.
UGH... IT'S THAT IDIOT AGAIN!
WHAT'S IT ABOUT?
> I can make sure it's you.
> I saw you fake the sign-over.
> I can give them the recording.
> You probably think that they need you too much, that they'll shield you. Well maybe they will...
> For a week or two.
> But if enough unpleasant truths come out, that'll change.
> Let's see how you like becoming a failure...
> You can watch it yourself.
> I've left a copy here. >>>/mapattached/>>>
NOTHING. ERR... IT DOESN'T MATTER.
GO & GET ON WITH SOME WORK.

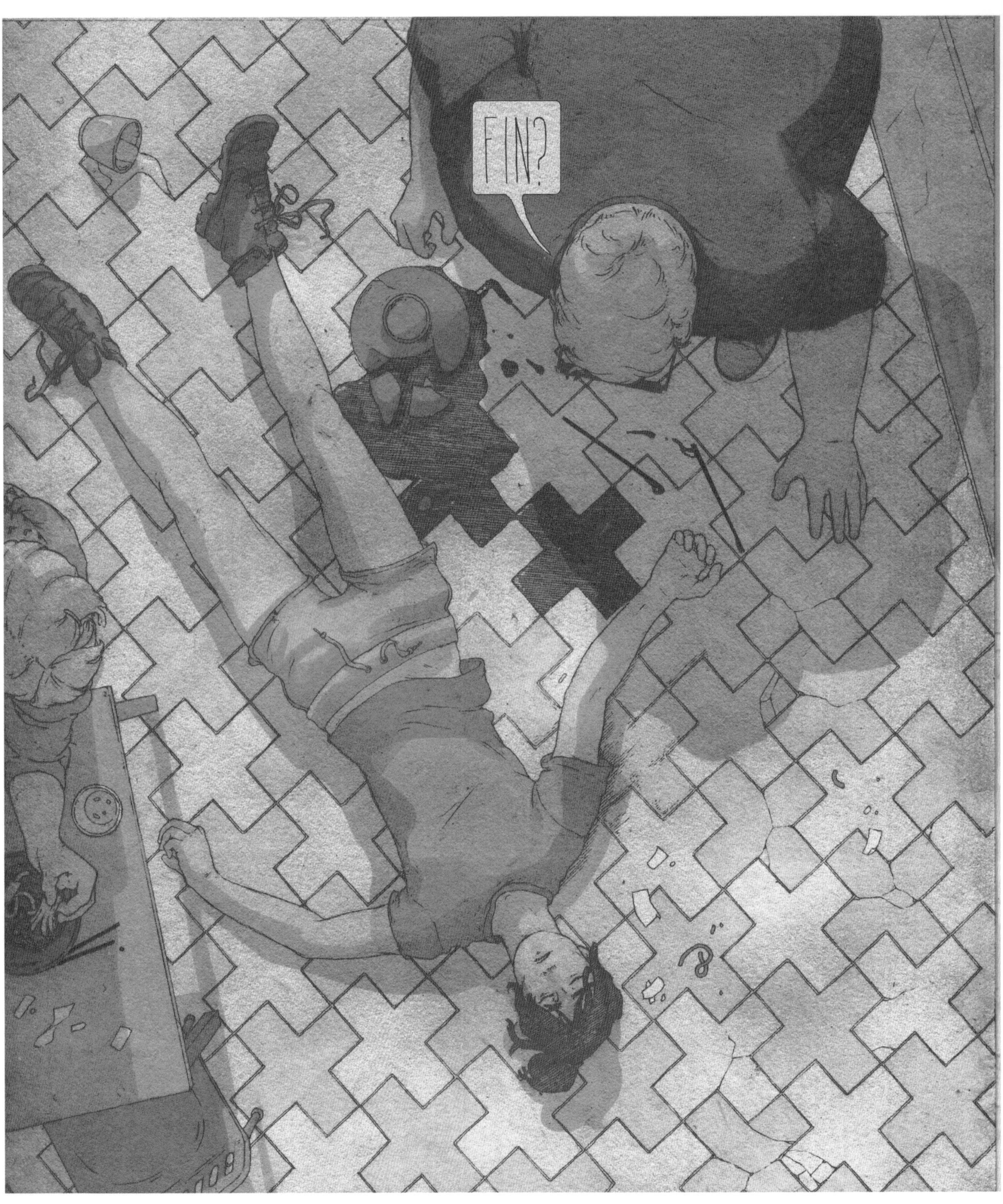
FIN?

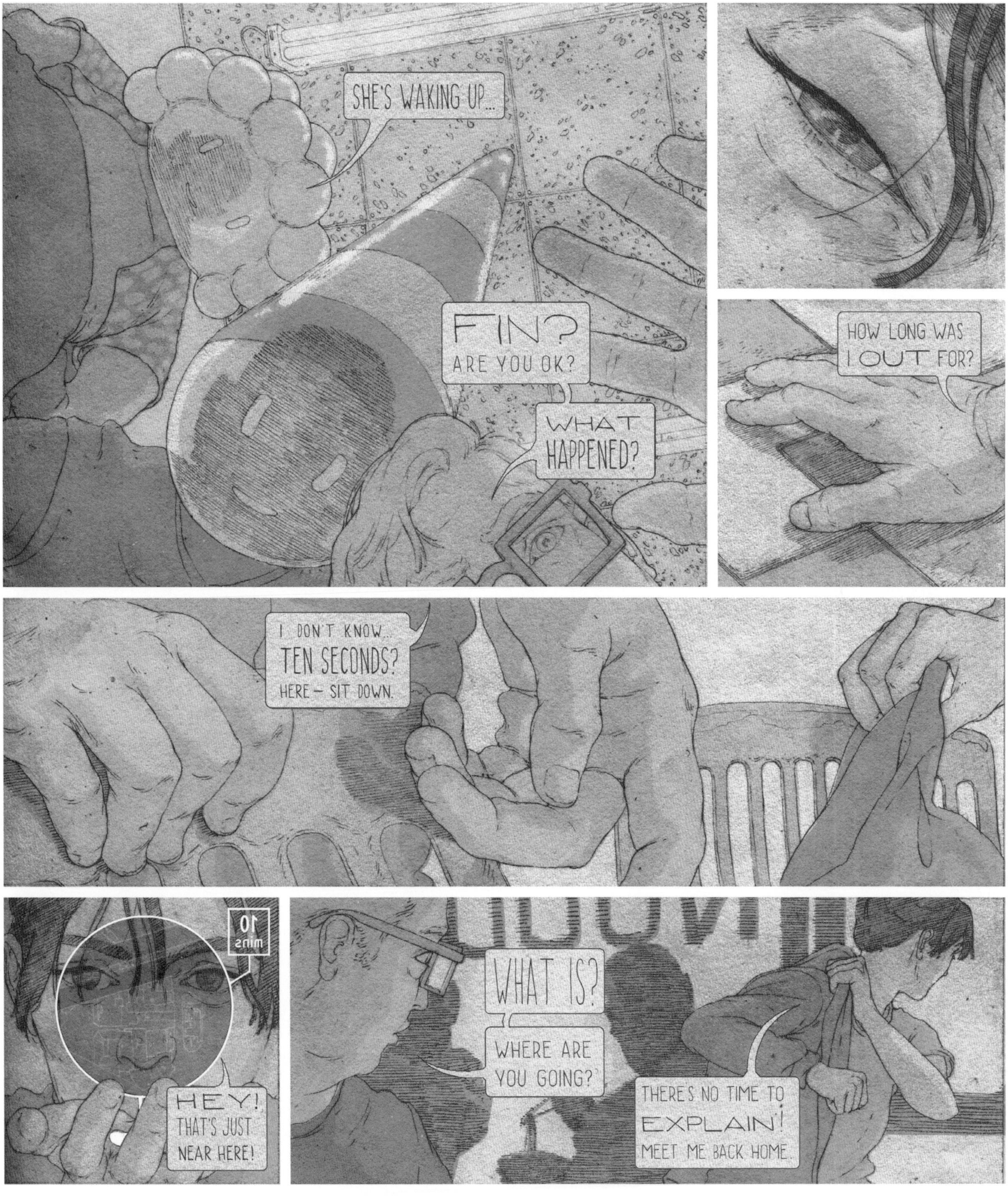
SHE'S WAKING UP...
FIN? ARE YOU OK?
WHAT HAPPENED?
HOW LONG WAS I OUT FOR?
I DON'T KNOW... TEN SECONDS? HERE – SIT DOWN.
10 mins
HEY! THAT'S JUST NEAR HERE!
WHAT IS?
WHERE ARE YOU GOING?
THERE'S NO TIME TO EXPLAIN! MEET ME BACK HOME.

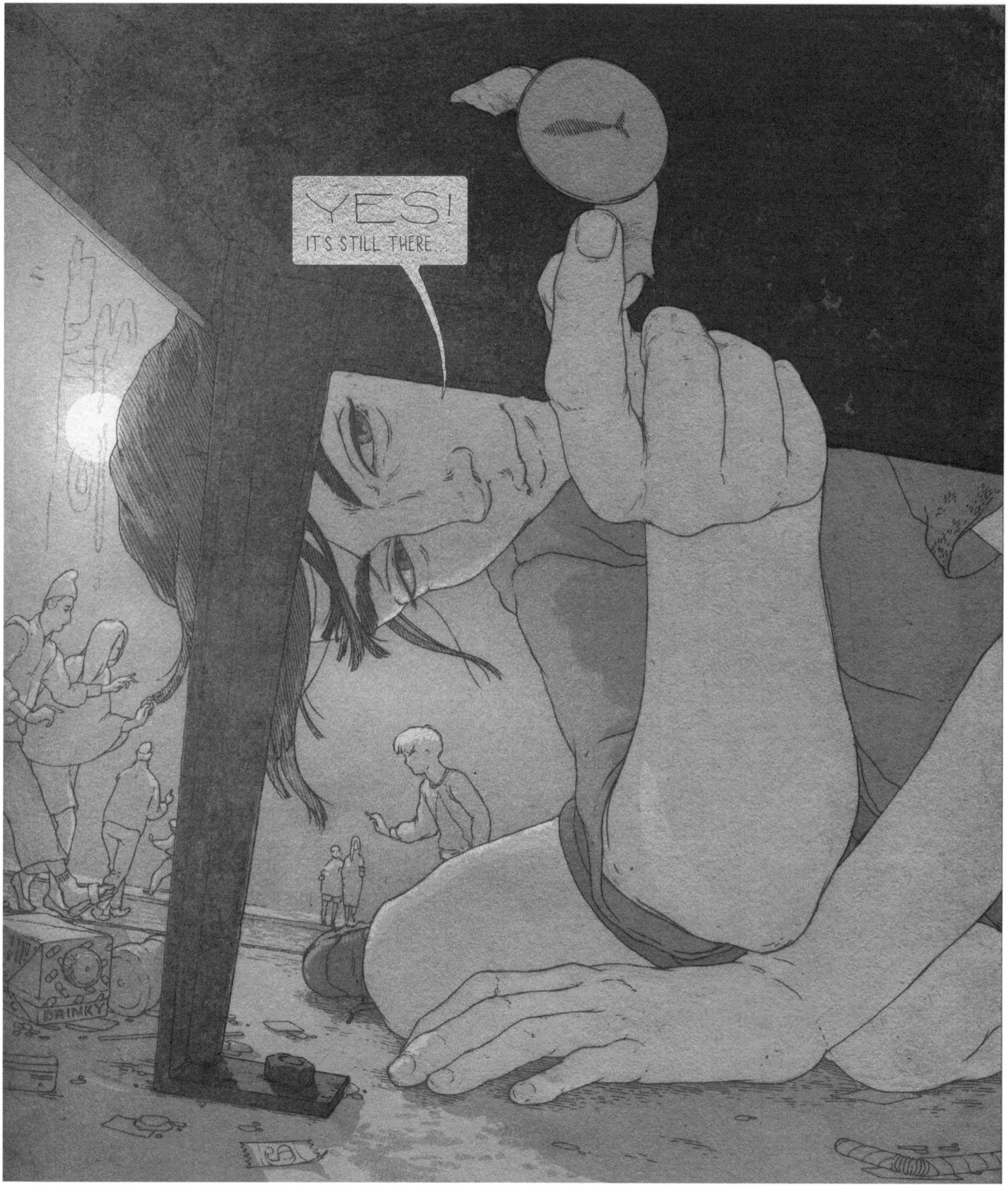
YES! IT'S STILL THERE...
DAINKY

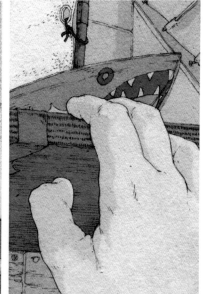
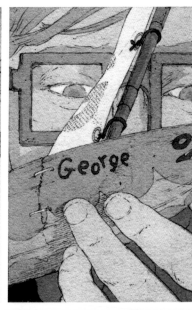

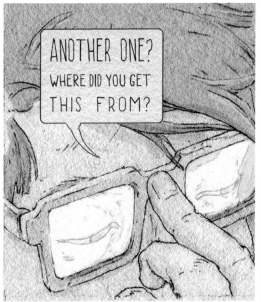

ANOTHER ONE? WHERE DID YOU GET THIS FROM?

WHILE I WAS OUT COLD... I SAW THIS BLACKMAIL MESSAGE & IT WAS REAL... THERE WAS A MAP.

WHAT...? A MESSAGE THAT TOLD YOU WHERE TO FIND THIS?

EITHER SHE DOES THIS NOW OR THE WHOLE BUSINESS GOES INTO LEGAL SUSPENSION.

IT SOUNDS CRAZY BUT SOMETIMES I SEE WHAT SHE SEES.

...SOMETHING LIKE THIS HAPPENED BEFORE I THINK... ... THERE WAS THIS BUG IN THE INTERFACE TO DO WITH CO-OPERATIVE MANIPULATIONS

BUT I FIXED IT IN CORVIS VERSION 2.

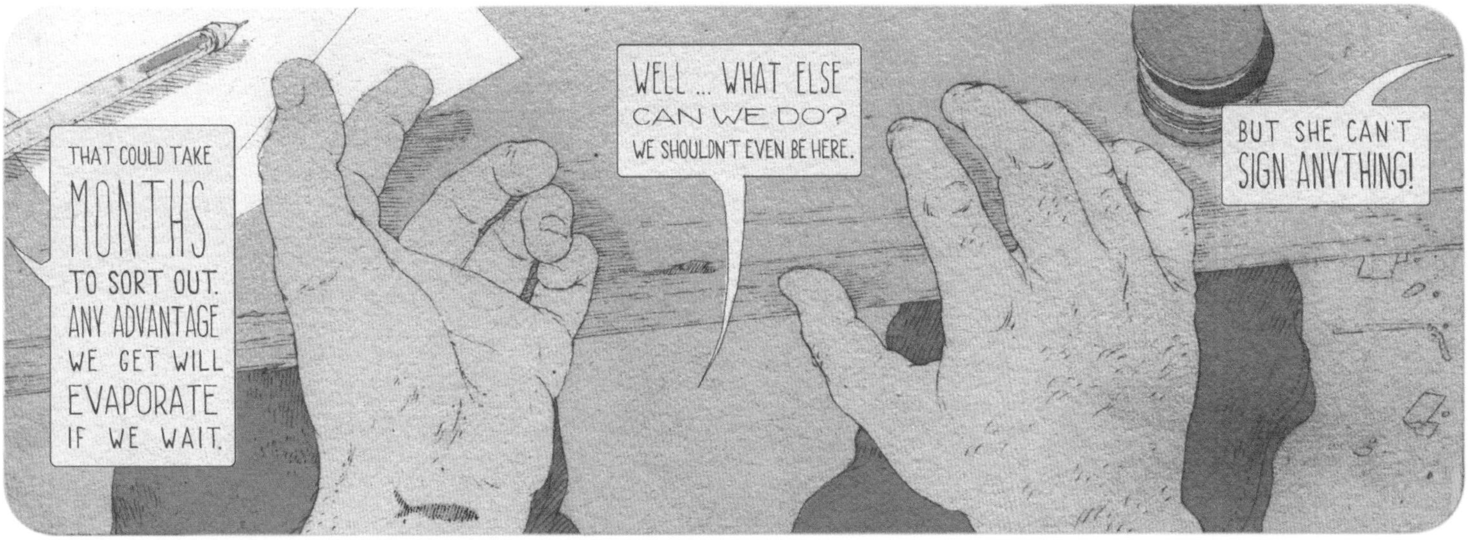
THAT COULD TAKE MONTHS TO SORT OUT. ANY ADVANTAGE WE GET WILL EVAPORATE IF WE WAIT.
WELL ... WHAT ELSE CAN WE DO? WE SHOULDN'T EVEN BE HERE.
BUT SHE CAN'T SIGN ANYTHING!

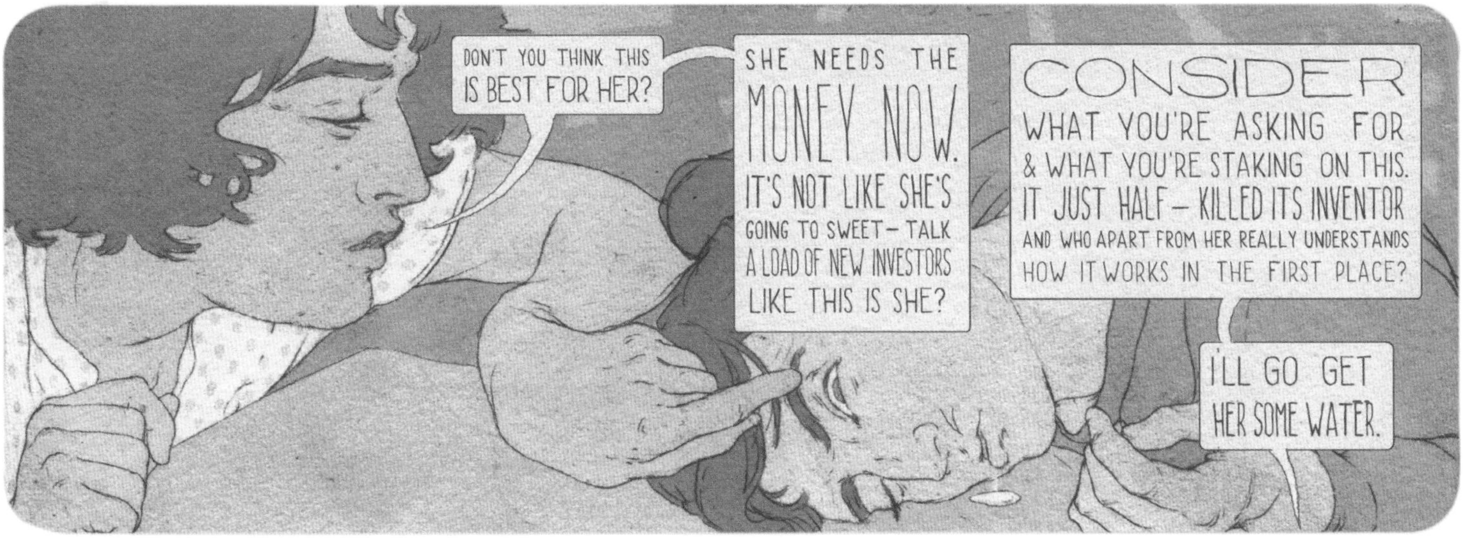
DON'T YOU THINK THIS IS BEST FOR HER?
SHE NEEDS THE MONEY NOW. IT'S NOT LIKE SHE'S GOING TO SWEET-TALK A LOAD OF NEW INVESTORS LIKE THIS IS SHE?
CONSIDER WHAT YOU'RE ASKING FOR & WHAT YOU'RE STAKING ON THIS. IT JUST HALF-KILLED ITS INVENTOR AND WHO APART FROM HER REALLY UNDERSTANDS HOW IT WORKS IN THE FIRST PLACE?
I'LL GO GET HER SOME WATER.

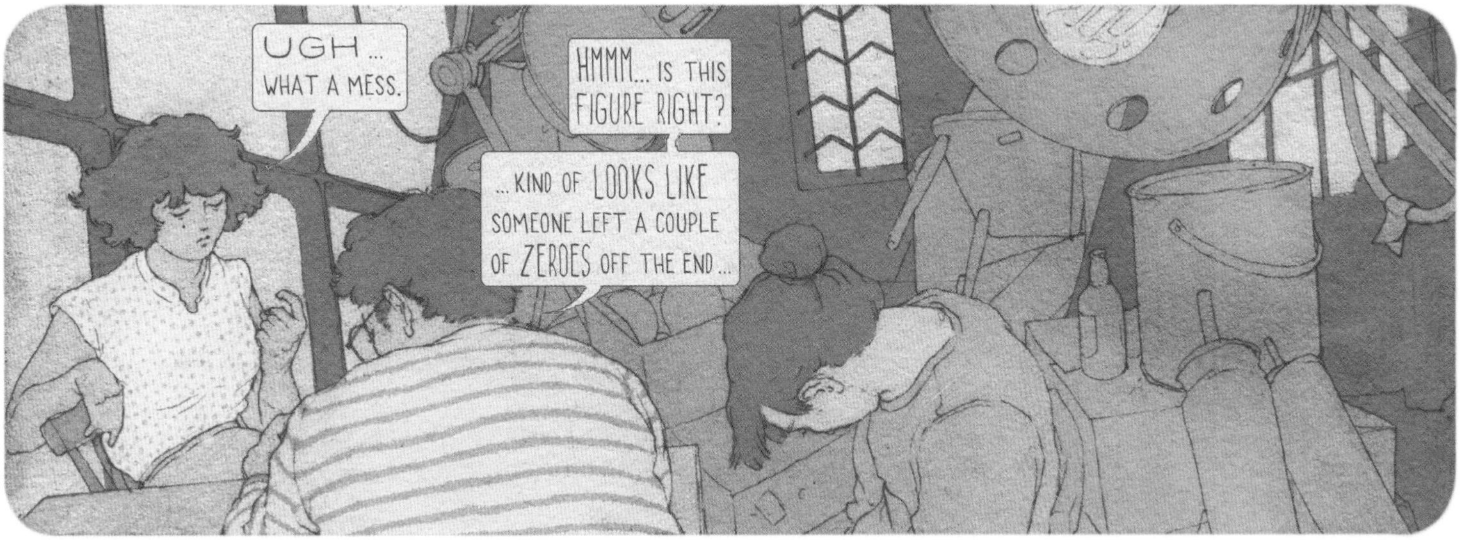
UGH ... WHAT A MESS.
HMMM... IS THIS FIGURE RIGHT?
... KIND OF LOOKS LIKE SOMEONE LEFT A COUPLE OF ZEROES OFF THE END ...

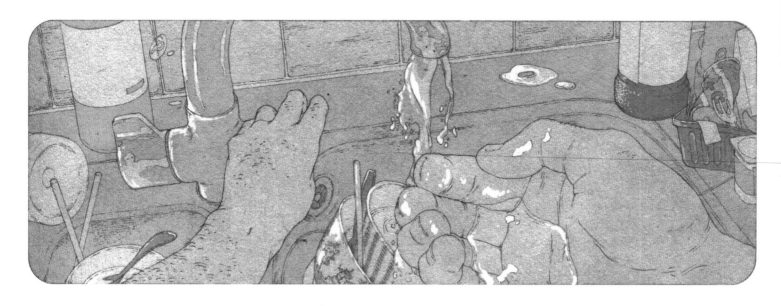

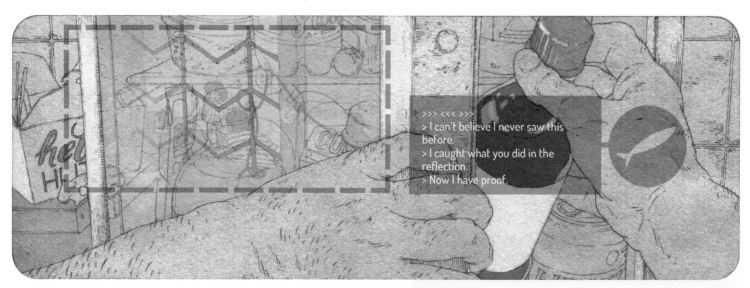

>>> <<< >>>
> I can't believe I never saw this before.
> I caught what you did in the reflection.
> Now I have proof.

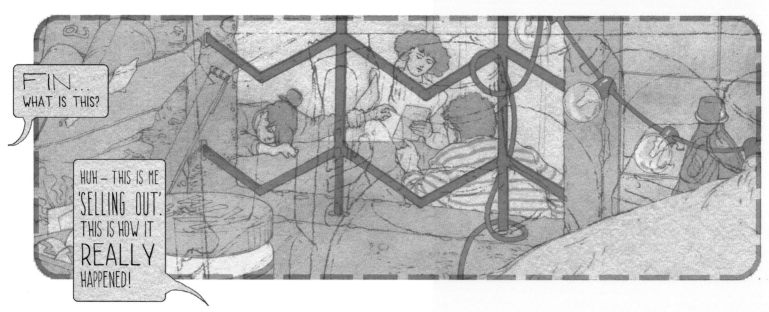

FIN...
WHAT IS THIS?

HUH – THIS IS ME
'SELLING OUT'.
THIS IS HOW IT
REALLY
HAPPENED!

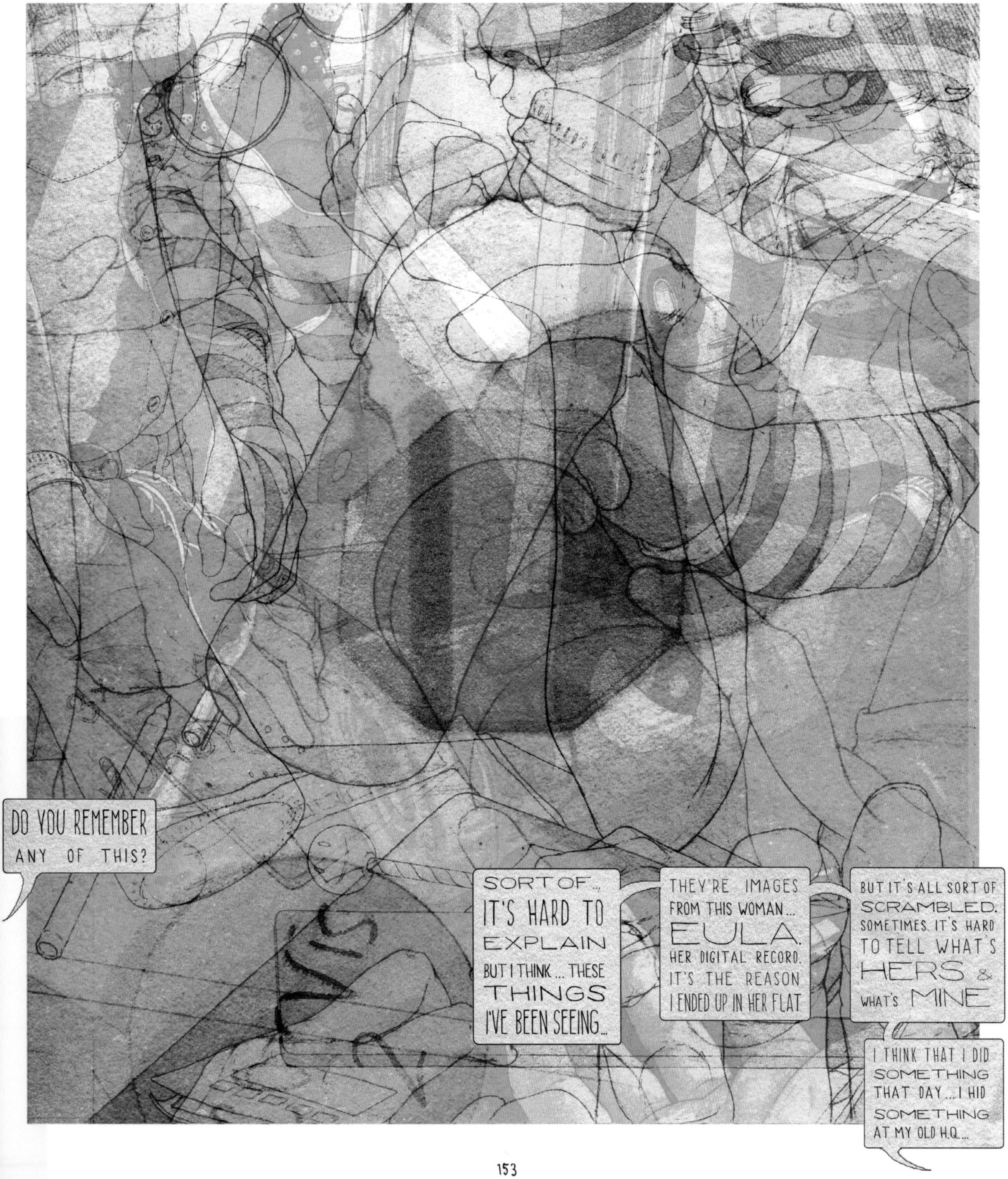
DO YOU REMEMBER ANY OF THIS?
SORT OF... IT'S HARD TO EXPLAIN BUT I THINK... THESE THINGS I'VE BEEN SEEING...
THEY'RE IMAGES FROM THIS WOMAN... EULA. HER DIGITAL RECORD. IT'S THE REASON I ENDED UP IN HER FLAT
BUT IT'S ALL SORT OF SCRAMBLED. SOMETIMES IT'S HARD TO TELL WHAT'S HERS & WHAT'S MINE
I THINK THAT I DID SOMETHING THAT DAY... I HID SOMETHING AT MY OLD H.Q...

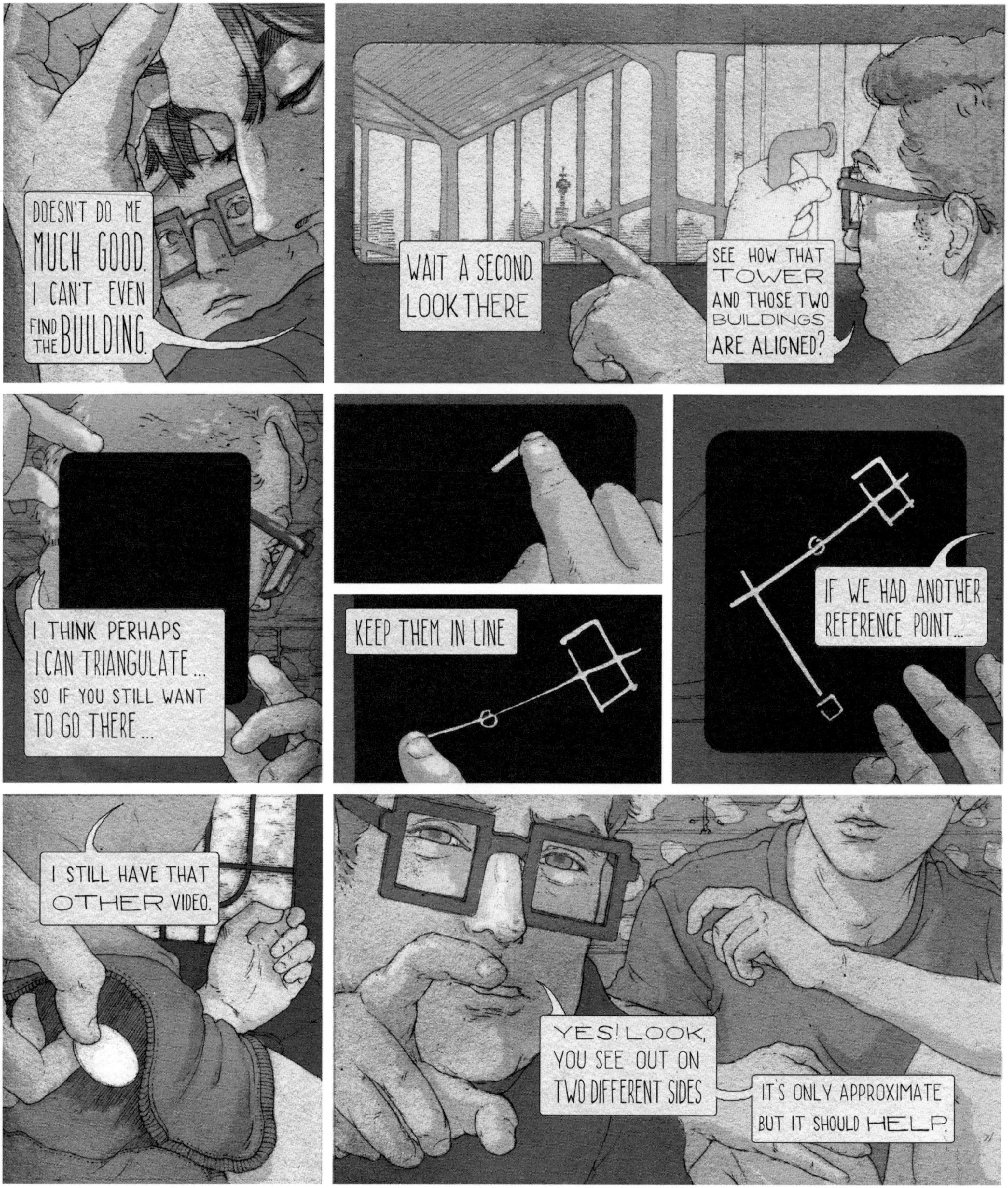
DOESN'T DO ME MUCH GOOD. I CAN'T EVEN FIND THE BUILDING.
WAIT A SECOND. LOOK THERE
SEE HOW THAT TOWER AND THOSE TWO BUILDINGS ARE ALIGNED?
I THINK PERHAPS I CAN TRIANGULATE... SO IF YOU STILL WANT TO GO THERE...
KEEP THEM IN LINE
IF WE HAD ANOTHER REFERENCE POINT...
I STILL HAVE THAT OTHER VIDEO.
YES! LOOK, YOU SEE OUT ON TWO DIFFERENT SIDES
IT'S ONLY APPROXIMATE BUT IT SHOULD HELP.

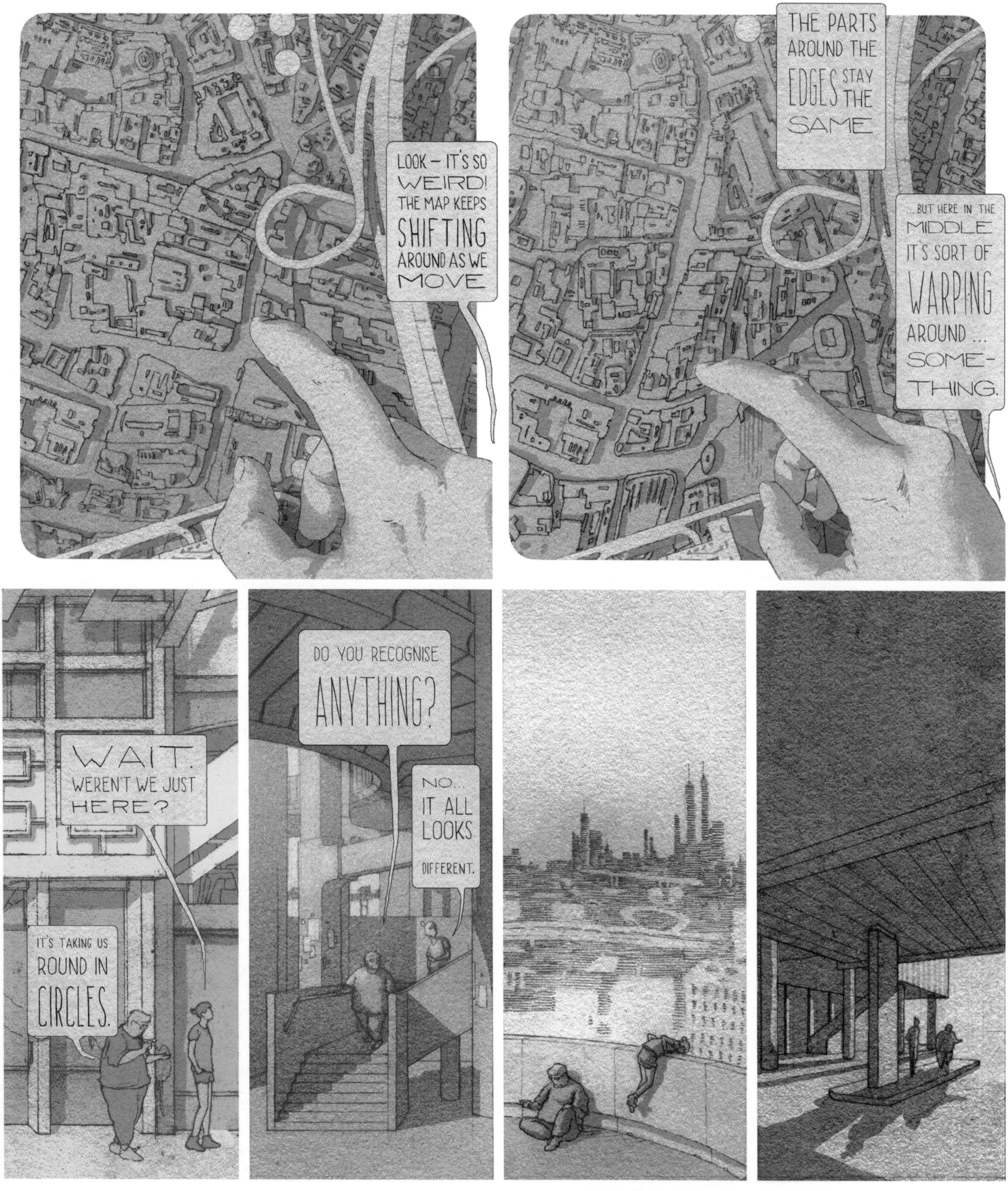
LOOK – IT'S SO WEIRD! THE MAP KEEPS SHIFTING AROUND AS WE MOVE
THE PARTS AROUND THE EDGES STAY THE SAME
...BUT HERE IN THE MIDDLE IT'S SORT OF WARPING AROUND ... SOME-THING.
WAIT. WEREN'T WE JUST HERE?
IT'S TAKING US ROUND IN CIRCLES.
DO YOU RECOGNISE ANYTHING?
NO... IT ALL LOOKS DIFFERENT.

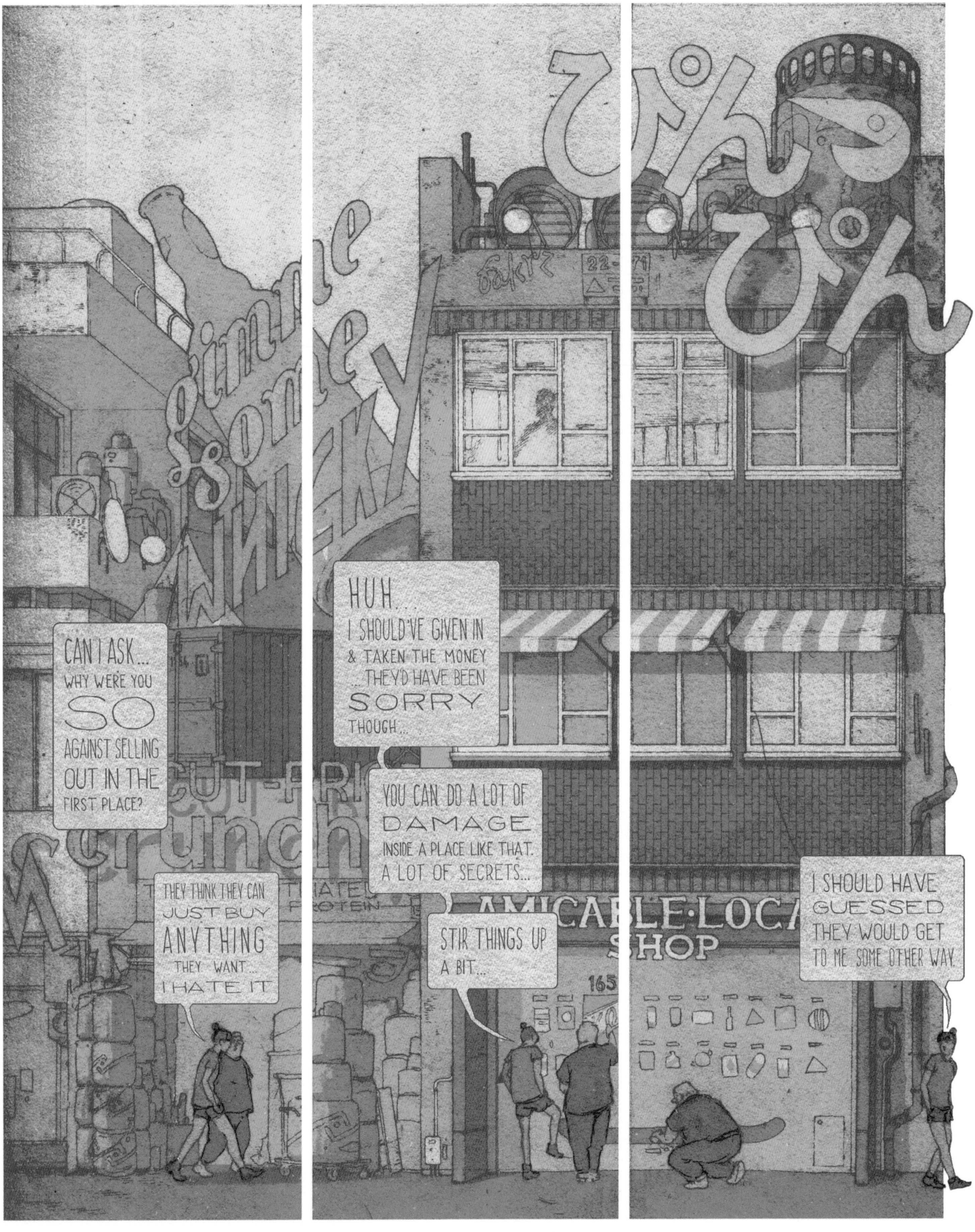
gimme some WACKY
CAN I ASK... WHY WERE YOU SO AGAINST SELLING OUT IN THE FIRST PLACE?
THEY THINK THEY CAN JUST BUY ANYTHING THEY WANT... I HATE IT
HUH... I SHOULD'VE GIVEN IN & TAKEN THE MONEY ...THEY'D HAVE BEEN SORRY THOUGH...
YOU CAN DO A LOT OF DAMAGE INSIDE A PLACE LIKE THAT. A LOT OF SECRETS...
STIR THINGS UP A BIT...
I SHOULD HAVE GUESSED THEY WOULD GET TO ME SOME OTHER WAY.
SHOP

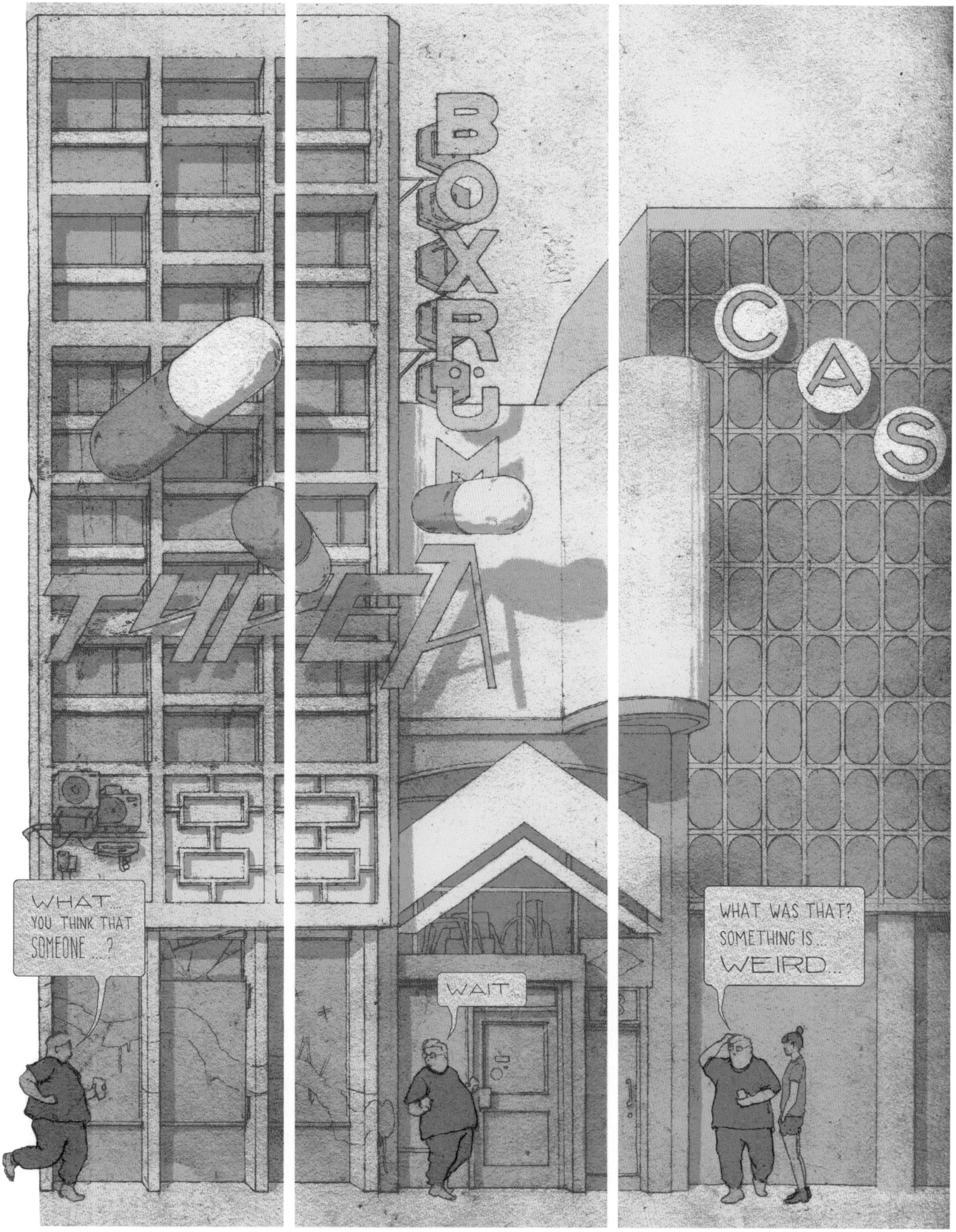
WHAT... YOU THINK THAT SOMEONE ...?
WAIT...
WHAT WAS THAT? SOMETHING IS... WEIRD...

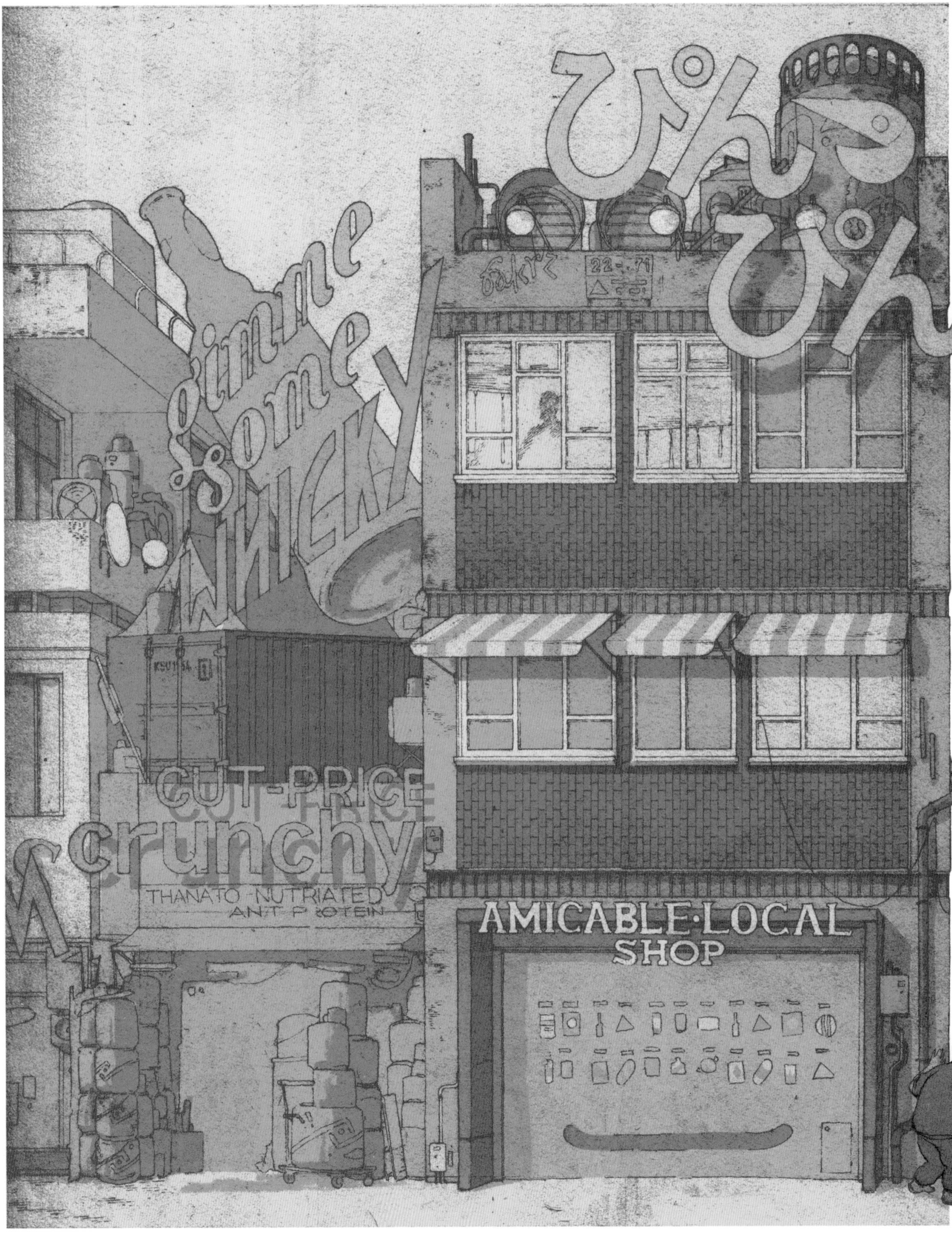
ぴんぴん
gimme some WHICKY
CUT-PRICE crunchy
THANATO-NUTRIATED ANT PROTEIN
AMICABLE·LOCAL SHOP

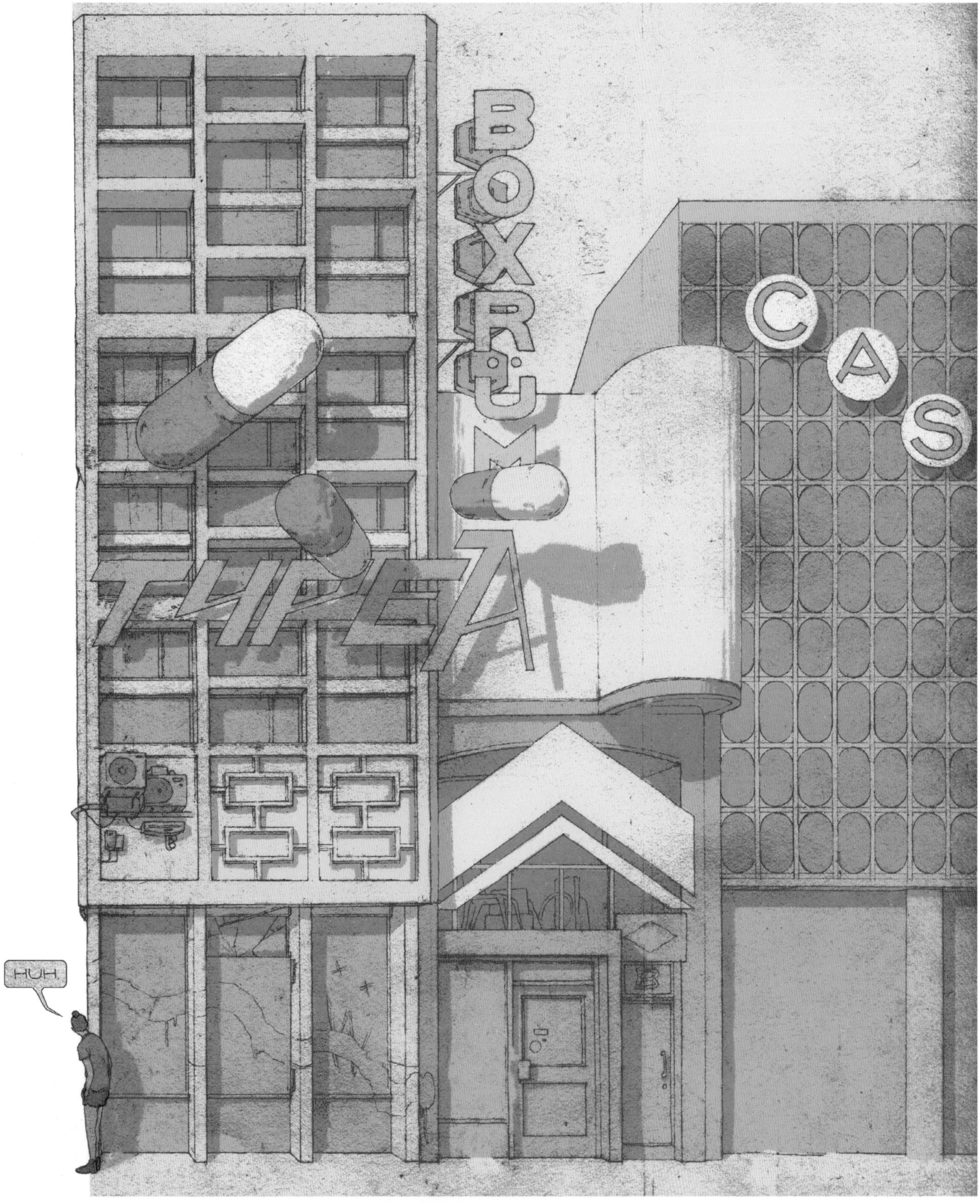
BOXRUM
CAS
HUH.

UGH — BE CAREFUL!
OOH I REALLY DON'T LIKE THIS. LET'S JUST...
FIN!

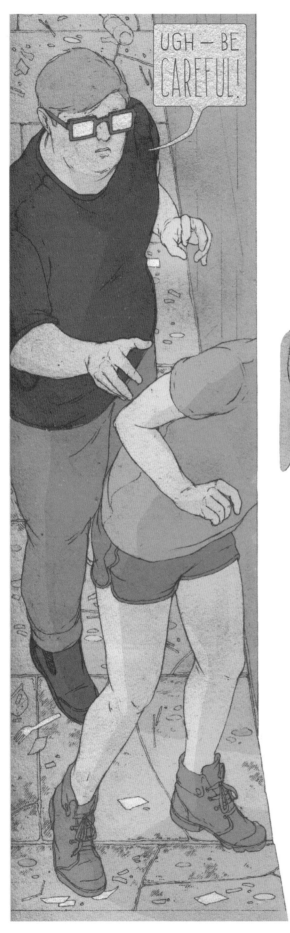

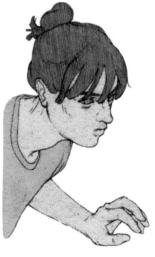

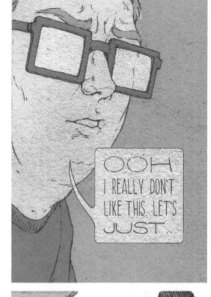

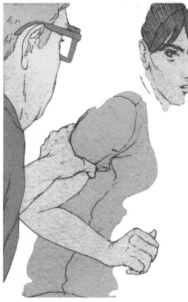

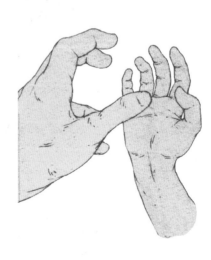

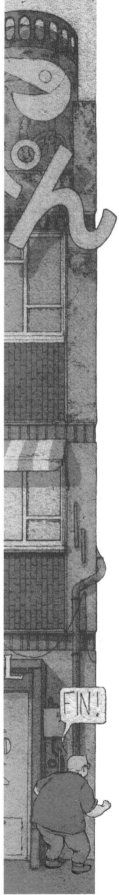

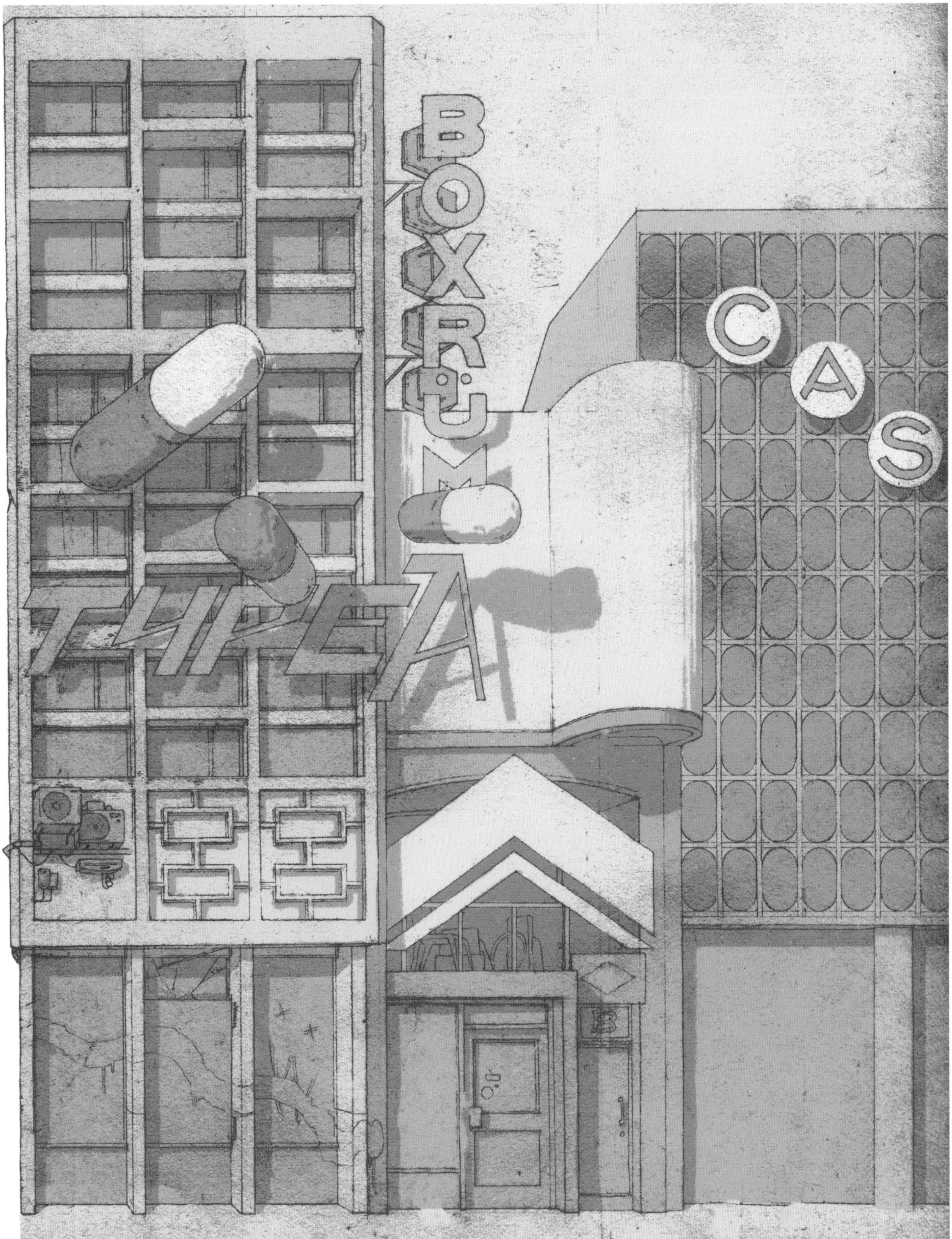
CAS

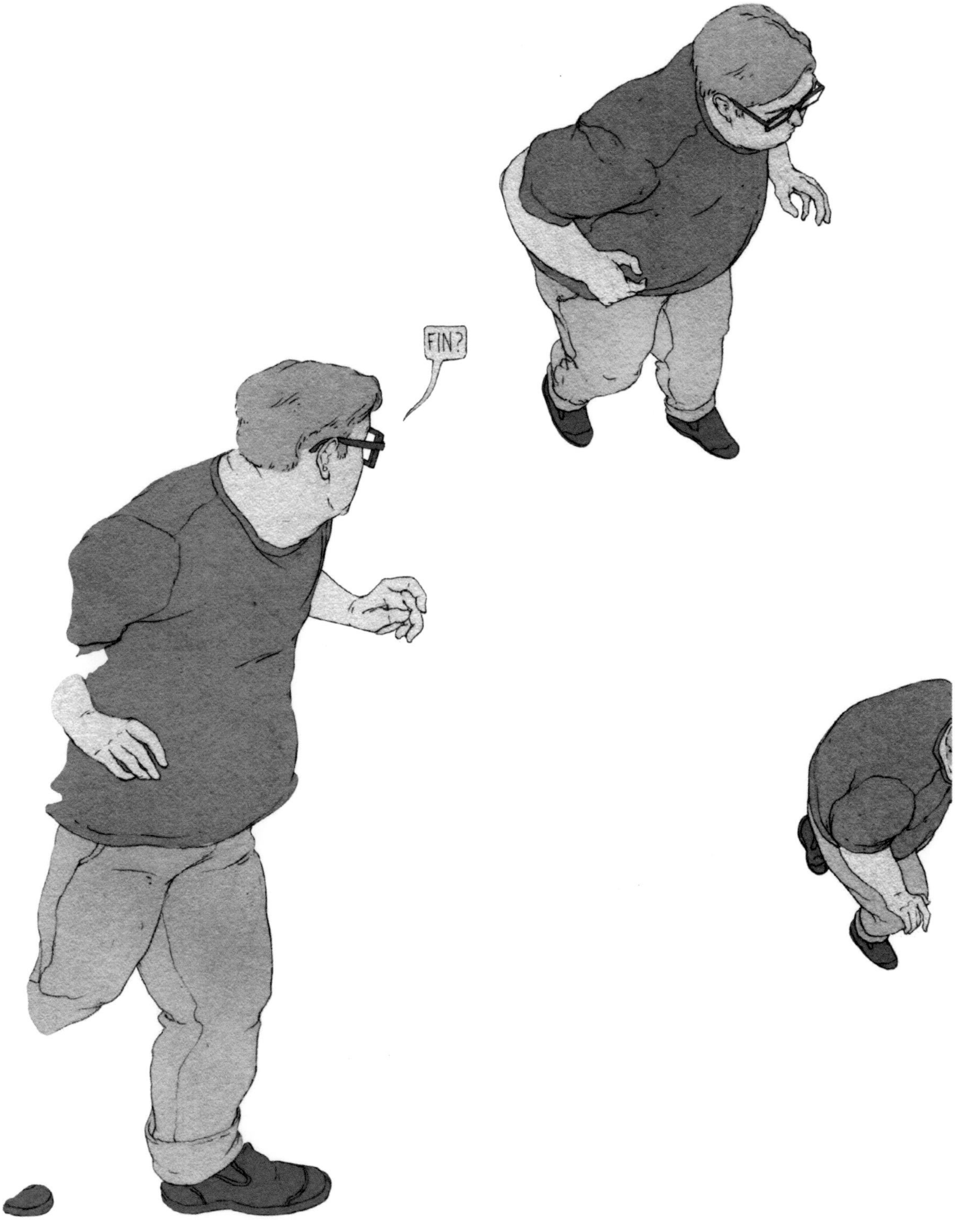
FIN?

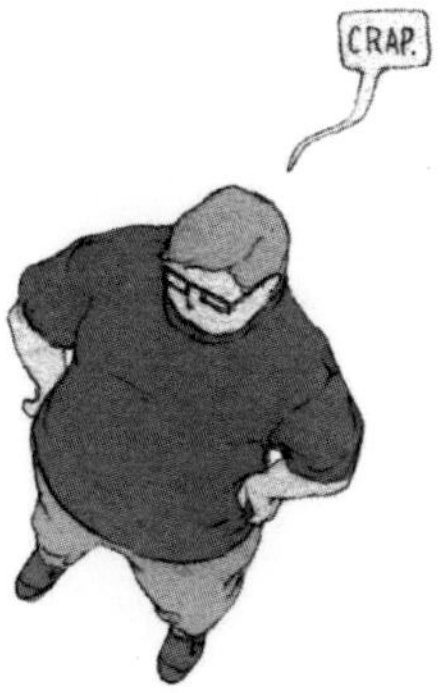
CRAP.

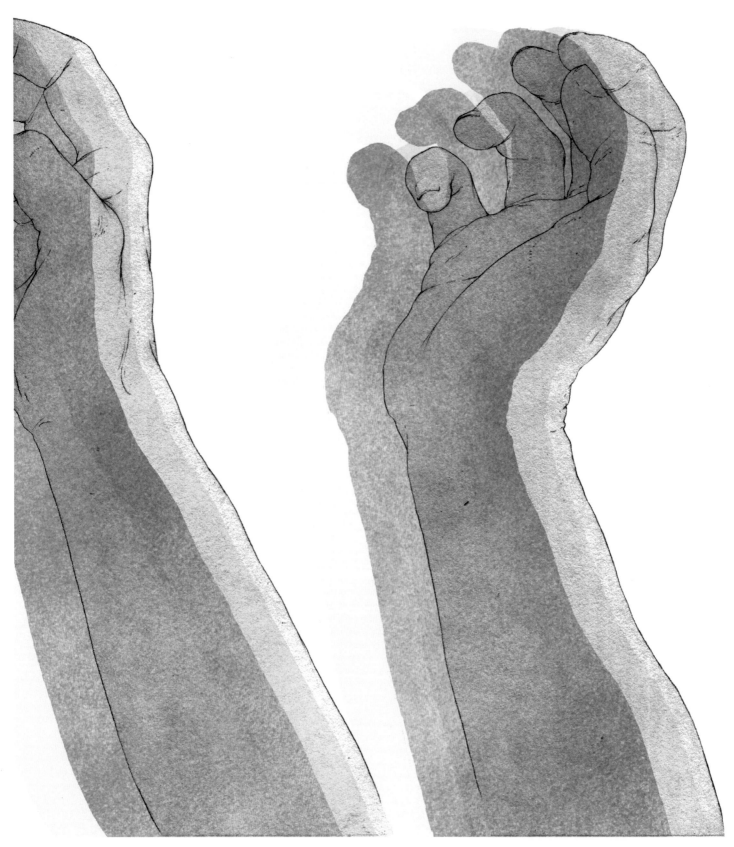

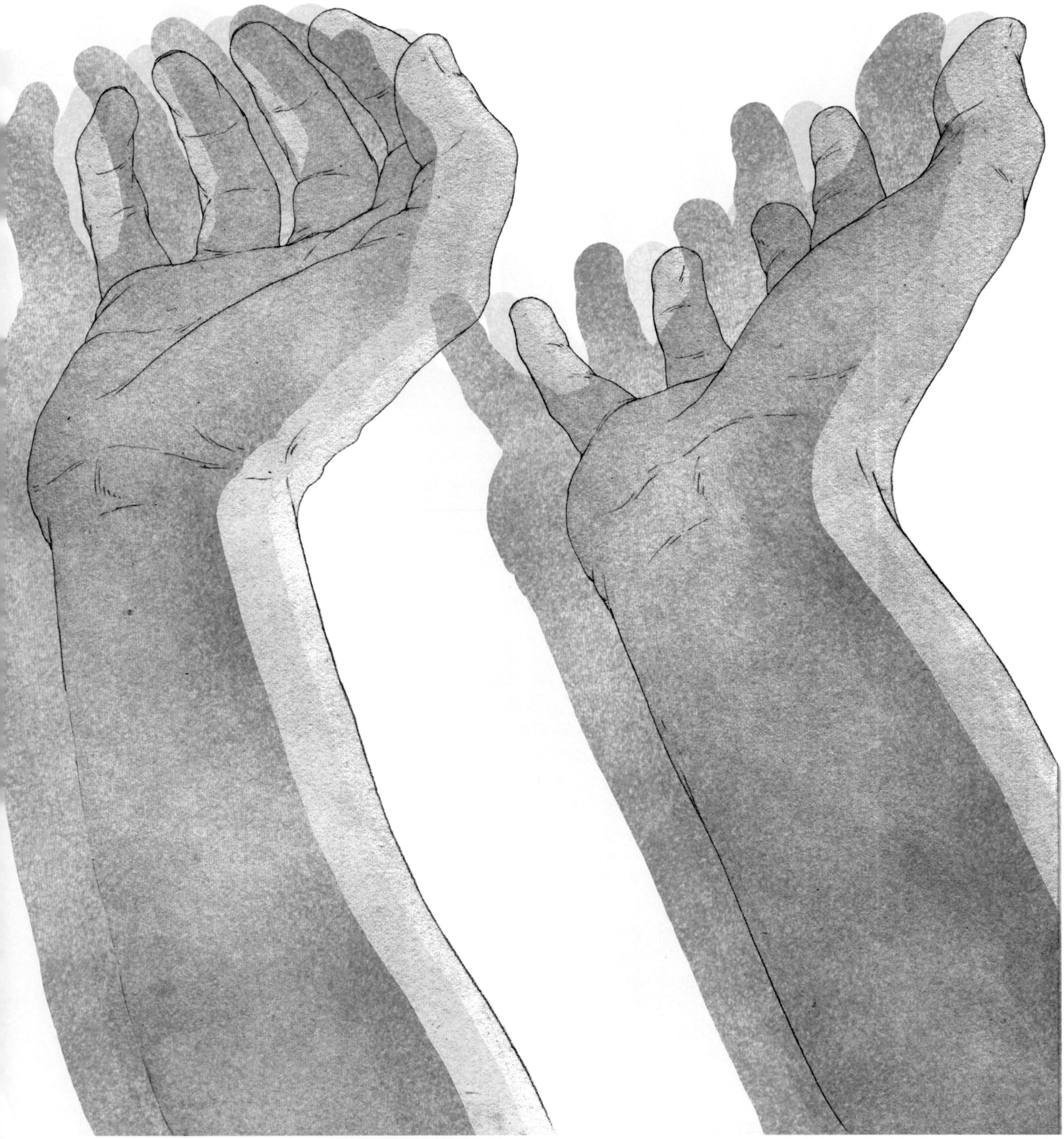

OW!
WHAT WAS...?
...MUD?

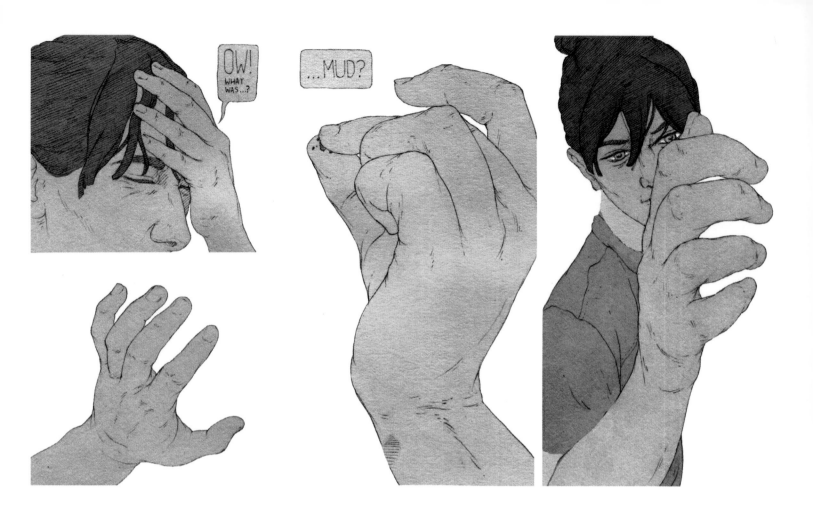

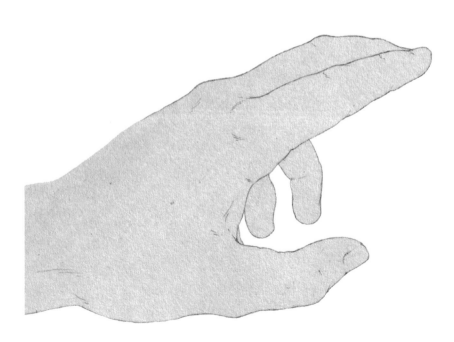

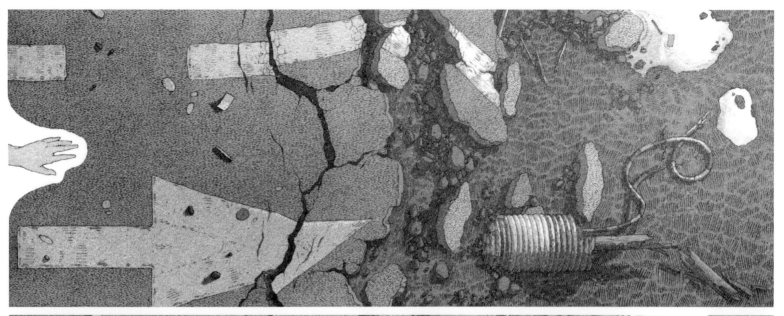

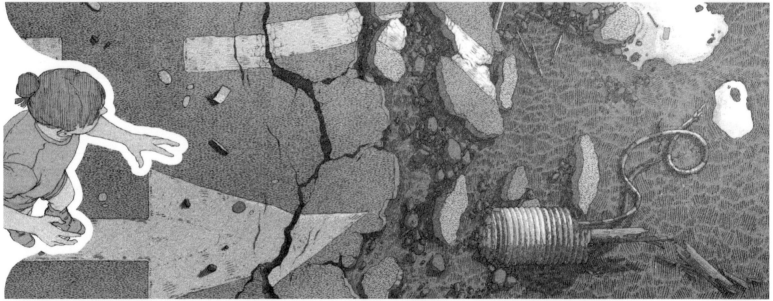

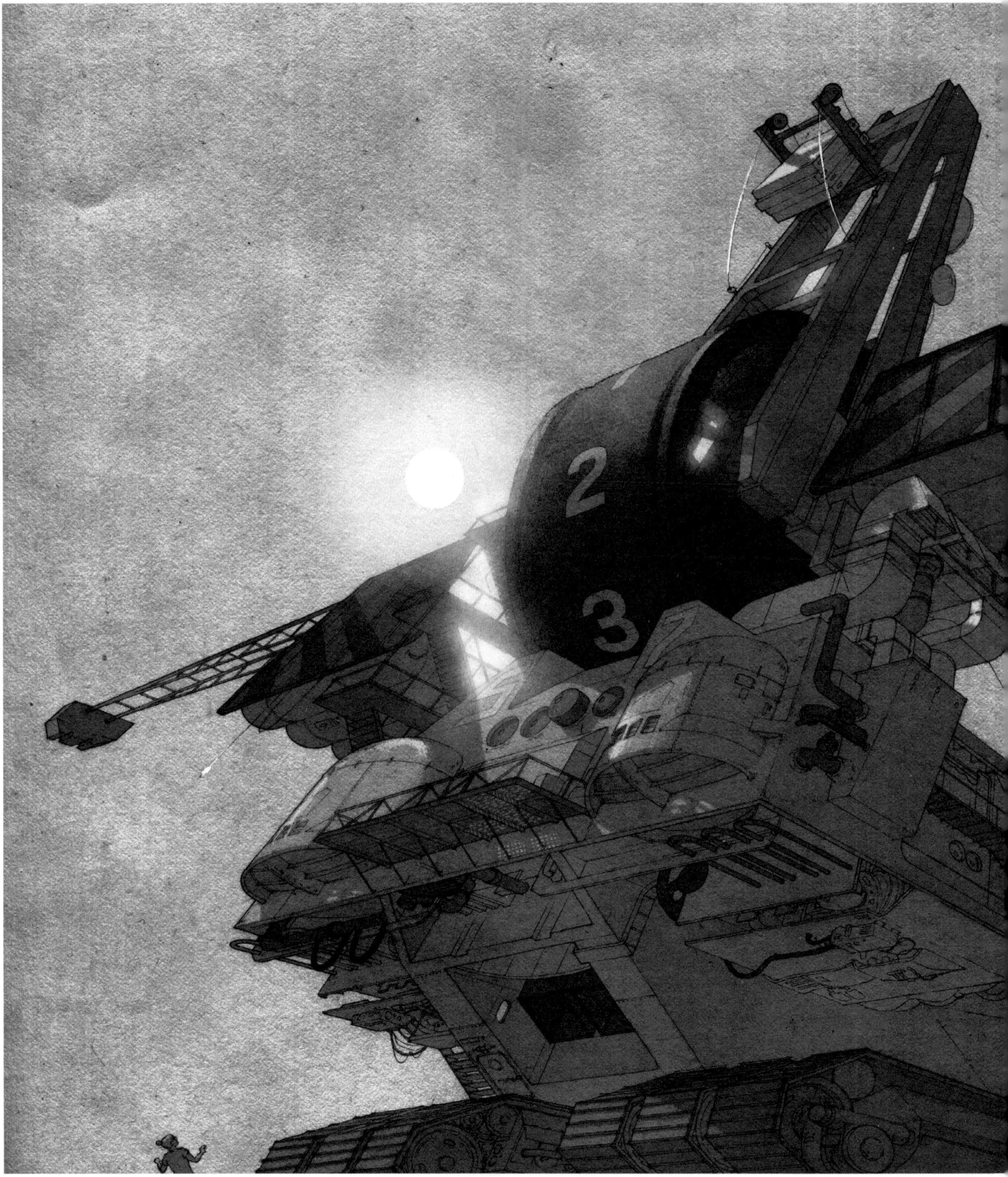
2
3

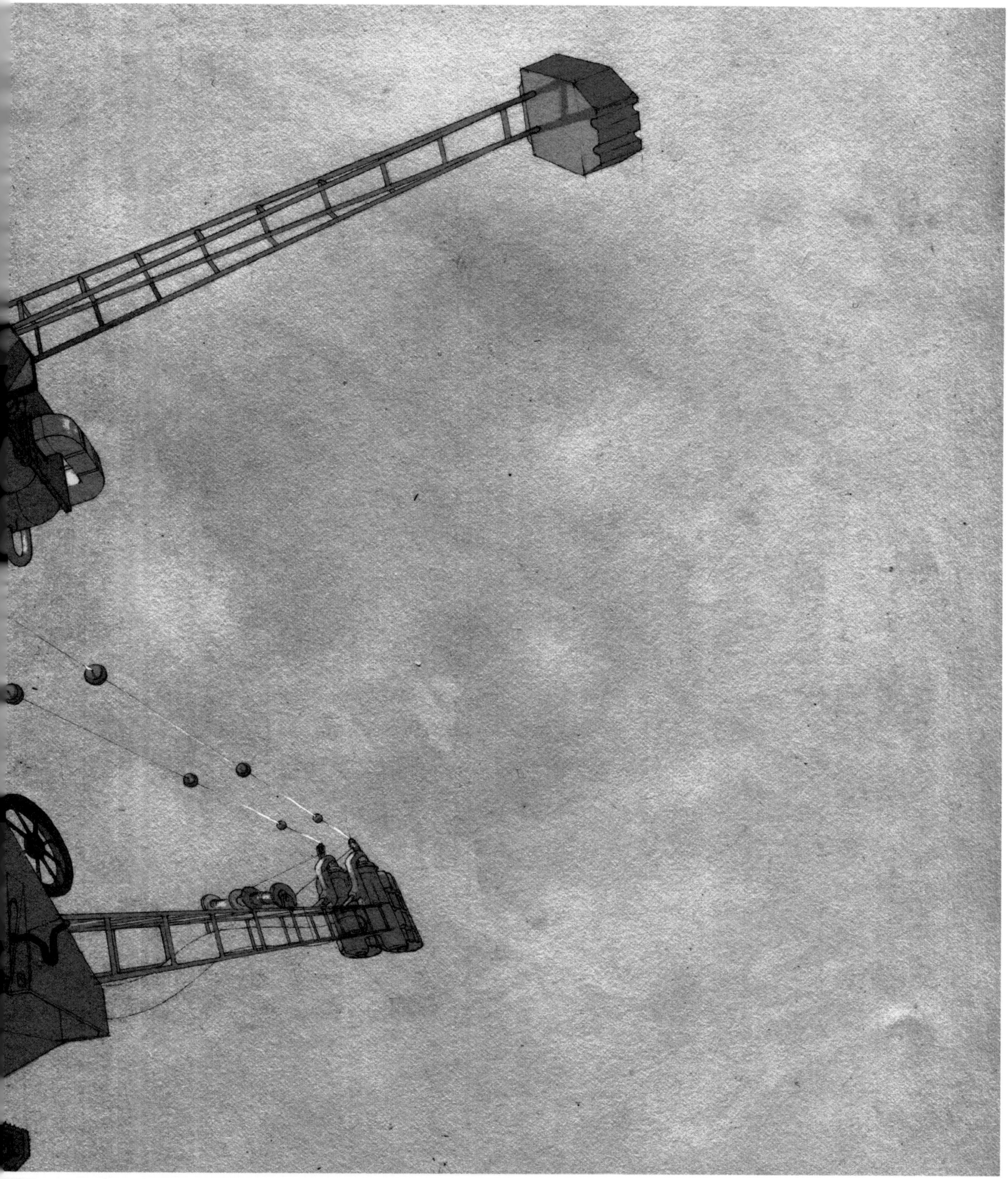

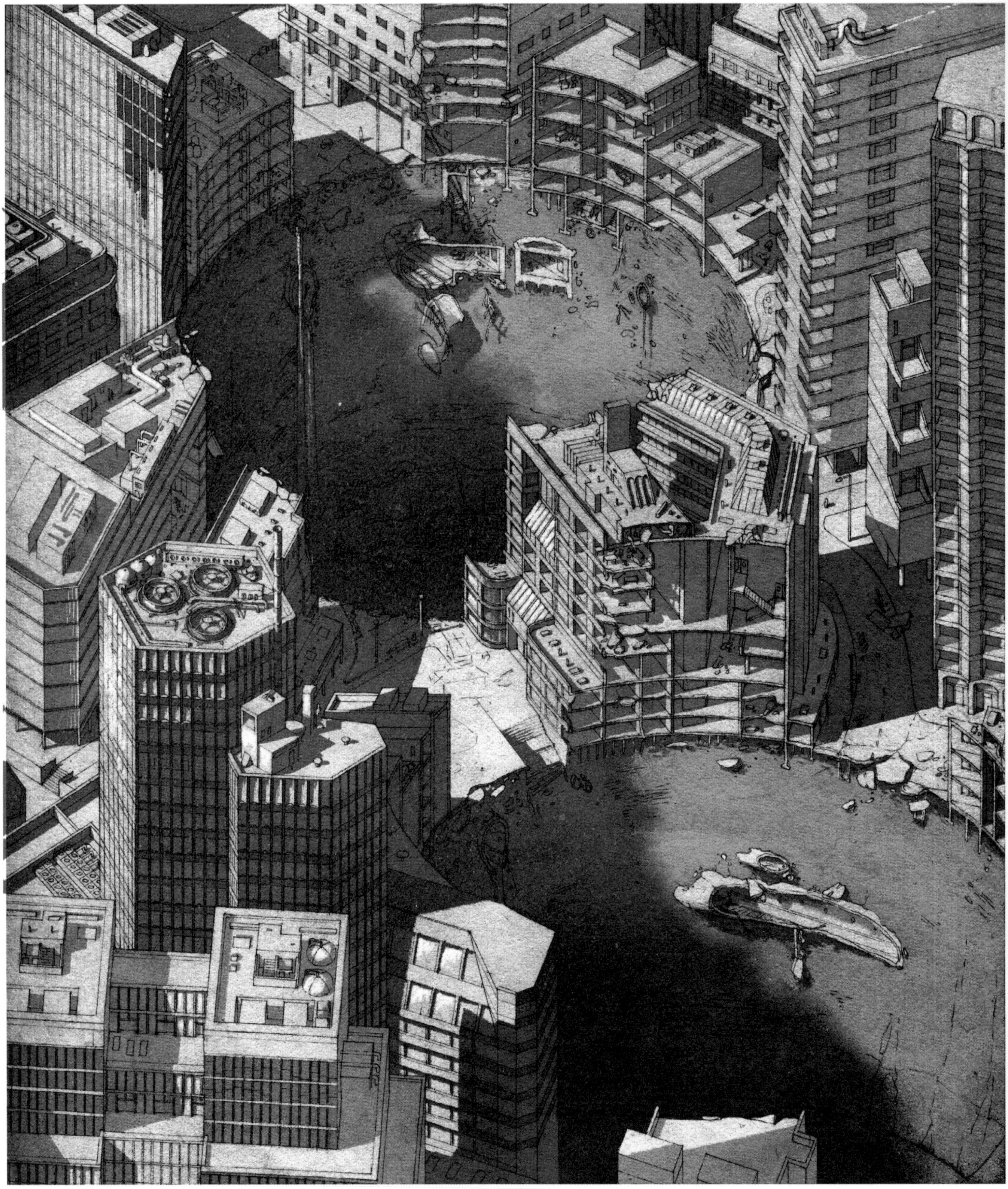

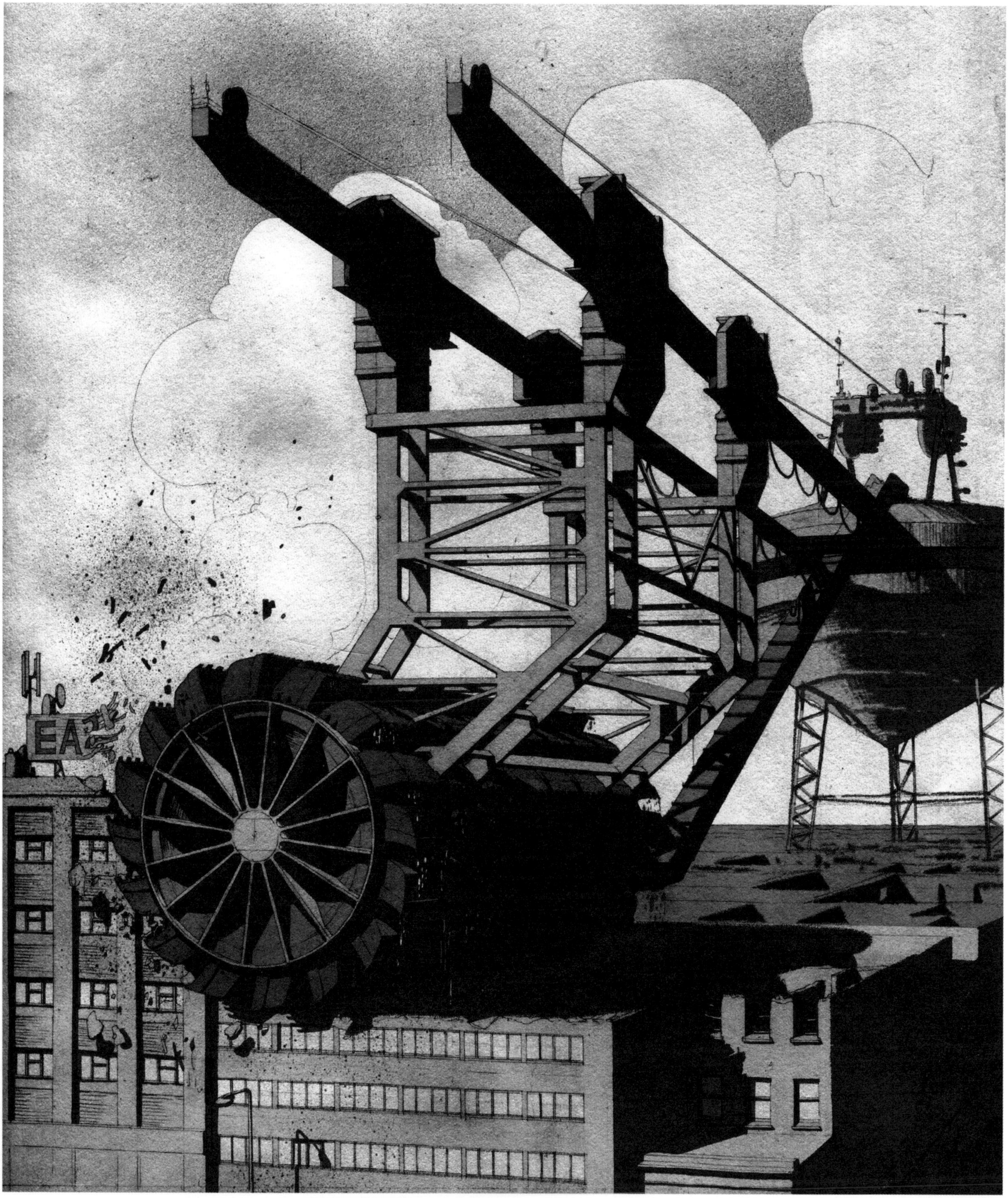
EA

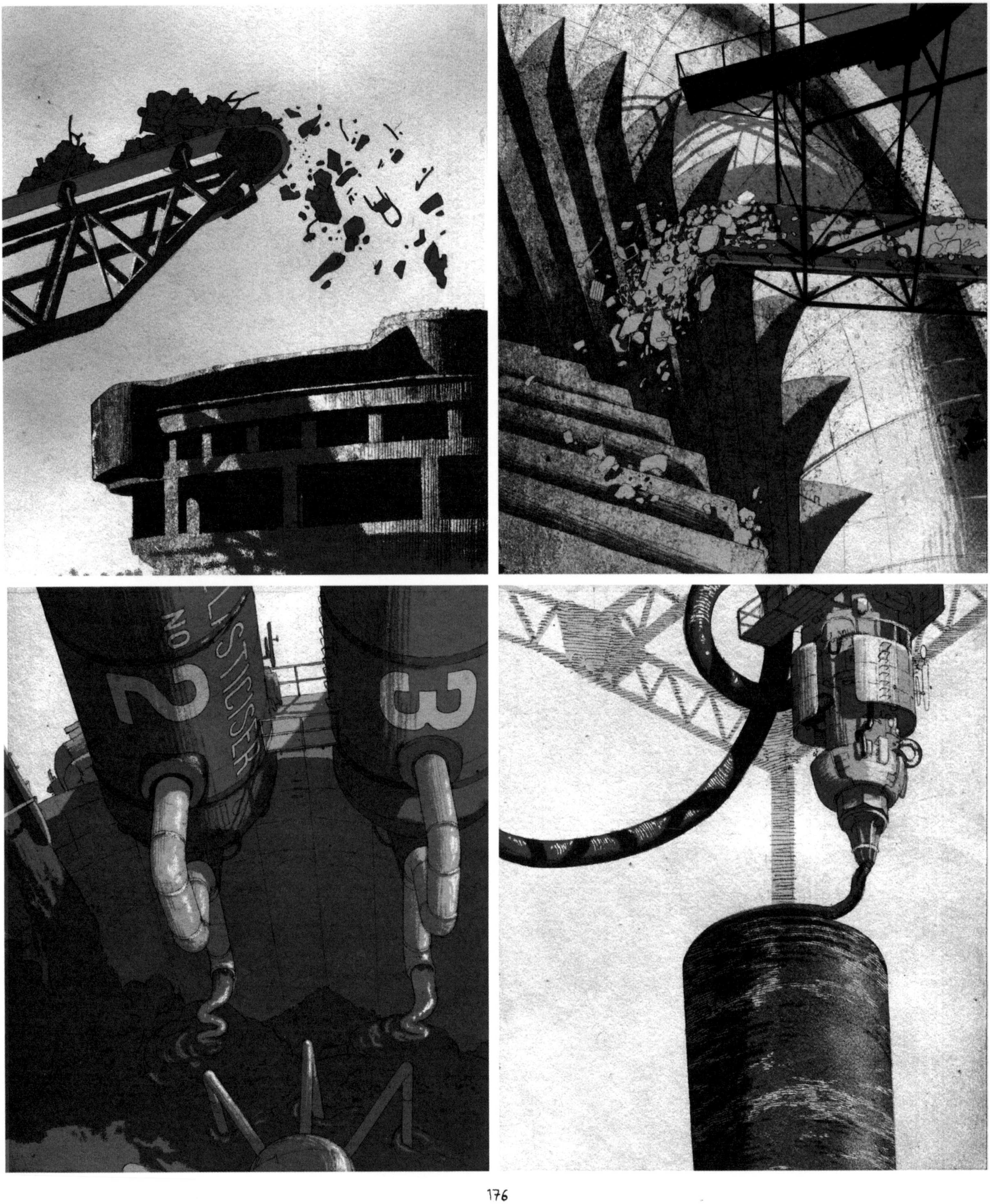
NO
2
3

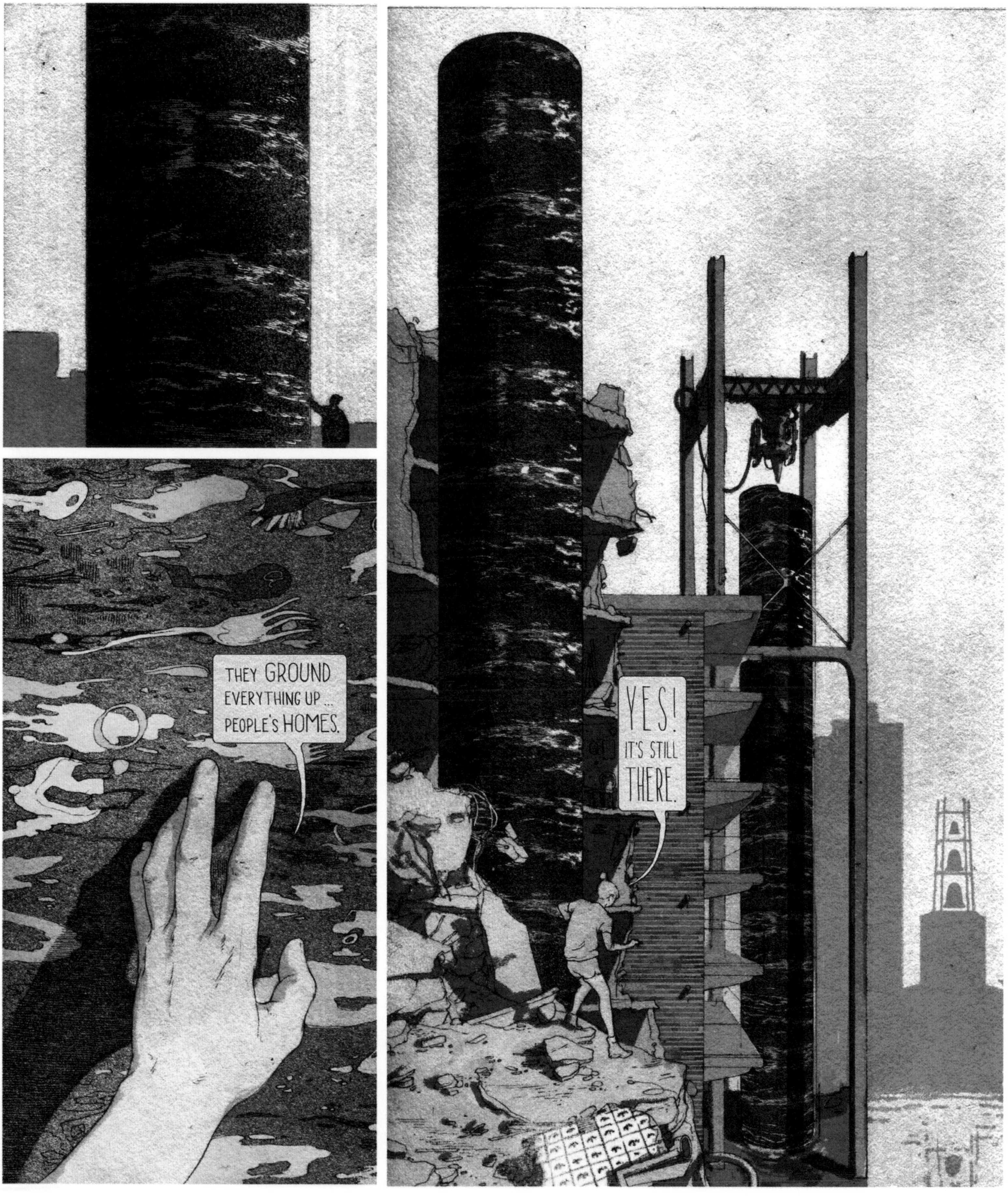
THEY GROUND EVERYTHING UP... PEOPLE'S HOMES.
YES! IT'S STILL THERE.

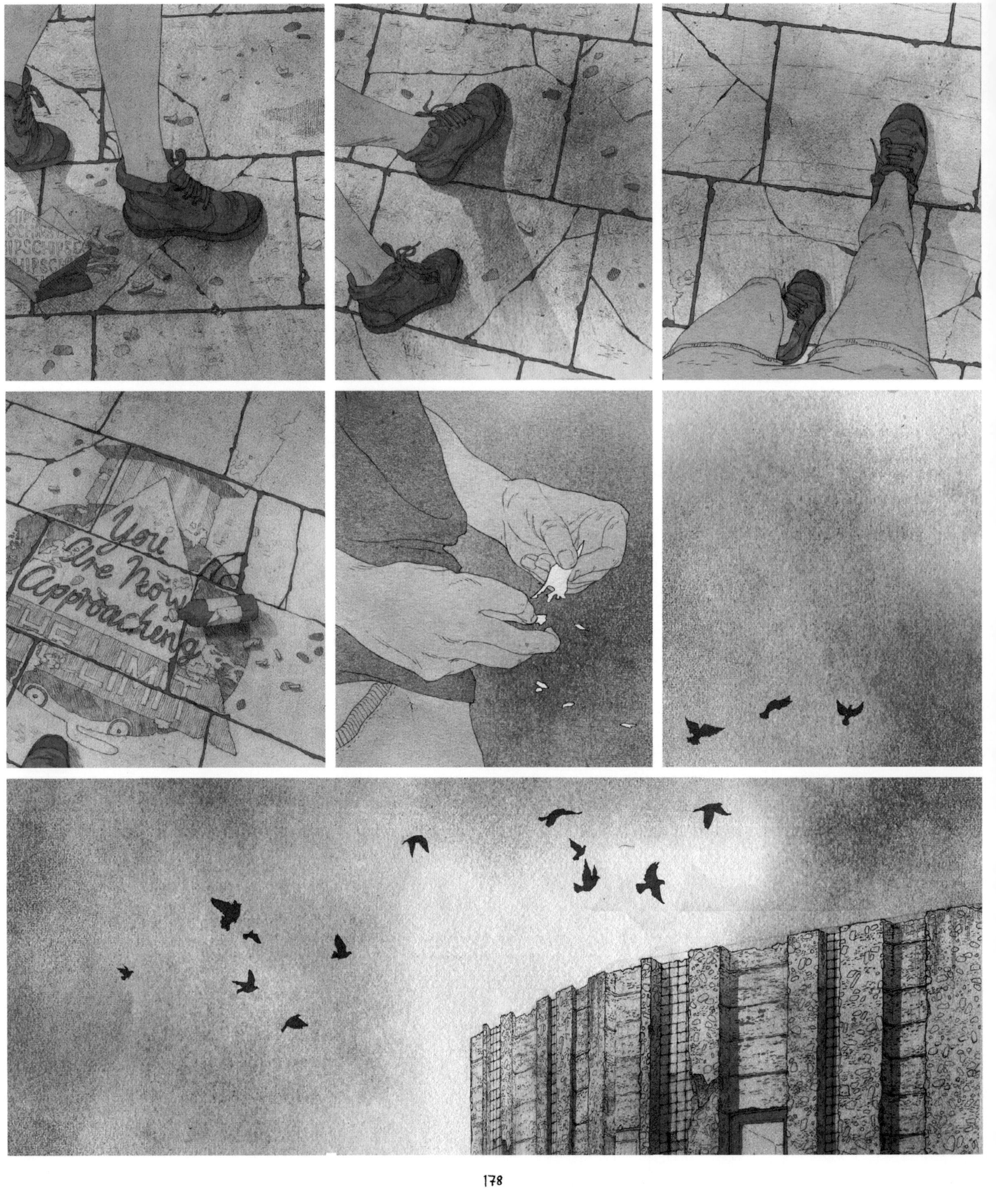
You Are Now Approaching

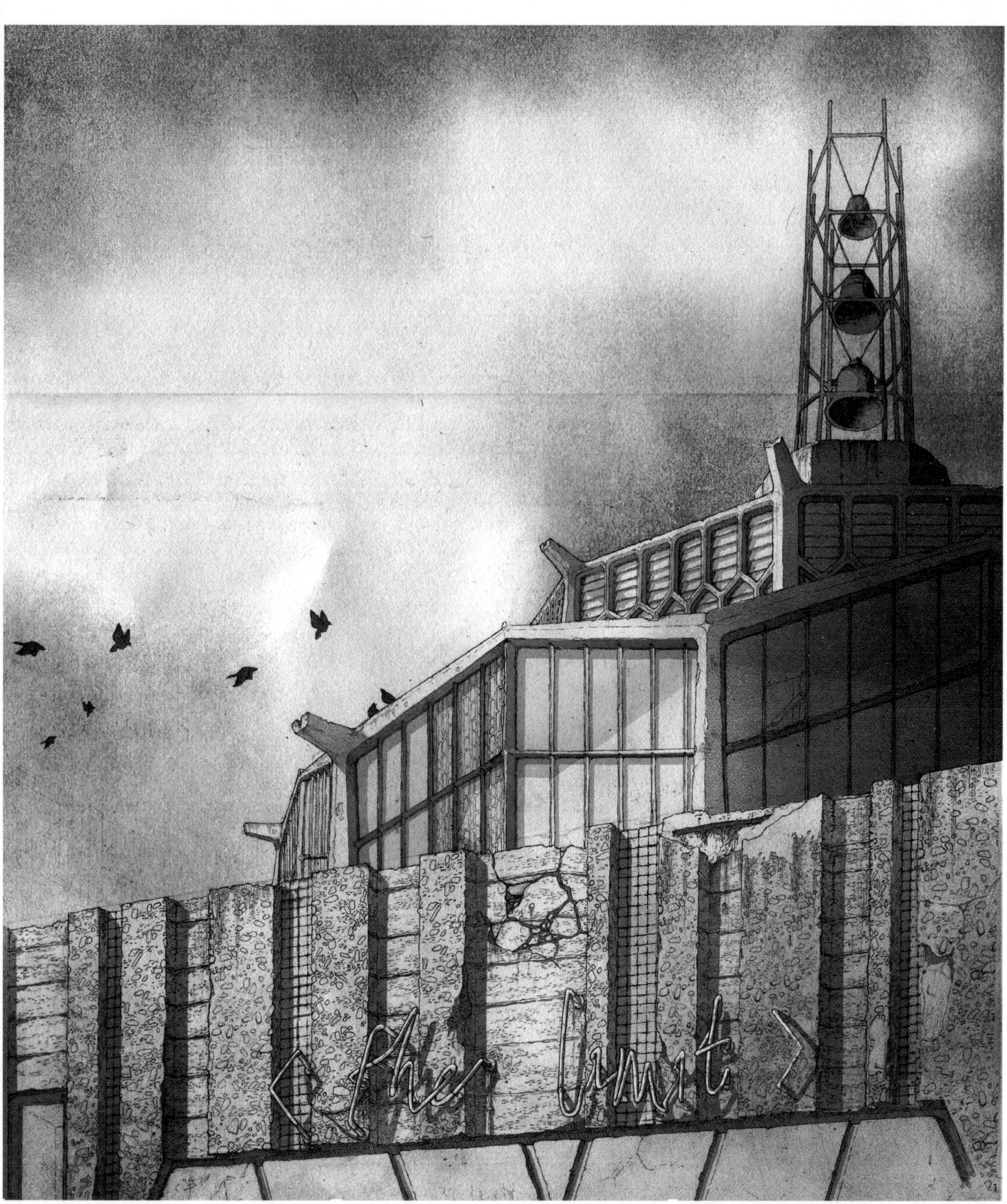

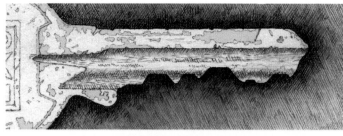

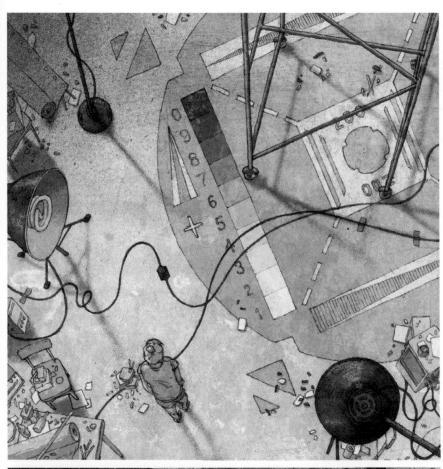
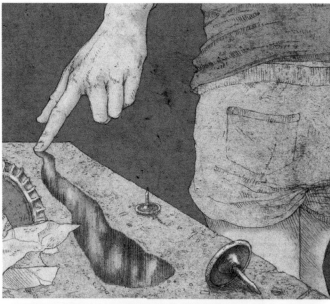
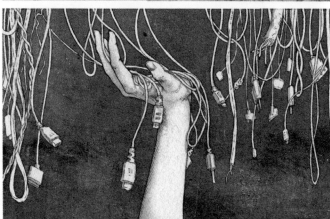

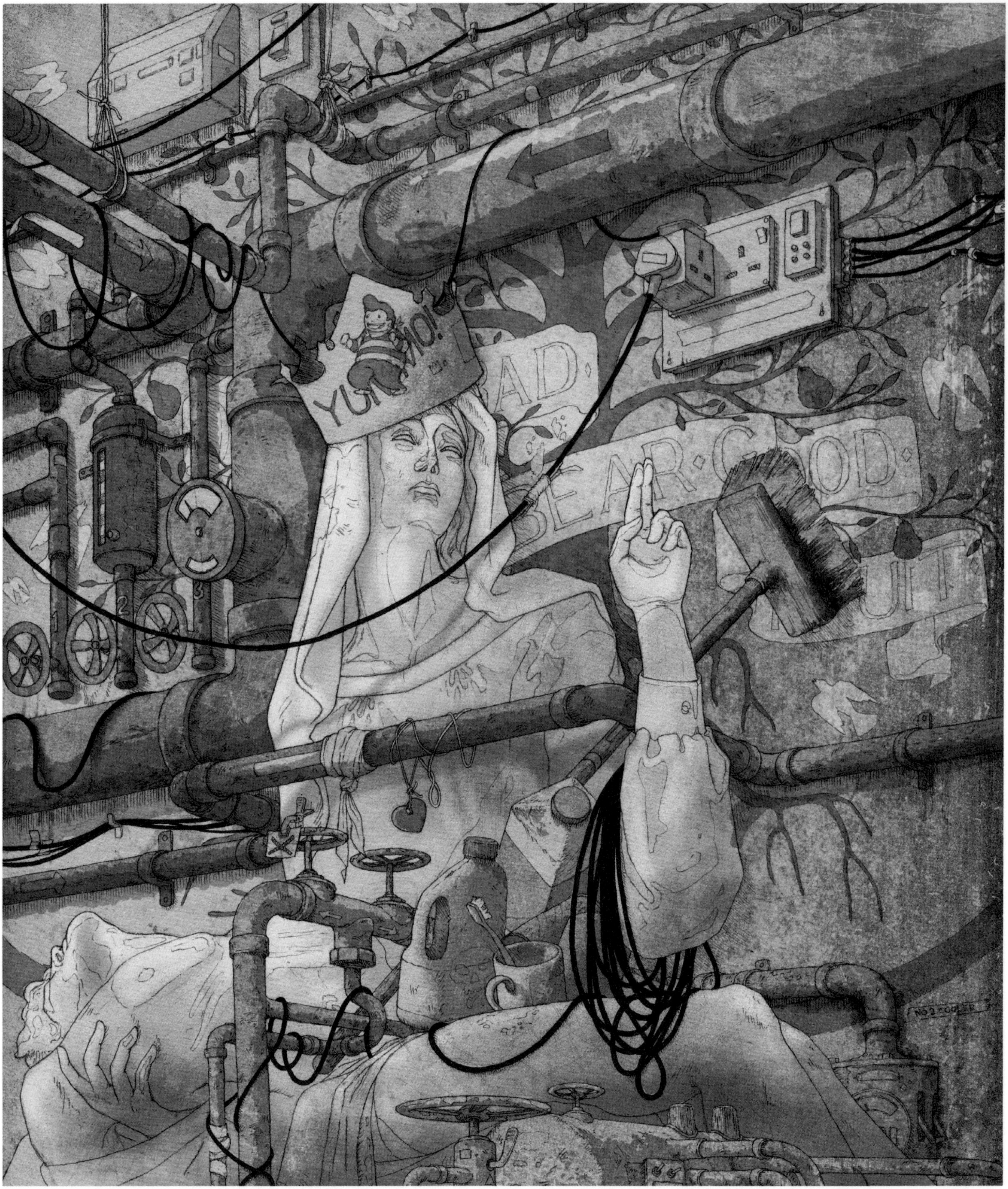
NO2 COOLER

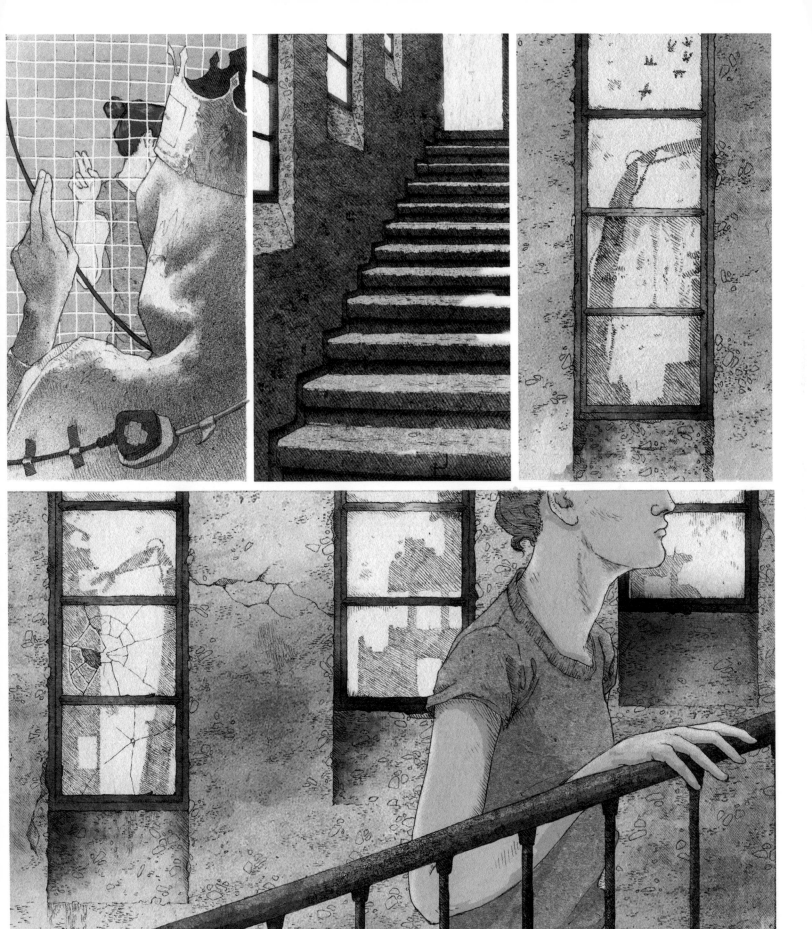

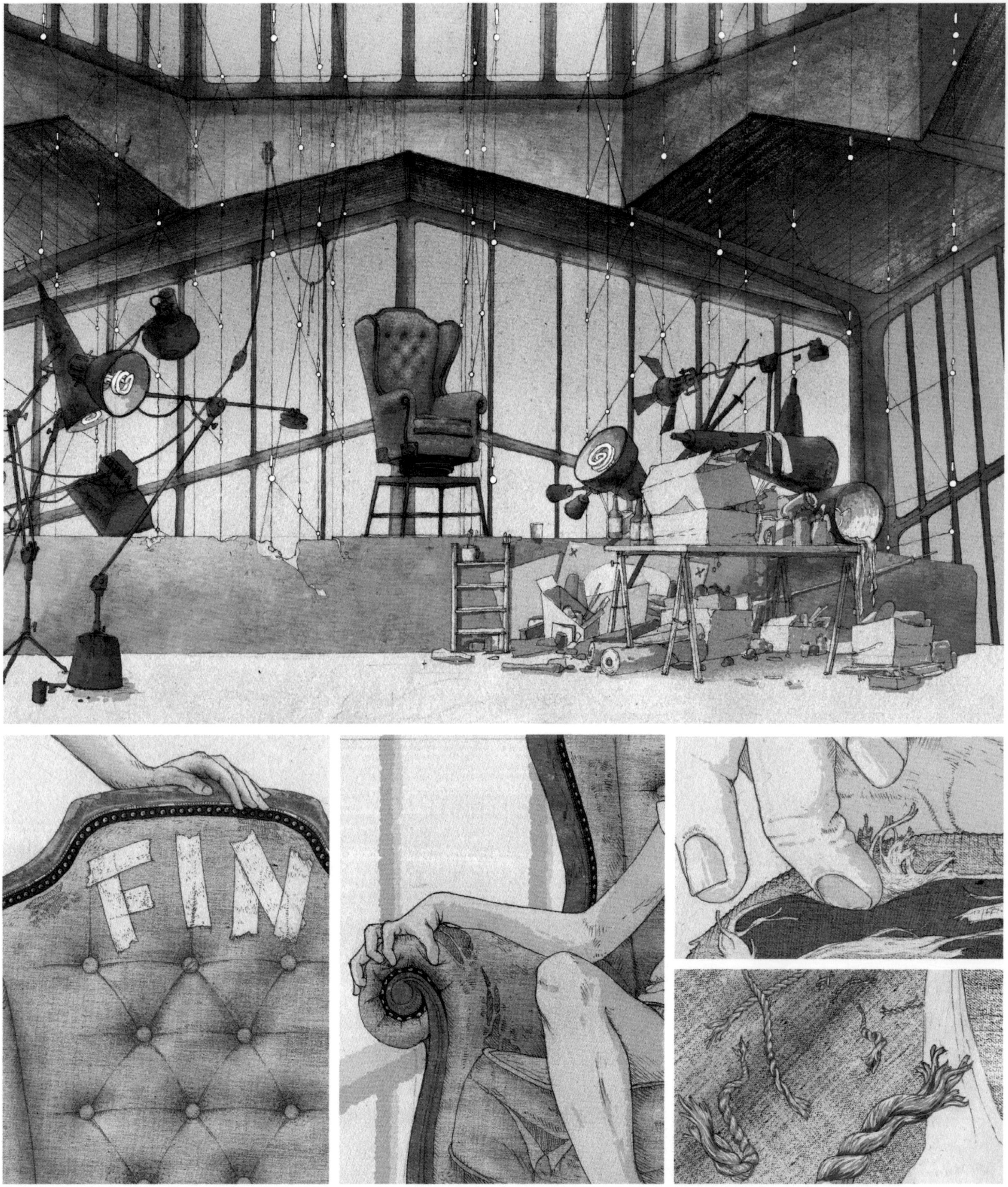
FIN

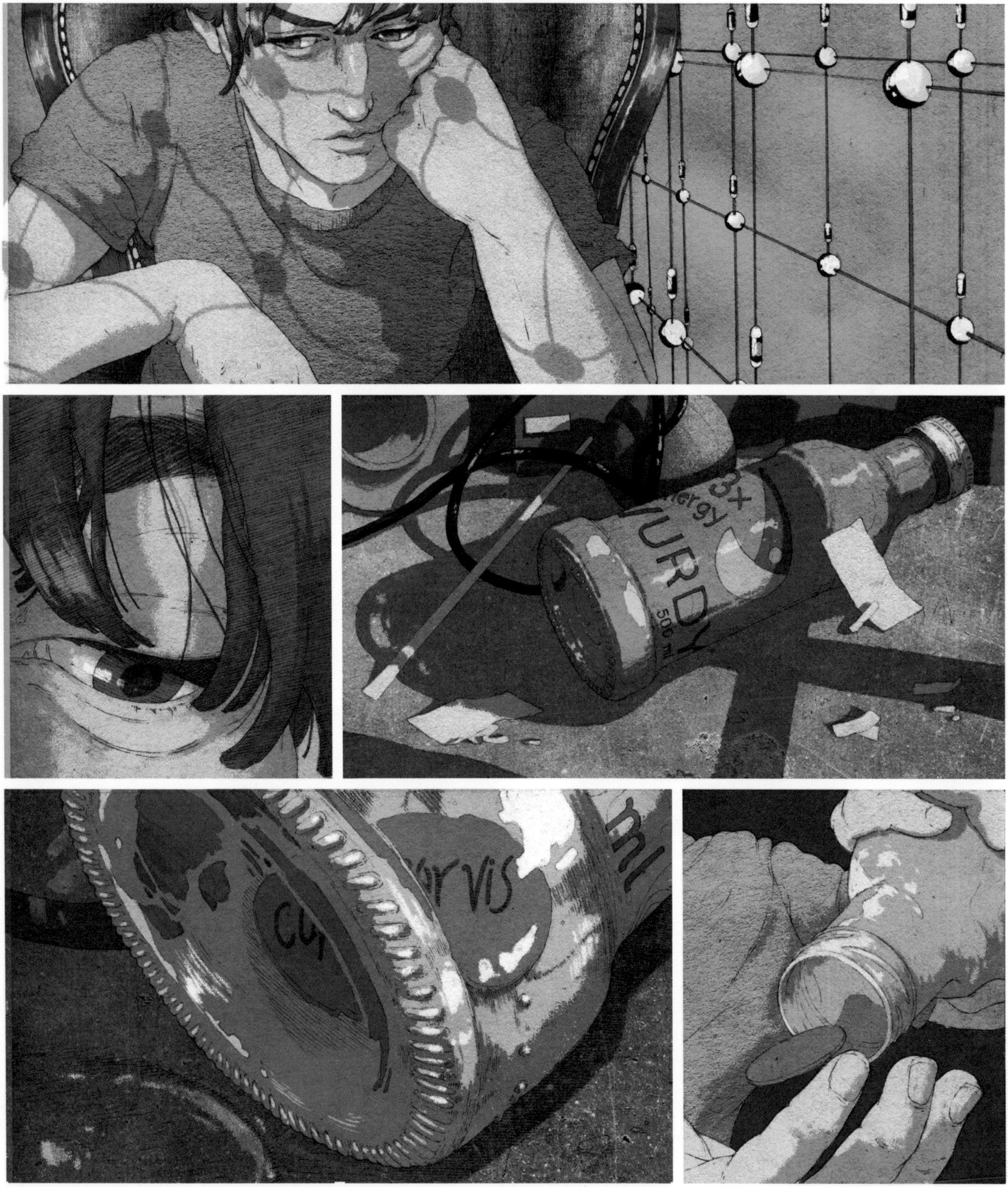
3x
500 ml

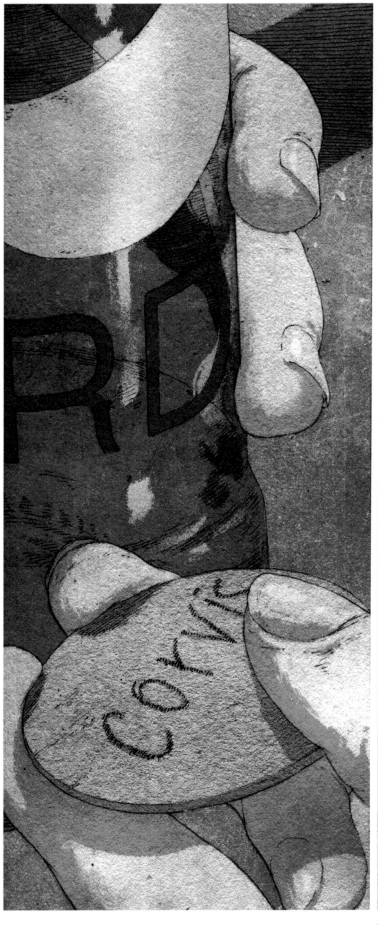
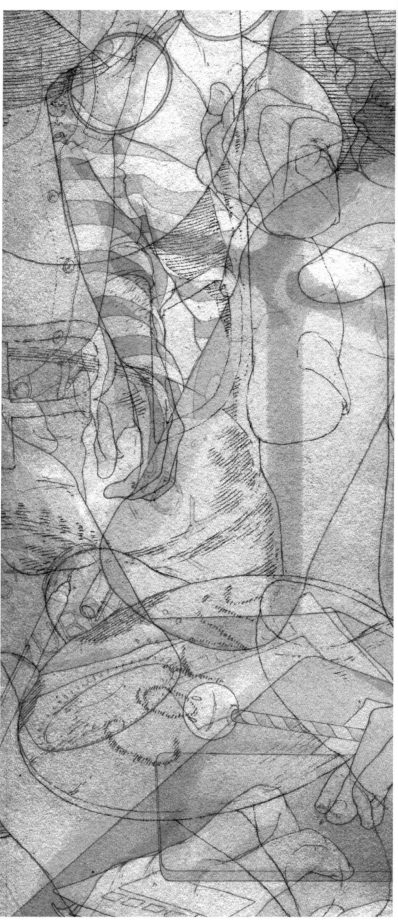

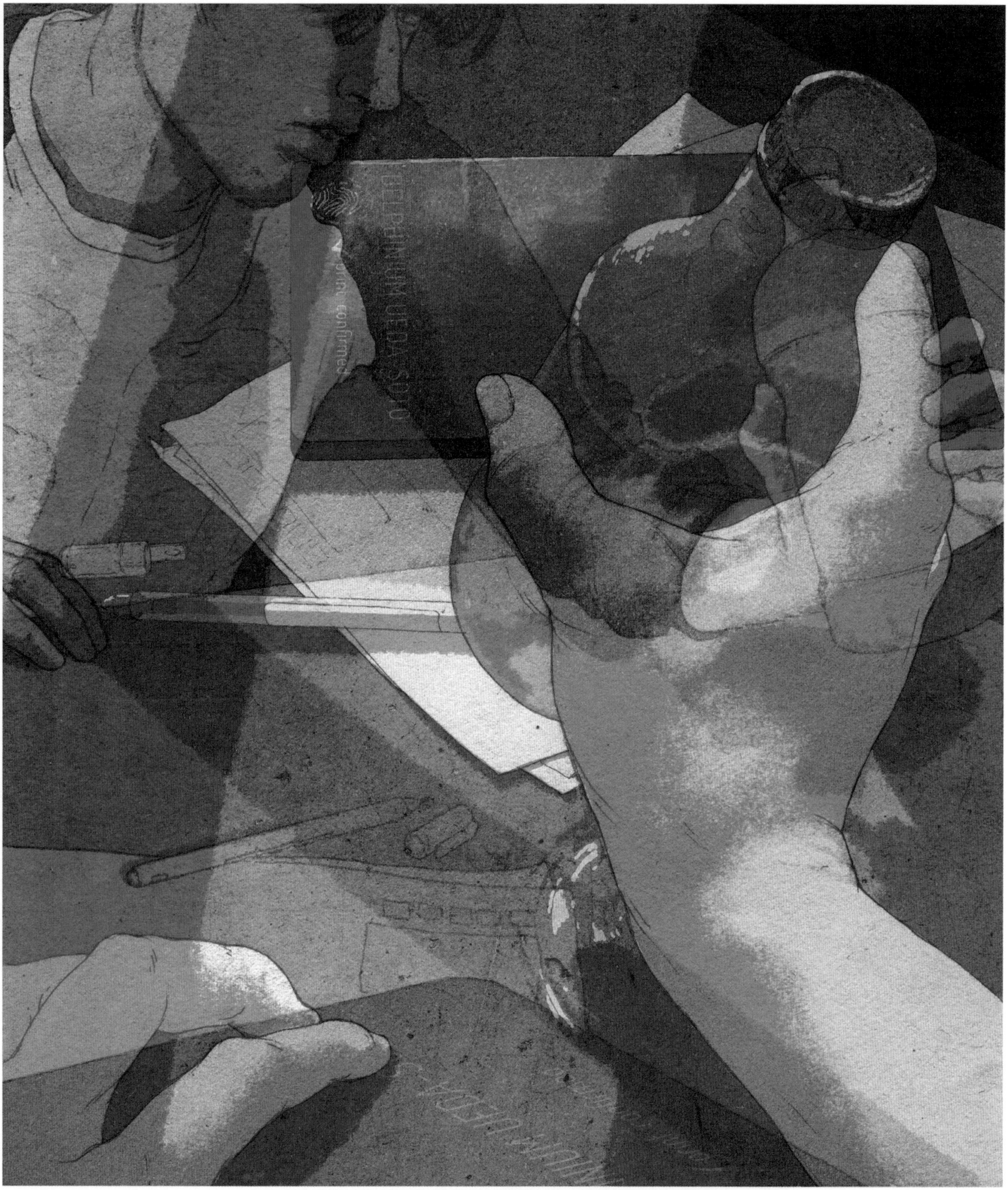

DELPHINIUM UEDA SOFU
print confirmed

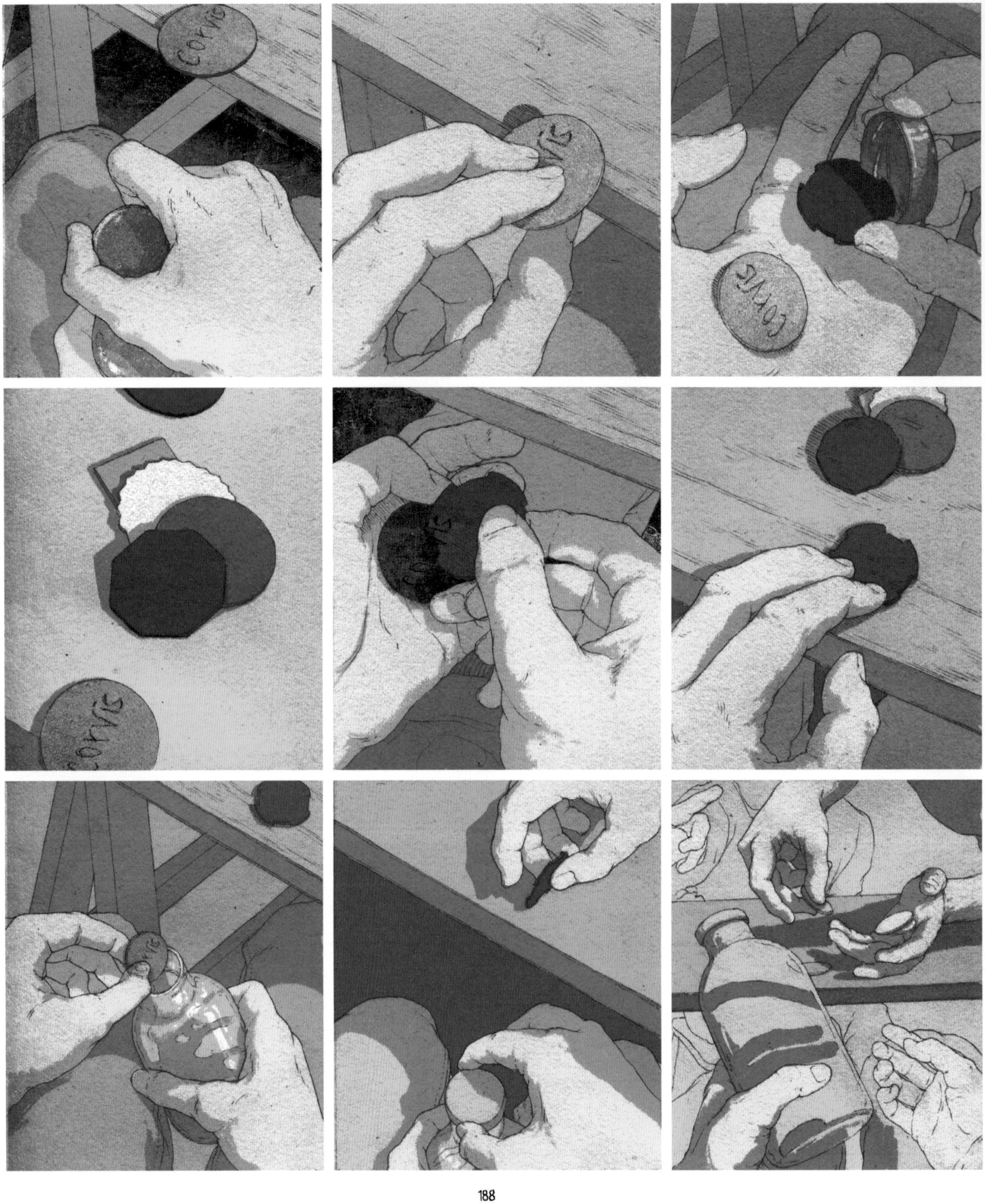

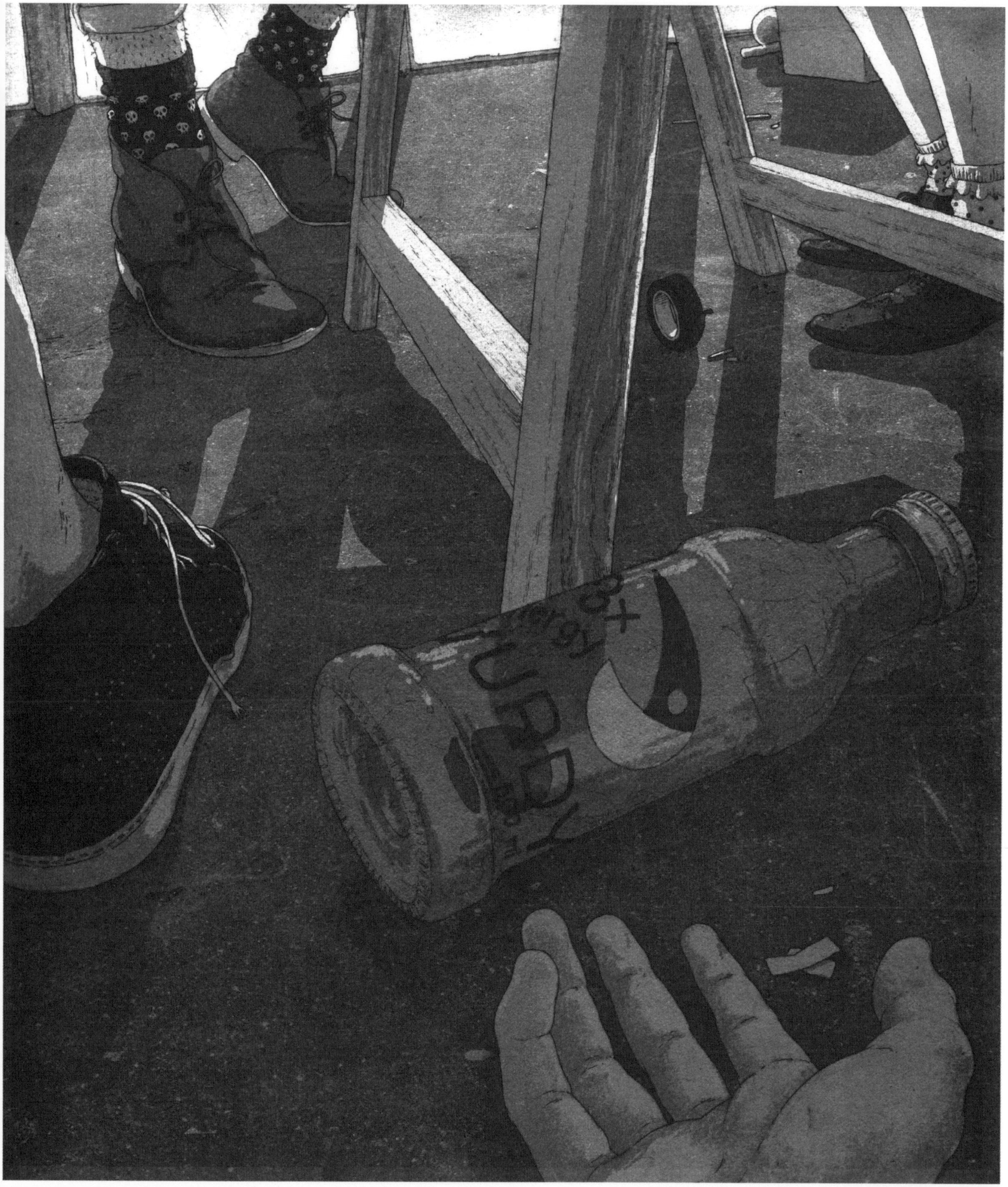

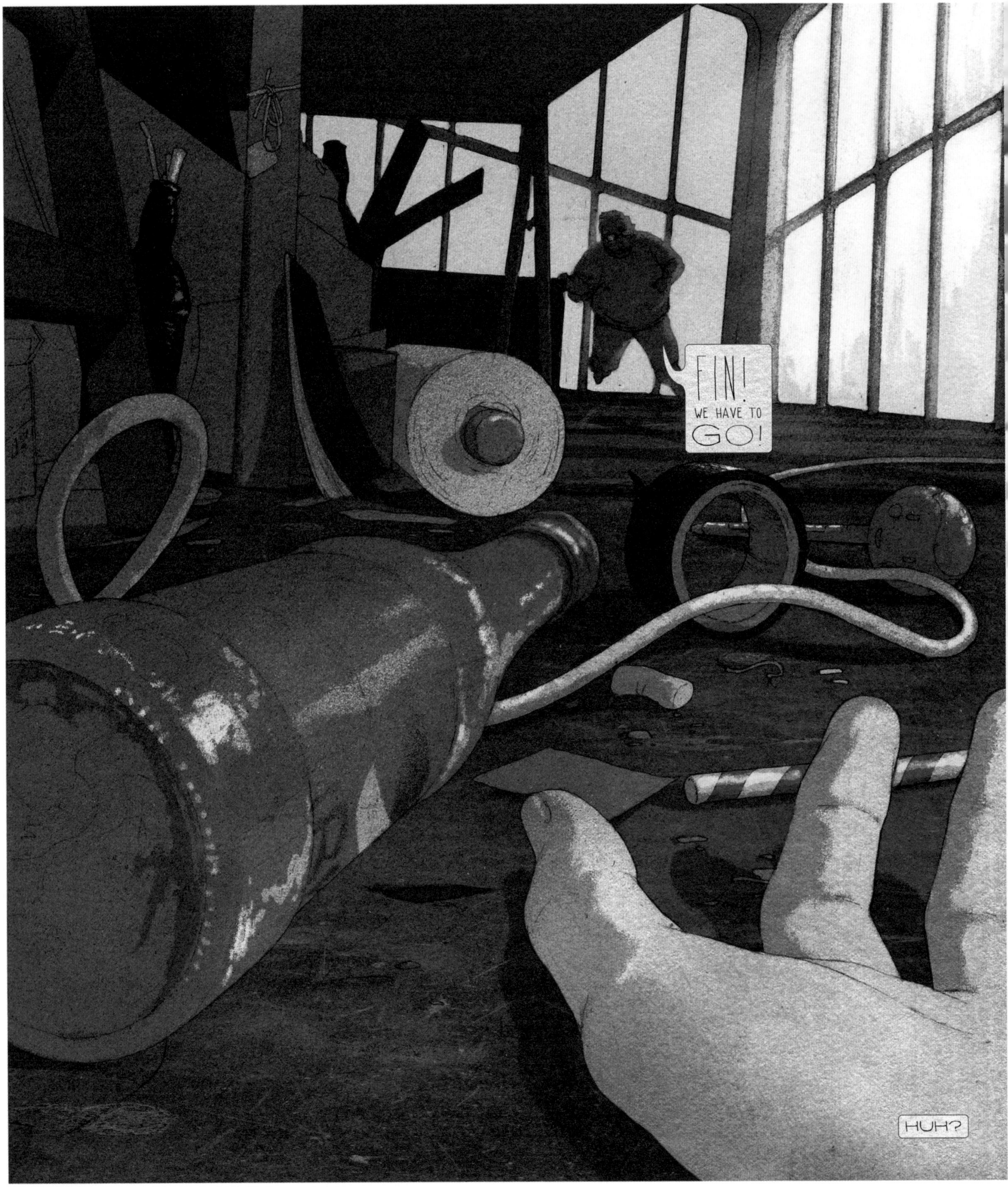
FIN! WE HAVE TO GO!
HUH?

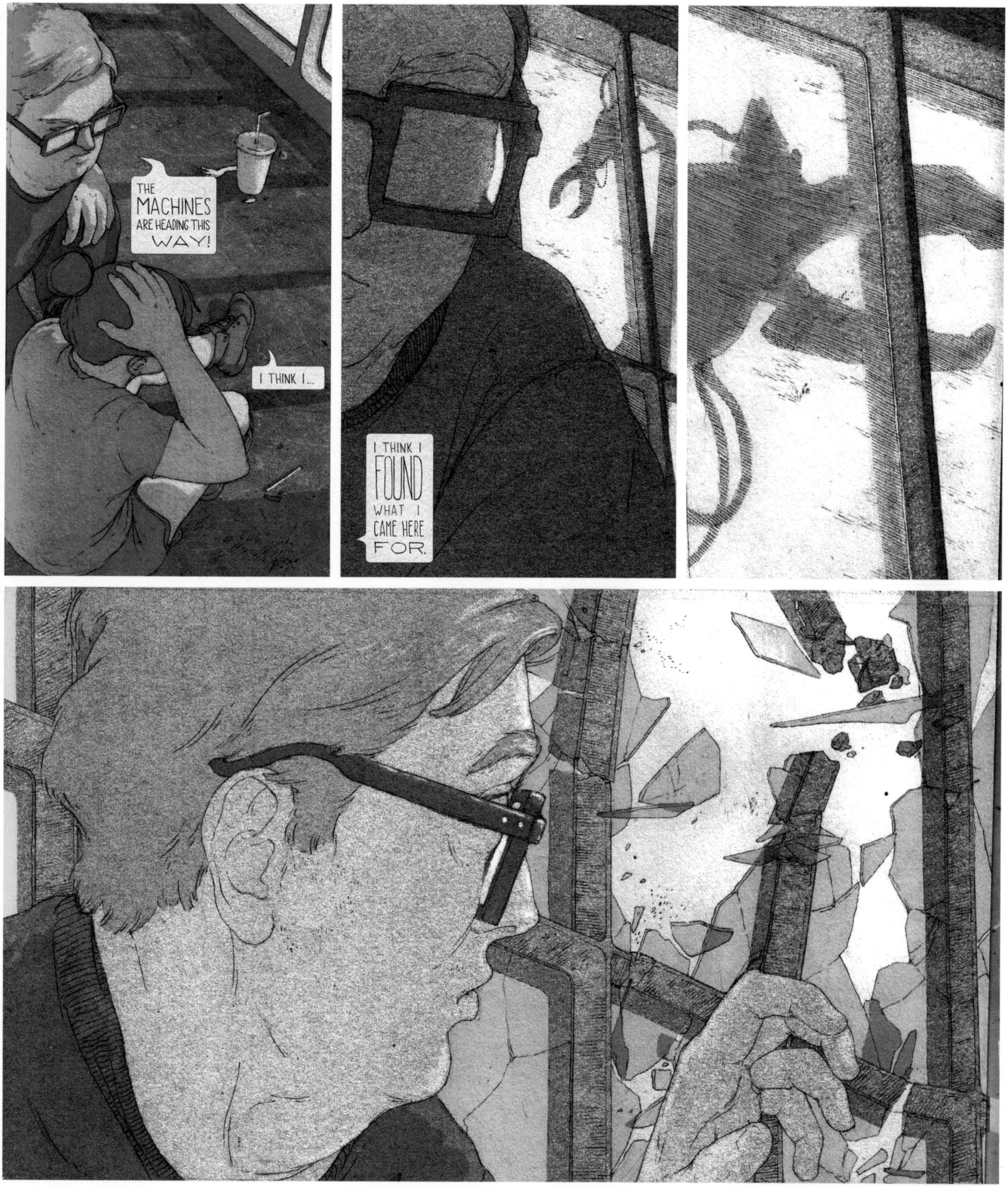
THE MACHINES ARE HEADING THIS WAY!
I THINK I...
I THINK I FOUND WHAT I CAME HERE FOR.

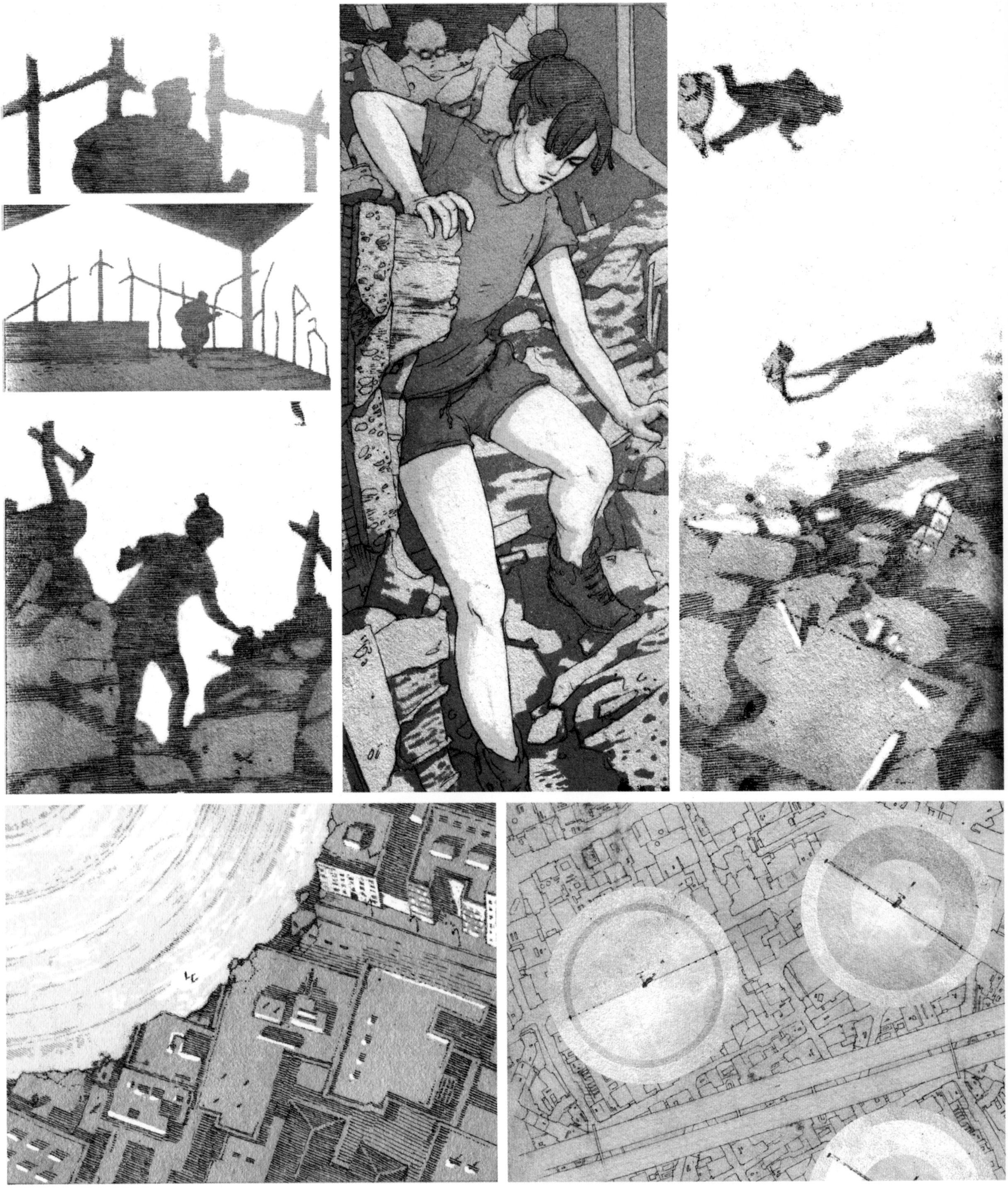

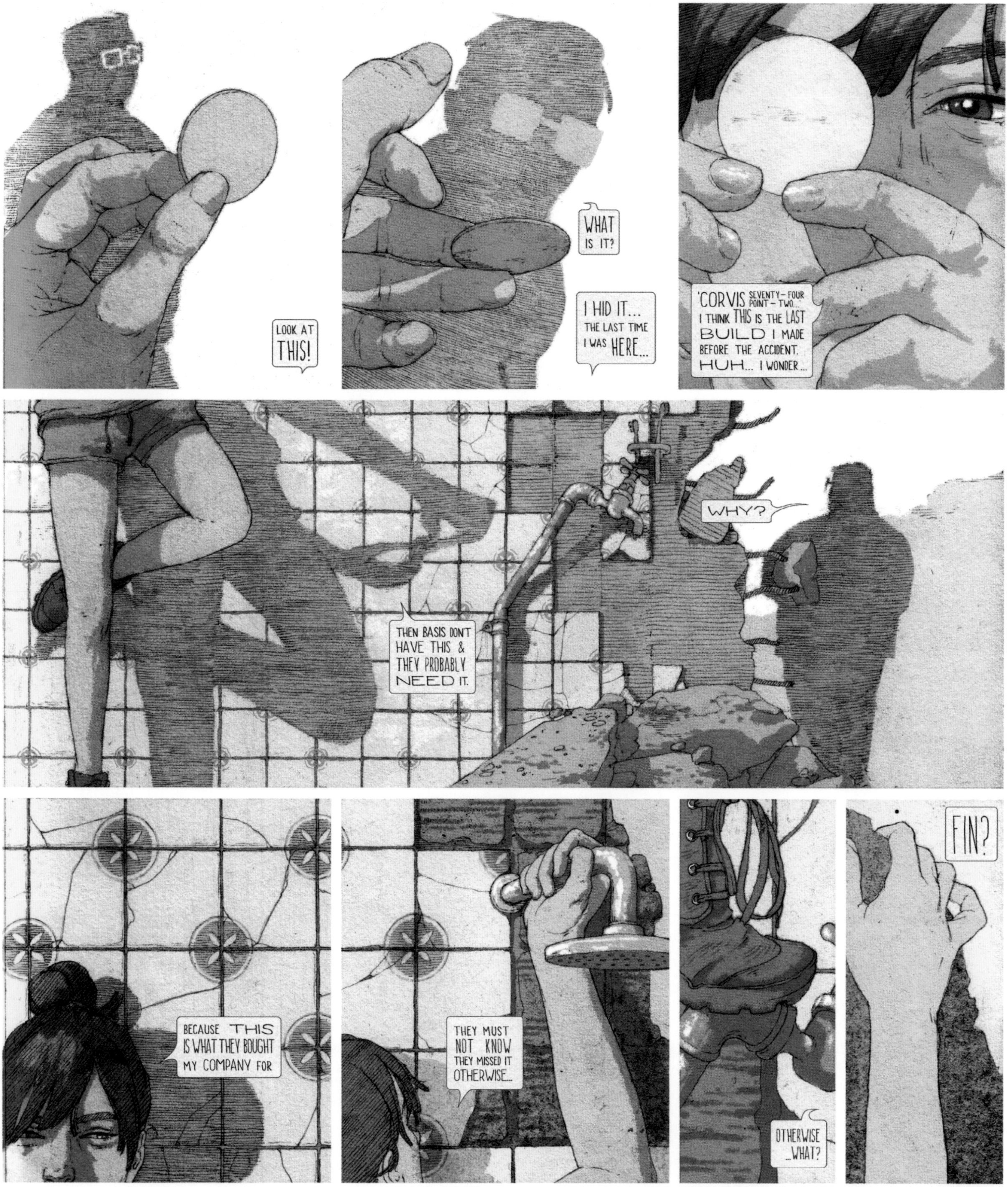
LOOK AT THIS!
WHAT IS IT?
I HID IT... THE LAST TIME I WAS HERE...
'CORVIS SEVENTY-FOUR POINT-TWO...' I THINK THIS IS THE LAST BUILD I MADE BEFORE THE ACCIDENT. HUH... I WONDER...
WHY?
THEN BASIS DON'T HAVE THIS & THEY PROBABLY NEED IT.
BECAUSE THIS IS WHAT THEY BOUGHT MY COMPANY FOR
THEY MUST NOT KNOW THEY MISSED IT OTHERWISE...
OTHERWISE ...WHAT?
FIN?

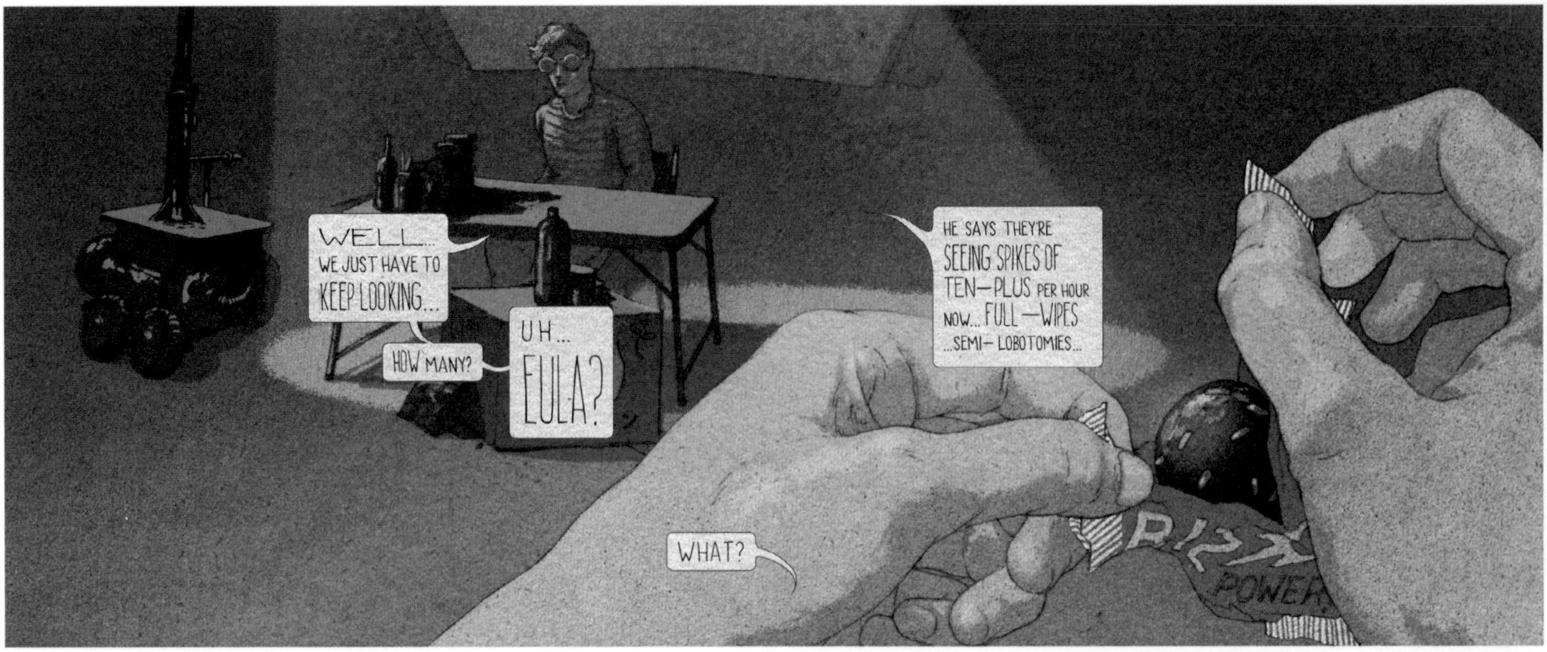
WELL... WE JUST HAVE TO KEEP LOOKING...
HOW MANY?
UH... EULA?
HE SAYS THEY'RE SEEING SPIKES OF TEN—PLUS PER HOUR NOW... FULL—WIPES ...SEMI— LOBOTOMIES...
WHAT?
BIZZ POWER
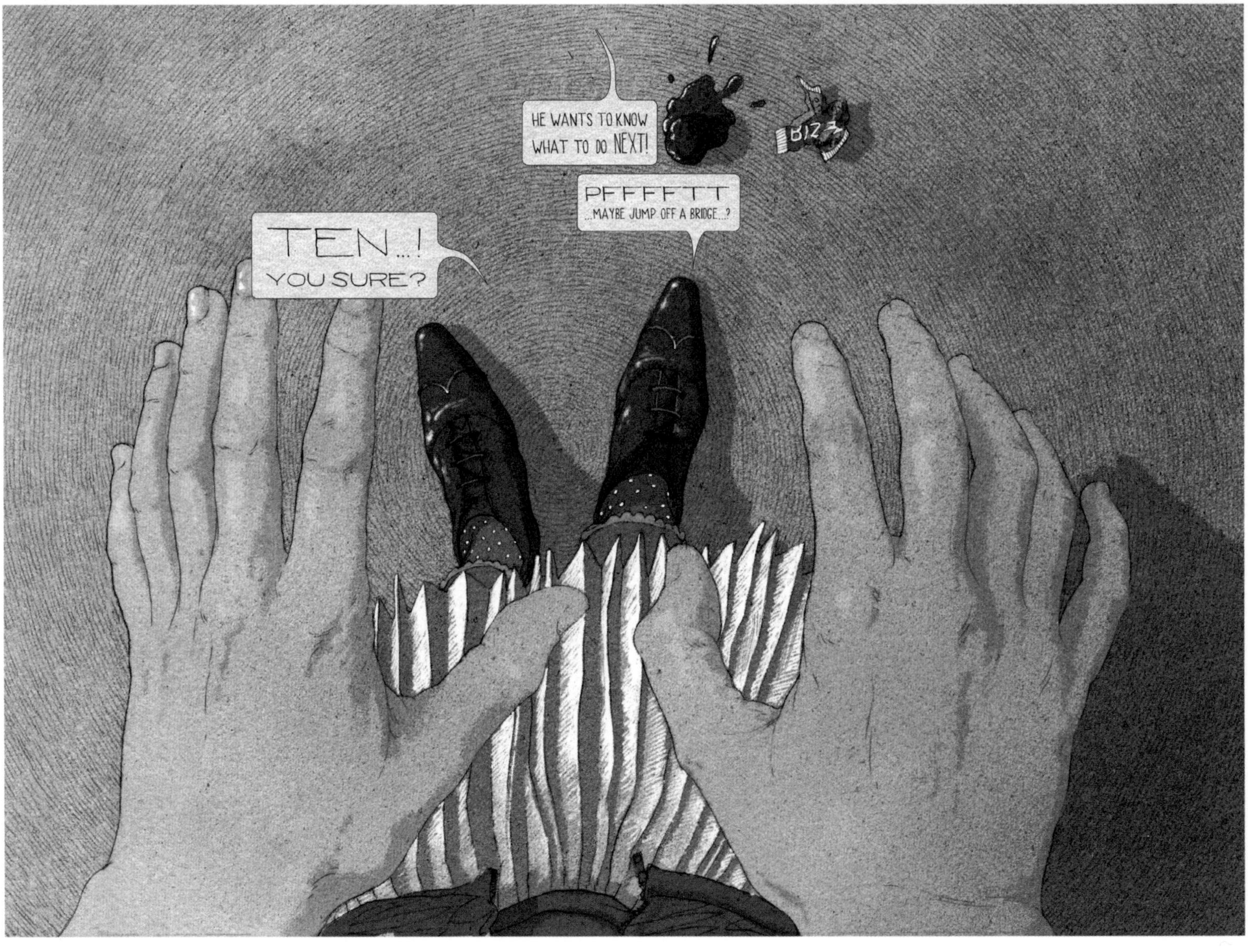
HE WANTS TO KNOW WHAT TO DO NEXT!
BIZZ
PFFFFTT ...MAYBE JUMP OFF A BRIDGE...?
TEN...! YOU SURE?

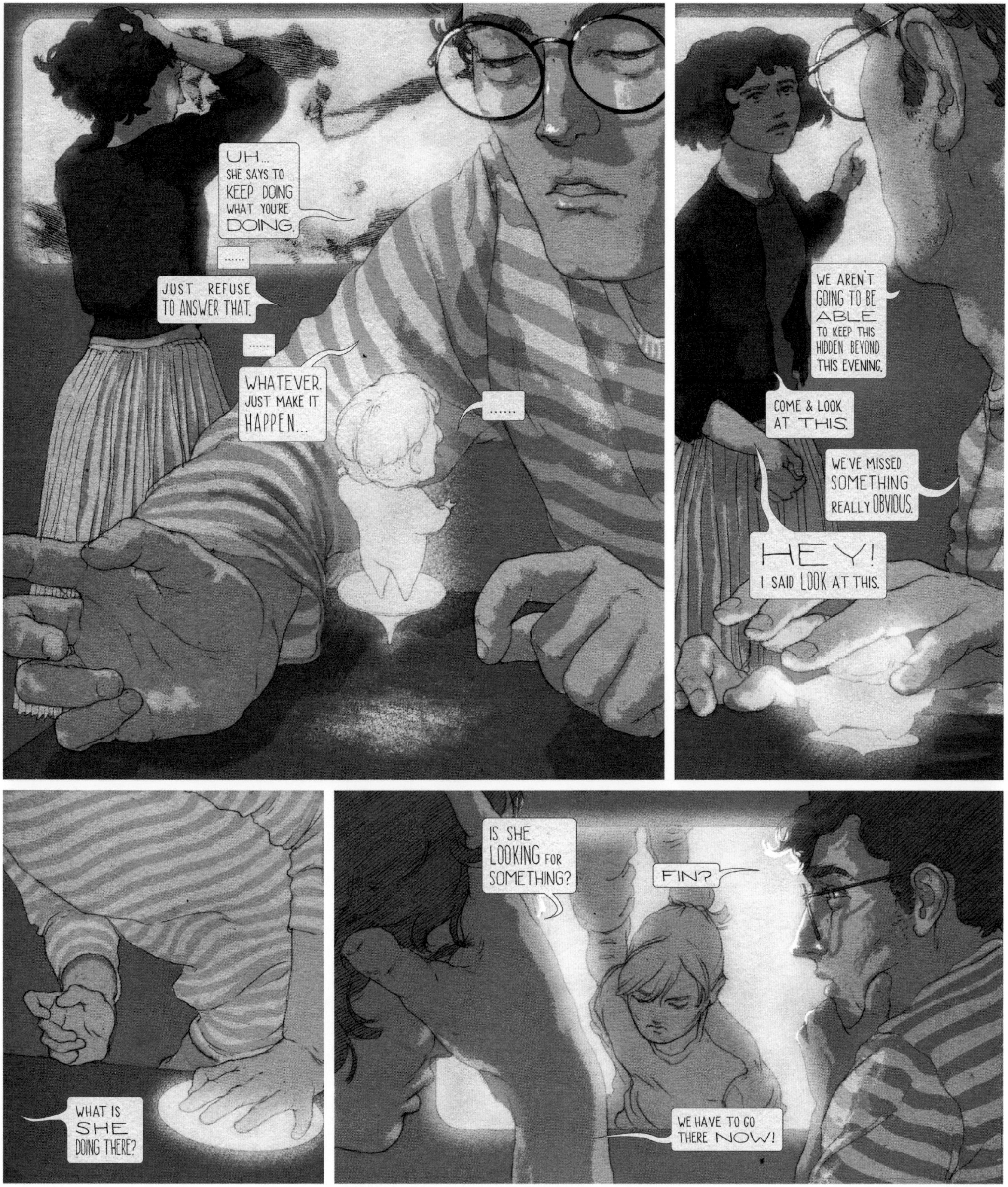
UH... SHE SAYS TO KEEP DOING WHAT YOU'RE DOING.
......
JUST REFUSE TO ANSWER THAT.
......
WHATEVER. JUST MAKE IT HAPPEN...
......
WE AREN'T GOING TO BE ABLE TO KEEP THIS HIDDEN BEYOND THIS EVENING.
COME & LOOK AT THIS.
WE'VE MISSED SOMETHING REALLY OBVIOUS.
HEY! I SAID LOOK AT THIS.
WHAT IS SHE DOING THERE?
IS SHE LOOKING FOR SOMETHING?
FIN?
WE HAVE TO GO THERE NOW!

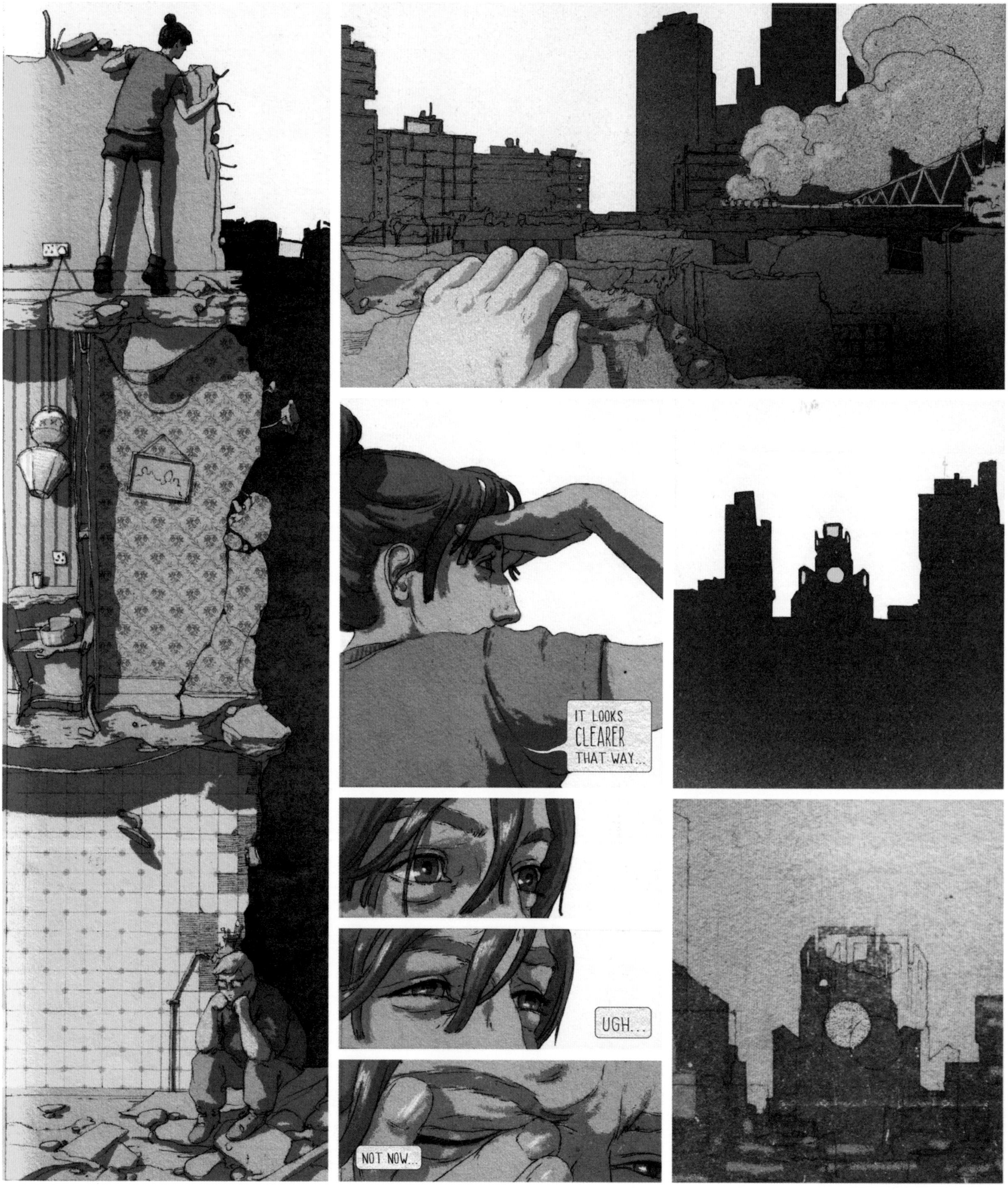
IT LOOKS CLEARER THAT WAY...
UGH...
NOT NOW...

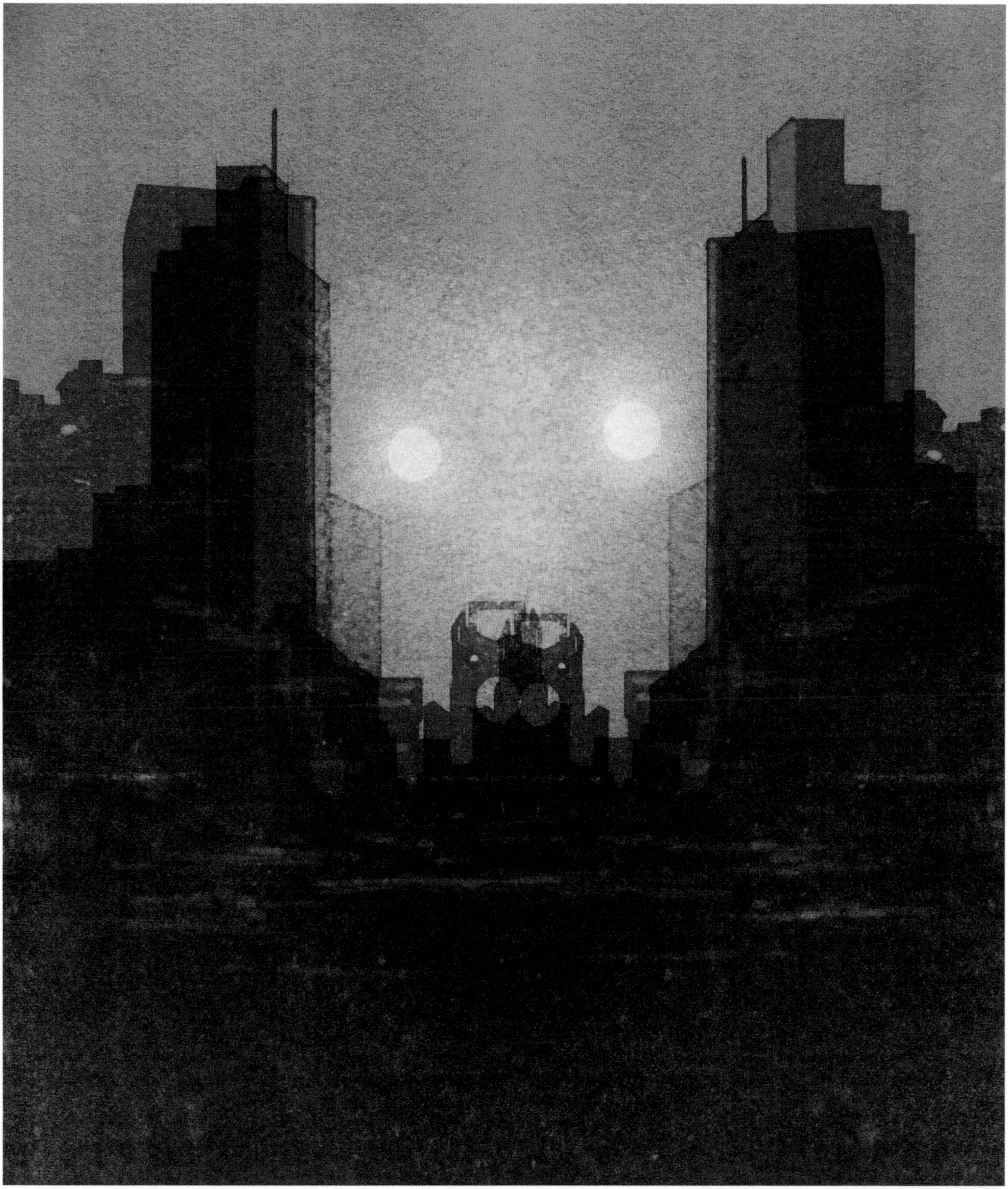

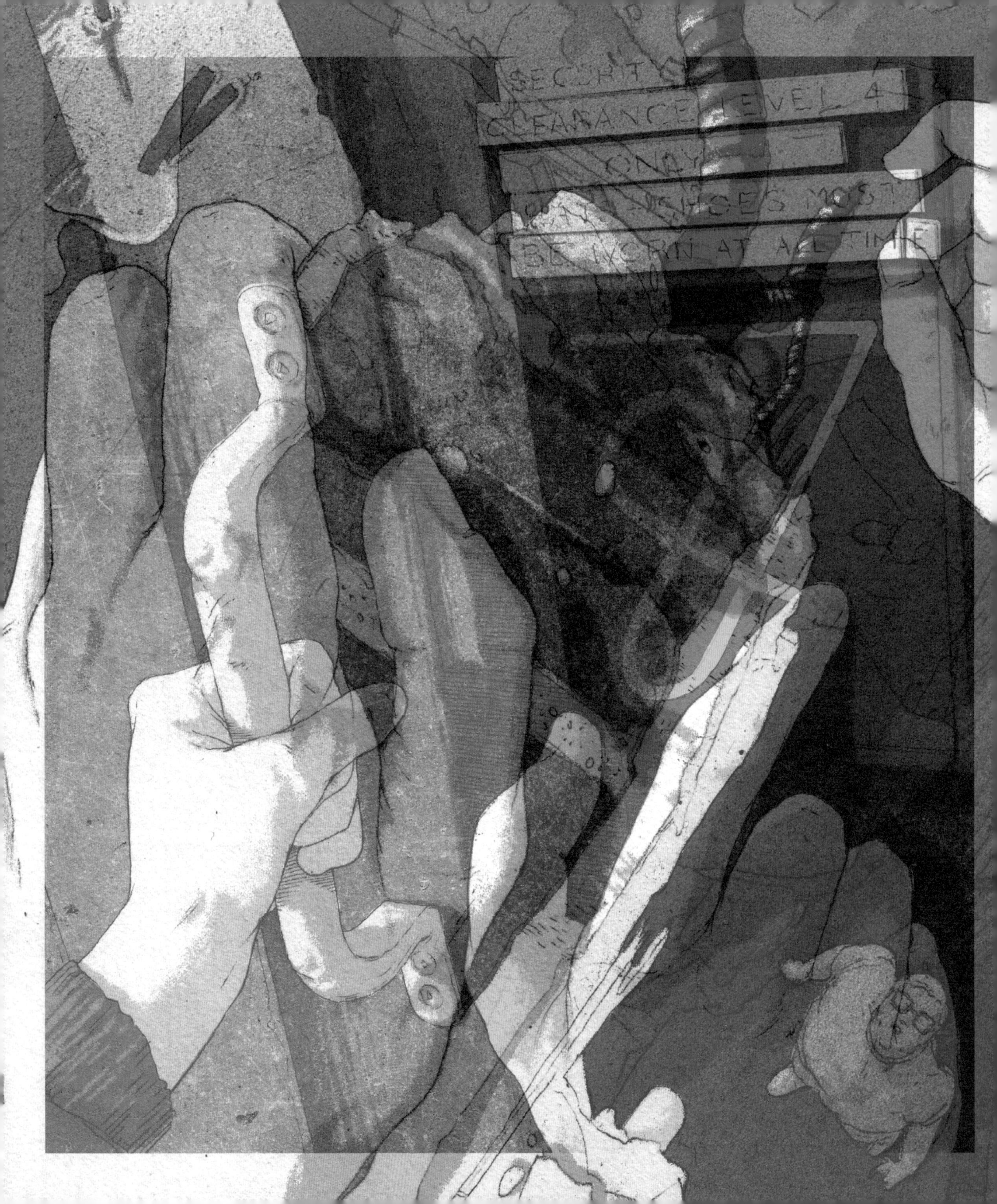
SECURITY
CLEARANCE LEVEL 4
ONLY
SHOES MUST
BE WORN AT ALL TIME

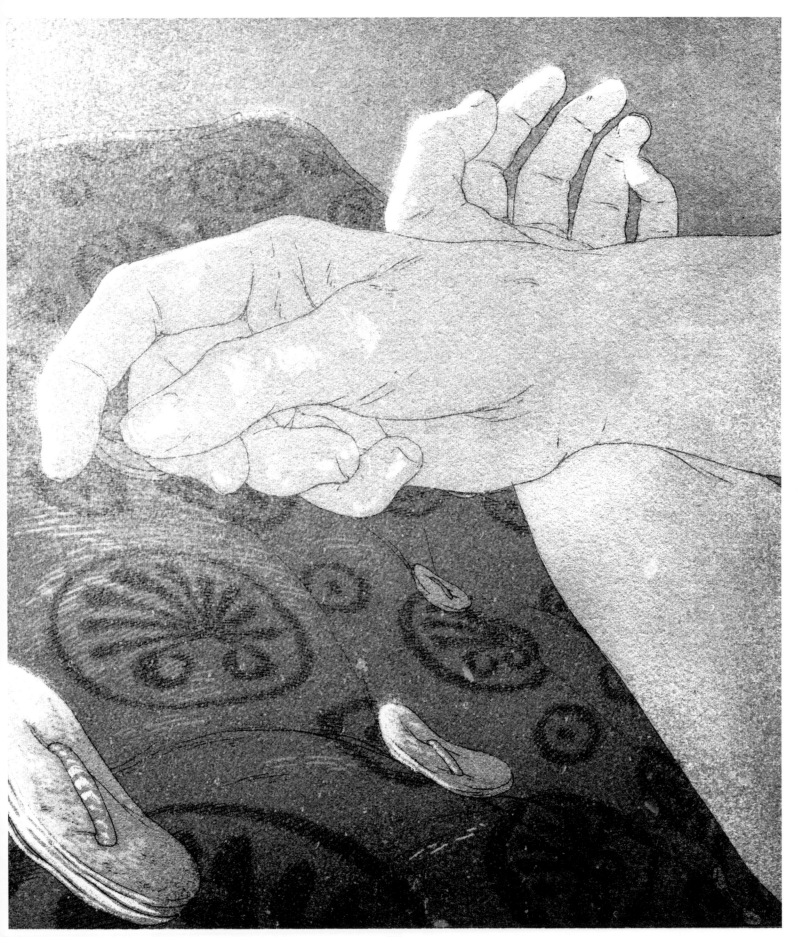

ARE YOU OK? YOU FELL!

IT'S NOTHING. JUST ANOTHER LEAK. I GET A BIT DIZZY WHEN IT HAPPENS.

BUT DOESN'T IT SCARE YOU? THESE WEIRD HALLUCINATIONS FROM SOMEONE ELSE'S HEAD?

I REMEMBER IT FROM BEFORE. IT'S NOT DANGEROUS

IT WAS JUST A BIT CONFUSING AT FIRST. LIKE A DREAM

IT MEANS THAT THIS WOMAN EULA IS USING THE INTERFACE I MADE – CORVIS

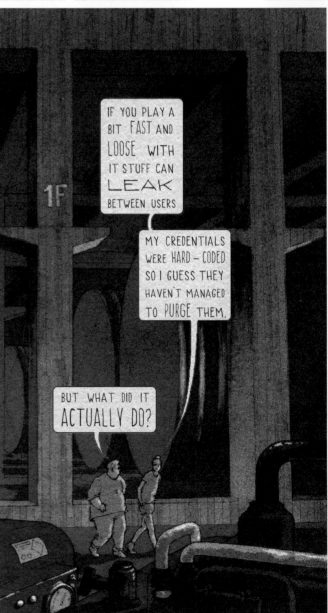

IF YOU PLAY A BIT FAST AND LOOSE WITH IT STUFF CAN LEAK BETWEEN USERS

MY CREDENTIALS WERE HARD–CODED SO I GUESS THEY HAVEN'T MANAGED TO PURGE THEM.

BUT WHAT DID IT ACTUALLY DO?

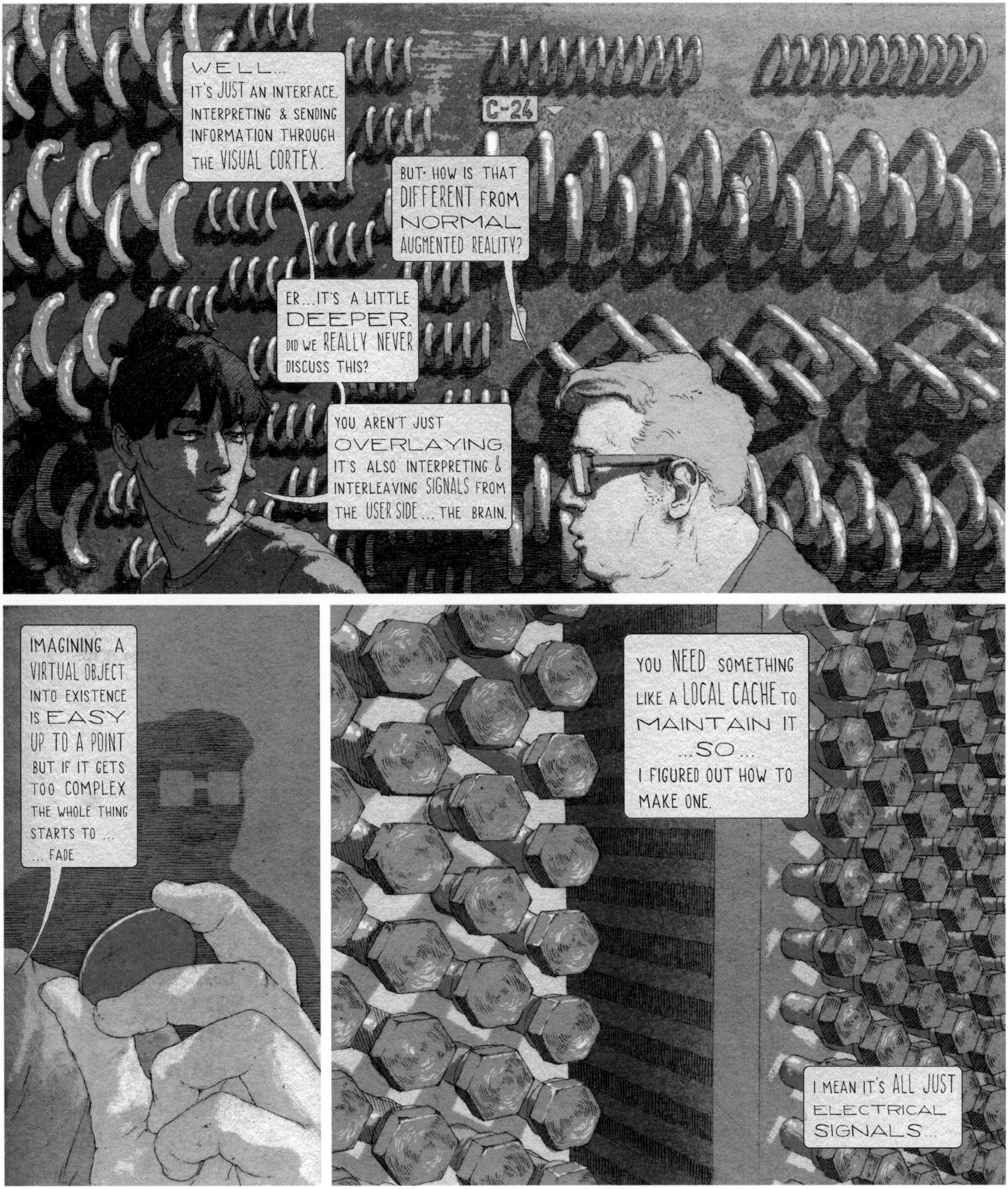
C-24
WELL... IT'S JUST AN INTERFACE. INTERPRETING & SENDING INFORMATION THROUGH THE VISUAL CORTEX.
BUT HOW IS THAT DIFFERENT FROM NORMAL AUGMENTED REALITY?
ER...IT'S A LITTLE DEEPER. DID WE REALLY NEVER DISCUSS THIS?
YOU AREN'T JUST OVERLAYING. IT'S ALSO INTERPRETING & INTERLEAVING SIGNALS FROM THE USER SIDE... THE BRAIN.
IMAGINING A VIRTUAL OBJECT INTO EXISTENCE IS EASY UP TO A POINT BUT IF IT GETS TOO COMPLEX THE WHOLE THING STARTS TO ... ... FADE
YOU NEED SOMETHING LIKE A LOCAL CACHE TO MAINTAIN IT ...SO... I FIGURED OUT HOW TO MAKE ONE.
I MEAN IT'S ALL JUST ELECTRICAL SIGNALS...

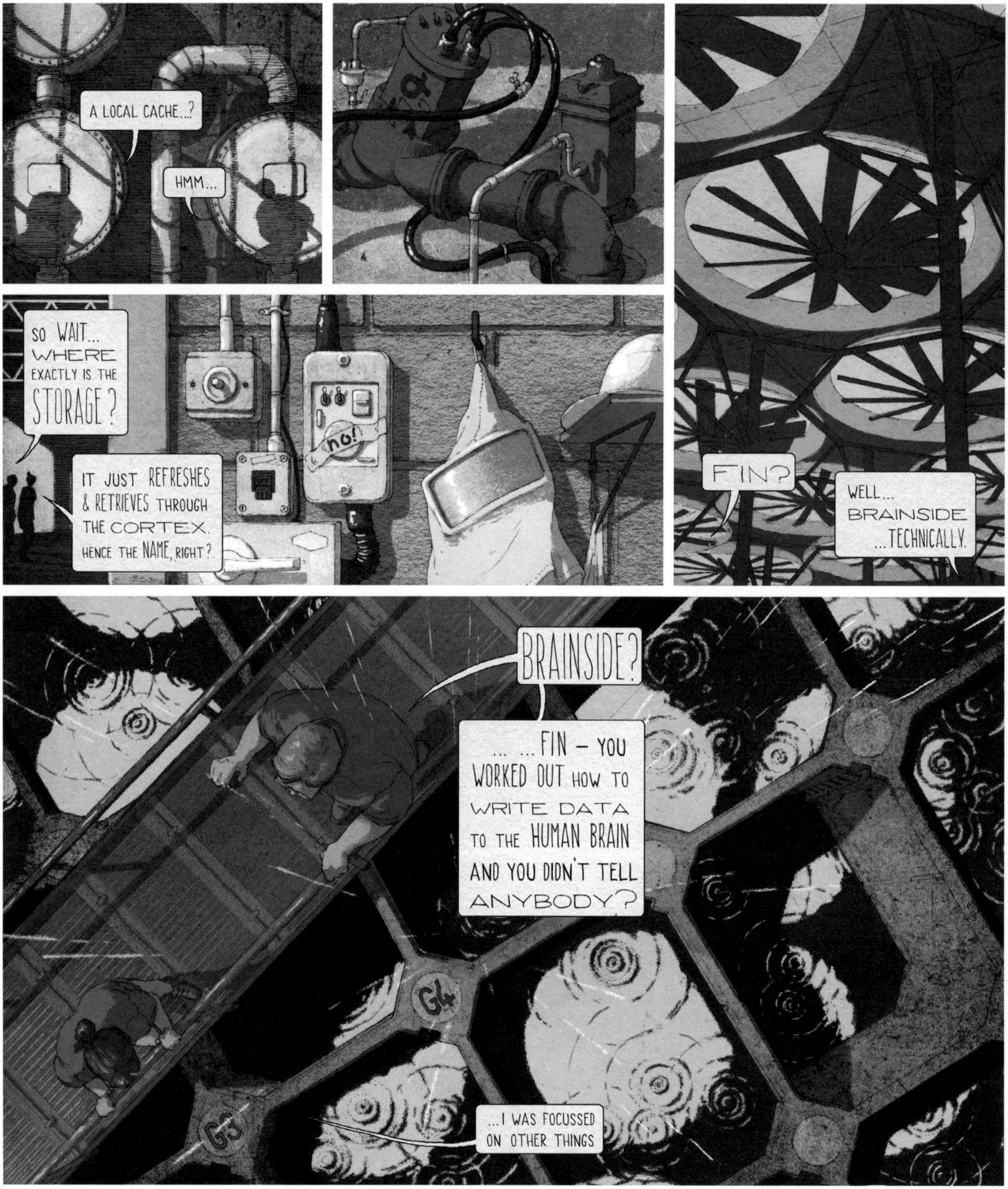
A LOCAL CACHE...?
HMM...
SO WAIT... WHERE EXACTLY IS THE STORAGE?
IT JUST REFRESHES & RETRIEVES THROUGH THE CORTEX. HENCE THE NAME, RIGHT?
no!
FIN?
WELL... BRAINSIDE ...TECHNICALLY.
BRAINSIDE?
... ...FIN – YOU WORKED OUT HOW TO WRITE DATA TO THE HUMAN BRAIN AND YOU DIDN'T TELL ANYBODY?
G4
G3
...I WAS FOCUSSED ON OTHER THINGS

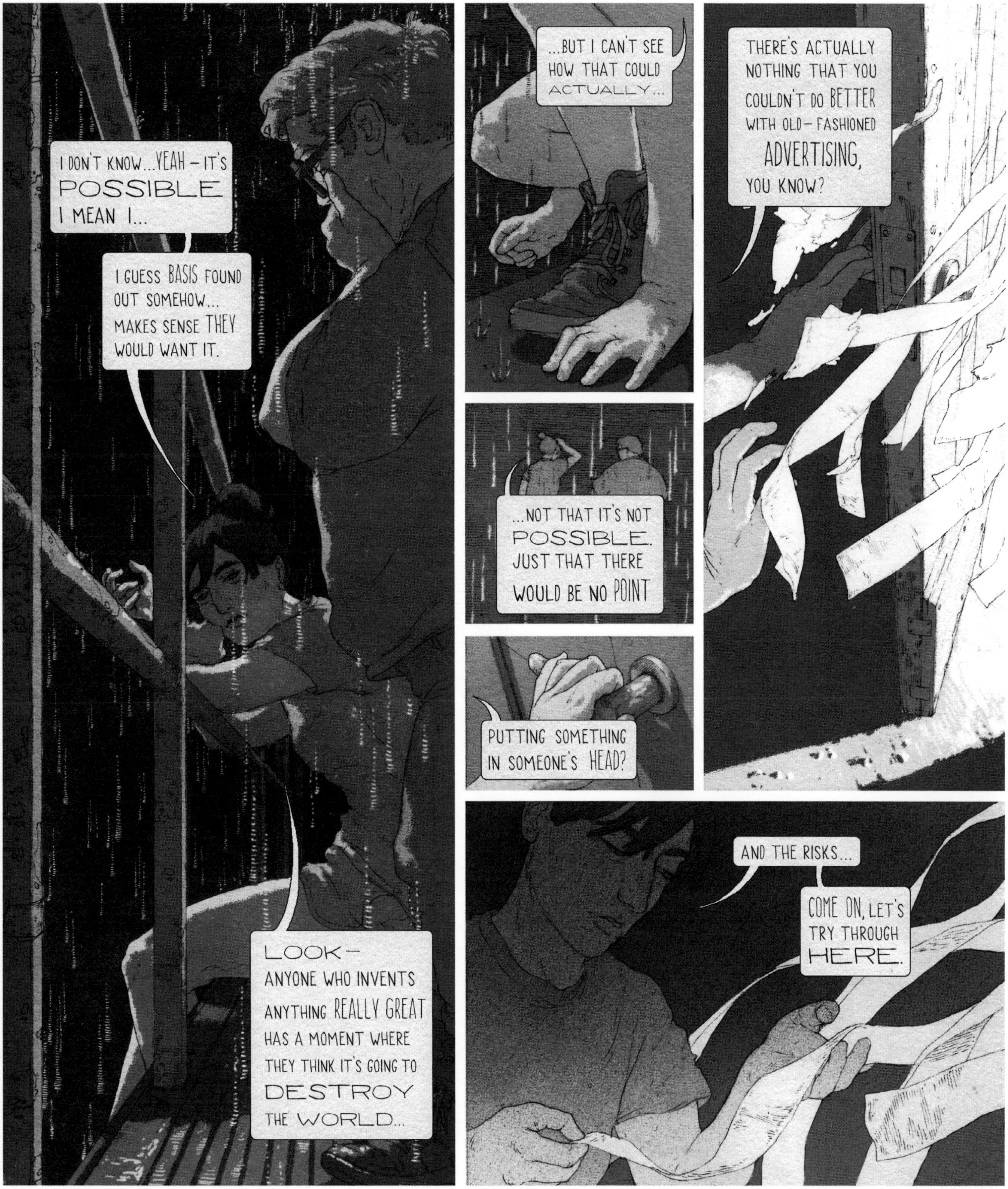

I DON'T KNOW... YEAH – IT'S POSSIBLE I MEAN I...
I GUESS BASIS FOUND OUT SOMEHOW... MAKES SENSE THEY WOULD WANT IT.
LOOK– ANYONE WHO INVENTS ANYTHING REALLY GREAT HAS A MOMENT WHERE THEY THINK IT'S GOING TO DESTROY THE WORLD...
...BUT I CAN'T SEE HOW THAT COULD ACTUALLY...
...NOT THAT IT'S NOT POSSIBLE. JUST THAT THERE WOULD BE NO POINT
PUTTING SOMETHING IN SOMEONE'S HEAD?
THERE'S ACTUALLY NOTHING THAT YOU COULDN'T DO BETTER WITH OLD-FASHIONED ADVERTISING, YOU KNOW?
AND THE RISKS...
COME ON, LET'S TRY THROUGH HERE.

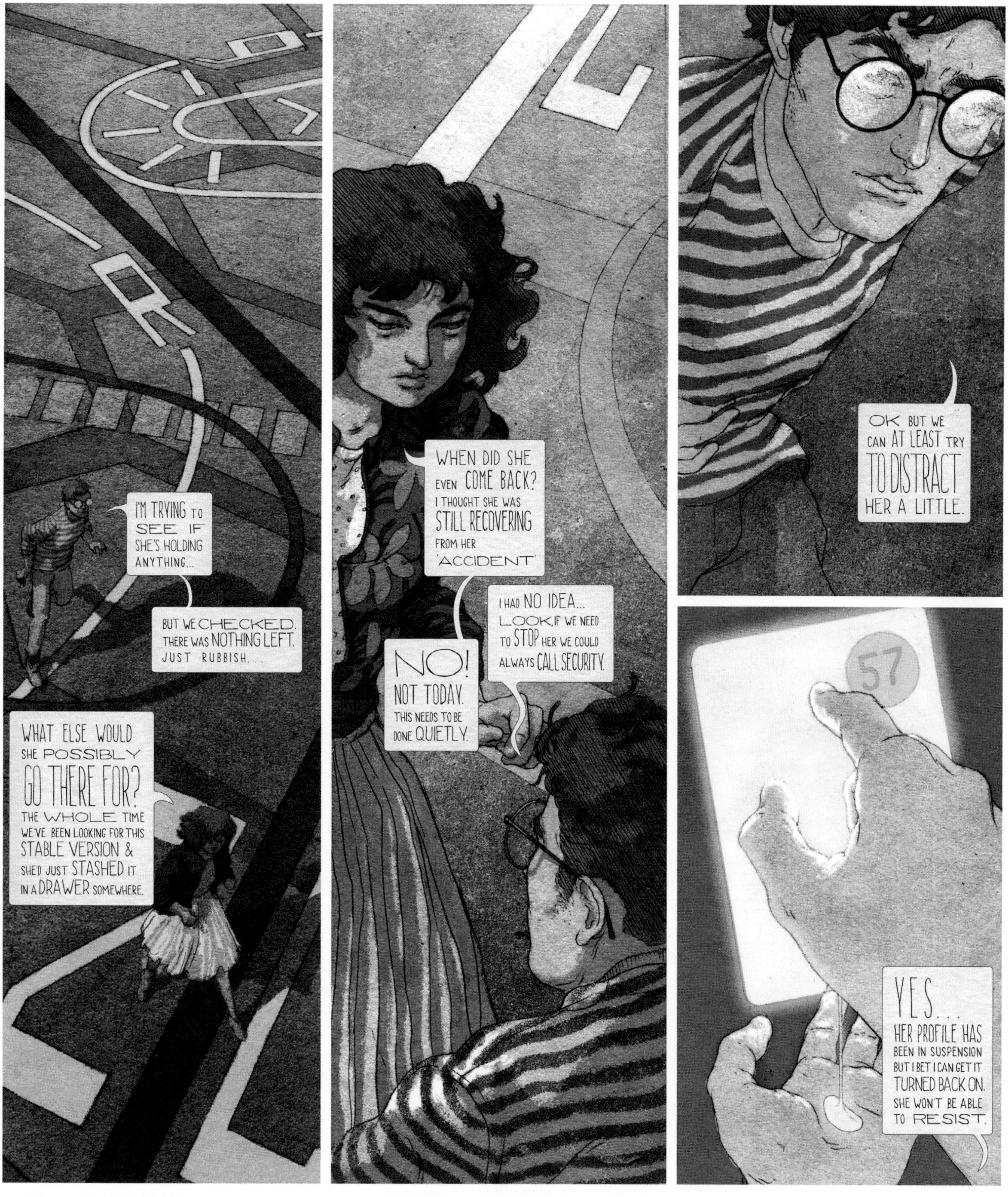
I'M TRYING TO SEE IF SHE'S HOLDING ANYTHING...
BUT WE CHECKED. THERE WAS NOTHING LEFT. JUST RUBBISH...
WHAT ELSE WOULD SHE POSSIBLY GO THERE FOR? THE WHOLE TIME WE'VE BEEN LOOKING FOR THIS STABLE VERSION & SHE'D JUST STASHED IT IN A DRAWER SOMEWHERE.
WHEN DID SHE EVEN COME BACK? I THOUGHT SHE WAS STILL RECOVERING FROM HER 'ACCIDENT'
I HAD NO IDEA... LOOK, IF WE NEED TO STOP HER WE COULD ALWAYS CALL SECURITY.
NO! NOT TODAY. THIS NEEDS TO BE DONE QUIETLY.
OK BUT WE CAN AT LEAST TRY TO DISTRACT HER A LITTLE.
57
YES... HER PROFILE HAS BEEN IN SUSPENSION BUT I BET I CAN GET IT TURNED BACK ON. SHE WON'T BE ABLE TO RESIST.

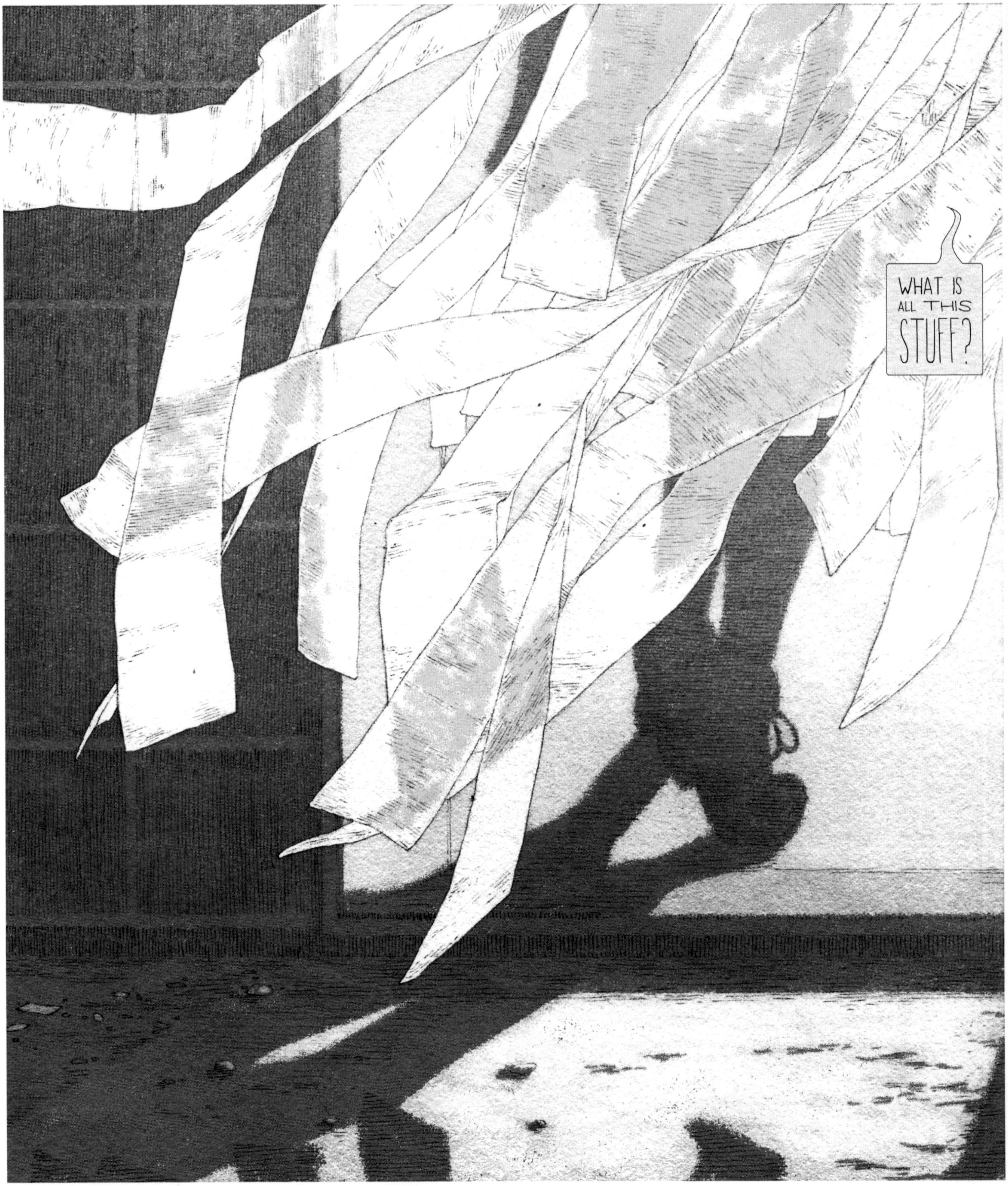
WHAT IS ALL THIS STUFF?

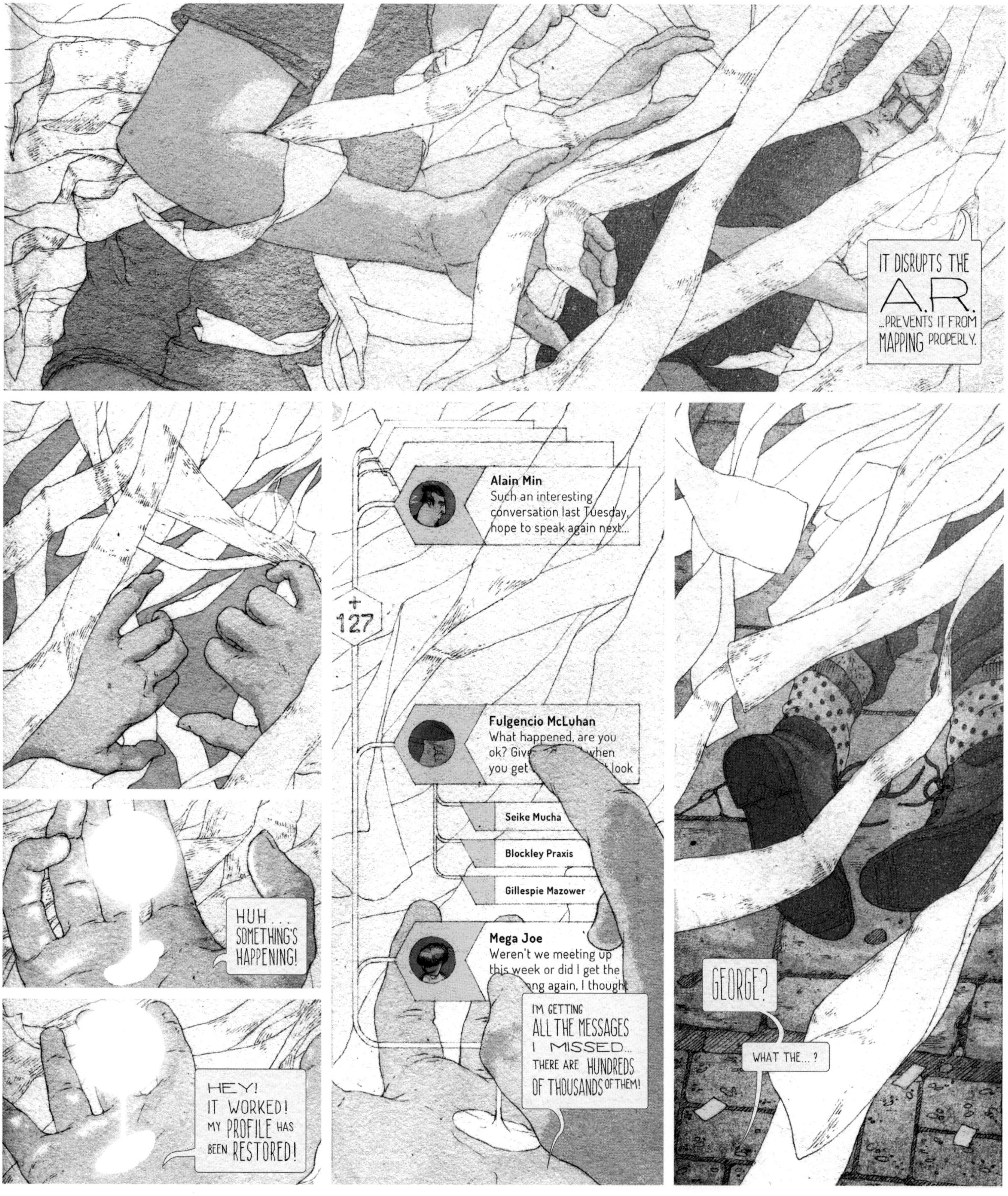
IT DISRUPTS THE A.R. ...PREVENTS IT FROM MAPPING PROPERLY.
HUH... SOMETHING'S HAPPENING!
HEY! IT WORKED! MY PROFILE HAS BEEN RESTORED!
Alain Min
Such an interesting conversation last Tuesday, hope to speak again next...
+ 127
Fulgencio McLuhan
What happened, are you ok? Give
when
you get
look
Seike Mucha
Blockley Praxis
Gillespie Mazower
Mega Joe
Weren't we meeting up this week or did I get the
again, I thought
I'M GETTING ALL THE MESSAGES I MISSED... THERE ARE HUNDREDS OF THOUSANDS OF THEM!
GEORGE?
WHAT THE... ?

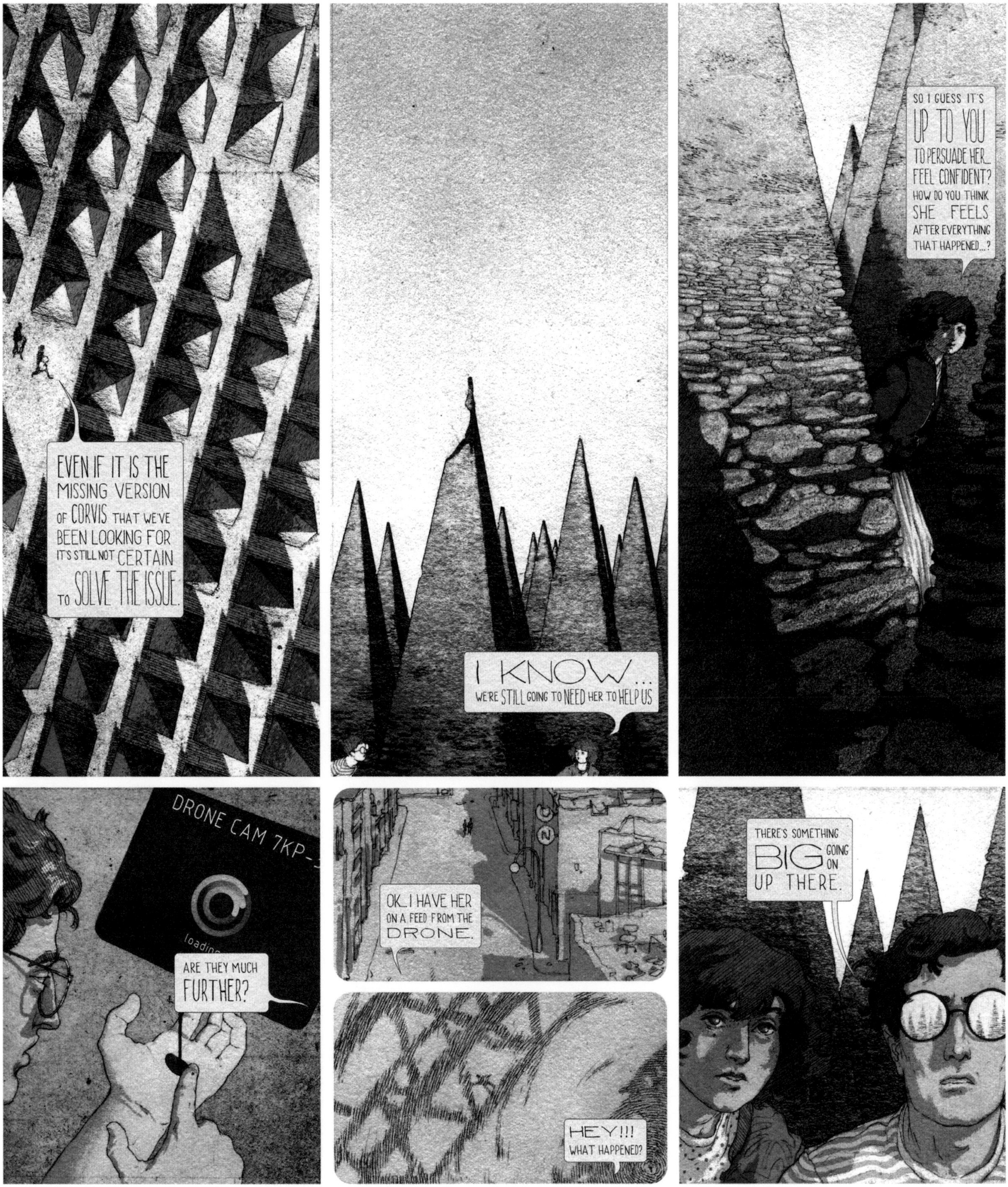

EVEN IF IT IS THE MISSING VERSION OF CORVIS THAT WE'VE BEEN LOOKING FOR IT'S STILL NOT CERTAIN TO SOLVE THE ISSUE.
I KNOW... WE'RE STILL GOING TO NEED HER TO HELP US
SO I GUESS IT'S UP TO YOU TO PERSUADE HER... FEEL CONFIDENT? HOW DO YOU THINK SHE FEELS AFTER EVERYTHING THAT HAPPENED...?
DRONE CAM 7KP-
ARE THEY MUCH FURTHER?
OK... I HAVE HER ON A FEED FROM THE DRONE.
HEY!!! WHAT HAPPENED?
THERE'S SOMETHING BIG GOING ON UP THERE.

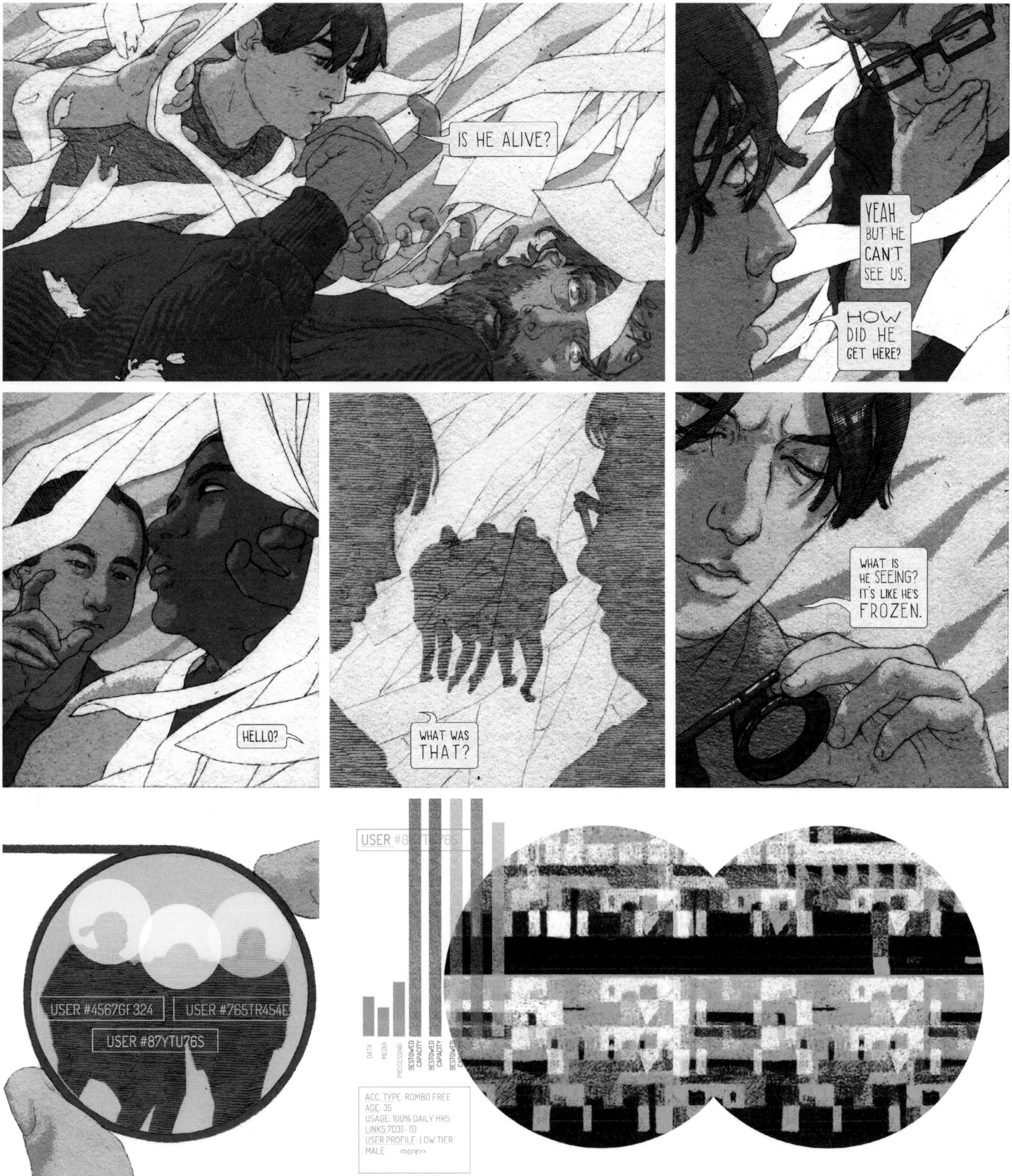
IS HE ALIVE?
YEAH BUT HE CAN'T SEE US.
HOW DID HE GET HERE?
HELLO?
WHAT WAS THAT?
WHAT IS HE SEEING? IT'S LIKE HE'S FROZEN.
USER #4567GF324
USER #765TR454E
USER #87YTU76S
DATA
MEDIA
PROCESSING
BESTOWED CAPACITY
BESTOWED CAPACITY
ACC. TYPE: ROMBO FREE
AGE: 35
USAGE: 100% DAILY HRS
LINKS:7D3)- !))
USER PROFILE: LOW TIER
MALE more>>

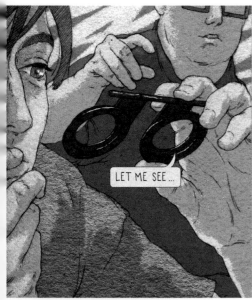

LET ME SEE ...

WEIRD.

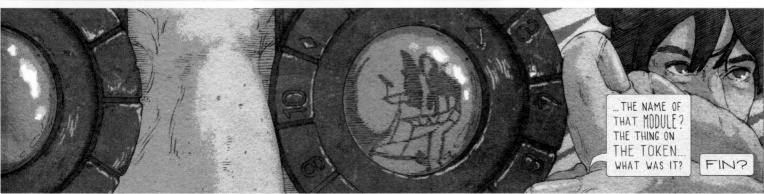

...THE NAME OF THAT MODULE? THE THING ON THE TOKEN... WHAT WAS IT?

FIN?

WHERE ARE THEY TAKING HIM?

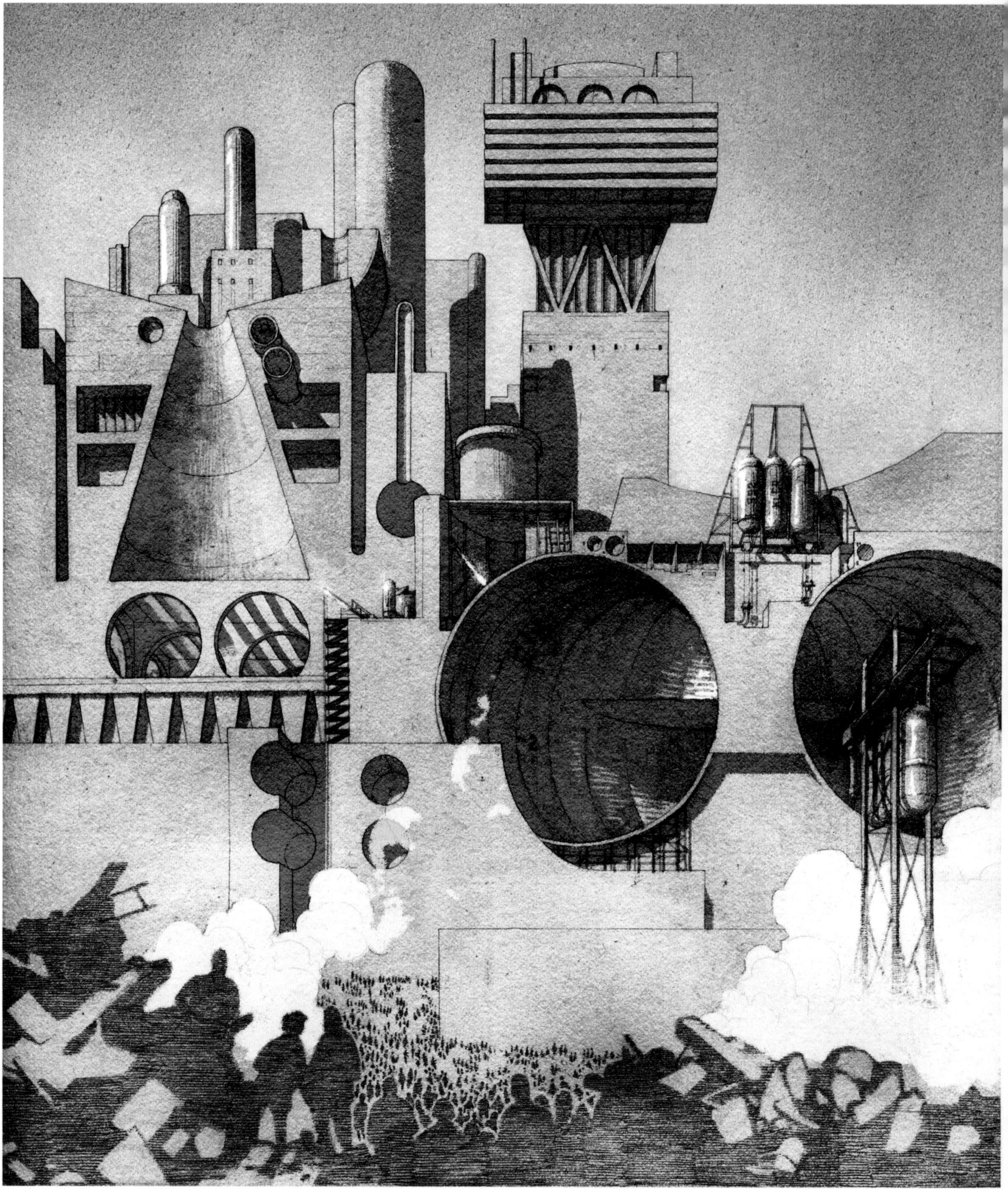

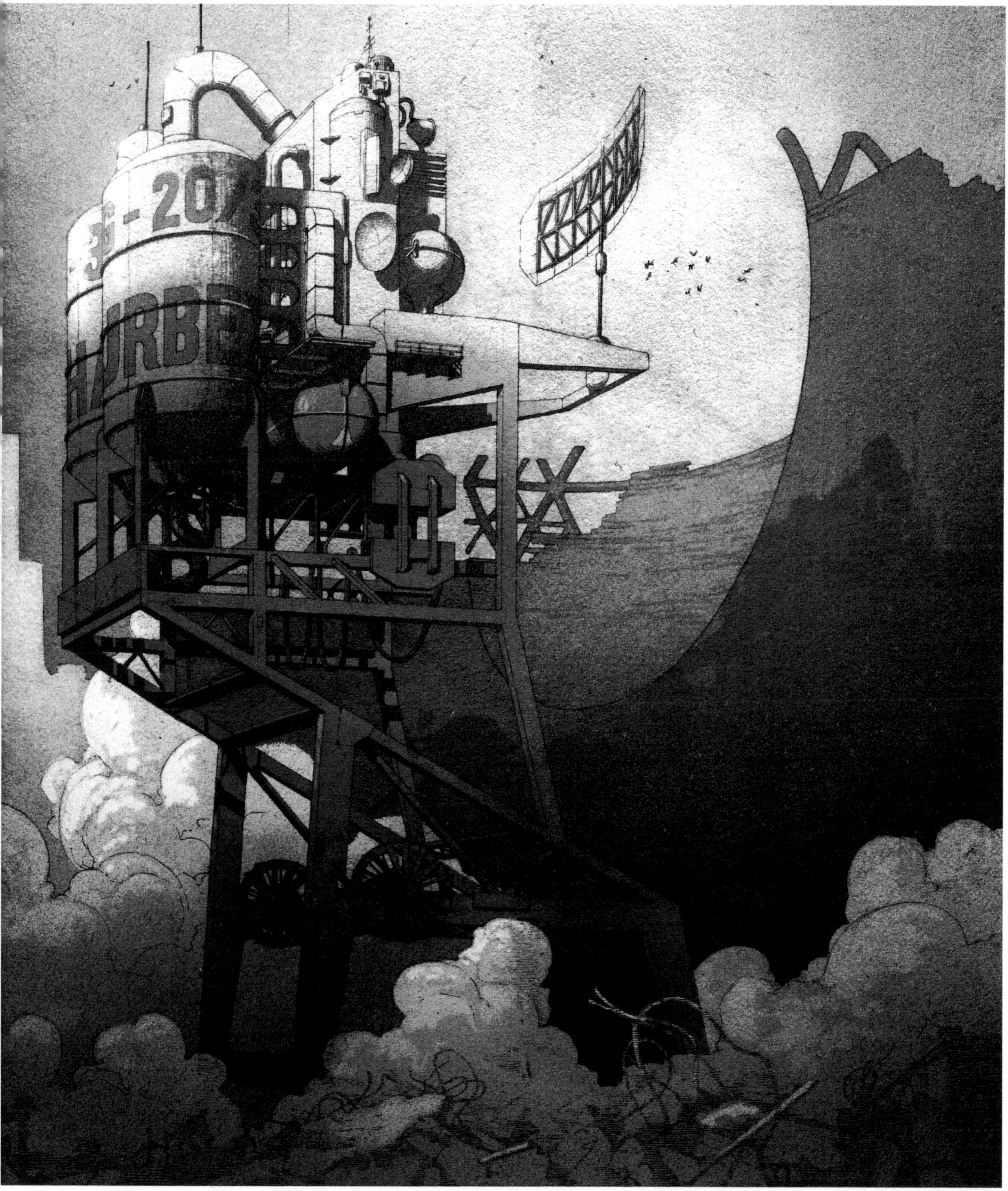

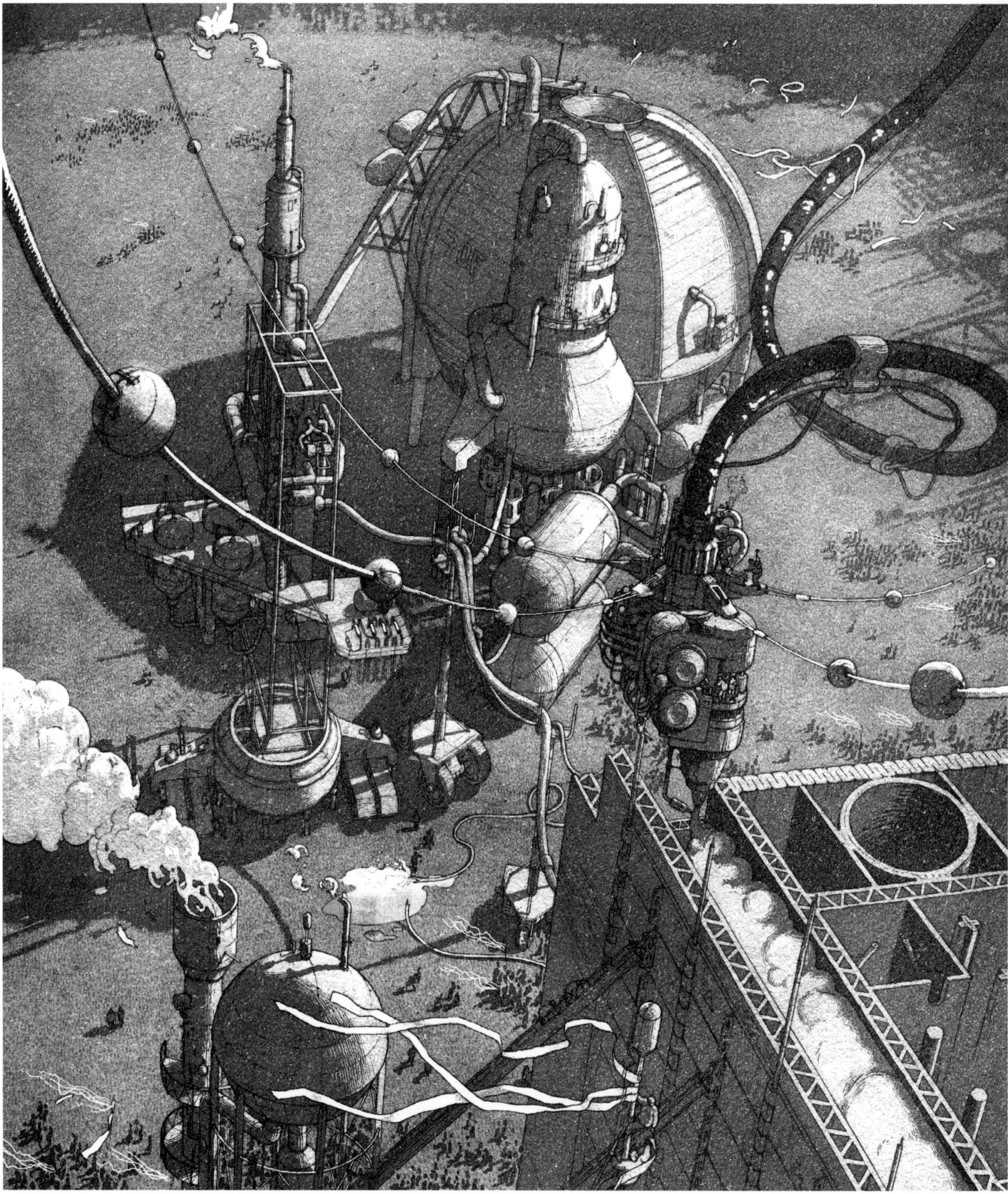

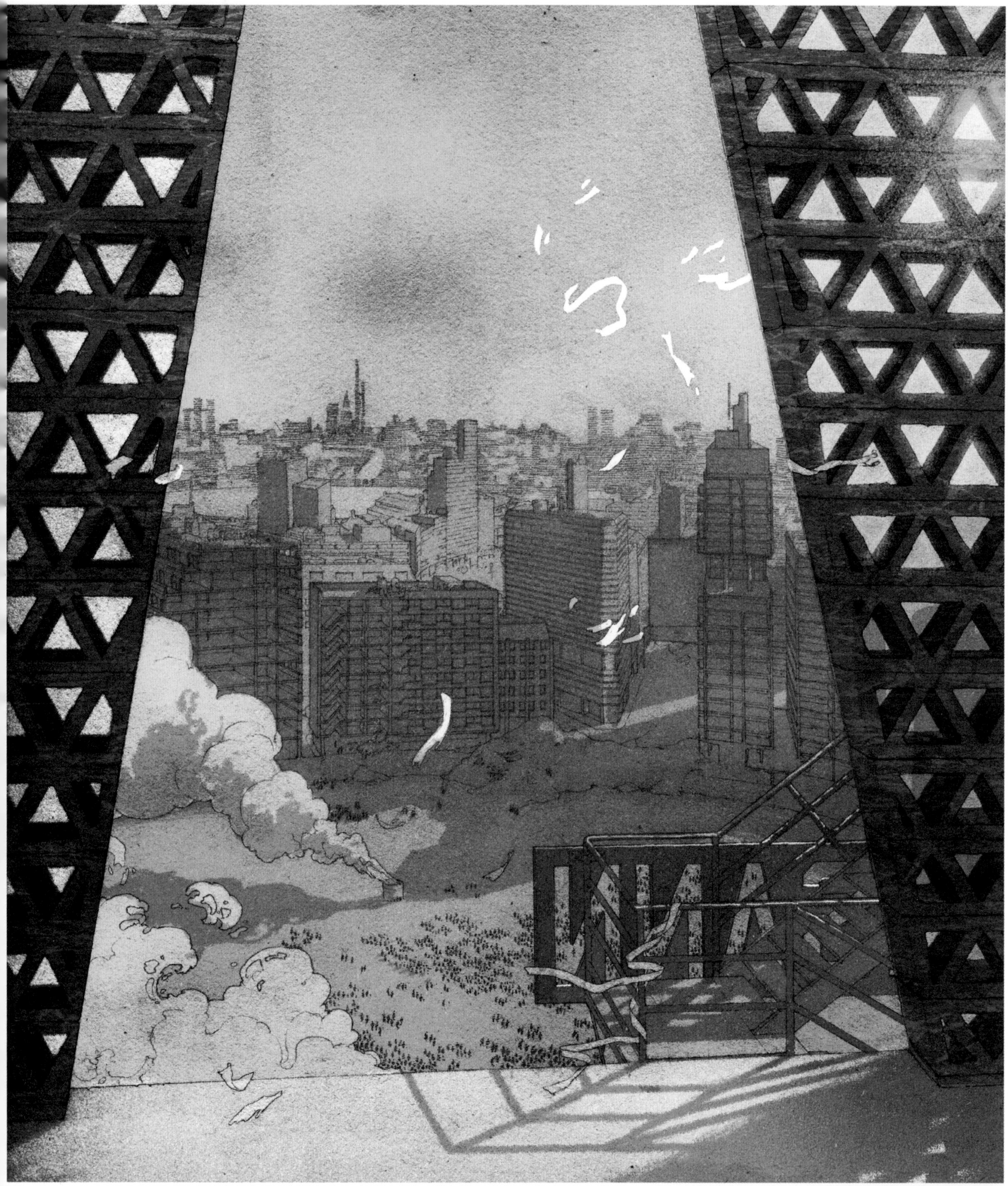

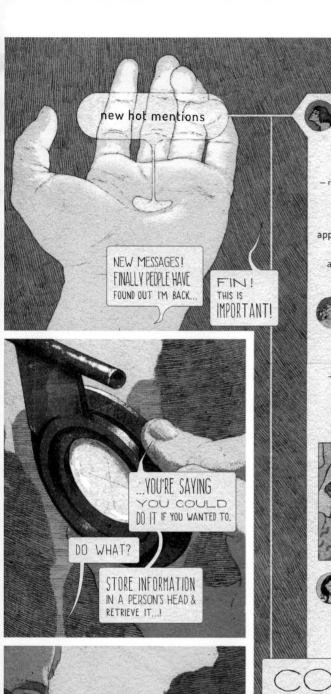

new hot mentions

NEW MESSAGES! FINALLY PEOPLE HAVE FOUND OUT I'M BACK...

FIN! THIS IS IMPORTANT!

so excited to hear my friend Fin Ueda-Soto is working on a new project... can I do anything to help... wherever you are babe.
— right this minute

a lot of speculation today regarding a certain new appointment at Basis. Not in a position to make any announcements. But soon.
— right this minute

hey n wld love to tlk about feature on yr recovery + return — so pleased — hit me back !

— right this minute

yeah, when your friend and biggest influence comes home and doesn't message you —at all — yeah that burns, and when you're basically the last person to ... it... ugh ... re to start

for ... ery exciting rumours about a tie-up between a certain high-profile inventor and the Basis Profound Upgrade program

... right this minute

COOL...! JOHN TELOS WANTS TO GET ME BACK ON THE SHOW FOR A COMEBACK INTERVIEW!

...YOU'RE SAVING YOU COULD DO IT IF YOU WANTED TO.

DO WHAT?

STORE INFORMATION IN A PERSON'S HEAD & RETRIEVE IT...!

YOU HAVE TO LOOK AT THIS PROPERLY. IT'S THE SAME ON ALL THESE PEOPLE!

HUH?

OK... IN THEORY MAYBE... BUT WHY WOULD ANYONE WANT TO?

LOOK AT THIS! THERE ARE HUNDREDS OF THEM AND THEY'RE ALL THE SAME!

FINE! BUT LIKE I ALREADY SAID THERE'S NO POINT! IF YOU JUST WANT TO MAKE SOMEONE THINK SOMETHING THERE ARE MUCH EASIER WAYS.

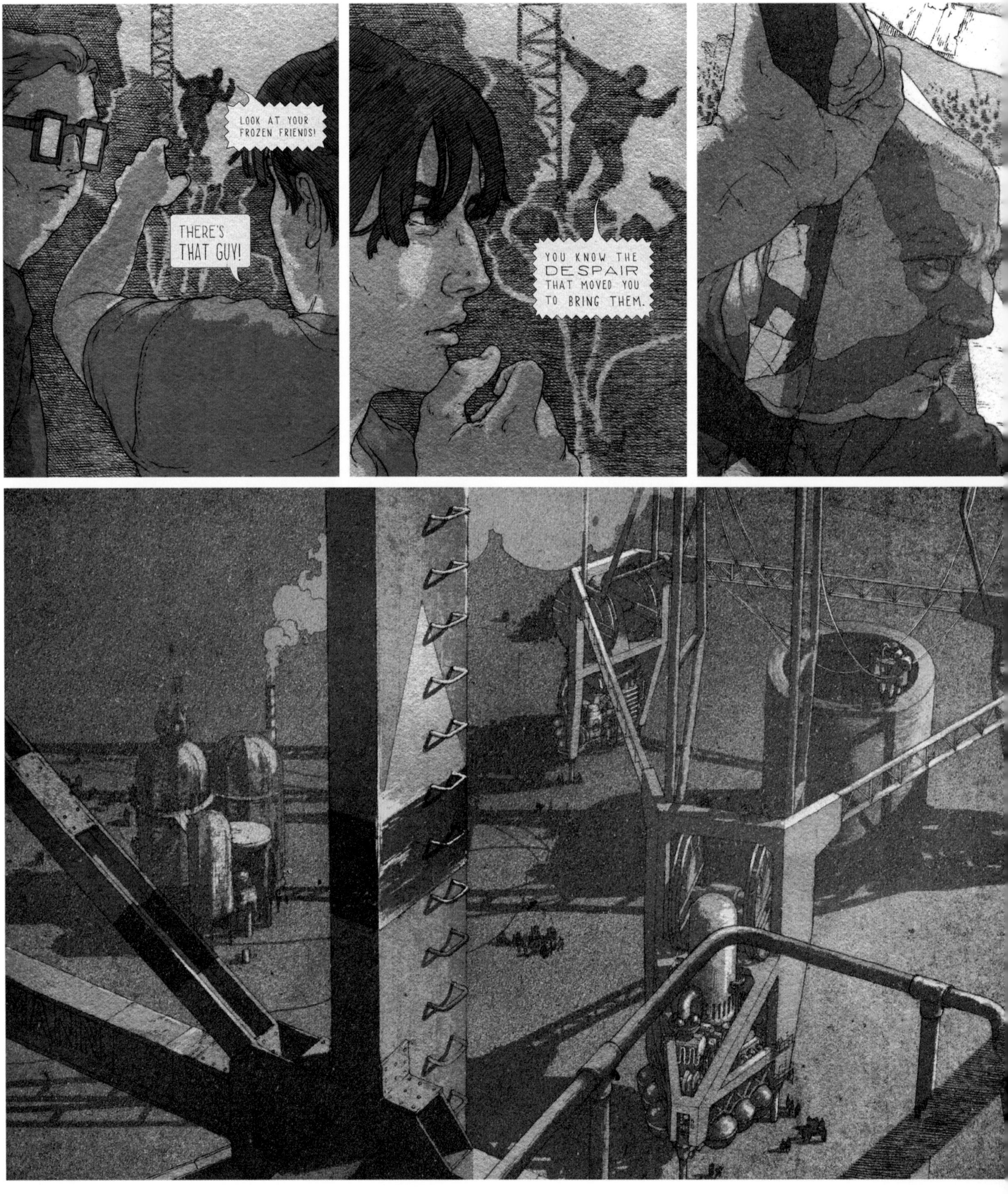
LOOK AT YOUR FROZEN FRIENDS!
THERE'S THAT GUY!
YOU KNOW THE DESPAIR THAT MOVED YOU TO BRING THEM.

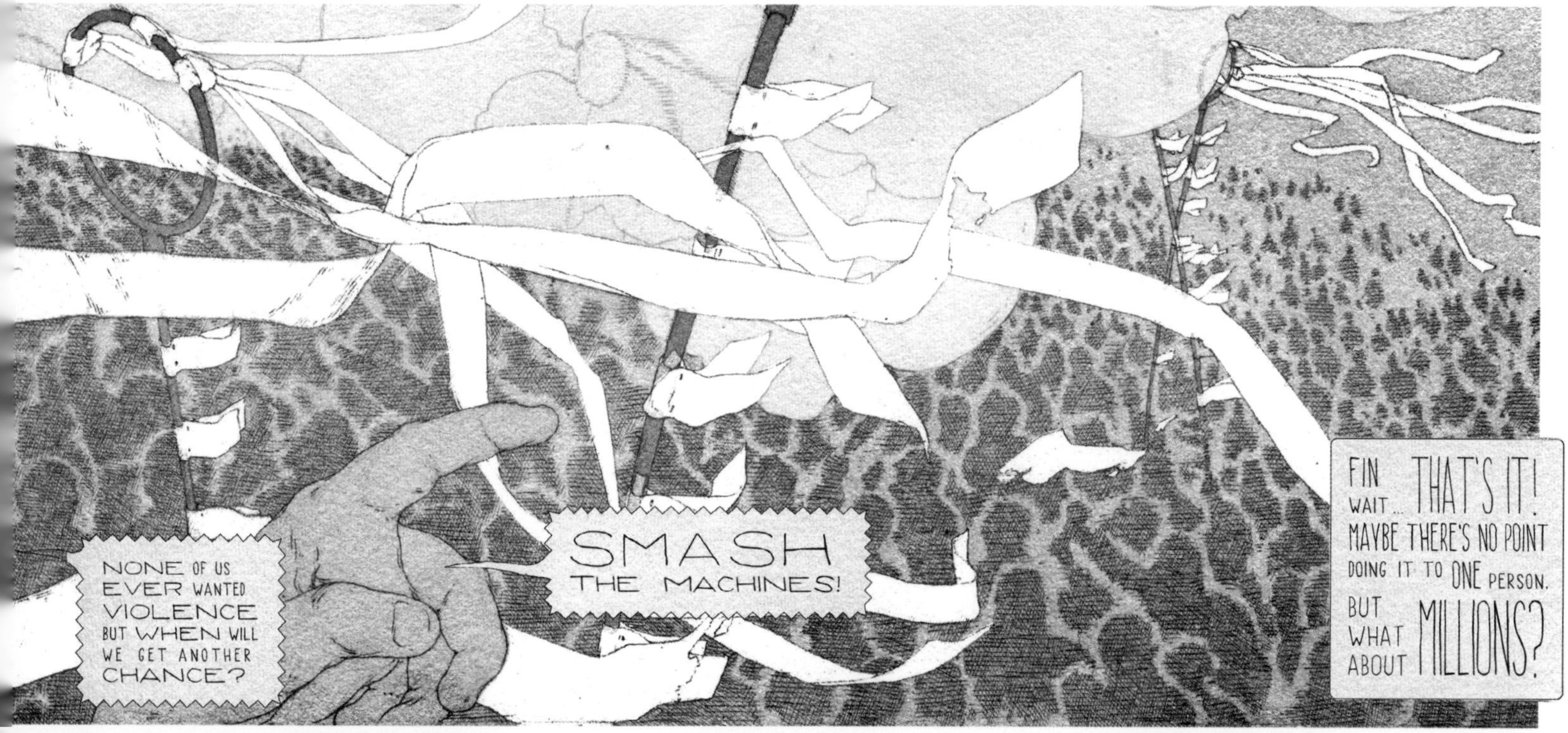
NONE OF US EVER WANTED VIOLENCE BUT WHEN WILL WE GET ANOTHER CHANCE?
SMASH THE MACHINES!
FIN WAIT... THAT'S IT! MAYBE THERE'S NO POINT DOING IT TO ONE PERSON. BUT WHAT ABOUT MILLIONS?

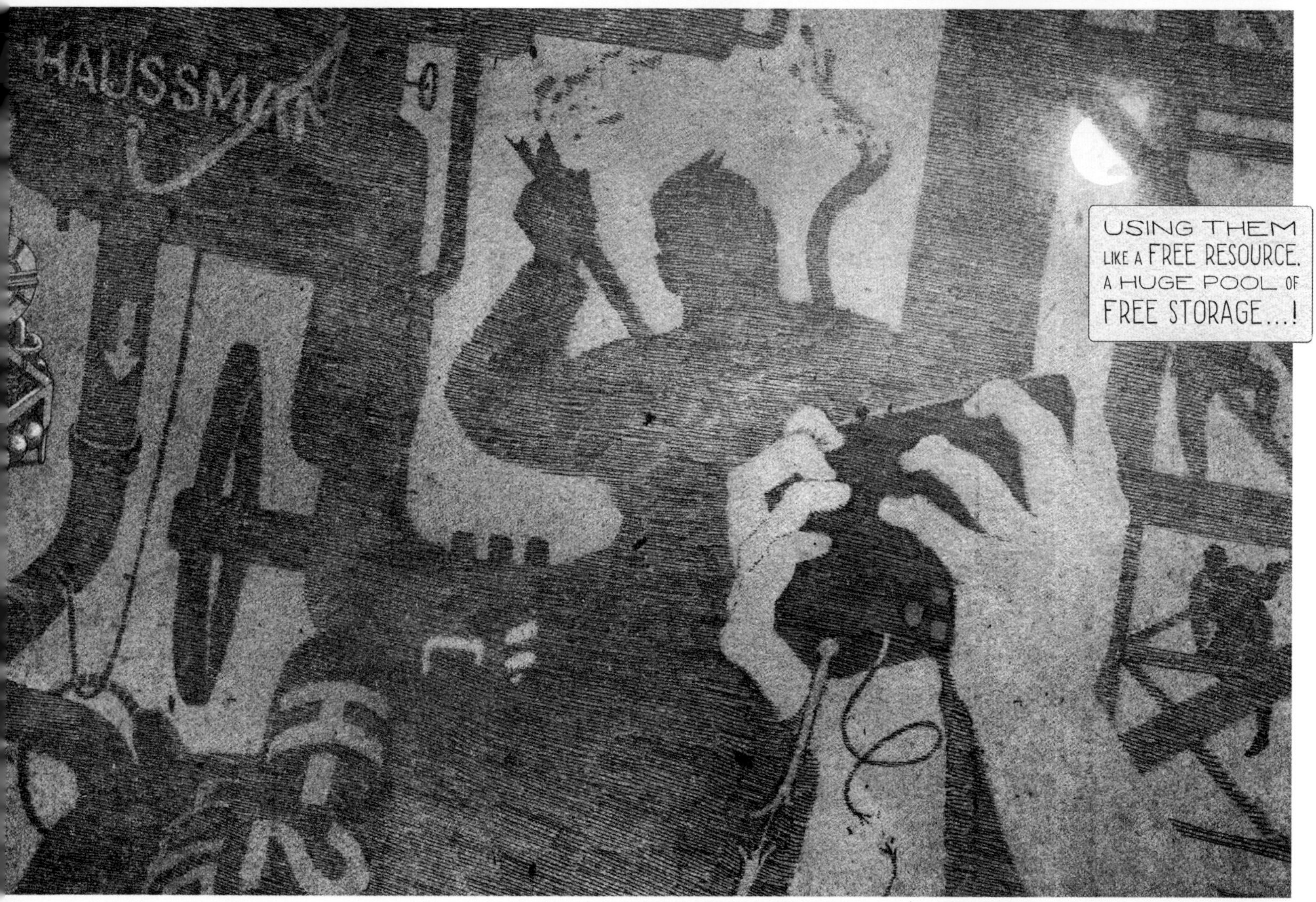
USING THEM LIKE A FREE RESOURCE. A HUGE POOL OF FREE STORAGE...!

WHAT'S GOING ON? NO ONE IS ALLOWED IN HERE THE AREA IS TOTALLY CLOSED!
WHAT IS WRONG WITH THESE PEOPLE?
WHAT ARE THEY SO ANGRY ABOUT? IS IT SOMETHING WE DID?
DON'T BE STUPID.
HOW WILL WE FIND THEM IN ALL THIS MESS?
WELL... IF SHE'S TAKEN THE BAIT I SHOULD BE ABLE TO FIND HER.
YES – SHE'S ACTIVATED. I SEE HER.
THAT'S BLEAK. IS SHE WORKING WITH THEM? SHOULD WE CALL SECURITY?
LET'S JUST GO DOWN & TALK TO HER.
GO DOWN THERE? ARE YOU MAD? IF THEY FIND OUT WHO WE WORK FOR...
OF COURSE IT'S ABOUT US!
I THOUGHT YOU SAID THIS WASN'T ABOUT US?

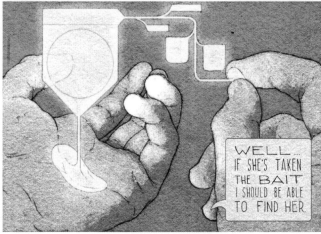

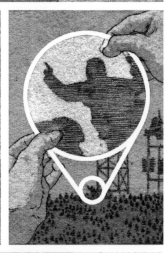

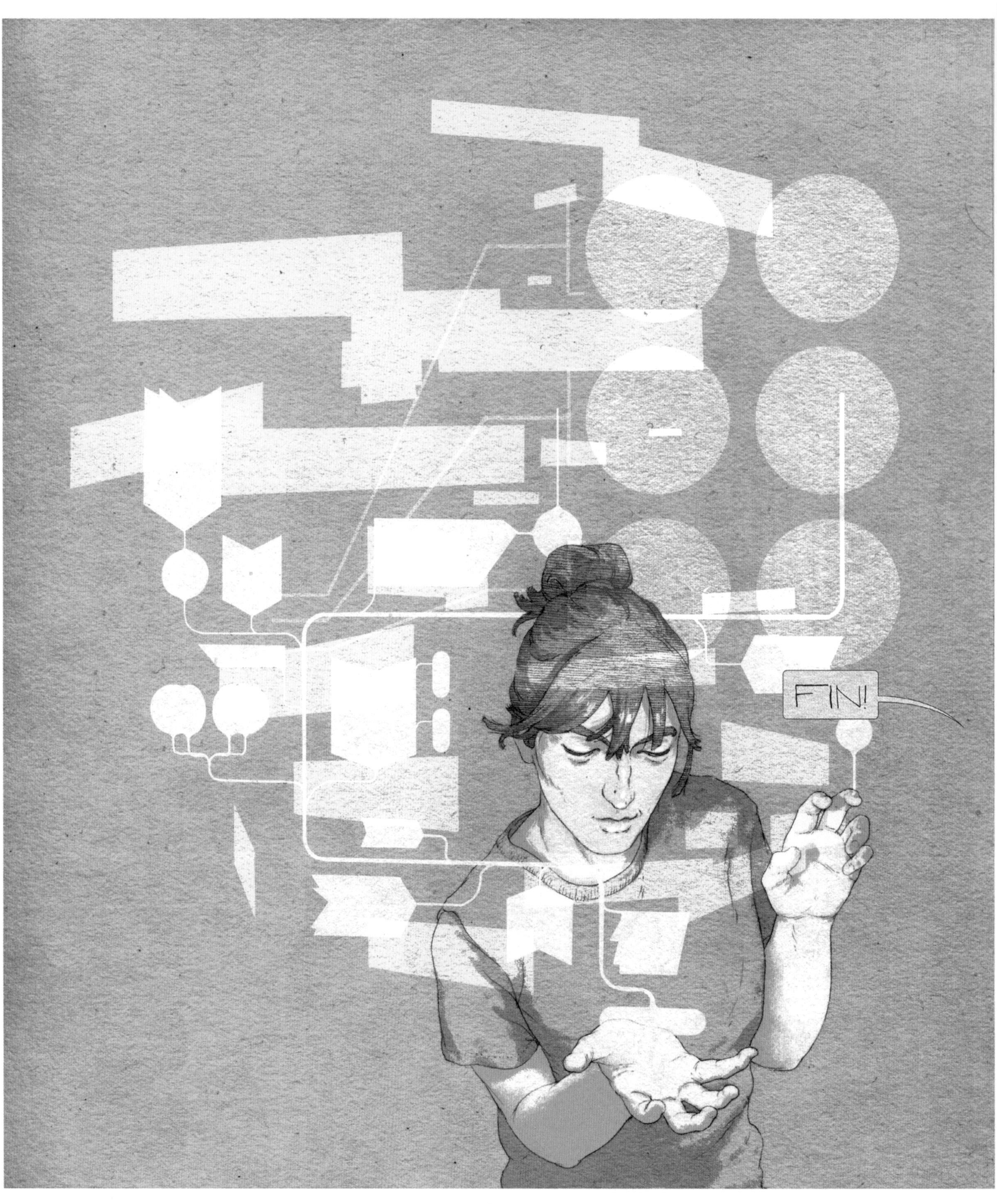
FIN!

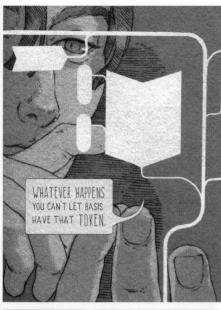

WHATEVER HAPPENS YOU CAN'T LET BASIS HAVE THAT TOKEN.

YOU SEE WHAT'S HAPPENING! THIS IS WHAT THEY'RE USING YOUR TECH FOR!

HMMM?

YEAH BUT WHAT AM I MEANT TO DO ABOUT MONEY?

WHAT ARE YOU GOING TO OFFER HER?

NOW CORVIS IS SHOWING UP IN ALL THESE BROKEN PEOPLE... SOMEONE HAS TO STOP THIS

THEY CAN'T UNDERSTAND IT PROPERLY... I BET I COULD MAKE IT WORK EASILY.

SHE'S A NARCISSIST. ALL SHE REALLY WANTS IS RECOGNITION.

OFFER MONEY. EVERYONE WANTS MONEY.

MAKE IT WORK! SURELY WE DON'T WANT THIS TO WORK!

I THINK WE COULD GET HER ONBOARD IF WE OFFER HER ENOUGH CREDIT

& NOW HER ACCOUNT HAS BEEN RECONNECTED SHE'LL REMEMBER HOW GOOD IT FEELS TO BE ON THE INSIDE.

UGH... NORMAL PEOPLE GIVE ME THE CREEPS.

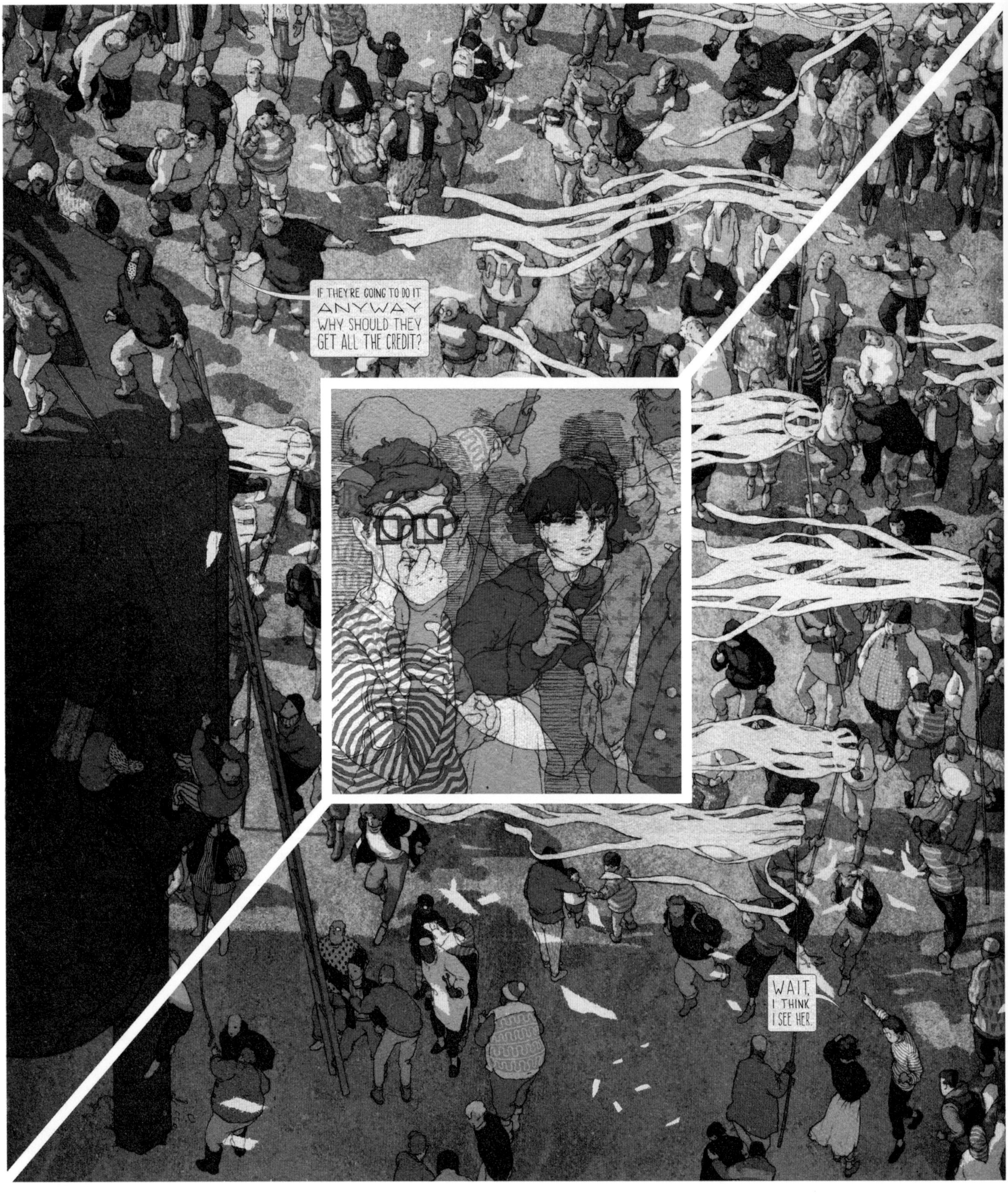
IF THEY'RE GOING TO DO IT ANYWAY WHY SHOULD THEY GET ALL THE CREDIT?
WAIT, I THINK I SEE HER.

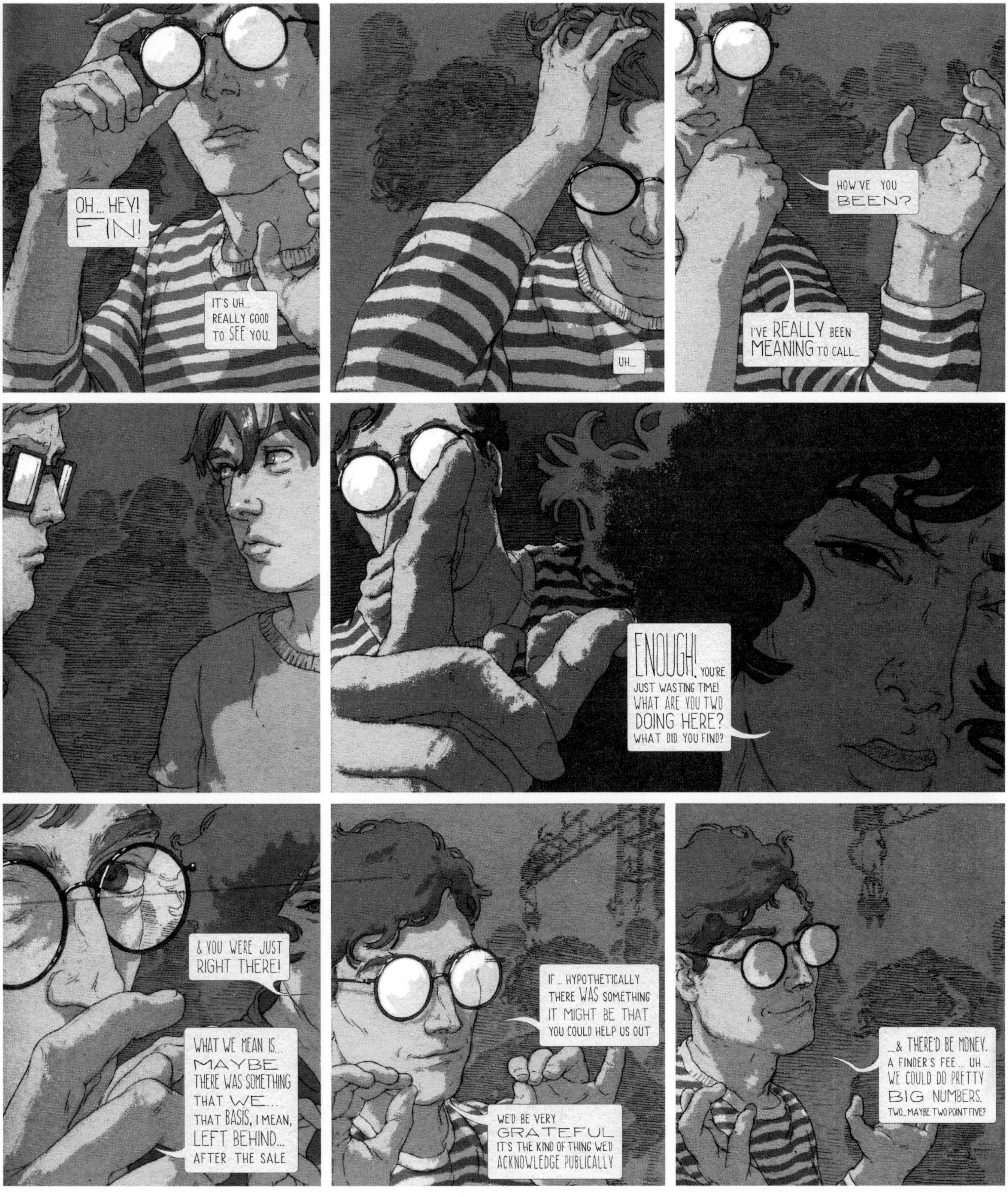

OH... HEY! FIN!
IT'S UH... REALLY GOOD TO SEE YOU.
UH...
HOW'VE YOU BEEN?
I'VE REALLY BEEN MEANING TO CALL...
ENOUGH! YOU'RE JUST WASTING TIME! WHAT ARE YOU TWO DOING HERE? WHAT DID YOU FIND?
& YOU WERE JUST RIGHT THERE!
WHAT WE MEAN IS... MAYBE THERE WAS SOMETHING THAT WE... THAT BASIS, I MEAN, LEFT BEHIND... AFTER THE SALE
IF... HYPOTHETICALLY THERE WAS SOMETHING IT MIGHT BE THAT YOU COULD HELP US OUT
WE'D BE VERY GRATEFUL IT'S THE KIND OF THING WE'D ACKNOWLEDGE PUBLICALLY
...& THERE'D BE MONEY. A FINDER'S FEE ... UH ... WE COULD DO PRETTY BIG NUMBERS. TWO... MAYBE TWO POINT FIVE?

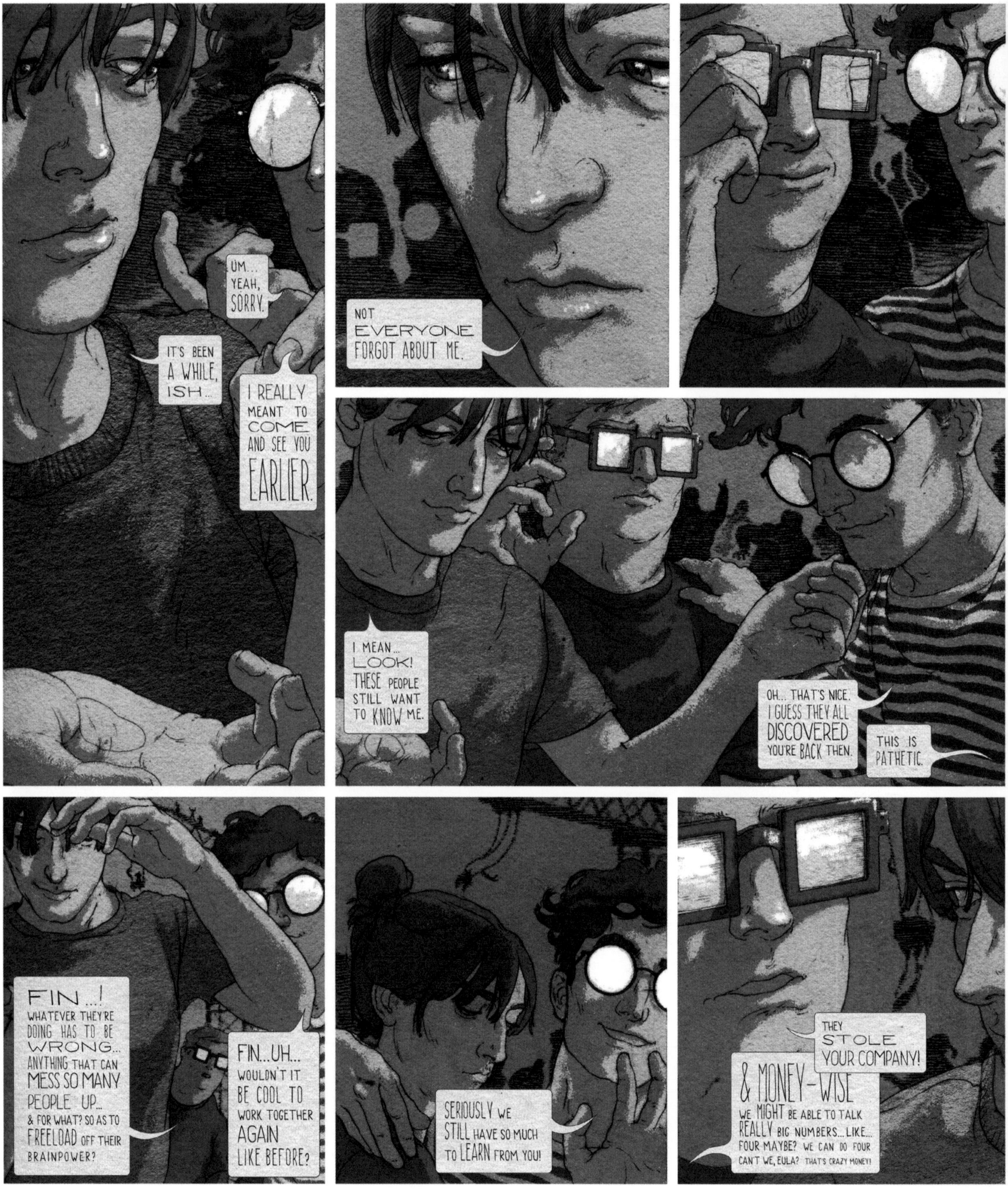
UM... YEAH, SORRY.
IT'S BEEN A WHILE, ISH...
I REALLY MEANT TO COME AND SEE YOU EARLIER.
NOT EVERYONE FORGOT ABOUT ME.
I MEAN... LOOK! THESE PEOPLE STILL WANT TO KNOW ME.
OH... THAT'S NICE. I GUESS THEY ALL DISCOVERED YOU'RE BACK THEN.
THIS IS PATHETIC.
FIN...! WHATEVER THEY'RE DOING HAS TO BE WRONG... ANYTHING THAT CAN MESS SO MANY PEOPLE UP... & FOR WHAT? SO AS TO FREELOAD OFF THEIR BRAINPOWER?
FIN...UH... WOULDN'T IT BE COOL TO WORK TOGETHER AGAIN LIKE BEFORE?
SERIOUSLY WE STILL HAVE SO MUCH TO LEARN FROM YOU!
THEY STOLE YOUR COMPANY!
& MONEY-WISE WE MIGHT BE ABLE TO TALK REALLY BIG NUMBERS... LIKE... FOUR MAYBE? WE CAN DO FOUR CAN'T WE, EULA? THAT'S CRAZY MONEY!

'STOLE'?
NOW HOLD ON, MR ... UH...
W H A T E V E R.
LISTEN... THIS WAS A VERY
STRINGENT LEGAL
UH... P R O C E S S...

& DONE.
I MUST SAY.
FOR EXACTLY THE
RIGHT REASONS.
WE NEEDED TO PAY
FOR HER CARE.

& ANYWAY THAT
TECHNOLOGY
CAN'T JUST ...
SIT IN A BOX
FOREVER
THE WORLD NEEDS IT.
UNLIMITED UTILISATION
OF DORMANT BIO-
PROCESSING CAPACITY.

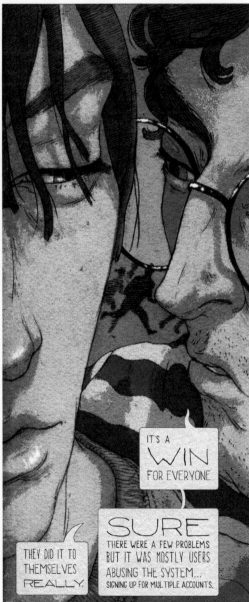

IT'S A
WIN
FOR EVERYONE

SURE
THERE WERE A FEW PROBLEMS
BUT IT WAS MOSTLY USERS
ABUSING THE SYSTEM...
SIGNING UP FOR MULTIPLE ACCOUNTS.

THEY DID IT TO
THEMSELVES
REALLY.

I DUNNO, ISH...
DIDN'T YOU
STEAL
MY COMPANY ONCE
ALREADY?

AREN'T YOU KIND
OF A LIAR?

LOOK
OUT!

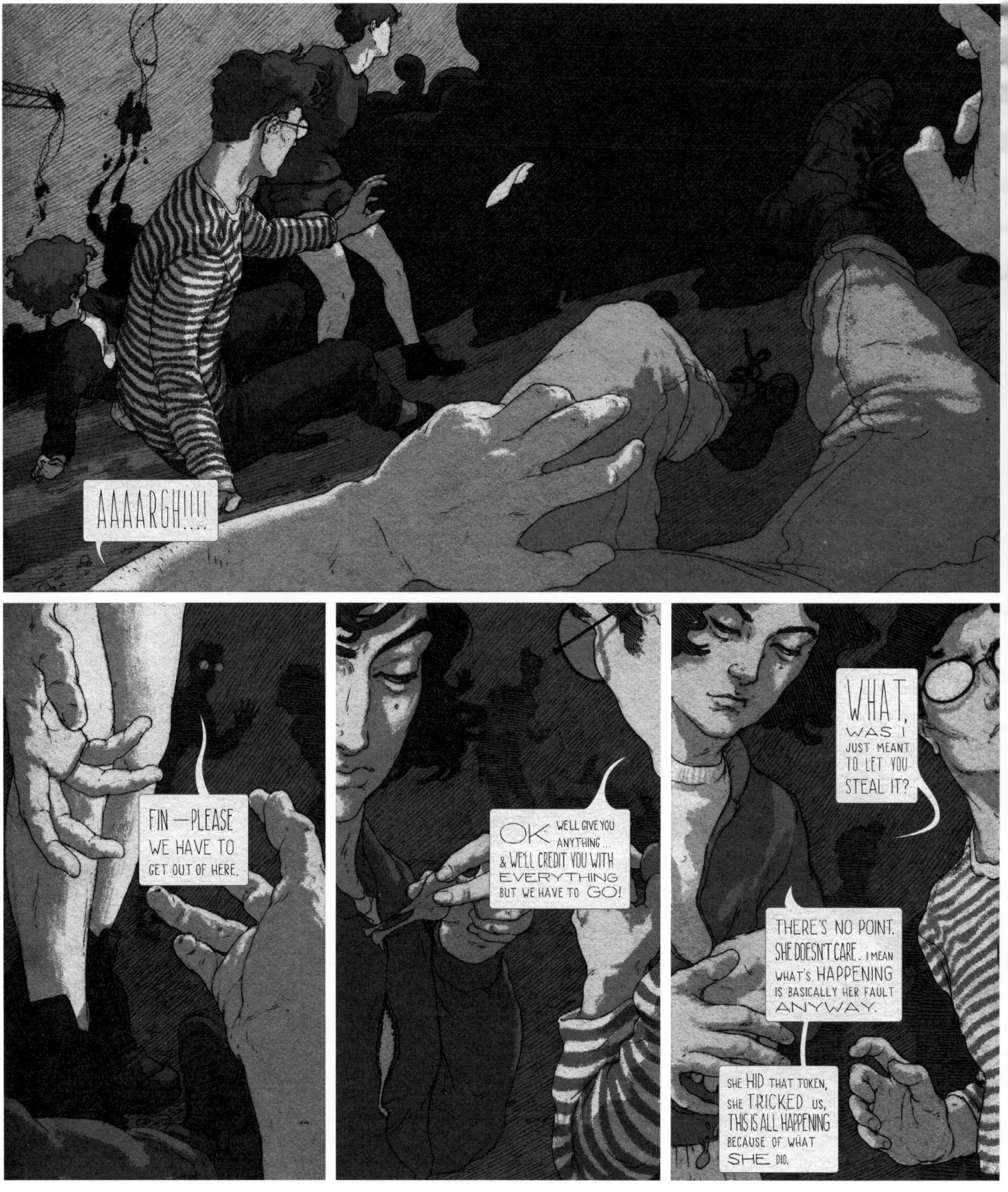
AAAARGH!!!!!
FIN — PLEASE WE HAVE TO GET OUT OF HERE.
OK WE'LL GIVE YOU ANYTHING… & WE'LL CREDIT YOU WITH EVERYTHING BUT WE HAVE TO GO!
WHAT, WAS I JUST MEANT TO LET YOU STEAL IT?
THERE'S NO POINT. SHE DOESN'T CARE. I MEAN WHAT'S HAPPENING IS BASICALLY HER FAULT ANYWAY.
SHE HID THAT TOKEN, SHE TRICKED US, THIS IS ALL HAPPENING BECAUSE OF WHAT SHE DID.

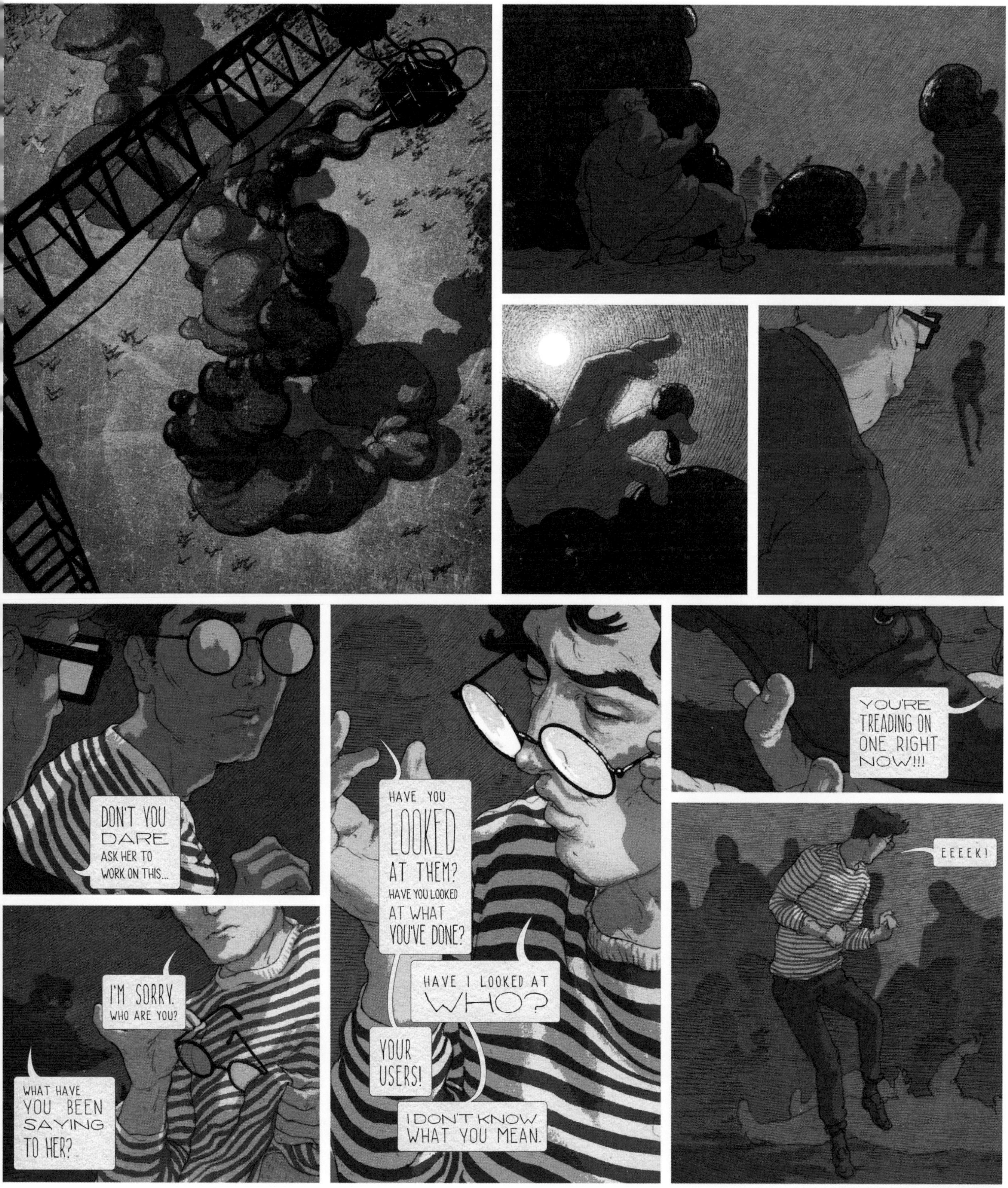
DON'T YOU DARE ASK HER TO WORK ON THIS...
I'M SORRY. WHO ARE YOU?
WHAT HAVE YOU BEEN SAYING TO HER?
HAVE YOU LOOKED AT THEM? HAVE YOU LOOKED AT WHAT YOU'VE DONE?
HAVE I LOOKED AT WHO?
YOUR USERS!
I DON'T KNOW WHAT YOU MEAN.
YOU'RE TREADING ON ONE RIGHT NOW!!!
EEEEK!

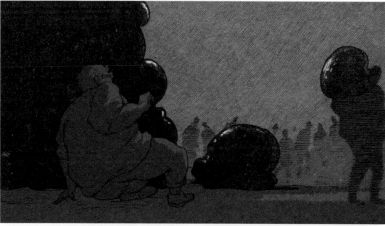

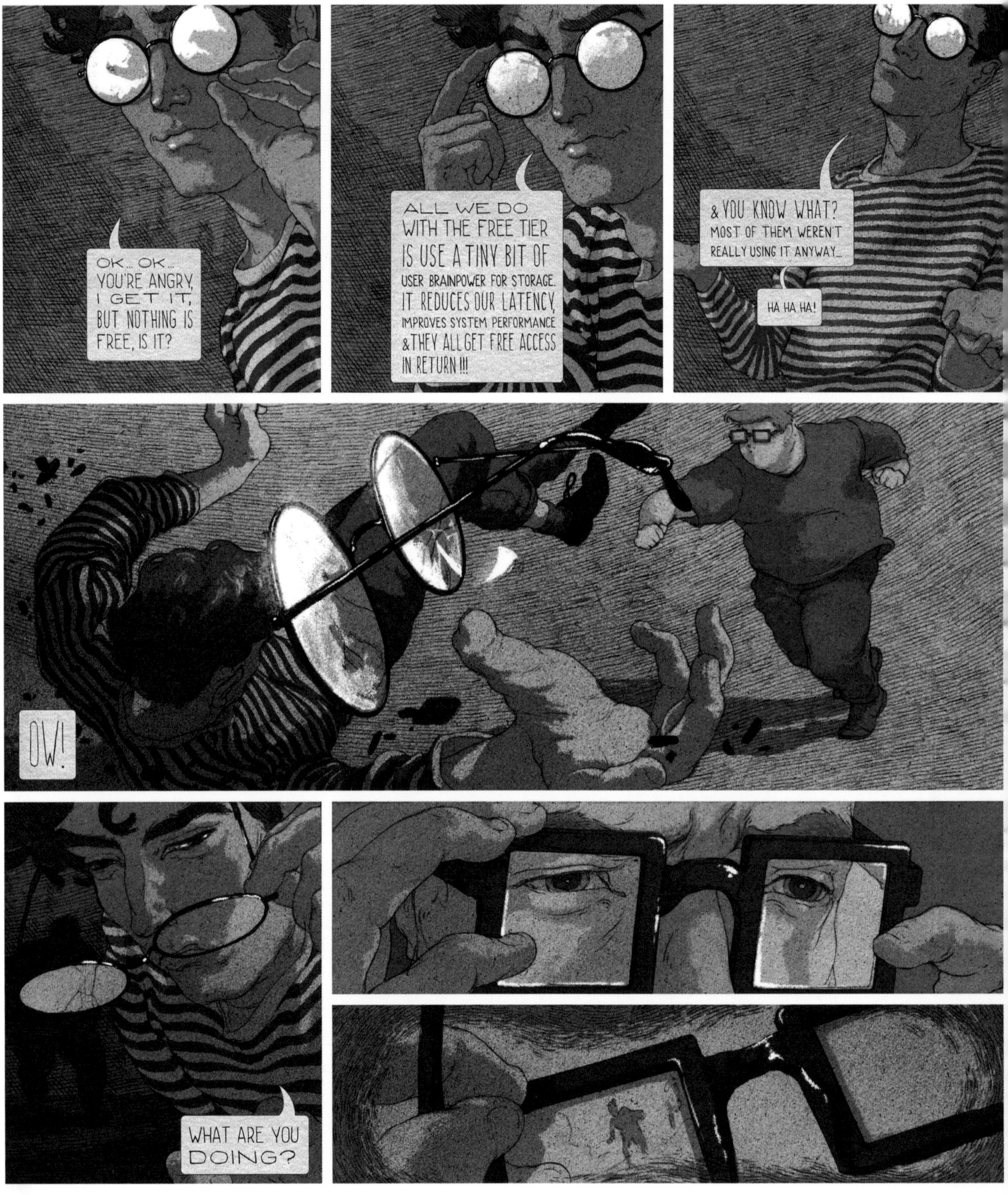
OK... OK... YOU'RE ANGRY, I GET IT, BUT NOTHING IS FREE, IS IT?
ALL WE DO WITH THE FREE TIER IS USE A TINY BIT OF USER BRAINPOWER FOR STORAGE. IT REDUCES OUR LATENCY, IMPROVES SYSTEM PERFORMANCE & THEY ALL GET FREE ACCESS IN RETURN !!!
& YOU KNOW WHAT? MOST OF THEM WEREN'T REALLY USING IT ANYWAY...
HA HA HA!
OW!
WHAT ARE YOU DOING?

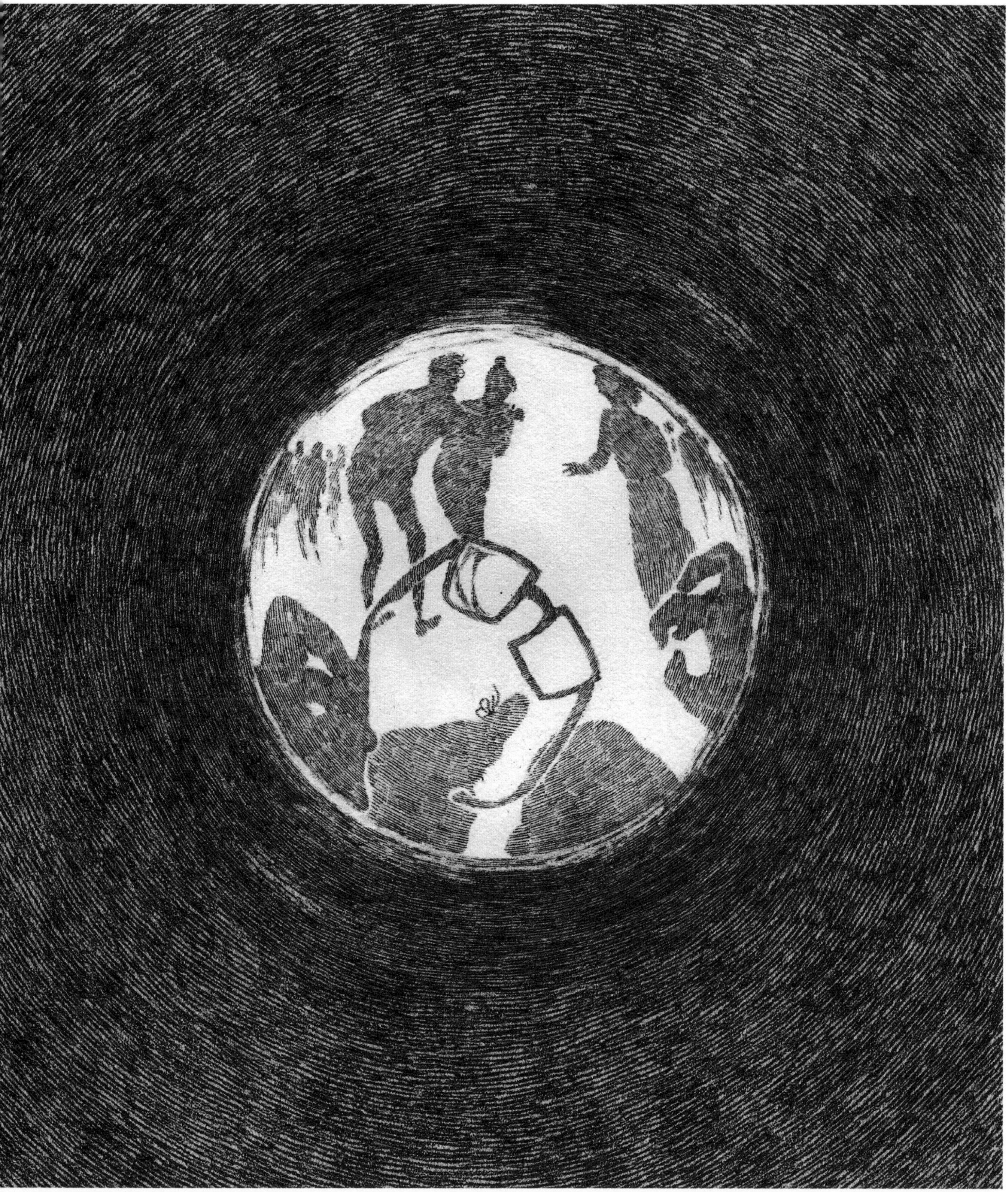

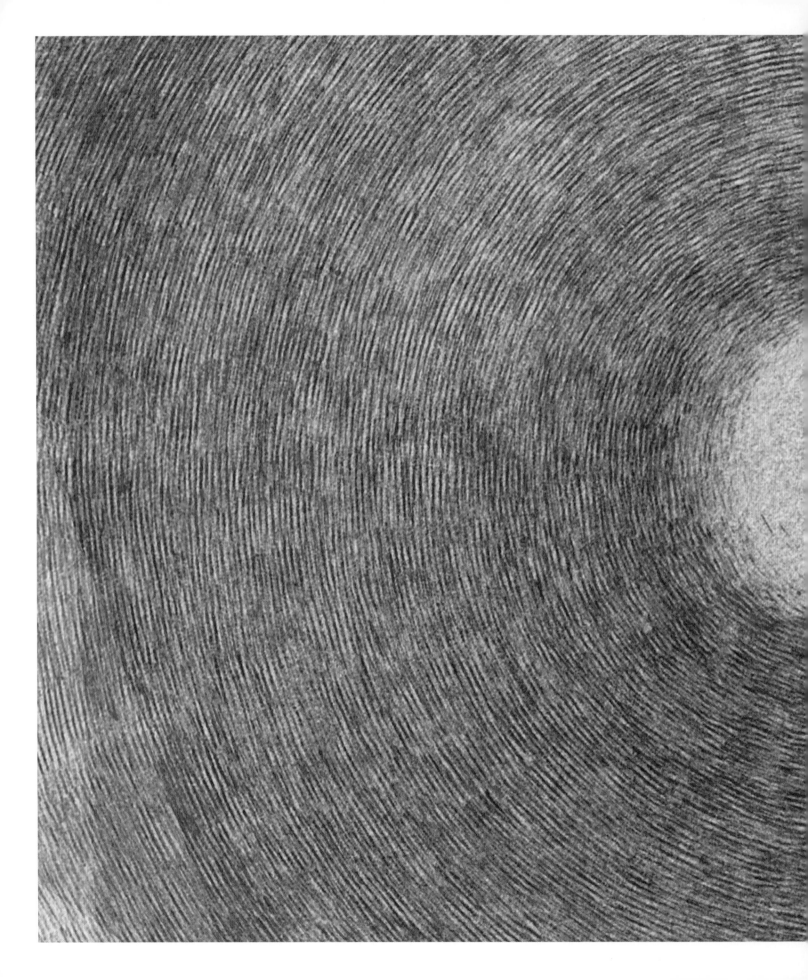

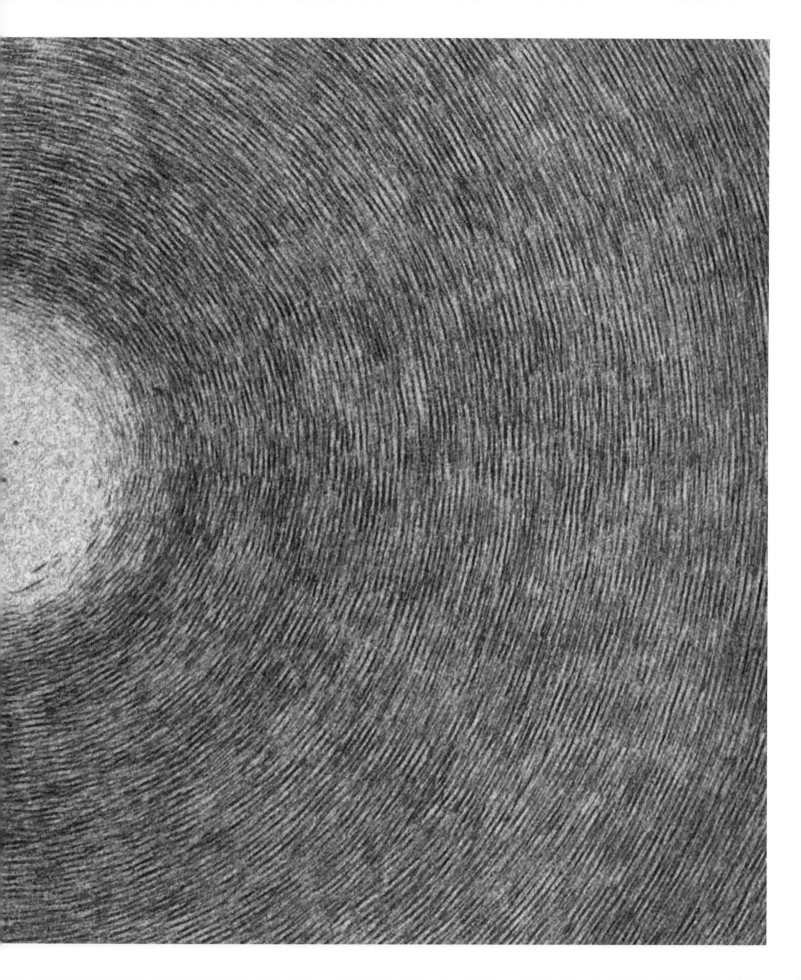

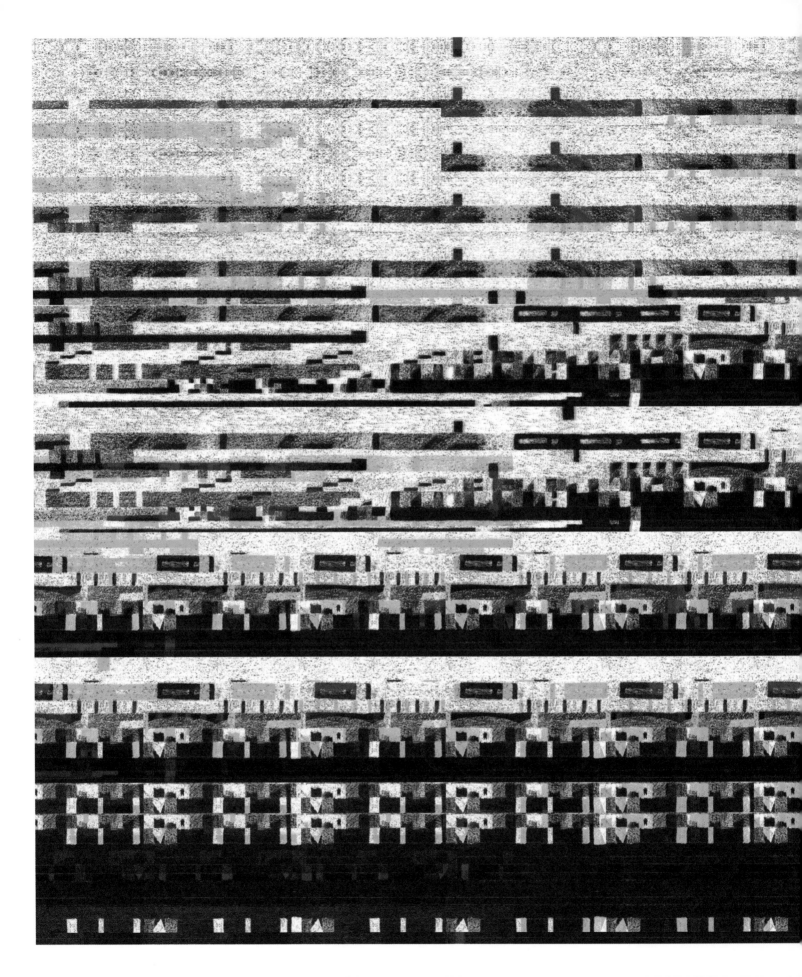

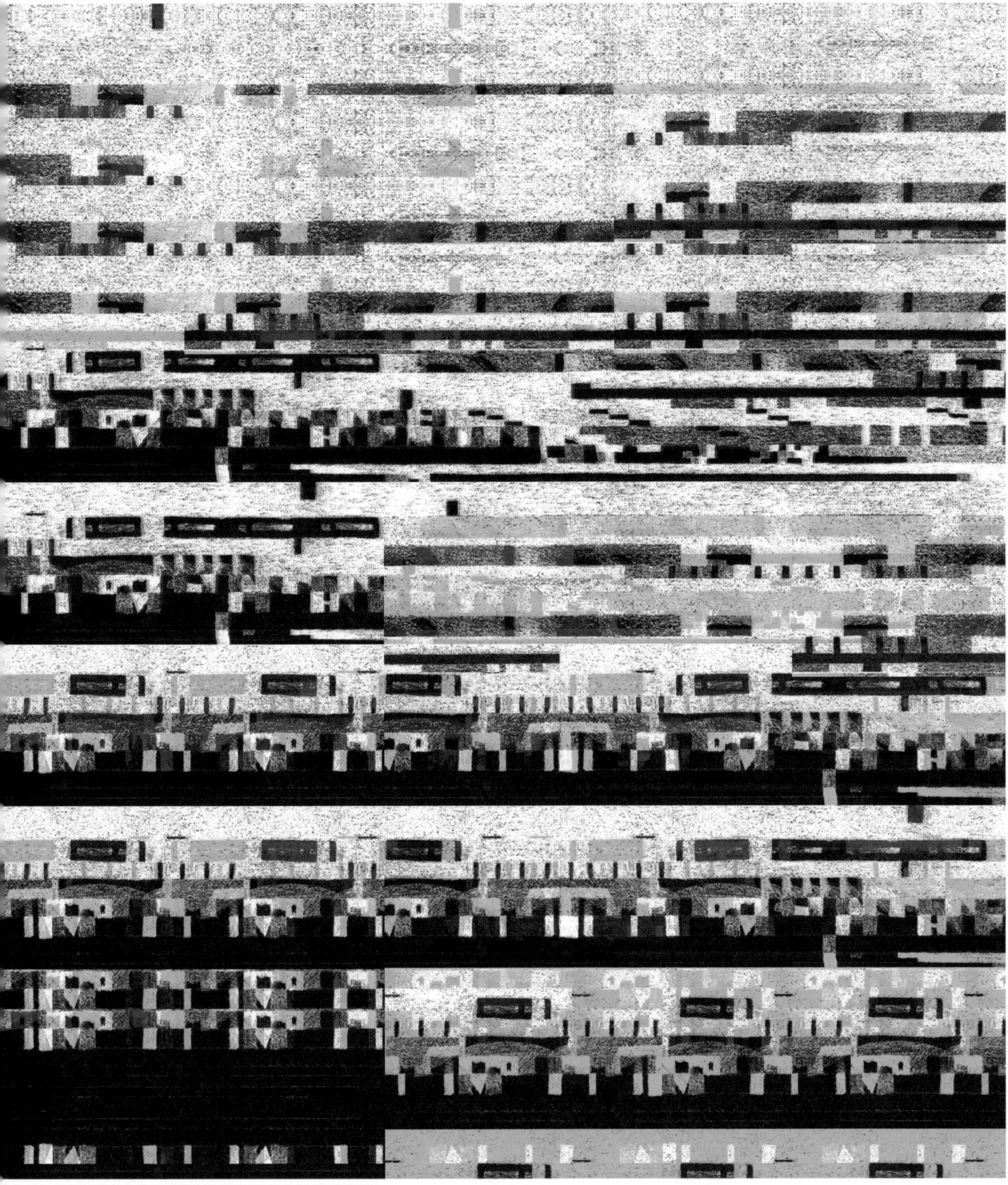

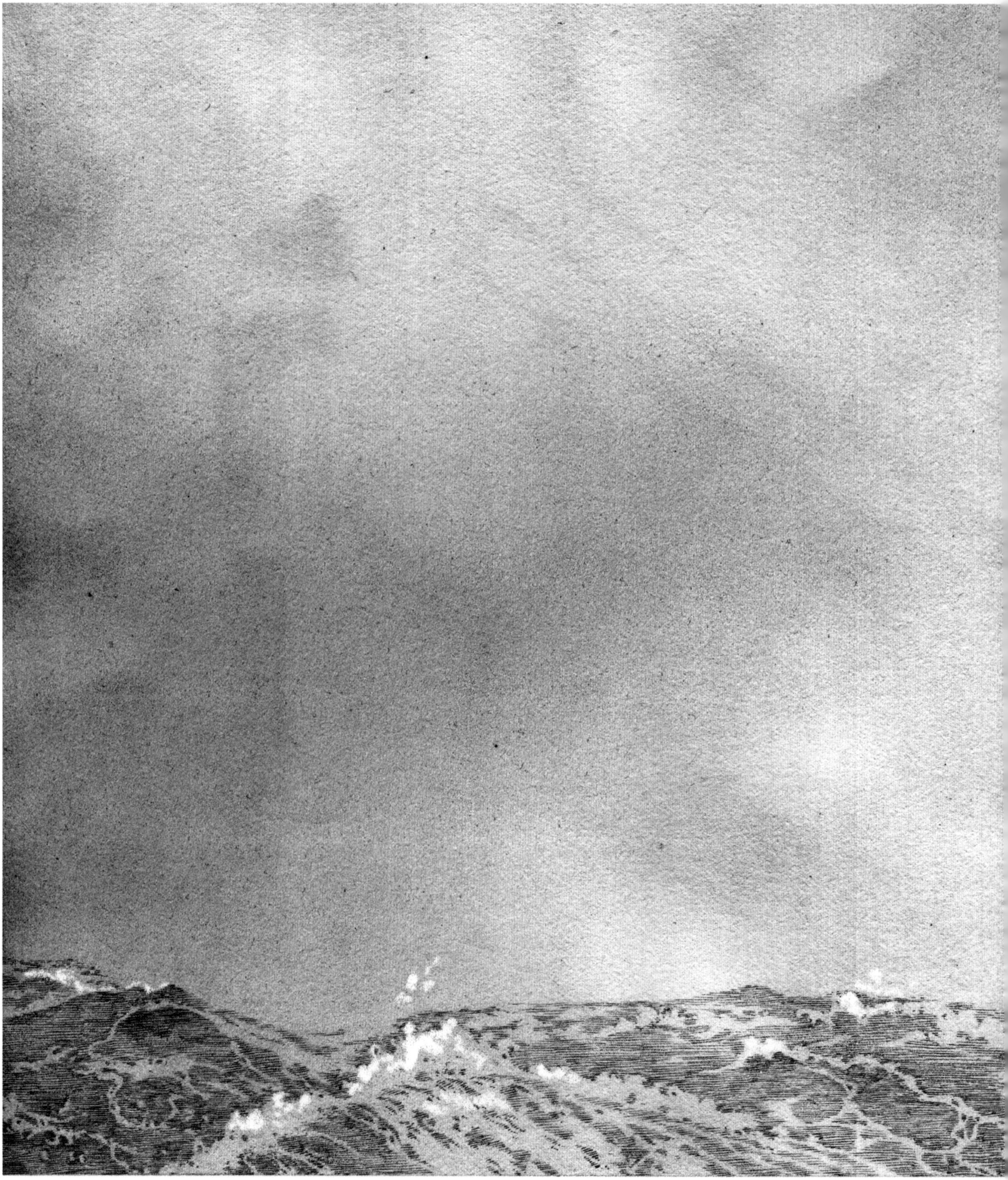

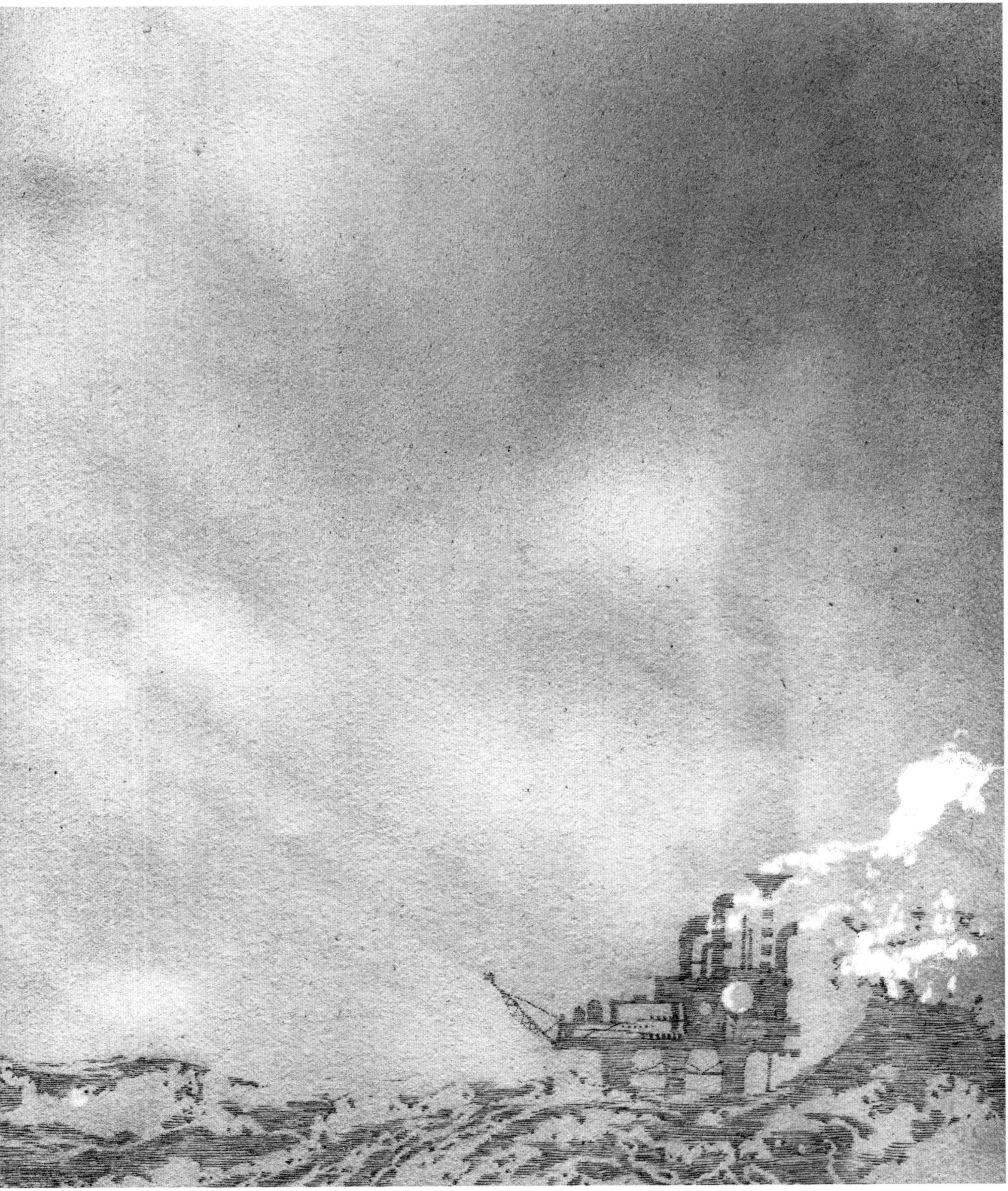

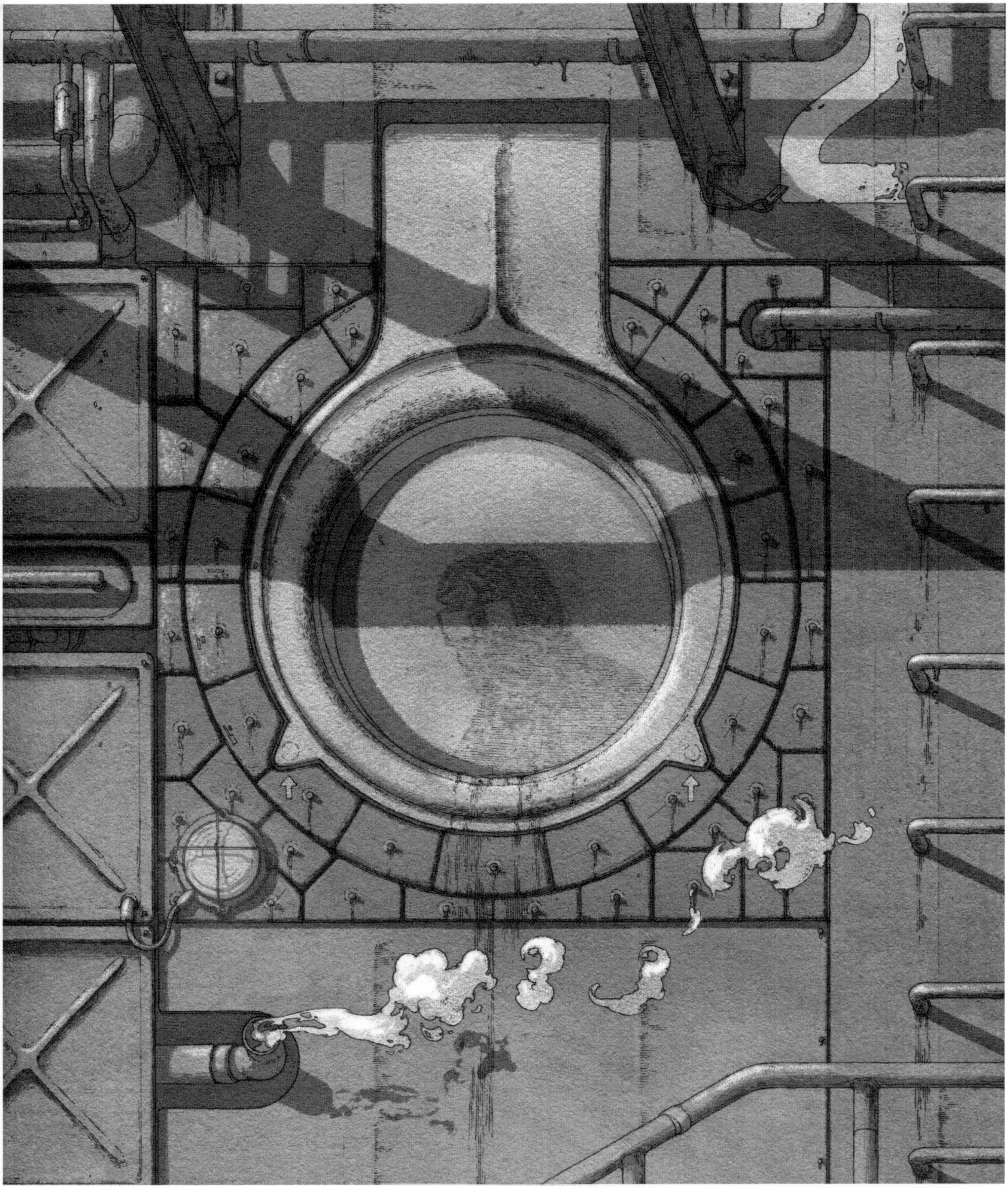

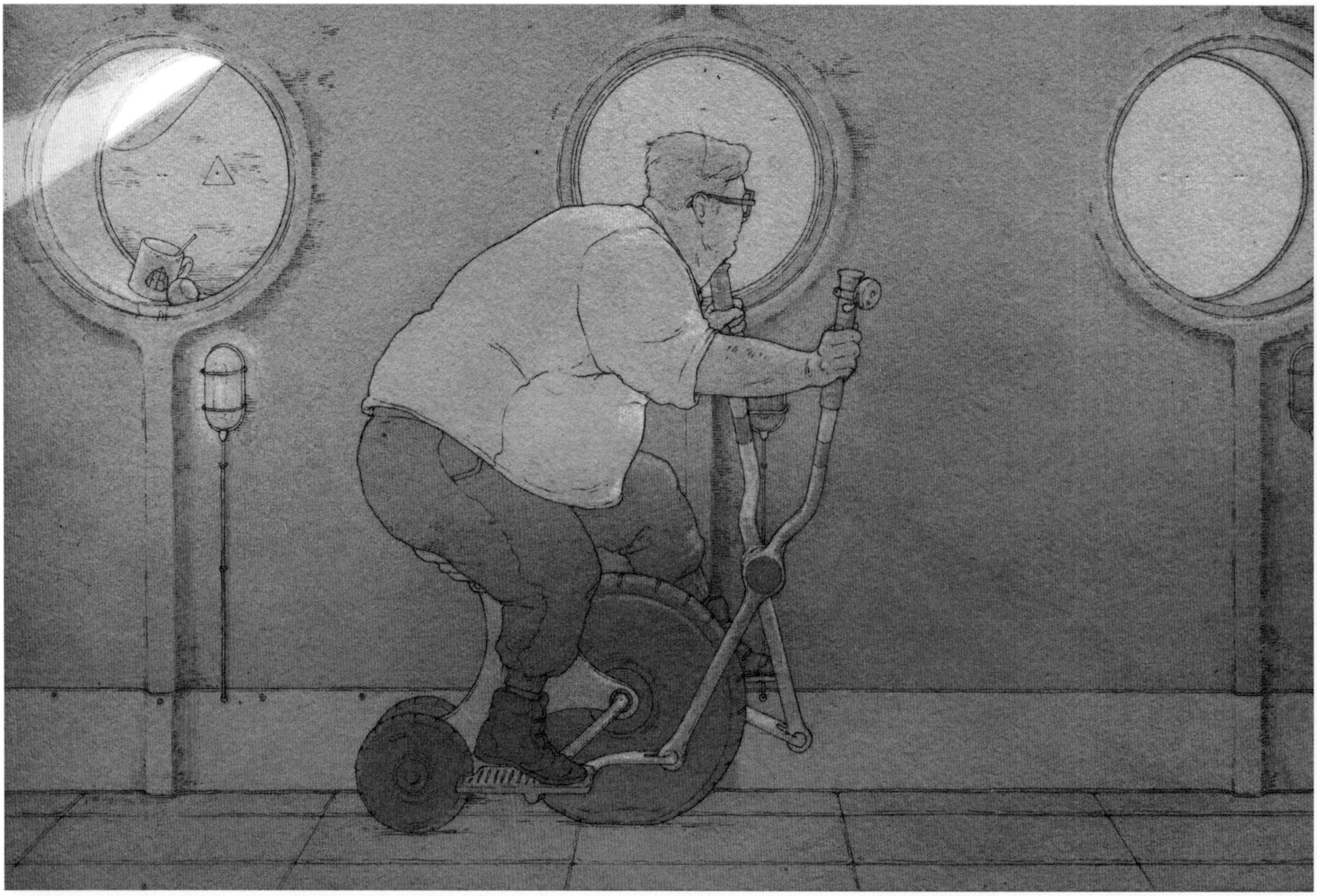

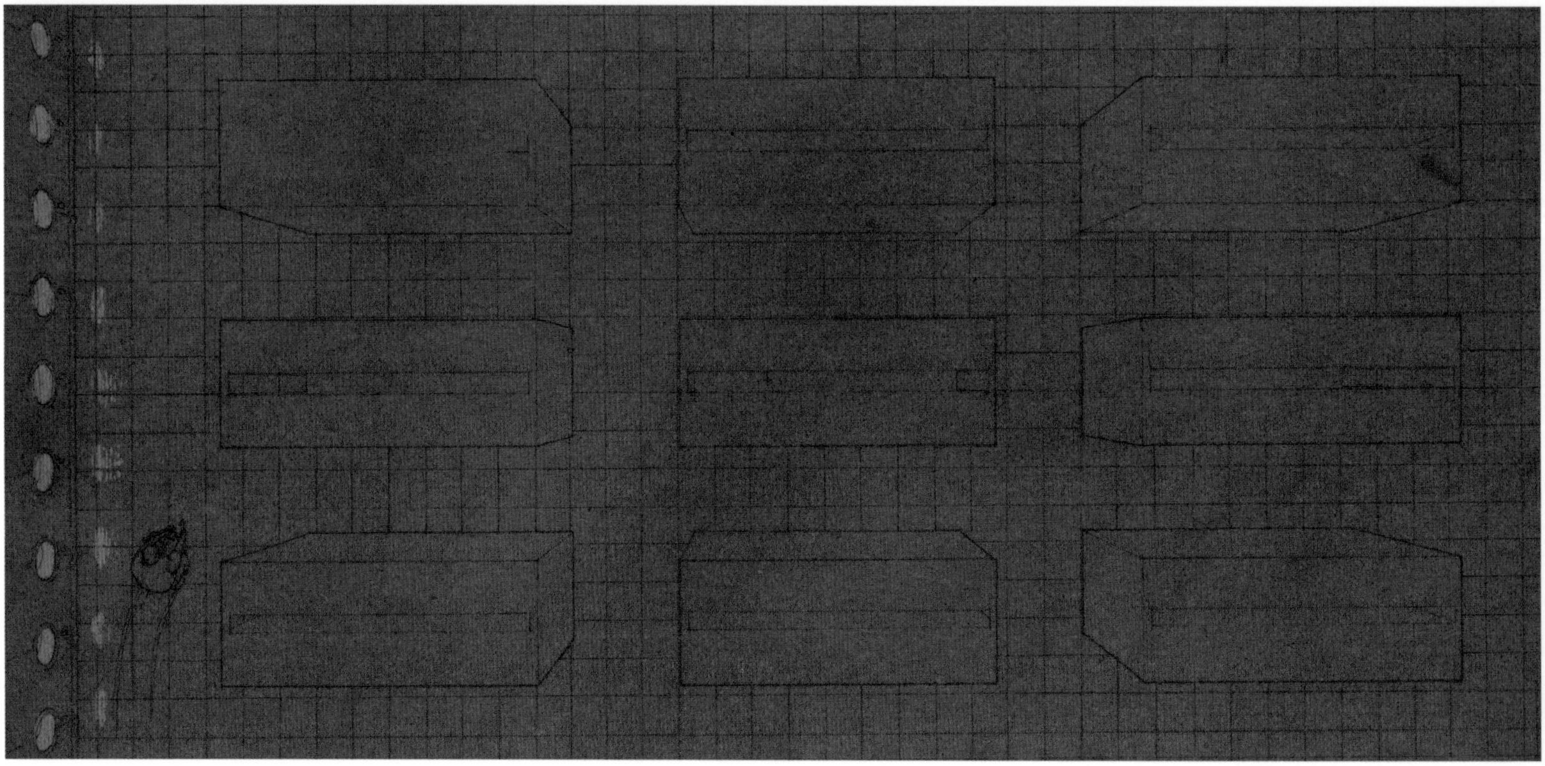

Basis - Clearnes
merger generating
'huge efficiencies'
Near universal
support for Upgrade
completion works
Urban terrorist's
trial scheduled f
month 6
FIN
UEDA-SOTO
1
from:
Fin
Ueda-Soto

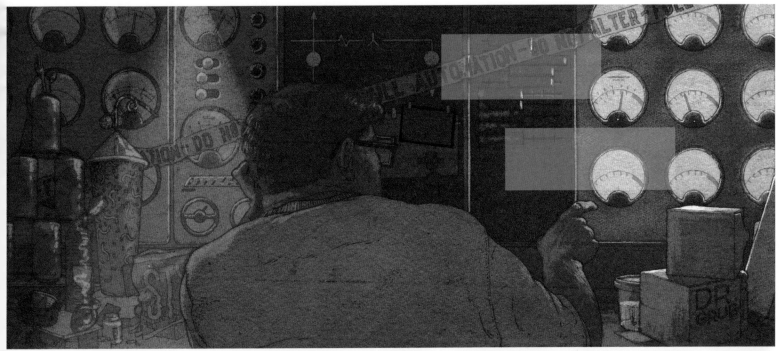

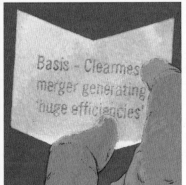

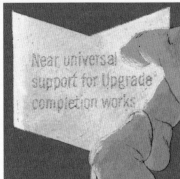

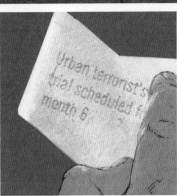

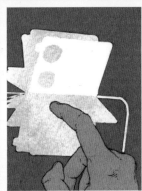

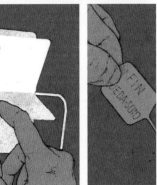

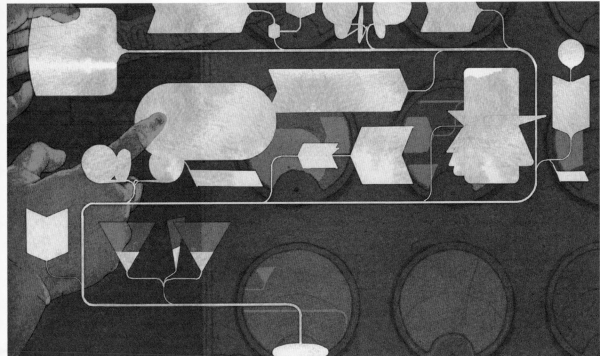

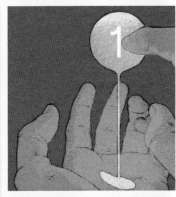

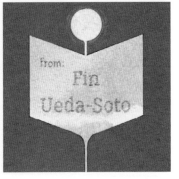

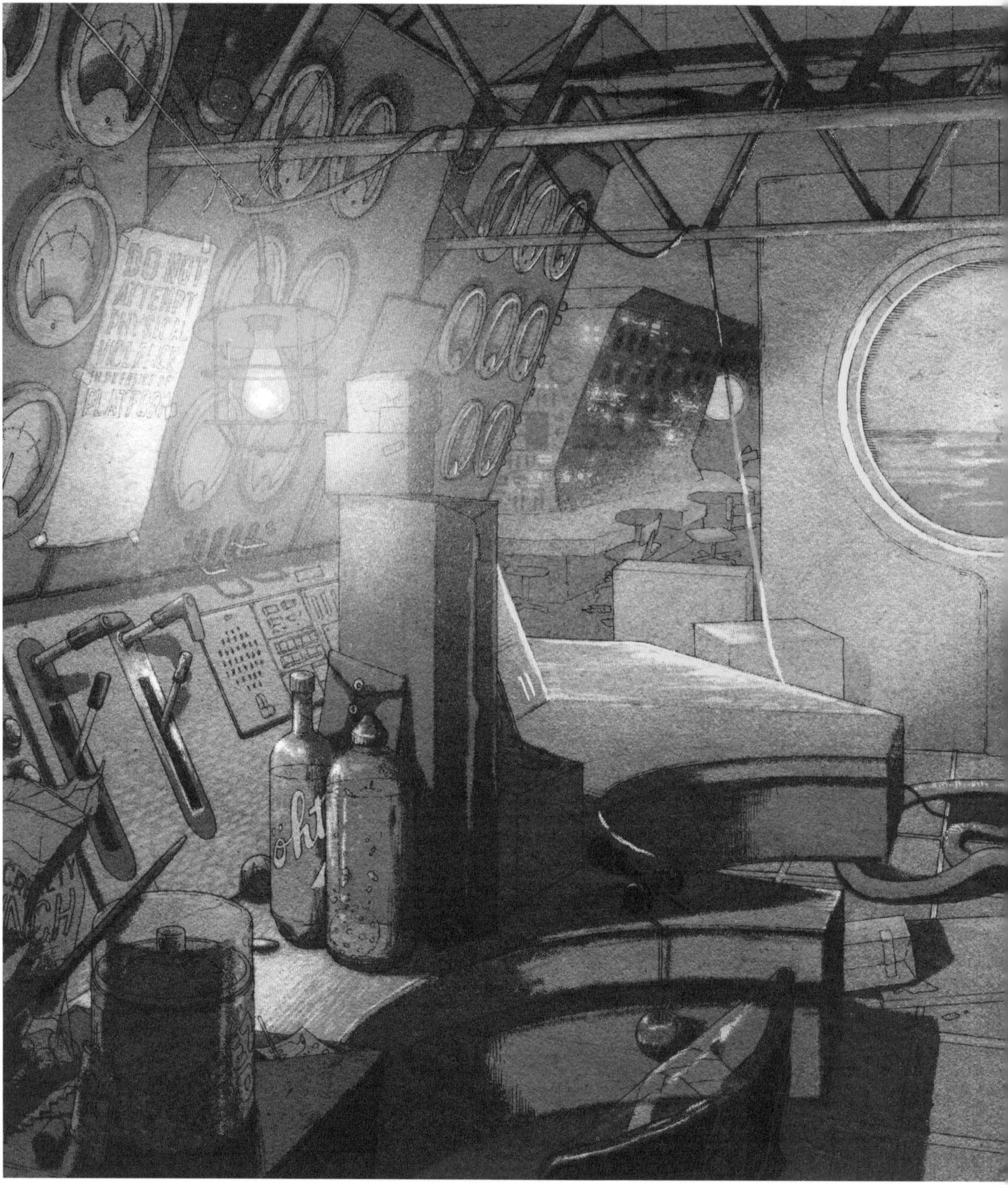
DO NOT
ATTEMPT
PHYSICAL
VIOLENCE
PLATFORM

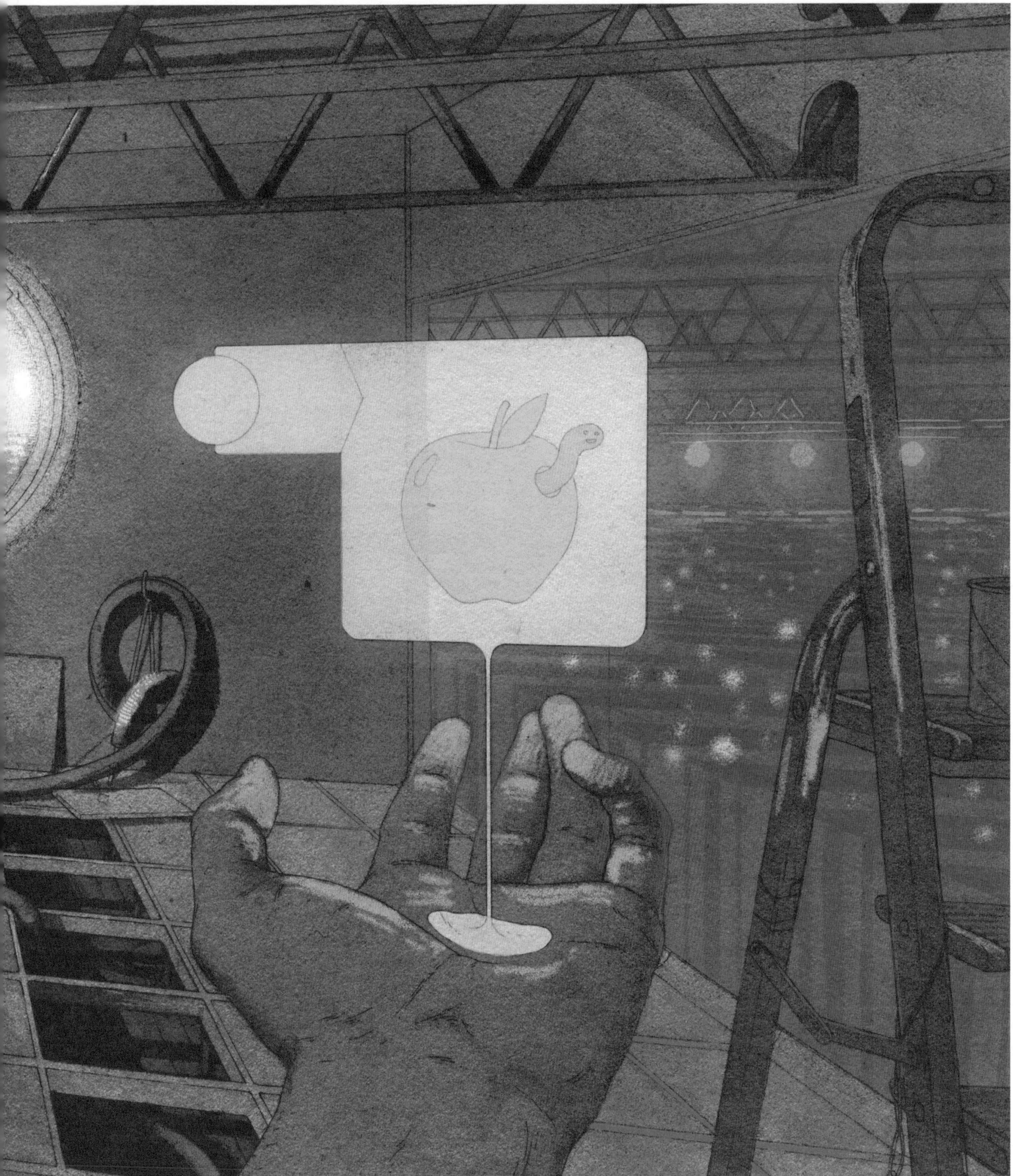

To our parents
Rod & June Mill   Mark Jones & Camilla Toulmin
who've given us their love of art and stories

Jan Kattein for being an inspirational tutor and friend
+ Chrysanthe & everyone at JKA who let me
share the studio for all these years

Jennifer D'Emanuele Fay Gibbons Catrina Stewart Lucy Jonas
Holly Gray Chris Burman Keiichi Matsuda George Carr
Jamie Mill Keiko Sumida
Sarah Fairbrother Agnes Jones William Jones
for all their support & advice

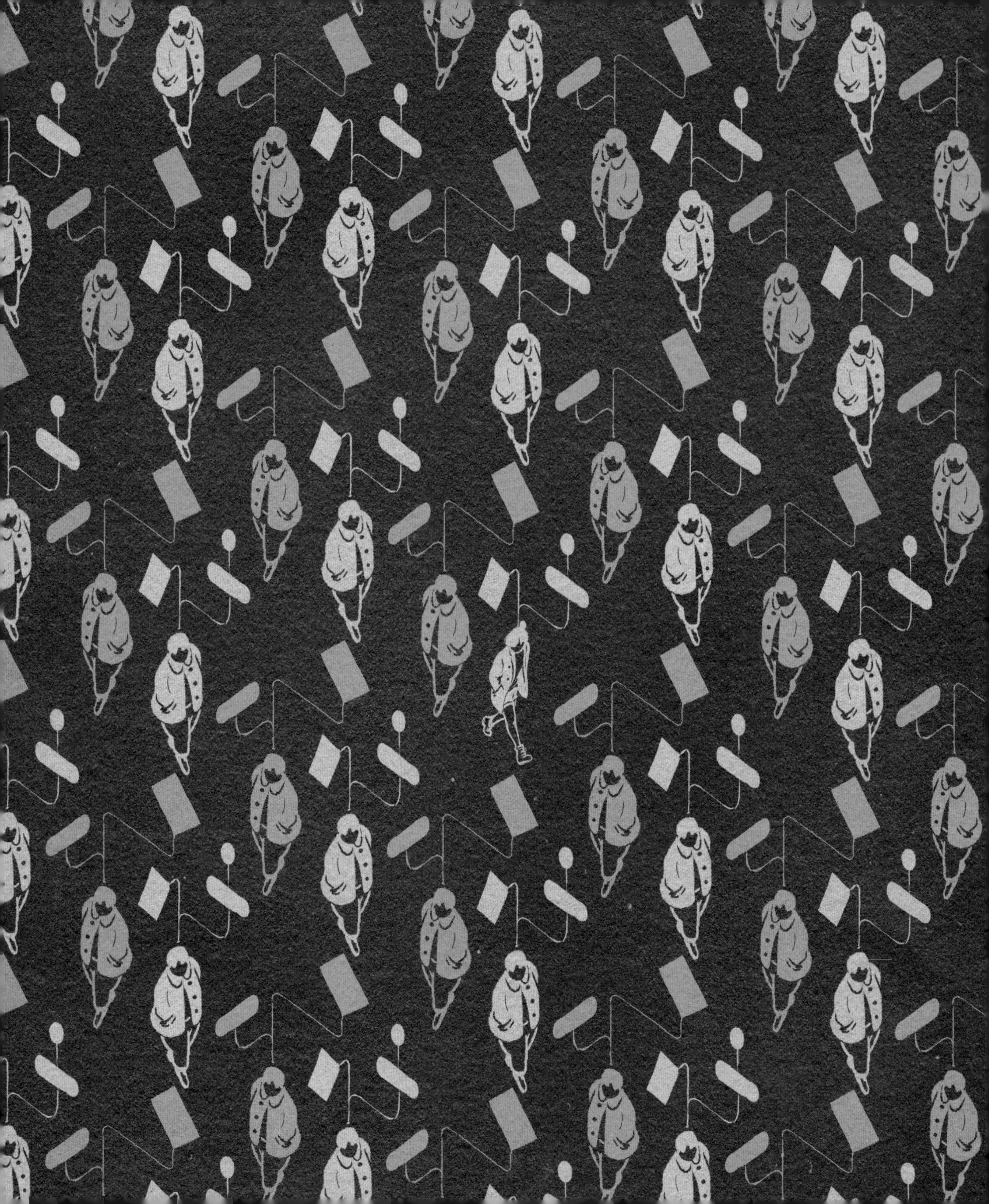